CAMP X

David Stafford

CAMP
X

DODD, MEAD
& COMPANY
NEW YORK

For J.C.

First published in the United States in 1987
Copyright © 1986 by David Stafford
All rights reserved
No part of this book may be reproduced in any form
without permission in writing from the publisher.
Published by Dodd, Mead & Company, Inc.
71 Fifth Avenue, New York, N.Y. 10003
Manufactured in the United States of America
First published by
Lester & Orpen Dennys Limited, Canada, 1986
First Edition

1   2   3   4   5   6   7   8   9   10

Library of Congress Cataloging-in-Publication Data

Stafford, David.
Camp X.

Bibliography: p.
Includes index.
1. Great Britain. Special Operations Executive.
Special Training School 103 (Whitby, Ont.)   2. World War,
1939–1945—Secret service—Great Britain.   3. World War,
1939–1945—Secret service—Ontario.   I. Title.
D810.S7S765   1987   940.54′86′41   87-5246
ISBN 0-396-09096-6

ABBREVIATIONS

BBC	British Broadcasting Corporation
BSC	British Security Co-ordination
CIA	Central Intelligence Agency
COI	Co-ordinator of Information
CSIS	Canadian Security Intelligence Service
CWAC	Canadian Women's Army Corps
FBI	Federal Bureau of Investigation
FIS	Foreign Information Service
GRU	Soviet Military Intelligence
MI5	British Security Service
MI6	(see SIS)
NKVD	Soviet Political Intelligence
OSS	Office of Strategic Services
OWI	Office of War Information
PWD	Psychological Warfare Department
PWE	Political Warfare Executive
RCMP	Royal Canadian Mounted Police
SIS	Secret Intelligence Service (also known as MI6)
SOE	Special Operations Executive
STS 103	Special Training School 103 (Camp X)
WIB	Wartime Information Board

CONTENTS

Acknowledgements **ix**

Introduction **xiii**

ONE   "A Good Place to Make Hooch": *The Farm on Lake Ontario*   **1**

TWO   "To Impress the Americans": *The Donovan Factor*   **25**

THREE   "A Born Salesman": *Brooker Takes Command*   **55**

FOUR   "All This Stuff": *Agent Training at Camp X*   **90**

FIVE   "Oh So Subversive": *Cloak-and-Dagger Operations* **117**

SIX   Policemen of the Airwaves: *HYDRA and the Radio Game* **139**

SEVEN   "Rackets and Balls": *Casting the Global Net* **167**

EIGHT   "Blood and Tears": *Missions Behind Enemy Lines* **202**

NINE   Final Secrets: *Dossiers and a Defector* **242**

TEN   Camp X: *Myth and Reality* **271**

Notes **293**

Bibliography **307**

Index **320**

ACKNOWLEDGEMENTS

The traveller setting off in search of the past has only a distant image of its shape and an imperfect view of the road. It takes many people at different stages along the way to ensure that the journey is completed, and all offer their own special help. There are those who point the traveller in the right direction at the beginning, provide maps of the general landscape, and then fade into the distance. Others, while perhaps unfamiliar with the ultimate destination, prevent the traveller from being diverted by attractive but misleading side-roads. Some people provide unexpected signposts to short-cuts along the way, and from time to time travellers bound for different places join in along the route and share their experiences and their knowledge. At all stages there are guides who help the traveller as the route disappears in the documentary underbrush or in the mists of time past. And then there are those who accompany the traveller all the way, having perhaps taken a similar route many years before in a different season. Some of these helpers wish for reasons of their own to remain anonymous, and to them I give my sincere thanks. They will know who they are.

As for the remainder, I wish to record my thanks to the following: Sir Francis Brooks Richards and the Special Forces Club in London, who first helped me locate members of the STS 103 instructional staff; Bill Brooker, Ramsey Rainsford Hannay, Hamish Pelham-Burn, and Cuthbert Skilbeck, commandants and instructors at Camp X, who, in personal interviews and correspondence, for the first time ever told their versions of the story and let me rifle their personal photograph collections; Christopher Woods, SOE adviser at the Foreign and

Commonwealth Office in London, who gave very generously of his time and expertise in helping me trace the documentary story from the SOE files; John E. Taylor, of the Military Archives Division of the National Archives in Washington, D.C., who provided a guide to the voluminous and newly released OSS operational files; Thomas F. Troy and Geoffrey Jones of the Veterans of OSS, who assisted in my search for American veterans of the Camp; and Alec Douglas, of the Historical Division of the Canadian Department of National Defence, who facilitated access to Camp X records in Ottawa.

Of those who trained, worked, or were otherwise directly involved with wartime operations at Camp X, I am also indebted to the following for personal interviews: Eric Adams, John Bross, George Carrothers, Cecily Cruess, Roald Dahl, Les Donaldson, Kenneth Downs, Norman Delahunty, George Glazebrook, Daniel Hadekel, Bill Hardcastle, Tom Hill, Douglas Hinton, Giles Playfair, and Bernie Sandbrook.

I also received considerable help and encouragement, particularly in the early stages of my project, from former members of British Security Co-ordination who helped fill in the larger BSC picture. Sir William Stephenson himself kindly received me at his home in Bermuda, while the following gave me their reminiscences and other assistance: Janet Fitzgerald; Harford Montgomery Hyde, who also gave me access to his personal papers deposited in the archives at Churchill College, Cambridge; Elizabeth Hunter; Charmian Manchee; Pat Thomas; Elizabeth Wood; and Helen Woolley. Cedric Belfrage, Sir William Deakin, Jean-Paul Evans, Grace Garner, Elsie Gatticker, David Ogilvy, Bill Ross-Smith, and Nancy Thompson, all former members of BSC, also kindly helped. Mrs. Mabel Drew-Brook and Mrs. Charles Vining gave me useful information about their late husbands, and also lent me photographs. Jean Crowe likewise told me about the experiences of her late first husband, William Paterson, at BSC, and provided some very valuable early clues, and support, to my searches.

Eric Dehn helped me with enquiries about his late brother, Paul Dehn, a chief instructor at Camp X, as did James Bernard. For permission to quote from Paul Dehn's poem, "Thirty Five", which appears in his collected poems *The Fern on the Rock*, I am grateful to

Hamish Hamilton Ltd. G.R. Roper-Caldbeck filled in some details about the career of his late brother, Terence Roper-Caldbeck, first commandant of Camp X, and William L. Cassidy helped me with enquiries about William Fairbairn. John Holmes both entertained and instructed me with his reminiscences of Tommy Stone, and Roy MacLaren, author of *Canadians Behind Enemy Lines,* generously put his notes at my disposal and suggested some early leads. Alois Vynhak kindly lent me his manuscript dealing with some of the more egregious myths about "Intrepid", and Roger Hall provided me with some fascinating material from the Ontario provincial archives. I am grateful to Times Books for permission to quote from Carleton S. Coon's poem, "Ode on Learning of the Death of Wild Bill Donovan", which appears in Anthony Cave Brown's book, *Wild Bill Donovan: The Last Hero.*

Others who helped in one way or another along the way were: Ada Arney, Joan Astley, Leif Bangsboll, Stevie Cameron, Ed Clark, Mrs. Norman Cockburn, Bob Cziranka, Elena Danielson, Ellen Devine, Chris Dwyer, Michael Finlayson, Michael Foot, Jack Granatstein, Barbara Harris, Bert Hart, Nora Herd, Lynn Hodgson, Kent Howarth, Jack Hyatt, Dave Kealey, Sir Edwin Leather, Jim Littleton, John Mezacks, Agnes Peterson, Heather Robertson, John Sawatsky, Peter Sichel, Bradley F. Smith, Harry Smith, John Starnes, Marion Stewart, Robert Stuart, who also kindly gave me access to material at the Camp X Museum, Peter Taylor, Jocelyn Thompson, Brian Winter, Gerald Wright, and Sir Peter Wilkinson.

Kate Hamilton patiently produced several drafts of the manuscript, and Terry Copp generously found time at an inconvenient moment to read it. Pruda Lood and Jeanne Cannizzo helped with the research, which was aided by a grant from the Social Sciences and Humanities Research Council of Canada. My colleagues at the Canadian Institute of International Affairs were supportive when the pressures on my time were at their greatest. The book might never have seen the light of day but for Malcolm Lester, whose idea it was, and for the subsequent efforts of Louise Dennys and my agent, John Duff. The Ontario Arts Council provided a writing grant. Finally, I wish to record my heartfelt appreciation for the contribution of my editor, Betty Corson, whose skill and encouragement were a tonic at the most wearying stage of the journey and with whom it was both an education and a pleasure to work.

David Stafford
Toronto
July 1986

INTRODUCTION

Algiers, North Africa: Christmas Eve, 1942. The assassin was young, in his twenties. He walked up and down the corridor, waiting. Suddenly the aide-de-camp appeared; beside him Admiral Darlan walked briskly. The boy touched the admiral on the arm and then fired three shots. Twenty-four hours later, as Fernand Bonnier de la Chapelle prepared to face a firing squad, he cried, "They will not shoot me. I have liberated France." He was dead before Darlan was buried.

The Kachin Hills, Burma: Monsoon, 1943. The trail through the mountain jungle disappeared in the mist; the wild orchids clinging to the trees were wet as the rain fell silently on the men of Detachment 101, on patrol, in the Golden Triangle. The Kachin headman in the lead stopped as the path divided. He plucked a hair from his head, tossed it in the air, and watched as it drifted slowly down onto the left fork. "There." He pointed. "The Japanese are down there," he said as the mist closed over the trail again.

Tang La Pass, The Himalayas: October, 1942. The Tibetan merchants were heavily armed, that much he could easily see. They were also well mounted on Mongolian ponies. But their intentions were harder to discern, for their eyes remained hidden behind painted masks and carved goggles. Protection against the wind, the sand, and the sun, and now against the inquisitive stare of the Feringhee. But the merchants stood down and let Major Ilia Tolstoy, professional adventurer and officer in the OSS, pass on down the road to the Forbidden City.

The Second World War was fought on a global scale and on many fronts. The most visible conflict was the conventional war between the armies, navies, and air forces of the combatants. But there was another war, the largely invisible struggle in the shadow realm of subversion, intelligence, and resistance. Since the beginning of recorded history the assassin has stalked his victim, the guerrilla has descended from the hills, and the spy has reconnoitred the unknown lands. But in the Second World War this shadow war assumed dimensions never seen before. Ever since, aided by the balance of nuclear terror, the shadows have lengthened and now give a grim reality to our contemporary world.

In June 1941, when President Roosevelt appointed General William ("Wild Bill") Donovan as Co-ordinator of Information (COI), the United States, still a neutral power, took its first step down the path leading to this shadow war. A year later, COI was transformed into OSS, the Office of Strategic Services, an organization that lasted until the end of the war, to be revived again shortly afterwards as the CIA (Central Intelligence Agency). The first phase of COI-OSS history was largely educational and experimental, and to learn the basics of the trade the Americans turned to the British. Much of this help involved Canada, and enabled Donovan to send missions into the field even before OSS was formally created in June 1942. Kermit Roosevelt, author of the *War Report of the OSS*, its official and now-declassified history, records that "some of these groups not only performed valuable service...but their operations became notable landmarks in COI/ OSS history later in the war."

These landmarks were scattered across the globe in North Africa, Burma, and Tibet, and they witnessed the assassination of Darlan, the struggles of the Kachin against the Japanese, and the entry into the Forbidden City of Lhasa. The routes that led to them were long and circuitous, sometimes crossing the high plains of visibility and at others snaking through the passes of obscurity that still cast their shadows of secrecy across the path. But each road was prepared by the British, and those who travelled its length began their journey at Camp X.

Whitby is a small Canadian town with a population of 45,000 that proclaims itself "the home of the marigold". On the north shore of

Lake Ontario, the smallest of the Great Lakes, it lies due north across the water from Youngstown in New York State at the entrance to the Niagara River. It possesses little to attract the casual visitor. Its main street, typical of small towns in this part of North America, consists of two- and three-storey red brick buildings constructed in the 1870s and 1880s, interspersed with parking lots, the occasional modern building, and several churches and a war memorial. The solidity of the older buildings once spoke of confidence in the future and a strong sense of identity. But somehow the future passed it by, and Whitby's identity has long been lost in the proliferation of fast-food franchises, car dealerships, shopping malls, and the neon and plastic jungle that has grown around every North American town since the war. Highway 2, the old King's Highway that links eastern and western Ontario and passes through the centre of town, has long been superseded by Highway 401, the six-lane highway that joins Toronto, thirty miles to the west, with Montreal, some three hundred miles to the east. Whitby's shops are distinctly modest, and the hub of local commercial action lies in the adjacent city of Oshawa, just three miles and as many minutes by highway to the east, a rapidly expanding conglomeration of businesses, shopping malls, and suburban subdivisions with a population of almost 120,000. Its main landmark is the huge General Motors plant, which is the city's biggest employer, making automobiles and trucks for the Canadian market. Not for nothing does Oshawa describe itself to the visitor as "the city which motovates [sic] Canada".

Halfway between Whitby and Oshawa, south both of the highway and of the tracks of the Canadian National Railways, and within sight of the lakeshore, lies a subtopian wilderness of industrial estates that is steadily encroaching on the remnants of recently agricultural land. Here, Thickson's Point juts out into the lake to form the western boundary of the small and heavily wooded Corbett's Creek. Immediately to the east of the creek stands a gigantic flat-roofed and windowless modern building, painted a greyish-beige, which resembles an aircraft hangar. It is, in fact, a 500,000-square-foot computerized distribution centre with a capacity of over 3 million cases of wine which belongs to the Liquor Control Board of Ontario. Its harsh and angular dimensions make it look even more temporary than it is against the soft and more irregular contours of the shoreline. At its

xv

southern end, just as the access road curves to the east towards the General Motors truck plant across the boundary dividing Whitby from Oshawa, is a small park. It consists of little more than a slope of grass running down to the lake ahead and to the creek to the west. In winter, the temperature here often drops to twenty degrees below freezing and the lake disappears from view behind driving snow, which can lie on the frozen ground from November to April. In summer, the temperature often rises to a baking heat, and the sun's reflection from the lake blinds the visitor. On clearer nights, however, the lights of Rochester and other towns on the American side of the lake glimmer across the water. An ugly sign on stilts gives the name of the spot: "Intrepid Park". In front of it runs a short curving wall moulded in grey concrete mounted with four flagpoles. Embedded in the wall is a bronze plaque. The inscription is simple, to the point, and only slightly inaccurate. It reads:

Camp X 1941-1946. On this site British Security Co-ordination operated Special Training School No. 103 and Hydra. STS 103 trained allied agents in the techniques of secret warfare for the Special Operations Executive (SOE) Branch of the British Intelligence Service. Hydra network communicated vital messages between Canada, the United States, and Britain. This commemoration is dedicated to the service of the men and women who took part in these operations.

Camp X was the first secret agent training school in North America. Established in Canada by the British, it was designed to help the Americans learn the arts of secret war. For that reason, it was built on a site with easy access to the United States. It opened its doors to recruits just two days after Pearl Harbor. For more than two years all three countries used it to train secret agents and others in the arts of clandestine war. The FBI and the OSS, SOE and SIS, BSC and the RCMP, all benefited from the training facilities and professional expertise carefully hidden on the north shore of Lake Ontario. By the time it closed down in 1944, the school had trained some five hundred students. Many became secret agents, spies, or guerrilla fighters in enemy-occupied Europe and Asia. Some became spy-catchers in the

United States or Canada. Others were sent to Central or South America to counter Nazi espionage and subversion against materials and shipping vital to the Allied war effort. Still others who worked at the Camp's HYDRA radio station transmitted some of the most sensitive intelligence material to pass between secret services on both sides of the Atlantic. This book tells the story of Camp X.

It has been known in the United States for at least a decade that in setting up the wartime OSS, and thus launching America on the path of the shadow war that led to the establishment of the CIA, the Americans depended heavily on the British. Ray Cline, a former CIA deputy director, and wartime OSS member, wrote in *Secrets, Spies and Scholars*, his 1976 history of the CIA, that American central intelligence "might never have come into being if it had not been urged upon the United States by the British and fashioned after the British intelligence system." "Perfidious Albion", after all, had far greater experience and expertise in the arts of secret and ungentlemanly war. The Secret Intelligence Service (SIS) had existed since before the First World War, and the Special Operations Executive (SOE), which specialized in subversive warfare and covert action, had been founded by Churchill almost as soon as he became prime minister. In its infancy and childhood the Office of Strategic Services learned a considerable amount from both of these agencies. Recognition of the importance of this side of the Anglo-American relationship surfaced during the cathartic investigations into the CIA in the aftermath of Watergate in the mid-1970s. The Senate established its famous Select Committee – the Church Committee, named after its chairman, Frank Church, a senator from Idaho – to look into the CIA in January 1975. As part of its mandate, the committee commissioned a history of the CIA, which closely examined its origins in the wartime OSS. Based on both public and classified sources, and on extensive interviews, the history was eventually published as a book in 1984 under the title *The Central Intelligence Agency: History and Documents*. "In real terms," it says of the OSS, "the British provided American intelligence with the essence of its tradecraft – the techniques required to carry out intelligence activities."

Meanwhile the CIA itself had produced its own internal account of the origins of the agency in the wartime OSS. Completed in 1975 and classified secret, Thomas F. Troy's *Donovan and the CIA* became publicly available in 1981. It, too, demonstrated how heavily the OSS had drawn initially on British advice and assistance, especially, Troy documented, "in regard to propaganda, intelligence and special operations." Both histories were in essence reinforcing the conclusion of the official war report of the OSS, which the CIA had finally declassified in 1976, after the Church Committee began its work. Written originally in 1948 under the direction of Kermit Roosevelt, who later engineered the 1953 CIA *coup* in Iran, it recognized that in training its agents the OSS had extensively learned from the British. "OSS was often assisted," Roosevelt noted, "in the development of its own techniques by experienced British agencies."

But how, and where, was this done? The official and semi-official sources that had appeared in print by the early 1980s were silent on the point. Hints that a top-secret British training school in Canada had a part to play in the story were available in scattered references elsewhere, and "Camp X" had long been a talking point in Canada. "Perhaps the best allied espionage school of World War II," wrote Ladislas Farago in *War of Wits*. "One of the most important places in North America," stated Richard Dunlop, a biographer of Wild Bill Donovan, who was more than ready to acknowledge that British Security Co-ordination in New York, headed by William Stephenson, a Canadian businessman, had taught OSS all it ever knew about foreign intelligence. The 1976 international best seller about Stephenson, *A Man Called Intrepid*, claimed that Camp X represented "the clenched fist" of all Allied secret operations in the Second World War.

It was this last book which above all set Camp X on the historical map of the Second World War, through its sensational portrayal of the training school as the centre of some of the most daring and dramatic events of the secret war against Nazi Germany. The author also connected the names of an extraordinary assortment of top Allied personalities with the Camp, and depicted its activities as ranging from underwater frogman exercises in Lake Ontario – which eventually inspired one of its alleged students, Ian Fleming, to create his fictional *alter ego* James Bond – to Lysander aircraft pick-up exercises used to rescue endangered secret agents in occupied France. Since then, others have made even more extravagant claims. According to a recent extraordinary account, the Camp was in existence long before anyone has hitherto even dreamed it was there. In *Enigma Tito*, a book published in Washington, D.C., in 1984, the author makes the startling claim that the Communist leader of Yugoslavia, Marshal Tito, was trained as a British agent at Camp X in 1927-28 as the first stage in a larger British and American operation to place Tito "on the throne of Bolshevik Yugoslavia".

How many of the stories about Camp X are true? Shortly after *A Man Called Intrepid* was published, professional experts on both sides of the Atlantic dismissed many of its claims about the extent and significance of Stephenson's wartime career as head of British Security Co-ordination in New York. Much of the criticism was justified. Stephenson's mandate never extended beyond the Western Hemisphere; he had no operational role in European activities; and he was far from being the intimate confidant and purveyor of top-secret intelligence for Churchill and Roosevelt that the "Intrepid" myth had painted. (Indeed, "Intrepid" was never his code-name.) By implication, and by most standards of plausibility, the account that the book gave of Camp X was also at fault. But improbability is in itself no proof of impossibility. In any case, even if some – or even all – of the claims were inaccurate, what was the reality? No one suggested that Camp X itself was a fictional creation. So what had happened there? What role had the Camp played in the creation of the close American-British-Canadian alliance in secret warfare and intelligence during the Second World War which had then continued into the peace? In what ways had Camp X and its instructors helped the OSS and thus indirectly helped to build the foundations of the CIA?

Finding out the basic facts and producing a detailed and accurate story of Camp X, of the agents who trained there, and of the expertise in secret warfare passed on by the British to the Americans, proved a more difficult, but in the end more rewarding, task than I first anticipated. Along the way it often seemed as though I was experiencing the frustrations and difficulties that many a wartime secret agent must have felt while trying to penetrate the secrets of the enemy. For the territory of Allied intelligence secrets, even those of four decades ago, is still an occupied country. As a professional historian who had already written a history of the Special Operations Executive, *Britain and European Resistance 1940-1945*, I expected to confront a certain amount of official secrecy and reticence. "Continued government secrecy," I had noted in 1978 in the foreword of my book on SOE, "perpetuates an absurdity...and must long since have lost any 'rational justification'." In the eight years since I wrote those words, a flood of books about SOE in particular, and also about OSS and Anglo-American secret wartime intelligence operations in general, has poured onto the market. Above all, the most closely guarded secret of the war, the breaking of enemy ciphers and the triumphs of Allied intelligence, has been thoroughly documented, even to the point where a massive three-volume official history of British intelligence operations has appeared. So when my publisher suggested that I write a book about Camp X, I anticipated that many of the problems created by official secrecy would have disappeared and that the basic documentary sources would be readily available.

Unfortunately, I had forgotten something else I had written in 1978. "The obsession with secrecy is perhaps the true English disease," I had said then, noting that "the cult of secrecy is one of the rituals whereby powerful and informal elite groups exercise and protect their influence in British society." Social change never comes quickly. In Britain it comes more slowly than elsewhere. I soon learned that the iron curtain of official secrecy about SOE in many ways remains firmly in place. It is true that since the 1970s there has been a certain *détente* in the relationship between the researcher and the official mind that determines access to documents. More windows of opportunity are now open for the diligent scholar, and I received considerable help from the current keeper of the SOE archive. But he, too, is bound by official policy and the SOE archive still remains a closed society. Visas are required to enter it, and the best the visitor can hope for is a carefully guided tour by its friendly and helpful official. Individual explorations into the documents themselves are still forbidden, and blanket searches untied to specific questions cannot be answered. Benevolent the process and its guardian may be, but a form of intellectual despotism it remains.

This jealous custody of the raw materials extends beyond the United Kingdom to affect all documents of British origin held in Canada and the United States. On the surface, the situation appears quite different in Ottawa and Washington. Unlike Britain, both countries have freedom of information legislation. Just as I began my investigation, the extensive OSS archives were released to the National Archives in Washington, making free-ranging explorations among the thousands of operational files available to anyone. In Ottawa, when some of the Camp X records became available in 1985, I felt confident that my search would be relatively obstacle-free. I was wrong. It soon transpired that the Canadian and American governments deferred to British sensitivities about their operations in wartime North America – and Camp X, for all that it was built in Canada and had a Canadian administrative staff, was a British, SOE, operation. I found out quickly enough that freedom of information in North America meant little when confronted with the English disease.

The most dramatic example of this came when I visited Washington in December 1985. The detailed records of the OSS schools and training division had just been made available and I expected to find considerable evidence about American wartime links with Camp X and its British training staff. Indeed, there turned out to be a certain amount of valuable material there, including a completely declassified history of the training schools which until only the previous year had had many crucial passages deleted by the CIA. But the substantial files about OSS relations with BSC – the administrative link between OSS and SOE in North America – were missing. Finally, on my last day in Washington, I was told that some forty-nine boxes of documents had just arrived. Fully expecting to find what I was looking for, I rapidly scanned the titles of scores of files until at last I came across two labelled "OSS Liaison with BSC." Victory, I thought. But when opened, the files contained nothing more than official slips of paper indicating in laconic bureaucratic language that the documents had been withheld by the CIA on the grounds of national security. There was, the notation said, a foreign government interest in the matter. The note was dated just three days before I had arrived in Washington – and over forty years since Camp X had been closed.

This, and somewhat similar experiences in Ottawa, where British interests sometimes appeared to present a welcome alibi for an even greater obsession with secrecy, might have deterred me, had I not had the benefit of having successfully overcome worse frustrations in writing about SOE a decade ago. Like the intelligence analyst, I feel disinclined to give in to the persistence of the other side in this exercise in obscurantism, or be deterred by the lack of every last piece of possible information. The files that have been released and that I have seen, as well as answers that the helpful SOE archivist gave in response to my specific queries while I was in London, have clarified a large number of very crucial issues. From what I have discovered in the three capitals, and from what I already know from working in the area of British wartime intelligence over the last decade, I have constructed what I believe to be a highly accurate, if not completely comprehensive, account of Camp X and its role in Allied secret warfare.

The documents, of course, are never enough. They can only provide the skeleton of a portrait. To flesh out the story and bring it to life I have turned to the eyewitness accounts of many of those who commanded, worked, instructed, or received their training at Camp X. This, too, has presented a challenge. The operation was international in scope, and the Camp's surviving alumni are scattered across Canada, the United States, Britain, and other parts of the globe. Some of them were killed in the missions they undertook after leaving the Camp. Many more after the war slipped into the obscurity of private life and have effectively disappeared from the historical record – protected, in some cases, by recently enacted privacy legislation. Others have died. It is, after all, over forty years since the Camp was in operation, and time has now removed most of the middle and all the upper echelons of the Allied war effort. This is not a process that slows down. In the course of my research at least two important witnesses with whom I had established initial contact, Ivar Bryce and Sidney Morrell, died before I could talk to them. Others, such as John Shaheen, an American graduate of Camp X who became a millionaire in New York, died before I even had the chance to contact them. Yet others, still loyal to their wartime oaths of secrecy, are reluctant or afraid to talk in spite of the enormous amount of once top-secret information now publicly and freely available to all and sundry. But here, too, the lessons that agents at Camp X learned about interrogation have helped me. People talk if it seems clear that you already know a good deal of the story. I did, and many of them have.

Another lesson also proved useful: never assume anything. Initially I focused on talking to many of the Canadians who had worked or trained at the Camp, and took it for granted that the British officers who ran it would have been of senior rank and thus unlikely to still be alive. I underestimated the longevity of those who had kept fit in the long Canadian winters of four decades ago. Fortunately, I had at the very beginning taken the precaution of making a carefully placed enquiry in London. Halfway through my researches this unexpectedly opened the door to Bill Brooker and Cuthbert Skilbeck, the two surviving wartime commandants of Camp X. Neither had talked to anyone about his experiences at Camp X before, both were dismayed by the outrageous public misinformation and myth about its wartime role, and each was more than willing to tell me his side of the story. In turn, they introduced me to some of the specialized instructors who had served under them. So I spent much of my time in various parts of the United Kingdom talking to eyewitness experts with vivid firsthand experiences of Camp X. One of them I met in one of the most historic guilds of the City of London; others I talked to among the peaks of the Scottish Highlands. In the United States, I talked to former OSS agents living in Washington and Virginia who had trained at Camp X, while throughout Canada, from Prince Edward Island in the east to Vancouver Island in the west, people with stories to tell gave freely of their time and information.

Many of those associated with the abortive Camp X museum project of the late 1970s willingly told me about both their own wartime experiences and the results of their own investigations into the subject. A number of the Canadian women who worked in the United States for British Security Co-ordination – and without whom it could never have functioned – gave generously of their recollections. Although few had had any direct connection with Camp X, they helped considerably in my understanding of BSC operations and its personalities and provided many crucial clues, the value of which neither they nor I necessarily appreciated at the time, but which proved important later.

Not surprisingly, reality turns out to be rather different from – although no less fascinating than – myth. The true story of Camp X is one of the most intriguing tales of covert Allied co-operation to have come out of the undercover battles waged by the secret armies of the Second World War.

A word of explanation about the title, "Camp X", which other historians might consider a misnomer. Extensive and deliberate wartime secrecy surrounding the Camp and its operations has created considerable postwar confusion. Official British documents describe the Camp as Special Training School 103, or STS 103. But those in Canada have other designations for it. On a day-to-day basis most of those who had anything to do with the school, whether British, American, or Canadian, simply referred to it as "The Camp" or, more frequently, "The Farm," for it was built on the fields of an old family farm. Such a plethora of names posed an obvious dilemma. In the end I decided that posterity should have the last word.

Rightly or wrongly, this Special Training School has become widely known as "Camp X" in Canada, the United States, and Britain. This is how the 1985 *Canadian Encyclopedia* refers to it, as does the commemorative plaque unveiled in 1984 that now marks the site in Ontario. To use one of the more technically correct titles would at this stage increase rather than diminish confusion where there is already too much. And finally, of the two surviving commandants of the school, one clearly remembers that "Camp X" was a term occasionally used, and neither finds the term inappropriate or unacceptable. If they can live with it – and between them they witnessed the entire life of the Camp – then so can the rest of us.

CHAPTER 1

"A Good Place to Make Hooch":
The Farm on Lake Ontario

Algiers, capital of the former French North African empire, was one of the jewels of Mediterranean culture. By late 1942 it had also become the headquarters of the Allied forces, which, in Operation TORCH, had landed all along the North African coast on the morning of 8 November. The French called the city *Alger la Blanche* – Algiers the White – because of the dazzling white terraces that rose steeply up from the palm-fringed boulevards of the sea front to the pine-studded hills behind the city. On one of these hills stood the luxurious Hotel Saint-George, which General Dwight D. Eisenhower, commander of the Allied invasion force, had made his personal headquarters. Just a little below it lay the *Palais d'Eté*, a splendid white Moorish-style mansion that was the official residence of the French governors-general.

On Christmas Eve, 1942, a young man in his early twenties arrived at the *Palais d'Eté* at two o'clock in the afternoon to find that its resident, Admiral François Darlan, was still at lunch. He waited patiently in an anteroom outside the admiral's office. Finally, an hour later, Darlan returned. As he approached his office the young man took out a revolver and fired. Darlan fell to the floor and died a few hours later in hospital. The young man, Fernand Bonnier de la Chapelle, was seized by Darlan's chauffeur and bundled off to a police station. Justice was swift. Found guilty by a French court-martial the day after Christmas, Bonnier was shot before dawn the following day.

Darlan's assassination caused both a crisis and a sigh of relief in Washington and London. A crisis, because he had been the highest French official in North Africa, and his death threatened civil order in the territory where the Allies were still establishing their control. A relief, because Eisenhower had paid what many critics had thought was too high a price to ensure that the local French military forces did not resist the Allied landings.

Darlan, Vichy's commander-in-chief and former prime minister to Marshal Philippe Pétain, the leader of Vichy France, had been in Algiers visiting his sick son, Philippe, hospitalized by polio, when the Allies landed. Through a deal with Darlan that left Vichy political control largely intact, Eisenhower had secured a quick armistice and an almost bloodless occupation. But "the Darlan deal" provoked international controversy and a storm of criticism. Vichy laws, including anti-Semitic ones, remained in place. Darlan was a particularly notorious symbol of French collaboration with the Nazis, for as a former Vichy prime minister he had signed arrangements on close co-operation with the Germans. At Berchtesgaden in May 1941 he had agreed to let the Germans use military bases in Syria, Tunisia, and Dakar. The American deal with Darlan seemed a betrayal of the very liberalism and democracy the Allies were supposed to be fighting for, a gratuitous offence to the British for whom Darlan had never disguised his dislike and fear, and a slap in the face to the French resistance for whom Darlan and Vichy were as much an enemy as the Germans. Lord Selborne, the minister in charge of SOE, protested bitterly to Anthony Eden, the British foreign secretary, that the deal "has produced violent reactions on all our subterranean organisations, particularly in France where it has had a blasting and withering effect."[1] But, as the old Balkan proverb has it and as Roosevelt put it to Churchill, "It is permitted to walk with the devil until you have crossed the bridge."

"Wild Bill" Donovan was one of the many Americans who strongly disliked the deal. To maintain American influence in France, he wrote on the anniversary of Pearl Harbor, "we have before us the very practical problem of eliminating the political leadership of Darlan."[2] The assassination, therefore, solved a problem. But who was behind it?

It took the French police in Algiers little time to learn that Bonnier de la Chapelle was a royalist fanatic and a member of a small military organization known as the *Corps Franc d'Afrique*, a group of young anti-Vichy volunteers. The *Corps Franc*, it turned out, was quartered at Ain Taya, a small base on the coast at Cap Matifou about thirty miles outside the city. Interestingly, SOE had made Cap Matifou the headquarters of its mission in North Africa, known by the code name MASSINGHAM; the British had recruited some of the young men from the *Corps* and given them sabotage and weapons training. Among the instructors was an American, an OSS man, who spent much of his time giving the students weapons and explosives instruction. He recalled after the war that "They were all young, enthusiastic and eager to learn. My job was to teach them all sorts of paramilitary actions, including tossing hand grenades and tying up prisoners. I taught in French and Arabic when needed. Being a professional teacher who missed his audience, I enjoyed it thoroughly."[3] Among his students was Bonnier de la Chapelle.

In Algiers the police quickly arrested one of the French instructors at Ain Taya on suspicion of complicity. They then learned that the OSS man had been seen in the vicinity of the *Palais d'Eté* at the time of the murder. That night they surrounded the SOE villa at Cap Matifou, but the OSS man had already slipped out of town. His name was Carleton S. Coon, one of the first Americans to have graduated from Camp X.

Coon's connection with the Darlan assassination is only one episode in a bizarre and exotic career as one of Donovan's "gentleman volunteers", a phrase Coon himself used in describing his life with the OSS.

"It is probably the secret ambition of every boy to travel in strange mountains, stir up tribes, and destroy the enemy by secret and unorthodox means," Coon wrote in a report for the OSS on his return to Washington in 1943.[4] Most boys grow up, but Coon, by his own admission, never did. He had to wait until his late thirties to fulfil his childhood ambitions, and in the meantime found a way to pursue his adventures in exotic places by becoming an anthropologist with eight field expeditions behind him by the time war broke out. His first field trip was to Morocco, shortly before the Riff rebellion against French rule in 1925, and his book, *The Tribes of the Rif*, published in 1931, gave him the Arab expertise that he was to use in the OSS. Later on, his book *Caravan* (1951) was to be widely used as a text by American diplomats concerned with the countries of the Middle East. A professor at Harvard, Coon became a leading anthropologist, but his robust and defiantly old-fashioned approach isolated him from the mainstream of opinion and often gave rise to allegations of racism. In his autobiography, published in 1981 just before he died and characteristically entitled *Adventures and Discoveries*, he complained bitterly that anthropology had become a forum for political criticism and unhealthy cultural introspection. "I have stood still," he noted, "and fads have risen and fallen around me."

There was little critical or introspective about Coon's view of his role in Donovan's OSS, which he seems to have regarded as merely another, if much more extended and exotic, field trip. "During these four years of excitement, boredom, good companionship, and the rare ecstasy of being on my own," he wrote, "I feel that I went through an ancient and fabulous rite of passage." When Donovan died in 1959, the CIA sent out a message to all its officials announcing: "The man more responsible than any other for the existence of the Central Intelligence Agency has passed away." Coon, on yet another expedition in The Riff, also heard the news, and immediately sat down in his tent and penned an adulatory ode to "Wild Bill" on the model of Homer's *Iliad*. Its last four lines read:

> How lucky we are that he came when he did in the lazy tide
> of history.
> Hail to Wild Bill, a hero of men and a name to hang myths
> on.
> As American as chowder, Crockett and Putnam
> A free fighter's hero, may God give him peace.[5]

Nor was Coon squeamish about solving the world's problems. He had once recommended to Donovan the formation of an élite corps of assassins, drawn from OSS and SOE, whose task it would be "to throw out the rotten apples as soon as the first spots of decay appear."

What path had taken Coon, an American, from his Harvard study via a secret agent training camp in Canada to the violent political whirlwinds that engulfed the British and the Americans in wartime North Africa?

The story went back to just over a year before, when Britain was still fighting for its existence and the United States remained a neutral power, but one that was increasingly fighting an undeclared war.

"We think the Americans are going to come into the war and they have to learn about all this stuff. Your job is to help train them and tell them everything we know." The date was September 1941, the location the headquarters of the British Special Operations Executive (SOE) at 64 Baker Street, London. The speaker was Colonel Colin Gubbins, the fiery and dapper Scot who was head of its training and operations directorate. Opposite him sat Major Bill Brooker, chosen by Gubbins from among the top SOE training staff in Britain to go out to Canada as the first chief instructor at Camp X.[6]

SOE was Britain's top-secret agency for promoting resistance against the Germans in Occupied Europe. Churchill had actively worked for its creation after becoming prime minister, and the War Cabinet had finally agreed in July 1940 when the whole of Western Europe was still reeling from the Nazi blitzkrieg victories of the spring. SOE was a hastily improvised expedient to channel the vast potential of European discontents against their Nazi overlords in Britain's favour. Eventually it grew to have a staff of over 10,000 men and women scattered across the globe, and was to train hundreds of secret agents who were infiltrated behind enemy lines to conduct sabotage and guerrilla operations in Europe and Asia. But in the fall of 1941 these successes were still in the unseeable future. Hugh Dalton, the minister in charge of SOE, a tall man with a booming voice and forceful character who belonged to the Socialist half of Churchill's wartime coalition, spoke of promoting revolution against the Nazis in Europe. When Churchill put him in charge of SOE, he had suggested that Dalton should "set Europe ablaze". But in the fall of 1941 SOE's achievements resembled a damp squib rather than a blazing conflagration.

Sir Frank Nelson, SOE's first executive director (code-named CD), was – in the words of Bickham Sweet-Escott, one of his colleagues who left a personal record of his experiences in his *Baker*

Street Irregular – "a man of great determination and utter ruthlessness." A fifty-six-year-old former India merchant, he had been a
Conservative Member of Parliament, but, more importantly, had had
considerable experience working with the Secret Intelligence Service
(SIS) while acting as consul in Basle in the 1930s. Nelson, a prodi-
gious worker, recruited several top-rank people to help run SOE, but
"setting Europe ablaze" proved a difficult task when the fuel supplies
were low. As Sweet-Escott later wrote, "It was impossible in the last
analysis to move faster than the Europeans themselves." And the
Nazis were often there first. While the first SOE agents had been
established in France, networks throughout the Balkans had been destroyed when the Germans had marched into Yugoslavia and Greece in
the previous April. Small arms being supplied to SOE by the War
Office were proving useless because there were not enough agents in
the field to use them.

On the wider canvas of the war, the picture was equally bleak that
fall. In the previous May, British forces had been driven from Crete;
in North Africa, Egypt was under threat. In the east, Hitler's armies
had launched their massive attack on the Soviet Union in June and
were slicing through Soviet defences with impressive speed. As
Gubbins sat with Brooker in his office, German armies had just surrounded Leningrad in the north and were pushing on to Moscow in
the centre. In the south, the city of Kiev had been captured three
weeks before. Britain's newfound ally seemed to be going the way of
France. To the west, things looked brighter but still remained un-
certain. The British depended heavily on the Americans to keep their
transatlantic lifeline secure, and in August Churchill and Roosevelt
had met off the coast of Newfoundland to sign the Atlantic Charter.
To all intents and purposes the United States was now conducting an
undeclared war against Nazi Germany. In Asia things were moving,
too. That summer Japan had turned Indo-China into a Japanese protectorate; in retaliation Roosevelt had joined with the British and the
Dutch in imposing an embargo on the sale of oil and steel to the warlords in Tokyo. The Anglo-American Alliance was in the making, but
it was still a common-law marriage. Gubbins and SOE were determined that, when it became official, it should extend from the realm
of regular military operations to that of secret war.

Colin McVeagh Gubbins was determined in practically everything he did. Code-named "M", he had been director of SOE training and operations since November 1940. Eventually, in September 1943, he was to become head of the whole organization. But long before that, he had been the mainspring for SOE. In outward appearance he was a stereotype, almost a caricature, of the Regular Army officer. A small, dark-haired, wiry Highland Scot in his mid-forties, he wore a toothbrush moustache, was always impeccably dressed, and spoke in clipped and staccato sentences. Born in 1896 in Japan, where his father was in the British consular service, he had been decorated for bravery in the First World War, in which he fought with the Royal Artillery in Flanders and France; afterwards he took part in the anti-Bolshevik campaign in northern Russia. A period of service in Ireland fighting in the anti-guerrilla campaign against the nationalists had followed. From these experiences Gubbins had been impressed, in historian M.R.D. Foot's words, "by the weakness of formal bodies of troops faced by a hostile population that was stiffened by a few resolute gunmen, and determined to exploit these impressions against the next enemy."[7]

History had helped to make him a man ahead of his time. Professional soldiers of strong anti-Communist views were common enough, but Gubbins combined this with fluency in languages, wide reading, and a strong interest and considerable expertise in guerrilla and unconventional warfare. In 1939 he wrote two pamphlets for the War Office, *The Art of Guerrilla Warfare* and *Partisan Leader's Handbook*, in the second of which he covered such practical points as how to organize ambushes and immobilize locomotives. Informers, he recommended, should be killed quickly. Then, in 1940, he had organized and commanded the "Striking Companies" that had covered the British retreat in Norway. All of this helped to ensure that he would quickly become a central figure in SOE's evolution and that its training and operations would reflect many of his own views on how to conduct ungentlemanly war. For behind the soft-spoken and quiet-mannered exterior was a strong personality of tireless energy for whom SOE had become a personal vision. "He was a man-at-arms," wrote Joan Bright Astley, who worked with him later, "a campaigner; the fires banked up inside him as glowing as those round which his Celtic ancestors had gathered between forays for glen and brae."[8]

Perhaps Gubbins's most successful campaign up to then had been to create from nothing an extensive and effective training system. Already, over 1,500 students had passed through some thirty SOE training schools, the majority recruited through old boys' networks or from volunteers already in the armed forces. It was a system that worked for the British, and Gubbins was now convinced it would work for the Americans.

SOE training has been described as a set of sieves, each one with a closer mesh than the one before. "One of the objects," writes M.R.D. Foot, "was to sieve out the unsuitables before they could wreak havoc abroad."[9] The standard training of an SOE agent – man or woman – consisted of three main phases. The first, lasting for two or three weeks, involved physical conditioning, elementary map-reading, and some basic instruction in pistols and sub-machineguns. Disguised as a commando training course and held at one of several country houses that SOE had requisitioned around the south of England, it eliminated many unsuitable candidates, some of them unable to resist the temptations of the deliberately well-stocked bars, others unable to take the physical pace. As techniques improved later in the war, this preliminary screening was replaced by an assessment board that examined students for psychological soundness.

Those who passed the first phase went on for three or four weeks of paramilitary training in Scotland, at one of the several big country houses that SOE had taken over in Arisaig, on the west coast of Inverness, close to where Gubbins himself was from. It was a wild and inviolate place, protected from prying eyes by lack of roads and the fact that the Admiralty had declared it a prohibited area. "A wretched, barren countryside, thinly populated; rain fell from a heavy sky that never cleared completely...a most depressing place," remembered Pieter Dourlein, a Dutch agent.[10] These schools were known as the Group A schools. Here, instructors taught agents more about small arms, silent killing, demolitions, sabotage, basic infantry training, fieldcraft, and elementary Morse code. There were plenty of practical exercises both by day and by night, some of them dangerous, and the recruits who passed the scrutiny of their instructors were thoroughly prepared for the challenges of their missions.

The jewel in the crown of the SOE training empire was Beaulieu, the spacious grounds of an old abbey set deep in the New Forest. Here, at the Group B schools, students passed through the third phase. Carefully segregated into national groups and isolated in various houses on and around the Beaulieu estate, agents received the final training in the finer points of their future clandestine lives. In essence, these B schools were the finishing schools. Students learned about the various branches of the German and Italian security forces and their relationship with various elements of the police in occupied countries. They received lectures on the Nazi Party and the German Army, and they heard from agents who had returned from the field how to deal with police controls and interrogation. Methods of security, cover, and disguise were heavily emphasized. In learning how to become invisible behind enemy lines, agents had to absorb thoroughly not only general principles of security but particular details of the country in which they would be working. What were local conditions really like? How should you dress to be inconspicuous? How should you behave in a bar or restaurant? What small points of daily behaviour, such as the way you held a cigarette while smoking or looking the wrong way while crossing a street, could give you away as an outsider?

Above all, they learned how to play a part, internalizing a false identity so well that they would merge undetected into the surrounding society. This required defensive skills quite different from the aggressive ones taught at Arisaig. Many of those who did well at paramilitary training failed to make the grade in the Group B schools. But those who did also learned about recruiting and running agents in occupied territory, message writing, secret inks, communications, and elementary codes and ciphers. There was also considerable education in the arts of propaganda.

Before finally leaving for the operational holding schools where they were kept immediately prior to going on missions, students would take part in practical exercises. For example, a railway junction several miles away would be targeted for destruction. Would-be agents had to lay explosives without being detected by the constabulary or military authorities or turned in by suspicious locals. In case of arrest they were provided with a cover story and, in the last resort, with a telephone number to call should their cover story not hold.

The training staff at Beaulieu were as intensely committed as their students to absorbing the skills that could mean the difference between life and death. They were a relatively small and homogeneous group who developed a powerful *esprit de corps*. They believed that the war against Hitler had to be fought on many fronts and in many ways, and that the arts of secret war could hasten the end of a far greater evil than the methods they used. In the hothouse atmosphere of wartime Beaulieu, friendships were forged that lasted a lifetime and a cadre of expertise and commitment created that SOE exported to its training schools across the world.

Even Kim Philby, the Soviet agent fighting his own special and silent war, recognized the achievements of the SOE training system. For a brief period in 1940, on his way to his ultimate goal of penetrating SIS, he worked for SOE at Beaulieu as a propaganda instructor. "Our staff of instructors," he wrote in *My Silent War*, the memoirs he later penned in Moscow, "had more than their fair share of intelligence and imagination…attacks on [SOE's] training establishment have been relatively and deservedly few."

The chief instructor at Beaulieu that fall of 1941 was Bill Brooker, a man with an ego as powerful as that of Gubbins himself. Eventually the two men were to develop conflicting views about what direction SOE should take in working with the resistance, and Gubbins would shunt Brooker to one side. But that September day in Gubbins's office, Brooker felt in complete harmony with the mission for which he had been chosen. Gubbins knew his man, and he had picked the perfect candidate for selling SOE to the Americans.

"Bill Brooker," wrote Sweet-Escott in *Baker Street Irregular*, "was a born salesman. He was a brilliant and convincing lecturer, and he had an immense fund of stories from the real life of a secret agent to illustrate his point." He was also a strong personality with a direct and forthright approach to issues and people and little respect for pomp, pretension, or position. Inside his large and powerful British frame was an American struggling to get out. It is hardly surprising that after he left Camp X he managed to get himself seconded to the OSS, for whom he worked in both the United States and Europe, and that after the war he was awarded the American Legion of Merit. Nor is it surprising that he succeeded in rubbing many of his British superiors the wrong way. Lacking an Oxbridge education, and with a background in European commerce, he mixed uneasily with many of the City-bred executives and professional soldiers who staffed the upper reaches of SOE. Many disliked him and some regarded him with suspicion. Brooker was unorthodox. He disagreed with the direction that SOE gradually took in favour of paramilitary warfare. Far better, he believed, to use Europeans already in place than to parachute large numbers of inexperienced agents behind enemy lines. He was not a man to keep such views to himself, and they made him enemies.

Brooker captivated his audiences with vivid accounts of what it was like to be a secret agent. He delivered his talks with such powerful conviction that on at least one occasion a high-level OSS official asked his British opposite number in Washington if Brooker was head of the British Secret Service. Brooker thrived on all this. Ironically, one of those who most appreciated Brooker's talent was his colleague Philby. Each made a strong impression on the other. Brooker to this day remembers Philby as "the cleverest man I ever met in my life", while in his memoirs Philby described Brooker as "the dynamic sales-man type with an inexhaustible armory of wisecracks and anecdotes, including a series in brilliant Marseilles argot...as far as I am aware he had never lived an underground life. But after a little research he could talk to trainees as if he had never lived otherwise." For once, however, Philby's intelligence was less than complete. Had he known more about Brooker's pre-war career, he might have appreciated an important source of Brooker's effectiveness as a lecturer in the skills of secret service. For it was not all a question of pure imagination or a natural flair for anecdote and drama. There was some lived exper-ience, too.

Brooker came to SOE with extensive firsthand knowledge of European life and languages. He had been born in France, where his father managed the Paris office of Thomas Cook's travel agency, and French was his first language. From the late 1920s he worked for the Nestlé company at their headquarters in Vevey, Switzerland. Throughout the 1930s he travelled extensively across Europe as an export salesman for Nestlé products. He had thus learned how to negotiate his way skilfully across the financial and territorial fron-

tiers of a rapidly destabilizing continent where officials regularly interrogated him about his business. The outbreak of the Spanish Civil
War found him in Barcelona carrying out an audit of Nestlé's Spanish
interests. He quickly left, but there remained the trickier problem of
getting blocked pesetas to Switzerland. "We got them out through the
Pyrenees, using couriers and clandestine routes," he later recalled. "It
took volumes of false papers and plenty of imagination."

When the Second World War was declared, Brooker immediately joined the Field Security Police. A course at the Intelligence Staff
College at Matlock, where his forthright and distinctly unmilitary attitudes to authority brought him into conflict with the commandant,
was followed by several weeks' work as a port security officer on the
rough Tyneside docks, where he learned a great deal about the techniques of interrogating and searching suspects. Following an interview by Gubbins, who immediately recognized him as a man after his
own heart, Brooker was recruited into SOE. Shortly afterwards,
Gubbins sent him to Beaulieu as an instructor.[11]

It was one thing for Gubbins and Brooker to talk about helping the
Americans to learn the arts of secret war; it was harder to arrange for
it to be done. It was not practicable for Americans to enter SOE
schools in Britain. For one thing, the British already had full hands
training their own recruits. For another, it would be time-consuming,
expensive, and wasteful of scarce resources – not to mention dangerous – to transport Americans across the Atlantic to enrol in British
schools when a predictable percentage of them were bound to prove
unsuitable. Not least of all, the United States was still a neutral power.
Should such a scheme become public knowledge, Roosevelt's administration would have an even rougher time than it normally did with
isolationist elements at home.

In any case, Gubbins envisaged far more than the training of
agents. He wanted to help shape the mental universe of those in the
United States who were preparing for American entry into the shadow war. Instead of the Americans coming to Britain, Gubbins
concluded, the British would have to go to the Americans. The obvious way was to establish an SOE training school in North America.
It would have to provide easy access to and from the United States but
without being on American soil. The obvious site: Canada.

The decision had been finalized only two or three days before Brooker was summoned to Gubbins's office. And because of the American dimension, the crucial meetings had taken place in the heart of New York.

St. Patrick's Cathedral in midtown Manhattan is one of the city's most famous landmarks, a place of worship and haven of calm amid the frantic activity of the city outside. Across from its main entrance on Fifth Avenue stands Rockefeller Center, a bustling complex of office buildings into which thousands of clerical workers pour every day. In the middle stands the International Building, which, like those around it, is largely occupied by the offices of airline companies, banks, and insurance agencies. In 1941 the thirty-fifth and thirty-sixth floors of the building were occupied by a British agency known officially to the United States government as British Security Co-ordination, or BSC. The plaque on the door of the main entrance to the offices on the thirty-fifth floor told the idle passer-by that this was British Passport Control, and indeed this is where those who had British passport or visa problems came to have them dealt with. But neither designation told the whole truth. BSC was an organization whose power stretched beyond the United States into the whole of North and South America, and its responsibilities covered far more than mere security matters.

Essentially, BSC was Britain's intelligence window in America, acting as representative of the major British agencies concerned with security and intelligence issues, and as their principal liaison in the United States with their American counterparts. The most important British agency was the Security Executive – officially designated the Home Defence (Security) Executive – created by Churchill almost as soon as he became prime minister in May 1940. Its creation owed a great deal to the panic that swept Britain during the rapid advances of the Germans through the Low Countries and France that month, aided, it was widely (and largely erroneously) believed, by an extensive internal "fifth column" of Nazi sympathizers. To avoid such dangers in Britain and to "find out whether there is a fifth column in this country and if so to eliminate it", Churchill appointed Lord Swinton (the former Philip Cunliffe-Lister, minister for air, 1935-38) to take charge. As the prime minister explained to the House of Commons later, existing departments concerned with national security "were not working smoothly. There were overlaps and underlaps, and I felt in that hour of anxiety that this side of the business wanted pulling together."[12]

Directly responsible to Churchill, the Security Executive, and its work, is still shrouded in secrecy, and its files have never been released. But while then, and now, remaining largely invisible, it was a powerful body that cast a wide net over the host of activities affecting national security: communications, censorship, travel, ports, shipping, and the internment of aliens. So far as British Security Co-ordination was concerned, the Security Executive was the parent body that laid down the guidelines it was to follow.

Although the Security Executive was established largely because of Churchill's dissatisfaction with the regular security and intelligence services, it did not replace them. M.I.5, the domestic security service that was also responsible for security in all overseas British territories, was considerably reorganized, given a new chief, Sir David Petrie, and put under closer supervision. It, too, used BSC as its representative in the Western Hemisphere. But the relationship was not an easy one, and in 1943 M.I.5 decided that BSC should no longer look after its interests in either Canada or the Caribbean.

SIS, or the Secret Intelligence Service (also known as M.I.6), was the third agency that BSC represented in the Western Hemisphere. Headed by Sir Stewart Menzies, SIS carried out intelligence overseas and also was responsible for counter-intelligence in non-British territories through its intelligence section, Section V. This latter function was particularly important where the United States was concerned, and BSC liaised extensively on counter-intelligence with the United States' authorities. Finally, after December 1940, BSC also agreed to act in the Americas on behalf of SOE, which at that stage of the war still had important responsibilities for propaganda.

These varying responsibilities were reflected in BSC's internal organization. There were four basic sections: Intelligence, Security, Special Operations, and Passport Control. A further section, that of Communications, was added later and assumed growing significance as the war developed. This was because BSC came to provide the main channel of communication for the distribution of top-grade intelligence between London and Washington. As we shall see in Chapter 6, it was also made responsible for arranging security measures that protected this highly sensitive source.

At the centre of this British secret empire in the United States stood its forty-five-year-old director, the diminutive "Quiet Canadian", William Stephenson.

Stephenson, who was later to be knighted for his wartime services, was a successful businessman with a superb First World War record as a fighter pilot. Originally from Winnipeg, he had left Canada after the war and become deeply involved in various business ventures in Britain, Europe, and North America. An unobtrusive man with piercing blue eyes and a legendary capacity for drinking dry martinis, Stephenson carried considerable punch – literally, because he had once been a successful amateur boxer, and figuratively, because he had a wide international range of business contacts and was adept at opening American doors that remained closed to his English counterparts. "He had the capacity," wrote Patrick Howarth in *Undercover*, his study of personalities involved with SOE, "for going straight to the heart of any problem and an inclination to go straight to the top of any organization with which he had to deal."

In the 1930s Stephenson had become involved with the so-called "Z" network of unofficial SIS contacts set up by one of its leading lights, Sir Claude Dansey, to provide information about German industrial capacity acquired during business trips to Germany. In May 1940 Sir Stewart Menzies, as newly appointed head of SIS, had sent him to act as head of SIS in the United States, where shortly afterwards he was reinforced by a professional SIS officer, Colonel Charles H. ("Dick") Ellis. An Australian by birth, Ellis (against whom so-far-unproven allegations of being a Soviet mole have recently been made) had been sent to New York by Menzies to run the secret intelligence division of BSC, and, according to some sources, to keep a watching eye on Stephenson, about whom some of the top SIS brass had reservations concerning his expertise. When Stephenson arrived in New York as station chief, it was under the then-standard cover as head of British Passport Control. A few months later Stephenson expanded his responsibilities into the security and special operations spheres. His organization grew from a small suite in Hampshire House, an elegant apartment hotel at the south end of Central Park, to a staff of several hundred occupying three entire floors in Rockefeller Center.

Stephenson never played the role of global spymaster that recent popular accounts have claimed. His responsibilities were confined to North and South America, and had nothing directly to do with either European or Far Eastern operations. Versions of history that have Stephenson planning operations in Occupied Europe are figments of the imagination. BSC was primarily a liaison agency with relevant American authorities, and both here and in other areas of the Western Hemisphere Stephenson operated within guidelines and under directives laid down by London.

Still, Stephenson did an excellent job in the limited but extremely vital task given him by Churchill, who understood how essential the Anglo-American relationship was. Stephenson was certainly not a professional spy himself and he knew little about the business. Neither did many of those he recruited to work for him. But for much of the really essential work that had to be done by BSC – liaison with the Americans and the early building of the Anglo-American security and intelligence relationship – Stephenson amply deserved his knighthood.

In late 1942 Commander Philip Johns, SIS head of station in Lisbon, was transferred to be head of station in Buenos Aires. Passing through New York, he spent several days meeting with Stephenson and various members of BSC while he waited for onward transport. Writing his memoirs *Within Two Cloaks* almost forty years later, he was extremely critical of popular versions of Stephenson's wartime role and eager to point out that, even from his SIS post in South America, he never reported to Stephenson on operational matters. Nonetheless, Johns had generous words to offer. "He radiated warmth and enthusiasm," he recalled. "He was exceptionally brilliant and enjoyed not only loyalty from his subordinates but deep admiration and respect for the job he was doing so well. No choice could have been more suitable for the extremely delicate position he held. Being Canadian helped a lot, and a 'Limey', however talented, would have had a much tougher task."

More recently, another former top SIS official, speaking anonymously, said of Stephenson that "he might have been a lousy spy...but he was a damned effective liaison man and did a first-rate job with the Americans."

Stephenson's wartime private suite was Number 1418 on the fourteenth floor of the exclusive St. Regis Hotel in midtown Manhattan. On the evening of Saturday, September 6, 1941, he invited a small group of friends for cocktails, and a couple of hours later the men moved to the rooftop restaurant for dinner. It was brief – the band was too loud and they could not hear themselves talk – so they quickly returned to Stephenson's apartment, where the conversation continued until after midnight.

Of Stephenson's guests two were British, two Canadian, and one American. The first of the Britons was a man called Tommy Davies, who had just flown in from SOE headquarters in London and in whose honour Stephenson was hosting the dinner. One of the top items he had come to discuss was the value of a training school for SOE in North America, and its possible location. Professor Noel Hall, director of London's National Institute for Economic and Social Research, who was now working as head of the War Trade Department in the British Embassy in Washington, was the second British guest. Hall's ministry in London provided cover for SOE – Hugh Dalton was the minister in charge of both – and their work often overlapped. In New York to have a couple of troublesome wisdom teeth extracted, Hall was accompanied that evening by the lone American, Dr. Blake Donaldson. Donaldson was a celebrated New York doctor who had recently caused controversy by suggesting in a book called *Strong Medicine* that America had too many doctors and not enough specialists, a thesis that understandably had not endeared him to his colleagues. Far more used to controversy was the fourth guest, the great Canadian arctic explorer Vilhjálmur Stefansson. The white-haired Stefansson was really the star of the evening, impressing the company with his forceful views on Russia's importance and that country's likely contribution to the war – a brave thing to do as the *Wehrmacht*'s pincers were closing around Leningrad.

The explorer, his face heavily lined by the arctic winds, was now in his sixties, but three decades earlier he had commanded the five-year Canadian Arctic Expedition to the frozen wilderness of the North. A great and controversial proponent of the strategic and commercial importance of the Arctic, Stefansson now lived in the United States and was about to reach an agreement with Donovan to establish a centre of arctic studies in the United States comparable to the Scott Polar Institute in Britain.

Inevitably, discussion soon turned to likely Japanese moves in the Pacific now that the German armies were distracting Stalin's forces in the war. Clearly the Americans were becoming more directly affected by Japanese expansionism, and their need for valuable strategic information made it all the more important that Donovan's new organization should succeed. "His speech is so clear, the facts always incisive," noted the fifth of the guests that night as he observed Stefansson's favourable impact on the visitors from Britain, "a great mind and very impressive to sound men like Hall and Davies."[13]

Sound men were always appreciated by Alfred James Towle Taylor, the other Canadian present that evening. This wealthy Vancouver businessman was an intimate friend of both Blake Donaldson and William Stephenson, and his presence at the St. Regis dinner and his meeting with Davies – whom he described as "a great fellow on Security just in from London" – were to be decisive for the story of Camp X. For it was A.J. Taylor who transformed the project from idea into reality.

Taylor's role in the history of British Security Co-ordination in general, and Camp X in particular, has until now remained unknown except to a small handful of those most closely involved with Stephenson. Having no official position with BSC and dying of a stroke almost as soon as the war was over, Taylor left little record of his contribution. Continued secrecy about the subject, combined with the distorting effect of myth, accomplished the rest. Only from his personal diary, still in the family's possession, can we trace in some detail the important part he played in this story.

"He has wide shoulders which deceive you by making him look short; busy hands; a direct approach to anything and everything; and thick dark hair where there is hair," noted journalist Gordon Sinclair, who interviewed him in 1940. He might also have noted Taylor's rimless glasses and the narrow, straight line for a mouth that helped to fix the portrait of this determined figure. When Taylor spoke, it was with a booming and deliberate voice that enunciated each word so clearly that it seemed to stand as a separate unit in itself rather than as a part of a sentence. Deliberate and careful construction might be said to have characterized much else about Taylor. He stood as an exemplar of a Canadian type who through ability and hard work had risen from being a self-employed engineer to being an extremely wealthy man who conceived it as his duty to put his power and influence at the service of the British Empire. "He can who thinks he can", "Life is what you make it", and "Take care of that which you seek, for that you shall surely have" were the platitudes of the self-made man that sprang as readily from Taylor's lips as the notes on his "disposition of time" that were carefully entered each day into his diary. Even his spare-time activities were of a utilitarian bent. His favourite pastime was the careful construction of gramophones, and his reading was confined to philosophy and biography. Novels and movies, he disliked.

The son of an Anglican clergyman from Victoria, British Columbia, he had started work at the age of fourteen in a machine shop on Vancouver Island, but by age twenty-five he had accumulated enough money to start his own engineering firm in Vancouver. In the mid-1920s he conceived the idea of using British capital to develop Vancouver by building a bridge across the First Narrows and creating an exclusive residential area on its North Shore. This visionary idea was met with scepticism in Vancouver but embraced by British financiers anxious to invest their money abroad – particularly the great Guinness brewery family whose money enabled Taylor to form British Pacific Properties, the syndicate that developed practically all of North and West Vancouver and of which he later became president. Taylor's vision materialized in 1939 when the Lion's Gate Bridge, a three-lane $6 million suspension bridge, was officially opened by King George VI on his royal tour of Canada. By then Taylor was a wealthy and influential man, a power broker in business contacts between Britain and Canada, and an anglophile go-getter with considerable and justifiable respect for his own achievements.

Taylor and Stephenson had known each other for several years through Stephenson's own financial interest in British Properties, and since the war they had been thrown even closer together. For now Taylor was working with the British Supply Council in Washington and was a frequent visitor to New York. The two men frequently breakfasted together, and about as often Taylor would drop round to the St. Regis after a day's work to exchange views and information about their respective work for the British war effort. "Bill has a great grasp of human affairs," Taylor wrote after one such meeting. "He is exactly fitted for his present job; moves about silently and in quite high places."[14]

Stephenson held little back from Taylor about his work in high places, and treated him as a professional confidant. It was a role of *éminence grise* that Taylor enjoyed. "I like being in on these plans before they become public," he confided to his diary after Stephenson had let him in on one of BSC's early schemes soon after "the Quiet Canadian" had arrived in New York. Particularly during the early period when Stephenson's organization was rapidly expanding, Taylor acted as the facilitator in many of his friend's administrative and personnel problems. Through his wide business contacts he helped to recruit a number of the young Canadian women who formed the bulk of Stephenson's administrative staff, and he arranged cover for some of the executives in the most sensitive positions. Kay, his own daughter – later to become a secretary to Lester Pearson at the Canadian Embassy in Washington – was one of the BSC staff. But his single most important contribution to Stephenson was his help in constructing Camp X.

The St. Regis dinner proved crucial in the history of Camp X. The following day, Taylor and Davis agreed to build the camp on the shore of Lake Ontario close to Toronto. Only two other people were present. Stephenson himself was occupied; instead, the BSC viewpoint was represented by two who worked in its Special Operations Section: Richard Coit and Ivar Bryce.

Coit was a man in his sixties with a pink and fiery complexion and a shiny pate with a halo of white hair. Known irreverently by his staff as "Coitus Interruptus" because he expected questions to be answered before they were asked, and once described by an acquaintance as "looking but certainly not behaving like a bishop," Coit had been placed in charge of the Special Operations Section at BSC the previous winter. Impatient, unpredictable, and distinctly idiosyncratic in running his section, Coit was to be replaced in the summer of 1942 by one of SOE's top London executives, Louis Franck, a wealthy Belgian banker whose favourite epigram suggested that he was eminently more suited to the world of subterfuge. "Truth," he was fond of saying to his colleagues, "is far too precious a commodity to be used lightly."

Coit's assistant, Ivar Bryce, was a lifelong friend of Ian Fleming who after the author's death wrote a book of reminiscences on their friendship entitled *You Only Live Once*. A wealthy and handsome young Englishman who by his own confession was remarkably indolent, and passing through a trough in what was always a tempestuous married life, Bryce had found himself at a distinctly loose end in 1939. Eventually he found his way into BSC, where Coit had given him the task of looking for likely recruits for secret missions into Occupied Europe from among immigrant communities in Latin America. "I recruited twenty such volunteers," Bryce wrote later. "About half never made it and for one reason or another were rejected."

It was Taylor who at that Sunday morning meeting suggested that Ontario would be an ideal site for Camp X. No one argued, and soon Davies had given Taylor a full picture of the facilities that such a camp would need. Taylor then proposed that he should be given a completely free hand to find a site and produce the buildings fully furnished and ready for occupancy by November. After Davies had agreed in principle, subject to London's approval, Taylor made three phone calls. The first was to his brother, E.G. Taylor, who owned a construction company in Toronto; the second was to a senior partner of Allward and Gouinlock, a Toronto firm of architects; and the third was to Washington's Union Station to book himself a berth on the next night's train from Washington to Toronto. By 4 P.M. the business had been completed.

In the next seven days there was frantic activity to make Camp X a reality. Stephenson was enthusiastic about the shift to Ontario. In Toronto, Taylor quickly consulted with business associates, including John Anderson, his "Man Friday" in British Properties, and his personal lawyer in Toronto, John Jennings, KC. They rapidly located land for sale in Whitby that offered easy access combined with relative isolation. By Wednesday of the same week Davies was able to cable full details to London. He particularly stressed the importance of access. "Toronto," he told SOE London, "is within two hours of New York by air with thrice-daily service, so that communications with HQ and with America are extremely convenient."[15] The additional advantage was that the land would be free because, Davies said, Taylor had agreed to provide it without charge for the duration of the war. The next day SOE gave him the go-ahead to spend up to £25,000 on preparing the site and putting up the buildings. Five days after that, Jennings, on Taylor's behalf, purchased the land from a small consortium of owners for the modest sum of $12,000.

Later on, myth would add its inevitable layer of mystery to the origins of Camp X. *A Man Called Intrepid* added its own special flavour by quoting the version produced later by Ian Fleming: that in the best spy-story tradition Stephenson had clandestinely acquired the site by the careful and discreet purchase of several small lots over a period of time. On the contrary. Only two lots were involved – Lots 17 and 18 in the Broken Front (lakefront) concession – and both were purchased simultaneously, with Taylor's money, in September 1941. It is true, however, that the land records concealed the site's purpose. When John Jennings sold the land just over a year after he acquired it for his powerful clients, it was not to British Security Co-ordination, or to Stephenson, or to the Canadian government, but to the modestly named "Rural Realty Company Ltd."

Unknown to any of those involved, history harboured its own secrets, which lent irony to the choice of this particular site as a scene for Anglo-American-Canadian wartime co-operation. Americans had been there once before in war – but as enemies, not friends. And treachery, not loyalty, had been the theme. Hidden in the land records was a story that went back to the War of 1812 between Britain and the United States. Lot 18 had originally been granted by the Crown in 1804 to one Adam Stevens, a "yeoman", who was almost certainly an American and one of the "late loyalists" who had left New York State in the early nineteenth century and arrived in Upper Canada hungry for free land. But the outbreak of war a few years later saw Stevens revert to his American loyalties and abandon the land – either driven out by hostility or having voluntarily thrown in his lot with the American forces. Whatever his personal fate, the land was forfeited to the Crown when Stevens was found guilty of treason in 1822, and Lot 18 was sold to a private purchaser shortly afterwards.[16]

"A good place to make hooch," observed Inspector George B. McClellan, head of the Toronto detachment of the RCMP, as he wandered one day around Camp X and saw the neglected apple trees of a once carefully cultivated orchard. Like the rest of the two hundred and sixty acres that officially comprised the Camp, the orchard had once been part of "Glenrath", a homestead belonging to the Sinclairs, a local family who had owned it since the late nineteenth century. With the death of Alexander Sinclair in the early 1930s, the property had passed into the hands of a small consortium, and the land gradually became derelict. But the old eight-room farmhouse and the few outbuildings were still usable in 1941, and served as storehouses for equipment and supplies once the Camp was built. Most of the site, however, consisted of a combination of flat, open field; rough woodland containing oak, chestnut, and pine; and, down by Corbett's Creek on the western edge of the site, swamp – ideal for SOE training requirements.

Camp X combined isolation and convenience. Highway 401 was still to be completed, and Toronto lay well over an hour away along the old King's Highway (Number 2) through a gently rolling and sparsely inhabited expanse of Ontario farmland. Whitby and Oshawa were still self-contained communities that retained their nineteenth-century small-town Ontario character: hard-working provincial towns untouched by commuters, where the Protestant work ethic remained dominant and local liquor laws turned drink into the devil's own work. Even with its huge automotive plant employing some 3,000 workers, Oshawa society was still small enough to be dominated by the legendary figure of Samuel McLaughlin – "Colonel Sam" – millionaire founder and first president of General Motors Canada.

Although in his seventies, McLaughlin was still actively involved in running the company, and the McLaughlin mansion was a centre of social life in the area where for the next three years officers from Camp X could expect to find generous hospitality and a welcome break from their isolated existence. For the NCOs and other ranks at the camp there were one or two bars in Oshawa – Whitby was too small to offer anything in the way of evening entertainment – and for those who wanted or could afford a meal out, there was Oshawa's only hotel, the Genosha, just east of the major crossroads on the main road.

It was a mile or so from the road south to the Camp, and to get there you had to cross the tracks of the Canadian National Railways, which effectively formed the northern border of the site. Access was by a small and barely noticeable dirt road that led from the highway to Lake Ontario, which with its low cliffs and rocky shore formed the southern boundary. Even during the Camp's existence the shoreline remained as it had always been – solitary and deserted, with nothing to attract the idle eye.

But for those who knew their destination, there was no problem getting there. Tommy Davies had been right in telling London how convenient it was to reach Camp X from the United States. The Canadian National Railways linked Toronto and Montreal with New York and Washington, so that visitors from Stephenson's or Donovan's headquarters could take the overnight train and be driven out to the Camp from Toronto the next morning. Or they could take a local train and get off at Oshawa about a mile away from the Camp and wait for a jeep to collect them. For the really urgent visits there were several daily flights to and from New York. But most of the visitors came by train, and Union Station in downtown Toronto soon became familiar territory to those who helped to run one of the best-kept secrets of wartime Canada.

CHAPTER 2

"To Impress the Americans":
The Donovan Factor

From the beginning, Camp X was more than a secret agent training camp. It was also a counter and symbol in a larger political game. One of its major players was "Wild Bill" Donovan.

Donovan has been described both as America's last hero and as its first director of central intelligence. Despite his silver-white hair and fifty-eight years of age, Donovan in 1941 was a man of crude and indefatigable energy and fertile imagination whose enthusiasm for action, adventure, and excitement placed an indelible mark on the American intelligence community for the next quarter of a century. "Bill Donovan," said movie director John Ford, who worked for OSS in Asia in 1943, "is the sort of guy who thought nothing of parachuting into France, blowing up a bridge, pissing in *Luftwaffe* gas tanks, then dancing on the roof of the St. Regis Hotel with a German spy."[1]

Like Stephenson, from whom in many other ways he was quite different, Donovan was a First World War hero and a self-made man. Born in Buffalo of a poor Irish immigrant family, he made his way up the corporate ladder to become a successful lawyer with a flourishing business on Wall Street. He served as acting attorney general under President Coolidge, unsuccessfully ran for the governorship of New York on the Republican ticket in 1932, and had powerful political contacts both federally and in New York State. In 1917 Donovan had joined up with the Fighting 69th Regiment of the New York National Guard, mainly made up of Irish Americans, and commanded a battalion in France, where his bravery in action won him the Croix de

Guerre, the Distinguished Service Cross, and the Congressional Medal of Honor. He came out of the war as one of the two most decorated American officers – the other one being Douglas MacArthur – and he had earned himself the sobriquet "Wild Bill" Donovan.

In the summer of 1940, following the collapse of France and the Dunkirk evacuation, when Britain "stood alone" against the might of the *Wehrmacht* and the *Luftwaffe*, Donovan visited Britain as Roosevelt's personal representative. He was received by the king, by Churchill, and by Sir Stewart Menzies, and helped to negotiate the historic "destroyers for bases" deal of September 1940 that linked the defence of Britain with that of the United States and marked the first major step towards the Anglo-American wartime alliance. Later in the same year Donovan returned to London, and in early 1941 spent several weeks visiting British forces in North Africa and the Mediterranean as well as examining the political and military situation in Yugoslavia and Greece.

In both missions Donovan gave high priority to the intelligence and counter-intelligence issues facing Britain and the United States. On his first trip he looked into the ways in which fifth-column activities had helped the Nazi victories in Norway, France, Belgium, and Holland that previous spring, and also discussed with top British officials how the U.S. Navy and the British Admiralty could collaborate more closely on intelligence to protect the vital North Atlantic shipping routes that provided Britain's lifeline. On his second trip he spent a considerable part of his time being briefed about SOE, the Security Executive, and SIS's counter-intelligence functions. Not only did he enjoy two long private discussions with Churchill, but he also made an extensive tour of SOE training facilities in England and discussed various special operations schemes with Hugh Dalton.

By the early summer of 1941 Donovan was seen by the British as one of their most powerful and sympathetic friends in the United States, and as the man through whom they could most effectively ensure that British influence be exerted on Roosevelt. And their best contact with Donovan was through Stephenson.

"Wild Bill" and "Little Bill" (Stephenson was several inches shorter than Donovan) had worked closely together in arranging Donovan's first visit to Britain in the summer of 1940. For all their differences, they were kindred spirits. Stephenson, well aware that an important part of his job in New York was to sell the British war effort to American public opinion and to cultivate pro-British Americans, had virtually sponsored Donovan's first visit to London, and had then personally accompanied him across the Atlantic on the second. By 1941 Stephenson saw Donovan as his single most important ally in the United States. "The co-operation between Stephenson and Donovan," writes British historian Christopher Andrew, "...was eventually to form the basis of a full-scale Anglo-American intelligence alliance."[2]

Donovan returned from his second mission to Europe in the early spring of 1941 and lobbied hard in Washington for the creation of a centralized intelligence agency. Finally, Roosevelt accepted the essence of Donovan's plan and on July 11, 1941, formally appointed Donovan Co-ordinator of Information (COI). "You can imagine," Stephenson cabled to London, "how relieved I am after three months of battle and jockeying for position in Washington that our man is in a position of such importance to our efforts."

On the surface, Roosevelt's appointment of Donovan as Co-ordinator of Information was unusual because of the Irish American's strong Republican connections. But Roosevelt had known Donovan as an acquaintance in New York politics for many years, and was temperamentally drawn to a man who shared many of his own deepest attitudes about America and its role in the world. Both men were optimists, enthusiasts, and anglophiles, both were activists and doers, and each of them possessed and admired courage. Besides, Donovan was a close and trusted friend of Roosevelt's secretary of the navy, Frank Knox, who himself was a Republican and had joined Roosevelt's Cabinet early in 1940. By 1941 Donovan had demonstrated convincingly to Roosevelt that he shared the president's views about the war and the need to fight a vigorous offensive against the forces of isolationism in American life.

COI initially concentrated on propaganda activities overseas and on the collection and analysis of strategic information. But Donovan, the ever-impatient activist, was soon making plans to extend COI's mandate to include espionage and special operations. Once again, he turned to Stephenson for advice.

Stephenson had originally been sent to New York solely as SIS representative, but when in December 1940 Sir Frank Nelson asked him also to act as SOE representative in the Western Hemisphere, Stephenson agreed. Shortly afterwards, SOE sent one of its top officials, Colonel Geoffrey Vickers, VC, a lawyer from the City of London solicitors Slaughter and May, to New York to see how best BSC could fulfil SOE needs. Vickers' directive, dated February 15, 1941, was to arrange for BSC to establish an SOE network throughout Latin America, to recruit likely SOE agents in the United States and other American countries, to help influence public opinion in the United States in a pro-Allied direction, to make contact with various European refugee and exile movements in the New World, and to help create secret communications channels for SOE networks.[3]

Stephenson and Vickers agreed that BSC should set up a small special operations section in its Rockefeller Center offices, and this, carefully disguised as the statistical division, developed slowly during the first six months of 1941. But Donovan's appointment as COI, followed by a meeting he then had with section heads of BSC in New York later that month, prompted Stephenson to ask London for greatly expanded facilities and new directives for Anglo-American intelligence co-operation.

In late July 1941 Stephenson once again took the long transatlantic flight back to London for personal discussions with Nelson and other SOE officials on how to expand SOE activities in North America. It was obvious that liaison with Donovan's new organization, as well as the growth of Britain's own plans for special operations in Latin America, would greatly increase BSC's job, and that there would have to be a significant increase in the size of BSC's head office and in the number of its field agents. London gave Stephenson the mandate he required. He returned to New York with instructions to enlarge his SOE activities, to give Donovan the fullest assistance possible in turning the COI into a full-fledged intelligence organization, and to create a strong framework for the Anglo-American Alliance in secret warfare.

The late summer and fall of 1941 saw close and intensive conversations between Donovan and Stephenson. The Americans turned to the British for advice and the British in turn worked to bind the Americans to the British ways of secret warfare. In August, Donovan requested Stephenson to provide him with experienced officers to help organize COI headquarters, and shortly afterwards Stephenson opened a small office in Washington with Dick Ellis in charge to facilitate daily liaison with COI headquarters. Donovan reciprocated by setting up a COI office in New York. Also based at Rockefeller Center, it was headed by a fellow New York lawyer recently recruited by Donovan for COI. His name was Allan Dulles. From then until Pearl Harbor the two men and their staffs were in almost continuous contact. "The Stephenson-Ellis duo," writes American historian Thomas Troy in his official CIA history of Donovan, "rendered really substantial assistance to Donovan not only in the formative period of COI but also well into the OSS years."[4]

It was in this hothouse climate of Anglo-American co-operation in the shadow war that the seeds of an idea for Camp X had first germinated and then came to full flower. From documents in the SOE archives in London, the story can now be revealed for the first time.[5]

The idea had been on the SOE agenda since the previous winter, but it had never been given a high priority. In fact, Stephenson had discussed the idea for the first time with Colonel Vickers in New York in February 1941 when the two men had agreed on SOE needs in North America. As a result, they had proposed establishing a special training school for SOE recruits found in Canada and the United States for infiltration into enemy-occupied Europe. Probably because of the winter weather and Stephenson's connection with Bermuda – he frequently spent the winters there – the island had struck the two men as an ideal site. But the British Admiralty, which controlled much of Bermuda as a naval base, eventually turned this idea down.

Thus it was that in late May 1941 Stephenson turned his attention to Canada. In a telegram to SOE headquarters on June 16, he told London that he had obtained agreement in principle from the Canadians and within a matter of weeks had come up with two possible locations: one on Prince Edward Island and the other on the south-east coast of Nova Scotia. By early June he had opted for Nova Scotia, and, as he put it to London, was "actively looking for a suitable site." SOE in London in the meantime had gone so far as to choose a prospective commandant for the camp, a Major Forster, and all seemed set to go. When Stephenson crossed the Atlantic in July, the topic was still on the agenda, but the whole idea was then put into the deep freeze, probably because SOE had second thoughts as to the camp's necessity and because Major Forster had proved unsuitable. He certainly showed little enthusiasm for a site in Canada. His one recorded contribution to the discussions was to observe that Canada was too cold; he preferred the West Indies.

It was the Donovan factor that in the end revitalized the Camp X proposal and explained the presence at the St. Regis dinner that September night of Tommy Davies. For he was the highest-ranking SOE official to have visited BSC since Stephenson had agreed to represent the agency the year before, and his visit was designed to help Stephenson carry out the rapid expansion of SOE in North America as well as to look personally at how Donovan's American plans were progressing.

In peacetime, Davies was a wealthy director of the huge textile firm of Courtaulds, a flamboyant, volatile character of great energy whose friendliness could suddenly metamorphose into violent rages. Brooker once saw him respond to some minor mistake by a secretary by shouting abuse and hurling a pen at her. At the outbreak of war he joined a special section of the War Office, known as MIR (for Military Intelligence, Research), which was responsible for studying methods of irregular warfare. Here he found himself one of the small group of men, including Gubbins, which, when merged with the sabotage section of SIS (known as Section D) in the summer of 1940, had become SOE. Davies' main job in MIR was primarily concerned with planning for Western Europe. After the German invasion of Norway, he decided that an attack on the rest of Western Europe was likely, and arranged for MIR to prevent Holland's huge stock of industrial diamonds falling into German hands. Personally crossing over to Holland on a destroyer, he returned carrying several large suitcases of gems. He also oversaw the destruction by the Dutch Central Bank of several million pounds' worth of sterling banknotes. Shortly afterwards he distinguished himself during the collapse of France by again crossing the Channel and removing several hundred thousand pounds' worth of platinum from the company's plant in Calais to prevent its falling into German hands. Not long afterwards

Sir Frank Nelson chose him to be one of his two deputy heads, with responsibility for all SOE supplies and training schools.

One of the first things Davies did after arriving in the United States was to see Donovan at COI headquarters in Washington. By now "Wild Bill" was in the full flood of his enthusiasm about launching America into secret warfare, and he had already begun to float the idea of creating a special American force to fight guerrilla warfare. Thus, when Davies asked him how SOE in New York could give him some practical help, Donovan immediately seized on the need for special training facilities such as those he had seen at SOE schools in England the year before. "Donovan," reported Davies to London, "insisted most emphatically on the establishment of a training camp and said it would be more convenient for him to have the men trained in Canada than, in the existing circumstances, to establish a camp for himself in America."[6] Donovan, of course, was referring to American neutrality and continued strong isolationist sentiment.

Back in New York, Davies raised the question with Stephenson, and the two men carefully reviewed the reasons for establishing a school in Canada. There were three compelling arguments in its favour. First, BSC was rapidly expanding its activities in both North and South America, and with the growth of the central headquarters and the number of field agents, there was obviously a need for a regional school. Second, BSC would certainly be recruiting potential agents from the Western Hemisphere for use in Occupied Europe, and it obviously made sense for them to receive preliminary screening and training before being sent across the Atlantic to more advanced schools in Britain. Finally, and most compelling of all, was the effect that a school in North America would have on the Americans. Stephenson strongly reinforced the basic message that Donovan had already conveyed to Davies. "A really efficient training school would impress the Americans," he said. "It would also provide us with valuable propaganda in obtaining their co-operation in the realm of subversive activities."[7] When measured against the huge potential gains of winning American support, and in the light of Donovan's barely contained eagerness to get involved in the whole realm of subversive warfare, any lingering doubts that Davies may have had about the value of a North American school quickly dissolved.

If anything further had been needed to impress Davies with the importance of the closest possible working relationship between Donovan and SOE, and of doing business with the Canadians, the St. Regis dinner and his meeting with Stephenson and Taylor had accomplished the purpose. The shift from Nova Scotia had been dictated by the need to accommodate the Americans. This left only one major problem: the Canadian government. It was a touchy subject, and everyone involved agreed it should be kept a highly guarded secret.

Such a secret, indeed, that Canada's prime minister, the eccentric, middle-aged bachelor Mackenzie King, almost certainly knew nothing about it. King was an enigma. A short and unimpressive figure who now stares at us anonymously from the wartime photographs of his meetings with Churchill and Roosevelt, King was nevertheless a master politician who laid the foundations of the Liberal domination of Canadian politics in the twentieth century. He was also a fervent believer in spiritualism, through which he held long conversations with his dead mother, and he led a richly repressed sex life. Prude and prudent soul that he was, King kept all this carefully hidden from public view. He felt the same way about secret intelligence. Indeed, in sharp contrast to both Churchill and Roosevelt, he thought ignorance of the whole business was the safest prophylactic, and preferred to delegate such matters to his subordinates. In turn they were only too happy not to disturb his peace of mind, and operated on the principle that, so far as their prime minister was concerned, "Knowledge if necessary but not necessarily knowledge" was the safest maxim to follow.

Canada was a dominion within the British Commonwealth, and like Britain had declared war on Germany in September 1939. George VI was Canada's king, Britain remained the principal and dominating point of reference for governments in Ottawa, and Canadians were still British subjects with a depth of patriotism for flag and Empire that often astonished visitors from Britain. For the first two years of the war Canada was Britain's most powerful ally. But the relationship was a deeply sensitive one. Canadians resented being patronized by the British as colonials, and, while eager to fight, were determined to do it on their own terms and as an independent country. Politically, the war presented King with a serious problem. His government depended for its survival on support in the province of Quebec, where francophone Canadians were much less keen than anglophone Canadians on fighting for Britain. Aware of this, King had carefully waited for a few symbolic days after Britain's declaration of war before following suit. He was also determined not to introduce the highly divisive issue of conscription unless absolutely necessary, and sought every opportunity to make it clear that this was Canada's war, not just a British struggle into which Canada had been drawn as a colonial dependency.

He, too, possessed Canadian sensitivities on this issue. Nothing demonstrated this better than his reactions to a previous British plan for using Canada as a wartime training ground. This was the British Commonwealth Air Training Plan (BCATP), proposed by the British government in 1939 to train British air force pilots on Canadian soil. It offered King a huge political gift in that it gave him the chance to implement a massive but casualty-free war effort, and in the end over sixty training centres were established. But King had been deeply offended by the arrogant approach of the British, "...amazing," he noted in his diary, "how these people from the Old Country...seem to think that all they have to do is tell us what is to be done." As a result, negotiations had been long and difficult.[8]

If this had been King's reaction to a scheme to train pilots, officials in Ottawa could easily guess what his reaction would be to a proposal to open a school run by the British mainly to train Americans in the arts of secret war. They decided, therefore, not to tell the prime minister the details and thus present him with a personal and political dilemma that he would certainly resolve by refusing. The whole subject, all those in the know agreed, was of the greatest delicacy and required careful handling. It should not even go to the Canadian Cabinet. Thus, Camp X is noticeably absent from the Cabinet records for the crucial period between September and December 1941.

Ironically, just the night before the St. Regis dinner – the eve of the decision to set up Camp X – King had flown back to Canada in a Liberator bomber after his first wartime visit to Britain. It had been a major success. King had attended several meetings of the War Cabinet, had been a personal guest of the Royal Family at Balmoral and of Churchill at Chequers, and had put his relationship with

Churchill on a sound and close footing. "There is no question," wrote Jack Pickersgill, editor of King's diaries, and whose brother Frank was to be executed by the Germans as an SOE agent, "that the visit established a sympathy between [Churchill] and Mackenzie King which had not existed before and which continued to the end of Mackenzie King's life."9 At their final meeting at 10 Downing Street, Churchill had impressed King with his vision of a future world controlled by the British and Americans. "You and I are helping in laying the foundation of that order," he told the Canadian prime minister. But so far as the record shows, King was unaware of at least one of the pillars of the structure being created. Stephenson in New York knew this only too well. Therefore, to help him in Canada, he turned to those whom he knew he could trust. The first of these was Charles Vining.

Charles Arthur McLaren Vining, like Bill Stephenson himself, was a Winnipegger. Born on September 4, 1897, he was the only son of a Baptist minister who had been responsible for the immigration of a hundred Armenian boys orphaned during the First World War. One of the conditions promised by the Reverend Vining was that the orphans would be thoroughly Canadianized; their names changed, they were to be "taught to salute the British flag [as] a daily privilege and duty". This fervent patriotism and a stern Nonconformist sense of duty and hard work were passed on to his son.

As soon as he graduated from Woodstock College, Ontario, in 1915, Vining volunteered for army service overseas, and by August 1916 he was in France with the Princess Patricia Canadian Light Infantry. The next year he was badly wounded at Passchendaele. Recovered from his injuries and back in Canada by the end of the war, he became a journalist after graduating from the University of Toronto in 1921 with a degree in political science. His first job was as a reporter with the *Toronto Daily Star* , where he made a good start by winning a personal interview with Canada's new governor-general, Lord Byng, even before the British general who had commanded Canadian troops at Vimy had been sworn in. Within two years the enterprising and ambitious reporter had become managing editor of the *London Advertiser* in London, Ontario. Five years later, in 1928, after a stint with the *Star Weekly* in Toronto, he moved to the public relations firm of Cockfield, Brown and Company. It was a turning point in Vining's career, marking his entrée into the business world revolving around the Toronto-Montreal axis. He now began to build a wide network of business and political associates, which later made him such a valuable asset to Stephenson's BSC empire. In 1934 a study he had done on the depressed fortunes of the Canadian newsprint industry led to his appointment as president of the Newsprint Export Manufacturers' Association of Canada, based in Montreal. For the next decade this influential position in Canada's commercial capital provided Vining with an important power base. At about this time he befriended two men crucial to the story of Camp X and BSC operations in Canada.

In the early 1920s Vining had met a young Toronto stockbroker called Tommy Drew-Brook and they became friends. In 1935, when Vining had to go to England on business, Drew-Brook gave him an introduction to one of his oldest friends, who then owned a farm just outside London. This turned out to be Bill Stephenson. The two men immediately liked and understood each other. Soon the couples were taking holidays together, the Vinings often spending long weekends with the Stephensons at one of their many homes in London, Jamaica, Bermuda, or New York. Vining learned a great deal about the business world from Stephenson, who in turn came to depend on Vining for advice about political affairs in the Canada he had left after the First World War.

In these years, too, Vining formed the second close friendship that is important in the Camp X story. As president of the Newsprint Association he met Colonel Layton Ralston, a Nova Scotian who had been a battalion commander in the Canadian Corps during the First World War and then a highly successful corporation lawyer in Montreal. By June 1940 Ralston had become minister of national defence in Mackenzie King's wartime government, where he was in a critical position to provide or withhold help to BSC and SOE. It was not just because of the office he held. Ralston, in the words of Canadian historian J.L. Granatstein, was "an honest, honourable, and simple soldier" who worked enormously hard for Canada's war effort, and among English-speaking ministers in the King government he enjoyed a personal and a national reputation that gave him immense influence. "Ralson was a very strong man," writes Granatstein. "Instantly upon entering the Cabinet he became, with King and Ernest Lapointe [the minister of justice and King's Quebec leader] one of the three most powerful men in the country."[10] Later on, when Ralston faced the crisis of his political career over the issue of conscription in 1944, it was to Vining he turned for advice. But in 1940 it was Vining who turned to Ralston for help on a quite different matter.

Vining had been approached by Stephenson and appointed the official Canadian representative of BSC, with code number 48/862, a position he held for several months during 1940 and 1941. His greatest achievement for BSC came as Royal Air Force pilots fought it out with the *Luftwaffe* over the fields of Kent during the summer of 1940. If the Germans prevailed in the Battle of Britain, the way was open for invasion. At Bletchley Park, home of the code-breakers who had cracked top German ciphers, buses waited to carry the experts to Liverpool and then on to the transatlantic safety of North America. In New York, Stephenson realized that his organization might have to expand and thus become far more important than originally intended. If that happened, certain operations would have to take place in Canada. Stephenson turned to Vining. "The Canadian government connection was ticklish," Vining wrote after the war. "We knew that King would not allow a British operation...to operate in Canada."[11]

The answer to the problem lay in his friendship with Ralston. As the decisive battle over Britain came to its climax on August 15, a "crucial day", as Churchill recalled in his memoirs, Vining turned to his old Montreal friend and, at meetings in Ottawa on August 14 and 15, 1940, told Ralston the whole story about Stephenson's operation and its security and intelligence needs in Canada. "He responded like the fine man he was," Vining wrote later. Ralston proposed that they should not tell Mackenzie King, who in any case was preoccupied by his forthcoming visit to sign the historic Ogdensburg Agreement with Roosevelt on joint U.S.-Canadian defence. "To tell him would merely add to the Prime Minister's heavy burden" was the fiction by which they agreed to conceal matters from Mackenzie King. Both Norman Robertson, the brilliant young under-secretary of state for foreign affairs, and Arnold Heeney, the secretary to the Cabinet, agreed after Ralston had promised to take full responsibility if anything became known.

As Vining himself put it, "getting suitable Canadians for top positions, and for secretarial, was a main job for me from late in 1940 to 1942; I rarely went to New York without bringing back a list of men wanted and we got some good ones." The job involved not only people for the propaganda and communications sections of BSC, but also the secretarial staff. In February 1941 he placed an advertisement in the *Toronto Telegram* asking for reliable young women competent in secretarial duties interested in working for "a Department of the British Government in New York City". "I ran it in the *Toronto Telegram* on February 10th 1941," wrote Vining later, "needing (and expecting) at that time only about half a dozen responses. But it drew some 300, most of them from women ready to give up high positions in Canada. All applicants were carefully checked and cleared by the RCMP.... Later on...we had over 1000 Canadian women on the BSC staff, mainly in confidential secretarial and communications work. Not one of them ever let us down as far as I can remember."

Vining also helped to establish a solid relationship between BSC and representatives of the Canadian government. Robertson agreed that the Department of External Affairs should provide the principal channel of communication with Stephenson in New York, and eventually a direct teleprinter link was established to facilitate and speed up direct communications between Ottawa and BSC headquarters. The mandarins of External Affairs thus became the facilitators of BSC operations in Canada. We therefore need to pause for a moment and look more closely at the personalities involved.

Robertson, the "Man of Influence," had a strong interest in intelligence and security issues. In 1940 he had spent hours personally looking over the lists of enemy aliens chosen for internment and as a result had earned the title of "Departmental Secret Service Operative". Although documents in Robertson's papers dealing with security and intelligence affairs are still withheld, it seems reasonable to assume that he had consulted the British on co-operation in person, probably during King's visit to London when he had accompanied the prime minister.

In any case, Robertson was exceptionally discreet, and committed as little as possible to paper. "Robertson used to operate under a special open door system," one historian has noted. "However, when his door was closed – which was rare – he was talking about intelligence matters...and no notes were left."[12] In these top-secret conversations, Robertson was invariably talking to one or more of a very small group of External Affairs officials to whom he delegated such sensitive issues. There were three of them: Lester Pearson, Tommy Stone, and George Glazebrook.

Pearson, Canada's prime minister from 1962 to 1968 and the leading architect of Canadian post-war foreign policy, had been a diplomat since quitting his underpaid job as a history professor at the University of Toronto in 1928. Posted to the Canadian High Commission in London a few years later, he left the British capital at the height of the Blitz early in 1941 to become second-in-command of the Department of External Affairs in Ottawa. The journey home gave Pearson his first taste of the world of secret intelligence, which he was to explore more fully when he got back to Canada. Hearing of his departure from London, a Foreign Office contact asked him if he would act as a courier and personally deliver some top-secret papers to BSC in New York. After duly collecting the plain brown official envelope containing the secrets, Pearson took the precaution of sleeping with it under his pillow during the stop-overs on his long flight to New York via Lisbon, the Azores, and Bermuda. He finally reached Rockefeller Center.

"As I got out of the elevator," he wrote in his memoirs, "I expected to be stopped and asked to produce my credentials.... Nobody bothered me. There was indeed a New York policeman in a chair outside the door of the office I was seeking. But he was dozing and ignored my entrance over his outstretched legs. Within the office a receptionist glanced at my credentials, signed for my envelope, thanked me, and said good-bye. This all seemed very casual for a secret service, a first impression of carelessness which I later found to be deceptive."[13]

Pearson indeed came to know a great deal more about BSC operations. But in his 1972 memoirs he was remarkably reticent about the security and intelligence work he did once he was back in Ottawa. "My duties," he wrote, "included problems of security and, in particular, the formation and development of a Canadian intelligence unit which worked closely with similar British and American agencies. Our unit was concerned with breaking enemy codes, not with the more glamorous work of snaring and shooting spies, but it did outstanding work in its own field."

That was all Pearson had to say about his involvement in the Examination Unit, Canada's wartime code-breaking centre. Little more was revealed about its activities until early in 1986, when documents released under Ottawa's Access to Information Act revealed substantial information about its operations. These voluminous documents show that Pearson was far more deeply involved in the affairs of the Examination Unit than was suspected, and that early in its life he was at the heart of a crisis that almost destroyed it.

The Examination Unit was set up in Ottawa in June 1941. Its task was to analyse enemy communications secretly intercepted from various sources. The messages included *Abwehr* communications to German agents in South America, material between Vichy France and the French Embassy in Ottawa, and a considerable amount of Japanese wireless traffic. According to a secret history of the Unit written by members of its staff in 1945, "the bulk of the material worked on came to us from BSC", which in turn had received much of it – as we shall see later – via the wireless facilities at Camp X. "Our general requests for traffic have changed frequently," the secret history noted, "and we have kept BSC advised as to what we wished to receive."[14] The rest came either from American sources or from intercept operations carried out by the Canadians themselves at monitoring stations across the country.

Controversy surrounds two men who worked for the Unit. The first, Herbert Norman, is still the subject of intense speculation as to whether he was a Communist agent. Norman was Canada's top Japanese scholar. He joined the Department of External Affairs in 1939 and in 1942 was made head of a Special Intelligence Section within the Examination Unit, set up largely at the urgings of Stephenson, who had first tried unsuccessfully to acquire Norman's services for BSC. With the help of one assistant and three support staff, he had to analyse intercepts and prepare intelligence reports on Japan and the Far East. After the war Norman went on to become Canadian ambassador to Japan, but by this time, because the Cold War was intensifying, his loyalties had become suspect. A pre-war Communist, Norman found himself under intense FBI and RCMP investigation as a possible

Soviet spy. Although the RCMP cleared him, Norman remained under suspicion in some quarters, and during the McCarthy hearings in the United States his name was frequently mentioned as a top-ranking Communist agent in the Canadian government. Although defended against these attacks by Lester Pearson, who by this time was Canada's foreign minister, Norman finally broke under the pressure. In March 1957, three weeks after his name had once again been mentioned in the United States as a possible spy, Norman jumped to his death from the top of a nine-storey building in Cairo where he was serving as Canadian ambassador. For Pearson, as for others in Canada, it was a profound and bitter shock. "My feelings never reached a lower point in my public career," wrote Pearson.

The crisis over the Examination Unit's top Japanese expert was a post-war affair. But Pearson was far more deeply embroiled in a crisis affecting the Examination Unit that occurred in the fall of 1941.

Lacking experts of their own to run the Unit, the Canadians had brought in the man who had been the top American code-breaker in the First World War, Herbert Yardley. It was an unfortunate decision that soon precipitated a major crisis, which the Unit barely survived. Despite the best efforts of Washington, Yardley had "spilled the beans" about the top-secret First World War operations in his 1931 book *The American Black Chamber*, and ever since then had been regarded by many code-breakers and intelligence experts on both sides of the Atlantic as thoroughly untrustworthy. When news of Yardley's appointment in Ottawa filtered back to London, the British cryptanalysts were horrified and quickly made it clear that they would refuse to co-operate with the Examination Unit and with Canada's code-breaking efforts until Yardley was fired.

Pearson was the man delegated by Robertson to deal with the crisis. After a visit to Washington only a few weeks before Pearl Harbor to talk with American and British officials about the Yardley problem, he produced a detailed nine-page report – classified until now – that made it clear that Yardley had to go. Otherwise, he advised, the Canadians would be completely shut out of all communications intelligence by their allies. "The U.S. Navy," Pearson reported, "would not touch Yardley with a ten foot pole." On November 22, 1941, in a painful half-hour interview with an outraged and angry Yardley, Pearson gave the American the bad news. "We had a most unpleasant half-hour," noted a colleague who accompanied Pearson. "Yardley accused us of bringing him up here and picking his brains dry and turning over into other hands various new methods of cryptographic problems which he had developed."[15]

Pearson's colleague during this final confrontation with Yardley was yet another of the Ottawa mandarins who play a part in the BSC and Camp X story. Indeed, he was the most important of all.

Tommy Stone, who eventually ended a distinguished diplomatic career as Canadian ambassador to The Hague, was a dynamic, popular, and eminently convivial figure. "A very curious fellow," one of Stone's closest wartime colleagues said later, "very imaginative, very lively, and always starting something new." John Holmes, Canada's eminent diplomat-scholar and another of Stone's wartime associates, remembers him as "a wonderful loyal friend" and as a man of enormous vitality with a gregarious and outgoing personality. "Tommy knew everyone and had friends everywhere," he now recalls. "He threw wonderful parties, loved to sit at the piano and thump out catchy tunes and songs, and always liked his food and drink."[16] A short, heavyish man with thick grey hair worn long, Stone also spoke beautiful and fluent French, but was a great mimic and loved to parody *franglais*, the language in which he produced some of his more risqué piano renditions. Eventually Stone's energy and inventiveness proved too much for his more stodgy co-workers, and in 1944 he was sent to exercise his talents in London, where he thrived even more. But for most of the war Stone was the main personality in External Affairs concerned with intelligence. He travelled to New York frequently for meetings with Stephenson. From time to time, although not very often, Stephenson would come up to Ottawa; when he did, it would be Robertson or Stone whom he saw.

Thomas Archibald Stone came from Chatham, Ontario. Educated at the University of Toronto and the Ecole Libre des Sciences Politiques in Paris, he joined External Affairs in 1927. He served mostly in Paris and Geneva, but then resigned in 1935 after marrying an American heiress who brought with her a plantation near Charleston and a large home in Maine. Clearly inventive and imaginative in his personal as well as professional life, Stone quickly recovered from his wife's unexpected death a year later and married her elder sister. From then on he had little to worry about and occupied himself on the estate he had inherited in South Carolina. But at the outbreak of war in 1939 he returned to Canada, where he began by reorganizing the External Affairs code-room, which had been overwhelmed by the massive increase in cipher traffic. From there he moved quickly to the centre of intelligence and security matters within the department. He controlled its responsibilities for censorship, became deeply involved in the intelligence derived from prisoners of war, and then established a Psychological Warfare Committee.

Stone hoped that Canada's contribution to Allied intelligence would lead ultimately to a full and equal partnership with the United States and Great Britain, and he even seems to have entertained hopes that Canada could make the Examination Unit equivalent to Bletchley Park. He certainly kept in close touch with Britain's top-secret code-breaking centre, and his co-operation with the British code experts was of the closest possible kind, suggesting a hitherto-unsuspected degree of collaboration in the field of communications intelligence between Canada and Britain. When he left Ottawa for a visit to North Africa in the fall of 1943, Commander Alastair Denniston, the first wartime head of Bletchley Park, provided him with the special set of one-time code pads needed for his secret communications with Ottawa. "I shall be glad if you will let me know whether, on my return to Canada, I should destroy these tables by fire or send them back to you," wrote Stone to Denniston in a "Most Secret" letter.[17] The reply is not recorded, but the query reveals a remarkable dependence by the Canadians on the British for such a sensitive matter.

The final member of this Ottawa group to note was George Glazebrook, enrolled by Pearson in early 1942 as a special wartime assistant. Glazebrook was a professor in the History Department at the University of Toronto, a former colleague of Pearson. He was fond of talking about "skulduggery", and his war was to take him far from his academic research and deep into security and intelligence affairs, and before he returned to his academic post in 1946 he was to be heavily involved in discussions about Canada's peacetime security needs. Within a week of his joining the group, Pearson asked him to take responsibility for intelligence and censorship matters.

Glazebrook went on to become an important figure in the BSC-Camp X story. He took over most of the routine liaison with Stephenson's office and, although he rarely went down to New York, he was visited at least once a month in Ottawa by Herbert Sichel, a member of the Sichel wine merchant family and the man from BSC headquarters mainly responsible for day-to-day liaison with the Canadians. As we shall see later on, Glazebrook came to know Camp X and its British staff quite well.

Here, then, were the handful of people who opened the doors in Canada to Stephenson's security and intelligence needs. They, and they alone, could facilitate the co-operation of the Canadian machinery of government. Through them the RCMP, the Canadian military authorities, and other official agencies could be mobilized to co-operate harmoniously with BSC in New York and, more immediately, with its representative in Toronto.

In 1941, Tommy Drew-Brook took over Vining's role as official BSC representative in Canada. The reason lay in Vining's growing commitments in Ottawa. In the fall of that year he began to work at the Wartime Prices and Trade Board with responsibility for public information and propaganda. From there it was a short step to becoming head of the Wartime Information Board, Canada's internal propaganda agency, in the summer of 1942. Only a few months after he took office Vining's health gave way; he continued to be close to Stephenson, but his role was now greatly limited – although, as we shall see, he played some part in Stephenson's post-war attempts to establish a Canadian intelligence agency. From 1941 until the end of the war Drew-Brook was Stephenson's right-hand man in Canada and a major figure among those Canadians who facilitated secret wartime operations in North America.

Tommy Drew-Brook was a quite different character from the slight, tall, compulsive, restless, and hard-driving Vining. He began and ended his professional life as a stockbroker. The outbreak of the Second World War found him comfortably and profitably ensconced as a partner in the Toronto firm of Wills, Bickle & Co., with an office in the heart of Toronto's downtown financial district on King Street West. As a child of six Drew-Brook had startled his family by announcing that his ambition in life was to own a Rolls-Royce. Business acumen granted him his goal, and later in life his Rolls-Royce became one of his most treasured possessions as well as a familiar sight in downtown Toronto.

For all his delight in the Rolls, Drew-Brook was an essentially modest man remembered with respect and affection by those who knew him. "Round, cheery and bright," said one of those who worked with him. "A little dynamo," thought one of the Canadian staff at BSC in New York. To the many young women he interviewed for BSC at his office, he was courteous, gentlemanly, and a good and careful listener. To the many visitors who came to Toronto and Camp X on official wartime business, he was a genial and kindly host who entertained them generously in his family home in one of Toronto's most exclusive and fashionable neighbourhoods. And to those who worked with him on BSC business, which ranged far beyond Camp X and into the realm of secret intelligence, he was the unassuming, hardworking and indispensable facilitator who found an answer to every problem. "What a nice level-headed conscientious little fellow he is," recorded Gerald Wilkinson, a BSC executive from Washington, after he had spent an afternoon talking business with Drew-Brook in Toronto.[18] Charles Vining, who might have claimed the credit for himself, readily conceded after the war that, so far as BSC was concerned, Drew-Brook "did a job second only to Bill Stephenson."

Tommy Drew-Brook was born on December 18, 1898, in Yorkshire, England, the youngest of five sons. When he was still a child the family immigrated to Canada, and Drew-Brook grew up in Toronto, where he went to the exclusive private school Upper Canada College. When war broke out in 1914 he returned to Britain and eventually joined the Royal Flying Corps. In the same squadron was another young pilot from Canada who was to have a hero's war, winning the Distinguished Flying Cross and the Military Cross. His name was William Stephenson, and from then on the two men were close friends. But Drew-Brook's war did not turn out so well. He was shot down and badly injured. Taken prisoner by the Germans, he spent several months recovering in a prison hospital; his convalescence continued after the armistice.

Back in post-war Toronto, he entered the brokerage business, began his rise in financial circles, and married Mabel Clark, the daughter of Joseph T. Clark, editor of the *Toronto Daily Star*. Her brother, Greg Clark, was to become a well-known Canadian journalist. It was through his in-laws that Drew-Brook and Vining first met, for it was at this time that Vining was making his way in the world of journalism. Whereas the latter's network eventually broadened to include Ottawa and Montreal, Drew-Brook's concentrated on the relatively small and homogeneous world of pre-war Toronto. Not only did he come to know everyone of importance in the city, but those of influence came to know him. His position prepared him well for his wartime task as faithful lieutenant in Canada to Stephenson in New York. "When Stephenson said 'jump', Tommy jumped," recalls Brooker. The man who at Upper Canada College had won an award for "cheerful submission to authority" was now more than content to place himself loyally and whole-heartedly at the service of his country's war effort and the mission of one of his oldest friends. "Bill and I were great friends," Drew-Brook told an interviewer shortly before his death in Toronto in 1977. "We flew together in the same squadron.... We kept in touch between the wars, of course, and when Bill came out to Canada in 1940, he came to see me. By then, Bill's operation [BSC] had grown enormously.... He wanted to have someone in Canada because he needed a base in a country that was at war, close to the United States and South America, where he had many operations."[19]

Drew-Brook continued the important task of interviewing and arranging the vetting of the large number of young women being recruited for BSC. His office in the Bank of Commerce Building began to receive a stream of visitors who, if deemed suitable, would be passed on for careful and discreet screening by the RCMP. For this, he turned to RCMP Inspector George B. McClellan, another key Canadian figure in the Camp X story.

McClellan has been described by journalist John Sawatsky in *Men in the Shadows*, his history of the RCMP Security Service, as "the father of the modern security service in Canada". After the war, as head of the RCMP's Special Branch, he established its first counter-espionage division – the initial step on the route towards Canada's present-day Security Intelligence Service. Later he was head of the RCMP itself. Much of what he knew about counter-espionage he learned from his wartime dealings with BSC and the dapper little Tommy Drew-Brook. There could hardly have been a greater contrast between the two men. McClellan had passed through the Royal Military College at Kingston and looked every inch a Mountie: his bulky two-hundred-pound frame and square face reminded his subordinates of the megaliths of Stonehenge. But the two men got on well together. The policeman's infectious sense of humour and first-rate story-telling abilities took him a long way. They won him frequent invitations to the Camp X mess, which he once claimed was the only decent place to get a drink between Montreal and Toronto.

More important, however, were the services he could provide. The RCMP did all the security vetting of those in Canada chosen to work for BSC, and the Mounties played an important part in recruiting agents from among various political groups in Toronto. Both Major Bill Brooker and Major Cuthbert Skilbeck, the first two chief instructors at Camp X, worked closely with McClellan in setting up and running the training exercises that took place outside the Camp. Because these often involved simulated sabotage and subversion, the Mounties had to be informed. In return for their help, Camp X instructors would often give the RCMP advice on security matters. Brooker, for example, produced a detailed report on security at the Welland Canal, and on potential counter-sabotage measures for industrial plants such as the large Massey-Ferguson factory. The RCMP was impressed and at the end of the war A.J. Taylor suggested Brooker's name as head of its British Columbia detachment – an offer that Brooker never pursued.

McClellan also helped to clear up problems created by the secrecy that surrounded the Camp. Brooker never forgot one incident of black farce that occurred in 1942. BSC sent a secret-ink expert from New York to give instruction at the Camp, but he turned out to be quite unsuitable for the job. Brooker called in Drew-Brook and asked him to take care of his undesirable guest. Drew-Brook was already using the basement of an empty Toronto house to store BSC wireless sets, so he set the man up in the house with a small secret-ink laboratory and hired a manservant to keep the place clean. Shortly afterwards the two men were joined by a German Brazilian being temporarily detained by the RCMP as a suspected spy. All went well until the day the manservant dropped dead of a heart attack while out doing the shopping. When the city police called at the house of the deceased, they found a "German", a dabbler in secret inks, and a basement full of wireless and other gadgetry. McClellan had some difficulty in convincing city police that they had *not* cracked a major German spy ring and that the press should *not* be alerted immediately.

"I had to get on the phone to Stephenson, he got on to Pearson, and in the end we got rid of the secret-ink man by sending him to Montreal," Brooker said.[20]

The second major job that Drew-Brook carried out for BSC was to provide a variety of clandestine services that could not be performed in the neutral United States. These ranged from the acquisition of arms to the printing and forging of documents, and they took the discreet and respectable stockbroker of King Street into strange and unfamiliar territory.

According to official BSC documents, "Station M", a centre for the art of "manufacturing" documents, was established in Canada in August 1941 – just four months before Camp X.[21] At its disposal was a scientist who, after studying forged documents with the help of the RCMP, settled into a small laboratory in downtown Toronto. One of the BSC officers most closely connected with the operation was Eric Maschwitz, the gifted lyricist of such famous songs as "A Nightingale Sang in Berkeley Square" and "These Foolish Things". He had been married to the actress Hermione Gingold, and for several years before the war had worked for the BBC as director of Variety. Later, he was story editor for the official British D-Day film *True Glory*, and he went on in the 1960s to become adviser to the controller of all BBC-TV programmes. He came into British Security Co-ordination via the Special Operations Executive and its predecessor organization, Section D of the Secret Intelligence Service. In his memoirs, *No Chip on My Shoulder*, he recalled that in his work for Station M he was "associated in turn with a German ex-Cabinet Minister, an astrologer, a South American professor, a stockbroker, an industrial chemist, and two splendid ruffians who could reproduce faultlessly the imprint of any typewriter on earth." It was Drew-Brook's task to find such ruffians. Thirty years after the war, in a tape now in the possession of his family, he recalled just such a job: "One morning Eric Maschwitz and Harford Hyde [Harford Montgomery Hyde, au - thor of several books, including *The Quiet Canadian*, and a wartime member of BSC] arrived at my office and told me about the LATI problem." The LATI (Linea Aerea Transatlantiche Italiane) airline, run by the Italians, was operating regular flights between Pernambuco in Brazil via the Cape Verde Islands to Rome carrying agents, couriers, propaganda, diplomatic pouches, and small amounts of raw materials and precious stones for the Axis powers. SOE wanted the airline closed down, but needed some extraordinary evidence to persuade the Brazilian government to withdraw landing rights. Maschwitz and BSC experts in New York concocted a plan. A forged and compromising letter signed by LATI's president in Italy would be leaked to the Brazilian authorities. The problem was to duplicate the LATI stationery, including the embossed heading, and then find a typewriter that could reproduce the type used in an original and genuine letter that had fallen into British hands.

Drew-Brook took personal charge of this aspect of the operation. First he travelled to Montreal to consult with Vining, an obvious expert in matters of paper and newsprint. His friend put him in touch with a small papermill in Ontario. One night, after the plant had closed down, Drew-Brook swore the manager to secrecy and explained what was needed. Three weeks later he collected the exactly duplicated paper. It was then embossed by stationers in Toronto, again after the mandatory nocturnal briefing and reading of the Official Secrets Act. Finally came the question of finding a typewriter. Here Drew-Brook sought the help of George McClellan. The burly RCMP officer put him in touch with two First World War veterans who ran a typewriter-servicing agency and often helped the police. Undoubtedly the two ruffians Maschwitz later remembered, they identified the typewriter used for the original letter as an Olivetti, and then spent two days carefully modifying one of their own machines to match imperfections in the original. All was now ready.

The next day Maschwitz and Hyde travelled from New York to Toronto with the carefully prepared text of the forgery, and the letter was typed out. It contained personal insults about the president, General Vargas, criticisms of Brazil's foreign policy, and suggestions that the Italians were subsidizing Vargas's political opponents. A microfilm was then sent to a British agent in Rio de Janeiro. Shortly afterwards a burglary of the LATI manager's house in Brazil was manufactured, the microfilmed letter was "found" and passed to an American journalist, who in turn forwarded it to the American ambassador. Believing it to be genuine, he immediately informed Vargas. The result was everything the British could have hoped. Vargas cancelled all LATI landing rights, confiscated their aircraft, and interned their personnel. It was one of Station M's more dramatic victories and testimony to this highly unconventional side of Drew-Brook's wartime activities.

More central to the story of Camp X, however, was his help in facilitating the purchase of land for the Camp and then ensuring that it was equipped in time for the arrival of its first commander. Drew-Brook was one of the first people A.J. Taylor had contacted on arrival in Toronto to look for a suitable site early in September, and as BSC's official Canadian representative he eventually took over complete responsibility for local arrangements.

Throughout October and November 1941 there was a flood of activity in London, New York, Ottawa, and Toronto to get Camp X ready before winter arrived. Taylor made several weekend visits from New York to Whitby to inspect progress with his brother, whose company had been given the contract to build accommodation for up to thirty students at a time, an instructional staff of a dozen, and about thirty support personnel.

Progress was slowed by bad weather and human error. During one visit, on "a miserable drizzly day with fog", Taylor, after breakfasting in Toronto with the food magnate Garfield Weston, discovered that the site foreman had misread the plans and some of the work had to be redone. Four weeks later, after yet another visit, Taylor "raised hell and fired the foreman". Stephenson himself visited the site in early November, taking the overnight train to Toronto from New York with his wife and Taylor. Tommy Drew-Brook and Charles Vining met them at the station, and after breakfast they all drove out to Whitby. Despite the grey and the drizzle, all of them felt pleased with the progress. By the end of the month, when Taylor returned to make another inspection, it was clear that the Camp was ready for occupation. The three most important buildings to house the students and staff were completed, and Taylor thought the job had been admirably done. The only black spot was that there had been a serious overrun on the estimate, to the tune of $20,000. "This takes away a good deal of the pleasure from the job," Taylor noted.[22]

Canadian military officials in Ottawa and Toronto worked equally fast to satisfy British requirements, as can now be traced in documents first released in Canada in 1985.[23] At Tommy Davies' suggestion, Gubbins had sent a Major Lindsay, his candidate as the

Camp's first commandant, out to Ottawa to discuss how the Canadians could help and to give a detailed and professional estimate of what he would need. He left Britain for Canada by air via Lisbon on September 24, and immediately on arrival in Ottawa discussed his needs with Layton Ralston and the commissioner of the RCMP, S.T. Wood, a dark-eyed, balding man in his late fifties described by one British visitor to wartime Ottawa as having "the sort of face that accompanies leather gaiters and austere shooting breeches".[24] Within two weeks Lindsay had travelled to Whitby to examine the site, met Tommy Drew-Brook, been introduced to Major-General Constantine in Toronto, commanding officer of Military District 2, and agreed with them all on what the Camp needed and how best to handle everything in the light of the overriding need for secrecy. Lindsay then flew back to London to make a personal report to Gubbins, to seek out the British staff he would need, and to prepare himself for the return to Canada in November.

In the meantime Ralston in Ottawa personally briefed a few key officers at National Defence Headquarters on the importance the British attached to the training school, and thereafter Norman Robertson provided them orally with most of the further details. Colonel W.H.S. Macklin, the director of staff duties in Ottawa who was put in charge of implementing the plan, noted with some exasperation: "Colonel [sic] Lindsay returned to the UK without coming in person to this HQ."[25] Still, despite being in the dark about the specifics of SOE's needs, from then on there was intensive communication classified "Most Secret and Personal" between Macklin and Constantine. The general had first heard about British plans in a letter from Macklin on October 24; he was instructed to offer all the support he could in terms of equipment and personnel. For while the British would provide the commanding officer and the entire instructional staff, the adjutant and twenty-six other ranks needed for administrative duties would be Canadians. So far as possible, Constantine was told, they should be men of low medical categories unfit for general service. "The Minister has approved all this," Macklin wrote, "and has also approved a proposition that we do not set this unit up as a distinct unit of the Canadian Army. This avoids approach to P.C. [Privy Council]." Furthermore, he instructed Constantine, "You should select [staff] carefully with a view to picking reliable men who can keep quiet about their duties...[the chief of the General Staff]... asked me to impress the need for every precaution as regards secrecy...the men do not need to know the purpose of the school."[26]

Once these general instructions were issued, Ottawa then ordered Constantine to negotiate the details with Tommy Drew-Brook. Until the British commandant arrived, Macklin told Constantine in another most secret letter dated October 31, "it will be in order for you to treat Mr. Drewbrook [*sic*] as the agent of the British Government so far as this school is concerned, and to deal with him in all matters affecting it, including financial matters."[27]

Drew-Brook was clearly the man in charge. By the end of October he had already arranged for the purchase of vehicles, beds, bedding, and crockery for the Camp, and early in November he travelled to Ottawa to iron out details of financial arrangements with senior officers at National Defence Headquarters which formed the basis of all subsequent co-operation between BSC and the Canadian authorities. The British officers and training staff were the exclusive responsibility of the British and were paid directly out of Drew-Brook's account; the Canadian support personnel were all to be nominally on the strength of Military District 2, but then allocated to the Camp for special duty – a fairly elastic and irregular arrangement that kept information about the Camp to a minimum, and above all had the advantage of keeping the War Cabinet in the dark. The British were responsible for the pay and allowances of the Canadians employed at the Camp, although the pay operations were actually carried out by Military District 2, which was then reimbursed on a monthly basis.

So far as supplies were concerned, the British were free to obtain them wherever they could. In practice, however, they usually obtained them from Military District 2. Again, they paid for them on a monthly basis. Drew-Brook received an account every month from the Treasury. Each month he would receive payment from BSC in New York and then reimburse the Canadian government through a bank draft in favour of the Receiver-General of Canada. So far as Camp X was concerned, Tommy Drew-Brook was not only a very likeable but also a very important paymaster.

How much did the Camp cost? So far as capital costs are concerned, the land cost $12,000, but as we have seen, this was not charged to the British government. During Stephenson's visit to London in July 1941 a provisional construction budget of $110,000 was approved, and in September SOE gave Davies authority to spend up to £25,000. But how much was actually charged against that amount is not clear. Other initial non-recurring costs, mostly relating to signals and wireless equipment, armament stores, and clothing, cost $28,000. So far as recurring costs are concerned, we have a rough picture from estimates prepared by the Canadian military authorities in October 1941 and finally released along with other Camp X documentation in 1985. They show an estimated cost for the fiscal year 1942-43 of some $74,800. The total recoverable costs incurred by the Canadians between March 1942 and October 1944 were almost $180,000. These do not include costs directly paid by the British themselves, either through Drew-Brook, Stephenson, or SOE in London. Nor do the figures include American expenditures that arose from the training of American recruits from the FBI or the OSS. These figures still remain obscured in the fog of secrecy that lingers around Camp X.

Secrecy, indeed, was the keynote. Tommy Drew-Brook dealt personally and directly with BSC headquarters in New York and took care of all the accounts with great discretion. Donovan and the Americans wanted their interests kept unknown because the United States was still, even at this late date, a neutral power and there would be a political backlash for Donovan if it became known he was training men to fight a secret war. SOE wanted the project kept secret because SOE itself was such a top secret that many British commanders were still unaware of its existence, and it masqueraded under a variety of cover names. So, therefore, did Camp X.

To SOE, Camp X was known officially as Special Training School 103, or STS 103, one of some sixty SOE establishments eventually scattered across the globe in Britain, the Middle East, North Africa, and the Far East. To the Canadians it was known as "Project J", or "J Force", and sometimes "Special School J" or even "Installation J". The file opened by Ottawa on the project was numbered Special 25-1-1, and eventually this designation, rather than "Project J", came to describe the Camp as well as the file series. Ralston had stressed the need for every precaution to be taken in connection with the Camp, and the file was given very restricted circulation in Ottawa. When the chief treasury officer of Army Services circulated copies of "the accounting procedure to be followed in connection with 'J' Force" on November 25, 1941, he gave instructions that once Drew-Brook had signed it "Concur" it should "be returned to me personally at my residence".[28] Likewise, Constantine in Toronto kept all correspondence with Macklin apart from even the routine Special 25-1-1 documents by locking it in a special drawer in his desk. All normal military auditing and equipment inspection procedures were suspended for the Camp. Site visits were banned, and special procedures were followed throughout the war that pre-empted the need for those not in the know to visit the Camp. Secrecy affected even the architects. Once the Camp was built, they were instructed to "forget" all about it and, to make sure, the RCMP descended on their offices one day and removed all the architectural drawings and other material relating to the Camp.

Despite this almost paralysing need for secrecy, Drew-Brook, Taylor, and the local military authorities succeeded in getting the Camp ready for its first training course by early December. There was one major hitch to be overcome before Camp X could begin to function.

Gubbins thought Major Lindsay was one of the soundest men he had. The major was an officer in the Irish Guards and commanded one of SOE's special training schools in England. He completed his preliminary visit to Canada and was back in London by late October. Gubbins had already chosen Brooker to be the Camp's chief instructor, and so in early November Lindsay and Brooker agreed to meet for lunch at White's, the exclusive London club in St. James's Street. But when Brooker arrived, it was to find Lindsay in a truculent mood. "Well," he told Brooker, "I've been to Canada and I'm damned if I'm going back." And this was the last Brooker saw of Lindsay, who almost certainly received his marching orders immediately afterwards from Gubbins.[29]

Gubbins had to search hurriedly for a replacement, and indeed within days came up with a man whom Davies described to Stephenson as "first class". More important for the job in hand, he had an American wife and knew the United States. All was finally ready. On November 11, 1941, Armistice Day, London cabled New

York that the training staff would leave for North America by fast convoy on or around the 23rd. It was less than three months since the meeting between Gubbins and Brooker. The British were on their way to the Americans "to tell them all about this stuff".

CHAPTER 3

"A Born Salesman":
Brooker Takes Command

What type of training was required to make an American un-American enough to stick the enemy in the back? No longer was there interest in the old tenet of standing up and fighting like a man. Now the accent must be laid on brutal, cruel, underhanded action, as definite as it must be deadly.[1]

The *SS Pasteur* had once seen luxurious days as a French liner carrying wealthy Americans on the transatlantic crossing between the United States and Europe. But by 1941 she had been stripped of her finery and was serving as a transport ship carrying raw materials and men across the deadly North Atlantic shipping routes. On November 21 she was anchored off Greenock in the safety of the River Clyde in Scotland, preparing for yet another run to North America against the packs of German U-boats that had turned the North Atlantic that year into a metal graveyard by sinking thousands of tons of Allied shipping and taking the lives of several thousand merchant seamen. Before the day was out, the *Pasteur* weighed anchor and slipped quietly down the Clyde to join up somewhere off the west coast of Scotland with a fast convoy bound for Canada. Aboard for the twelve-day crossing to Halifax in Nova Scotia was the initial training staff for Camp X.

The nine men were led by Lieutenant-Colonel Terence Roper-Caldbeck, found by Gubbins at the last minute to replace the defiant Major Lindsay as commandant of SOE's first and only special training school in North America. Roper-Caldbeck had been commanding STS 41, an SOE holding school for Norwegians on the River Thames near

Henley, when he was told he was going to Canada. An elegant, dark-haired, and hatchet-faced Scot who invariably wore a Glengarry and a kilt, he had been a Regular Army officer in the Argyll and Sutherland Highlanders before joining SOE. Educated at Harrow and the Royal Military Academy at Sandhurst, he had served overseas with the Shanghai Defence Force and had then served two tours of duty in West Africa. SOE had first recruited him in August 1941 to head STS 46, their holding school for Poles and Czechs at Chichely Hall, a fine red-brick early Georgian mansion in Buckinghamshire close to the Bletchley code-breaking centre. With an American wife and the experience of two training schools behind him, he seemed ideally suited for the special requirements of Camp X.

Major Bill Brooker was the second-ranking officer of the British group, but as chief instructor he had the most important role to play. It was he who had the job of training the recruits and the main responsibility of impressing the Americans, and whose task it would be to adapt the SOE training syllabus to the special requirements of Camp X. To help him he had Captain Fred Milner, the third officer of the group, a soldier from the Dorsetshire Regiment who had already worked at several SOE schools in Britain as a demolitions expert. Milner stayed at Camp X until 1943, when he was posted back to Britain, and he ended up being parachuted into Burma as an SOE field agent in March 1945.

Of the six remaining members of the group, the one who was to make the strongest impact on early batches of recruits at Camp X was Sergeant-Major George de Rewelyskow, whose specialty was unarmed combat. A small, dark, dapper man with a moustache and in peacetime a professional wrestler, de Rewelyskow was the son of an Olympic wrestling gold medallist of White Russian background who had founded a family all-in wrestling business in the north of England. Like Milner, de Rewelyskow left Camp X in 1943 on being reassigned to SOE duty in Britain. The remainder of the group was made up of two sergeants and three corporals, for a total of nine men – one short of the official war establishment approved for Camp X in London.

The most memorable event of the crossing was the lifeboat practice that took place shortly after they left Greenock. Assembled on the deck with their life jackets in an icy wind, the group was told by the officer in charge that it was really all a waste of time. "If you survive the attack," he said grimly, "the U-boats will get you. And if *they* don't, the water will." After this less than encouraging start, followed by the inevitable tension of the voyage and a rough passage, the group was glad to arrive in Halifax on 2 December. For all except Roper-Caldbeck, it was their first sight of North America. The word that came to Brooker's mind was "plenty". There was plenty of food, plenty of warmth and hospitality, plenty of cars, plenty of everything. The contrast with wartime Britain was both shocking and pleasurable, and the group had several hours in Halifax to enjoy it before boarding the train for the trip to Toronto. This journey threatened to be more dangerous than the Atlantic crossing because the train derailed not far from Halifax. But none of them was hurt and within several hours they were on their way again. Once they arrived in Toronto, they immediately reported to 159 Bay Street, headquarters of Military District No. 2, a stone's throw from Tommy Drew-Brook's office in downtown Toronto. "Roper-Caldbeck arrived yesterday and is looking about," Major-General Constantine told Ottawa; "he seems very pleased with arrangements so far."[2]

The date was Sunday, December 7, 1941.

That same afternoon in New York, while Stephenson and his wife were lunching with A.J. Taylor at the St. Regis, Donovan was at the New York Polo Grounds watching a football game between the New York Giants and the Brooklyn Dodgers. It was shortly after two o'clock when he heard a message over the loudspeaker requesting him to call Operator 19 in Washington. When he finally got through to the capital, it was to hear Roosevelt's son James telling him the news that Japanese planes had attacked the U.S. Pacific fleet in Pearl Harbor. Hurriedly he left the stadium and headed for LaGuardia and the military plane that awaited him. Shortly after midnight Donovan found himself being ushered along with CBS correspondent Ed Murrow into the Oval Office. The president, still shaken by the attack, was sitting at his desk in the semi-darkened room. The three men discussed what the situation implied for America's ability to fight the war, and Donovan seized the opportunity to press on the president some of his ideas about guerrillas and subversive warfare. But the main topic of conversation was public opinion: would the American people finally accept war with the Axis powers? Roosevelt wondered. Donovan and Murrow thought they would.

It was 2 A.M. when Donovan finally left the White House. Later that same day the United States declared war on Japan, and three days afterwards, Americans also found themselves at war with Germany and Italy. The long wait was over. It was now up to "Wild Bill" to prove that his agency could collaborate in the secret war with the British on a full and equal basis. The moment had come when he could actually plan his own secret and special operations.

While the British and the Canadians were setting up Camp X, the Americans themselves had been far from idle. During the summer of 1941, from his headquarters in the former home of the National Health Institute at the intersection of 25th and E streets, a dreary neighbourhood of downtown Washington close to the Potomac, Donovan had created the basic structure of COI by setting up two of its main divisions: the Foreign Information Service, based in New York under the direction of the playwright Robert Sherwood, and the Research and Analysis Branch, later headed by the distinguished historian William L. Langer, which concentrated on the collection and analysis of strategic information.

But this was not enough to satisfy the restless and wide-ranging imagination of Donovan, to whom almost any unorthodox way or plan of fighting, however far-fetched, seemed a good idea. After talking to the top intelligence experts in Britain, he had returned determined to set up similar services in the United States. But in contrast to the British, who had a separate agency for each service – SIS for intelligence and SOE for special operations – Donovan planned to include both within COI. But what was involved? What were the basic principles underlying secret intelligence and subversive warfare? How could they be made operational? Neither Donovan nor anyone else in the United States had much idea, and history provided little help. Spies and espionage had played an important part in America's history ever since Captain Nathan Hale went to a British gallows in 1776 for spying behind enemy lines during the American Revolution. And during the First World War Major General Ralph Van Deman of the U.S. Army had earned himself the title of "Father of American Military Intelligence" by recruiting such talents as Herbert Yardley, the great code-breaker, and by bringing national co-ordination to American's intelligence efforts. But as William Corson wrote in his study of the rise of the American intelligence empire, *The Armies of Ignorance*, "Prior to the outbreak of World War II in September 1939, America's intelligence heritage can best be seen in terms of the records of individuals...rather than by the institutional history of the early, essentially makeshift wartime intelligence organizations which faded out of existence once the various wars were ended." As for special operations involving sabotage, subversion, guerrilla warfare, and other forms of covert action, it was virtually unknown territory. "Very few Americans," recorded one OSS official history, "knew anything about espionage outside of the work of Messrs. Oppenheim, Greene and Ambler."[3]

Donovan initially turned to Stephenson, who could provide experts to deal with all the questions Donovan had to ask. The "Quiet Canadian" responded with enthusiasm. It was not just that he had immense personal faith in Donovan. As director of BSC, he needed a strong pro-British ally in the United States to help him fight bureaucratic battles in Washington, and Donovan was nothing if not a fighter. Furthermore, as the discussions to set up Camp X have revealed, Stephenson was under strong pressure from SOE in London to please Donovan. "Although SOE was careful to be discreet," OSS historian Bradley Smith wrote in *The Shadow Warriors*, "it had become as eager for American support as any other British organization. Not only was it short of arms and aircraft, it required an active ally who could help open up full-scale subversive operations."[4] So Stephenson threw himself into the task of aiding Donovan as fully as he could by telling him how the British secret services worked, by passing on valuable pieces of intelligence when COI still lacked independent sources of its own, by lending him some of his own experts, and by assisting SOE to establish Camp X. And while A.J. Taylor was commuting between Washington and Toronto to ensure that the Camp was ready as soon as possible, Stephenson helped Donovan to set up his own special operations division. One way he did this was by arranging for the man Donovan had appointed his deputy on special operations to visit SOE schools in Britain.

Lieutenant Colonel Robert Solborg already had some experience in the shadowy world of secret intelligence. The son of an army general, he was born in Warsaw while Poland was still a part of the Russian Empire. After being wounded with the Russian cavalry in the First World War, he was sent to New York to work for the Russian military purchasing commission, and he stayed on after the Bolshevik Revolution. Solberg became an American citizen and then joined the Armco Steel Company; by 1939 he was its managing director for Britain and France. It was the kind of position that provided excellent cover, and Solborg used it to help British intelligence by reporting on what he had learned about German war production on a visit to Germany he made during the first year of the war. He undertook a similar job, also under the cover of his Armco job, for U.S. Army intelligence in 1941, when he made an extensive tour of Portugal, Spain, and the Vichy French territories in North Africa.

When Donovan began to cast around for someone to set up COI's "operations and special activities" branch by putting out feelers to BSC and army intelligence, Solborg's name was mentioned by two men. The first was Major Preston Goodfellow, one-time president and publisher of the Hearst-controlled Brooklyn *Daily Eagle*, who was looking after Donovan's relations with army intelligence and knew about Solborg's undercover experience. The other was Stephenson's deputy and right-hand man, Dick Ellis. Through his first wife, a Russian *émigrée* whom he had married in the early 1920s, Ellis had long-standing connections in White Russian circles, and through these he had met Solborg, whom he described as an "old friend" when recommending him to Donovan in mid-September.

Eventually Solborg and Donovan were to have a monumental falling-out. Like a lot of other people, Solborg soon concluded that Donovan was a hopeless administrator, and before the year was out was complaining bitterly of the "haphazard way and stuntlike propensities of Donovan's procedures". There was a row, after which Solborg left to head up COI operations in Lisbon in February 1942; after a further violent quarrel Donovan refused even to see Solborg and then fired him.

But in the fall of 1941 all was harmony: on October 9 Donovan put Solborg in charge of special activities with orders to go to London, and arranged for Stephenson to help him. Solborg immediately paid a visit to BSC in New York, talked to the SOE experts there, and quickly produced some preliminary ideas. "The oppressed peoples," he told Donovan, "must be encouraged to resist and to assist in the Axis defeat, and this can be done by inciting them, by assisting them, and by training and organizing them." But, he added, "sabotage is not enough. It must be accompanied by efforts to promote revolution." Here was the language of SOE, of Dalton's own vision of a democratic European revolution against Nazism, and of Churchill's stirring injunction to Dalton to "set Europe ablaze". Solborg was soon to absorb much more of the SOE spirit. He told Donovan that the British training system had much to teach them and for that reason he proposed to study the problem "very minutely". In late October he left for Britain and, while the Canadians were putting the finishing touches to Camp X, made an extensive tour of the SOE training schools in England and Scotland – "the first time," author Nigel West claims in *M.I.6,* "that an American had been allowed prolonged access to a secret British department." Solborg, in William Corson's words, "was dazzled by what Colin Gubbins...and his band of commandos, saboteurs, and 'thugs' showed him.... The demonstrations of special operations techniques were almost too exhilarating for Solborg, but fortunately the British demurred in granting his request to become an active participant in the 'training' they had him observe. He was given 'honorary' commando status, a swagger stick, and a black beret."5

Camp X opened only two days after Pearl Harbor. Ironically, American entry into the war fundamentally altered its original purpose. SOE had created it mainly to train American recruits and help Donovan to lay the foundations for an American capability in secret warfare. But now, with Donovan able to set up his own full-scale outfit, including training camps, in the United States, what was the Camp's point?

Oddly enough, Pearl Harbor made Camp X even more important. Donovan's need for expertise and advice was more urgent and immediate than before. The Camp, with its nucleus of British experts and training facilities, was a godsend. Furthermore, with the American, British, and Canadian alliance now a reality, the door was open for even more comprehensive co-operation. "The supreme world event", as Churchill described Pearl Harbor, had transformed the face of the war.

The prime minister's visit to Washington and Ottawa immediately afterwards symbolized the new transatlantic alliance. Staying as a personal guest of the president at the White House, Churchill addressed the American Congress on the day after Christmas, 1941, and extolled the British and American peoples. "It is not given to us to peer into the mysteries of the future," he told the throng of senators and representatives gathered to hear him. "Still, I avow my hope and faith, sure and inviolate, that in the days to come the British and American peoples will for their own safety and for the good of all walk together side by side in majesty, in justice, and in peace." Two days later he travelled by overnight train to Ottawa to stay with the governor-general, Lord Athlone. On December 29 he attended a meeting of the Canadian War Cabinet, and the next day addressed the Canadian Parliament. "We could all rejoice," Churchill later recorded in reflecting on his two speeches, "at the creation of the Grand Alliance with its overwhelming potential force."

But how was this potential force to be applied? This was a question hammered out by the British and American military chiefs during Churchill's Washington visit, in the code-named "Arcadia" discussions. As a first step the Allies agreed to form a Combined Chiefs of Staff to formulate a common war strategy. More important for Donovan and SOE, they endorsed propaganda and subversive activity as having an important part to play in wearing down enemy resistance before the final attack.

For the SOE experts who had just arrived at Camp X, the decision was important in two respects. In the first place it reaffirmed the British commitment to special operations as an important part of the war effort, and it was more than appropriate that it was in Canada that Churchill should have spelled this out most fully. There were three phases in the war that lay ahead, he told the Canadian Parliament. First was the period of consolidation as the Allies gathered their forces for the great and final phase, the "assault upon the citadels and homelands of the guilty". In between lay the second phase: liberation. "We must look to the revolt of the conquered territories," he said, echoing his 1940 command to SOE "to set Europe ablaze"; "no nation or region overrun should relax its efforts for the day of deliverance…where active resistance is impossible, passive resistance must be maintained."[6]

Second, the Washington discussions meant that the Americans were committed to a similar goal. Donovan could now anticipate greatly increased resources for his "special activities." He was not to be disappointed. Even before Pearl Harbor, Roosevelt had authorized COI to spend $2.5 million on counter-espionage and secret activities in Europe. Now, while Churchill and his military chiefs were still in Washington, Donovan was given another $1 million to carry out special projects in Asia. Shortly after that, in late February, the American Joint Chiefs of Staff put their own official stamp of approval on Donovan's plans by formally authorizing him to organize and conduct secret and subversive operations.

Characteristically, Donovan had been proceeding at full speed in any case. Solborg returned from his visit to SOE installations in Britain early in the new year of 1942, his head full of ideas for the setting up of America's own service for subversion, sabotage, and guerrilla warfare. Its operations, he told Donovan, should include the dissemination of black propaganda, the sabotage of enemy transportation, communications, and military installations, and the "fomenting, organizing, equipping, training, and leading of disaffected elements under enemy rule". Donovan immediately gave him the go-ahead. Solborg's row with Donovan shortly afterwards hardly affected things: in his place Donovan appointed Major Goodfellow. With the headquarters now organized, Donovan urgently needed trained agents to carry out his plans for operations behind enemy lines. Camp X would provide them.

Kenneth Downs was one of the first group of Americans to arrive at the Camp for training. Pearl Harbor had found Downs, a thirty-two-year-old war correspondent, kicking his heels at Shepheard's Hotel in Cairo, on a brief breather from the Western Desert, where he had been for a fortnight covering the ebb and flow of the battles between the British Eighth Army and Rommel's *Afrika Korps*.

Downs was a staunch isolationist when Hearst International News sent him to France as chief of the Paris Bureau in January 1937. For two years he reported on the march of events that led to the outbreak of the Second World War. Then he covered the fall of France. That, dramatically, converted him overnight to an ardent interventionist. He was convinced that the United States would have to enter the war;

it was only a question of when and how. He resolved that when the time came, he would volunteer for military service.

Covering successively the London Blitz, the German occupation of France, and the Middle East campaign only served to harden his commitment to his course of action when his country became a belligerent. So, when news came of the Japanese attack on December 7 he resigned as a correspondent and began to look for transportation to Washington.

During the days of waiting for available space on a plane, he mulled over his plans: join the army and opt for service in the armoured corps if possible. The unexpected arrival of a distinguished guest at Shepheard's changed these plans. The visitor was an old friend, William C. Bullitt, the American ambassador to France during Downs's years there and now an ambassador-at-large sent by Roosevelt on a secret and special mission to the Middle East.

At breakfast one morning Bullitt asked Downs about his plans. He then suggested that he see Donovan instead. Downs, having only a vague notion of what COI was, protested that he did not want to go home only to work on propaganda.

"There's a lot more to COI and Bill Donovan than that," said Bullitt. "Do me a favour and look him up before you make a commitment."

Back in the American capital early in the new year, Downs did. After a talk in Donovan's office, he found himself two days later a member of COI with an army commission. "We've got the Foreign Information Service, we've got counter-intelligence, and we've got research and analysis," Donovan told him. "But I think you'd be better in special operations." Downs jumped at the chance. Watching the war in Europe, he had become obsessed with America's lack of experience and expertise in all aspects of intelligence, and now that Donovan was finally getting things organized he wanted to be in at the beginning. It went a bit against the grain for a New World idealist to accept that America should take the same path as cynical old Europe, but this was war and the enemy had to be fought on his own terms and with his own ungentlemanly rules.

In any case, Downs had already enjoyed a slight taste of the cloak-and-dagger world. Less than twelve months before, International News Service had assigned him to a brief stint in Vichy, capital of unoccupied France. He soon found that he was on a hopeless assignment. Suffocating censorship prevented him from even hinting at the suffering of the French population from cold and hunger and the persisting deep trauma of the 1940 defeat. There was clear evidence everywhere that the Germans, through severe rationing and control of the currency, were bleeding France white. None of this could be reported.

Paris was in Downs's heart and on his mind. When his repeated requests for permission to go to the Occupied Zone were refused, he decided to go on his own, illegally. In Lyons, he tracked down Paul Thiriert, a brilliant and fearless young Frenchman who had been on Downs's Paris staff until joining his cavalry unit in 1939. He agreed enthusiastically to join Downs in the venture and to make arrangements to cross the demarcation line between the zones.

On the morning of the agreed day, they left Lyons in a hired car after Thiriert had inspected Downs in his worn trenchcoat, heavy muffler, and beret. "Okay," said Thiriert, "you'll pass as a Frog."

They drove through farm country to the north until they reached a hamlet, where they dismissed the car. Two lean guides whom Thiriert had engaged met them, and the four men went into a bistro and had a couple of cognacs. After receiving their 1,000 francs (about $50) and a bottle of cognac apiece, the two guides led Downs and Thiriert through the wooded countryside until they reached a point where a country road crossed their line of approach about 100 yards away.

"That's it," said one of the guides. "A patrol will come along in about five minutes. When it disappears, you can go. Don't run. Walk slow and easy. When you get across the road, you'll be in the Occupied Zone. Then you're O.K."

Exactly five minutes later, the patrol passed, two young Germans on bicycles with rifles slung across their backs. After the soldiers disappeared from view, the guide said, "O.K. *Allez-y.* Remember, slow and easy. *Merde!*"

The crossing was easy and Downs and Thiriert walked to a village where they caught a local train to Dijon. From there, they hurried to the main line station to catch an express to Paris. On the platform they met a sight that suddenly "focused their attention". Most of the waiting passengers strolling up and down in the dusk were German officers. They seemed a relaxed and happy lot, conscious of their smart appearance in their black boots and peaked caps. Fortunately, they showed no interest in their French fellow passengers, including the phony one. The train was full of soldiers, but the trip was uneventful.

Downs and Thiriert arrived in a semi-blacked-out and eerily silent Paris, full of strangers. Day after day in what seemed a surrealist world crammed into an old familiar setting, they impressed facts and sights into their memories. They discreetly visited a score or more of old friends, any one of whom could have betrayed them. After about ten days they decided not to press their luck any further, and boarded a night express for Cannes. Their luck still held and they arrived without incident. Downs then bade a sad farewell to his friend and without delay went on to Lisbon, from where he dispatched a series of uncensored reports on life under German occupation in both zones of France.

In the safety of North America he was soon to experience a train journey of a very different kind. Less than a month after he had joined COI, he was summoned to the office of Colonel Garland Williams, right-hand man to Preston Goodfellow in the Special Activities Division and the man whose job it was to decide how best to train Donovan's new recruits in special operations. Williams had long experience in police and undercover work as former director of the New York Bureau of Narcotics, and he brought to the new job much of the zeal and impatience with routine he had exhibited in the old one.

Originally from New Orleans, Williams spoke with a broad Louisiana accent. "Gentlemen," he drawled portentously to Downs and the half-dozen other men gathered in his office, "you are going on a mission. You will proceed by train to Canada. I have the tickets here. You will take the train at fifteen hundred hours to New York and board the overnight train to Toronto. That's all I can tell you. You'll be met at the station. Travel separately and ignore each other on the journey. Don't tell anyone else you're going and remember this is top secret."

Williams then introduced everyone in the room to everyone else by his first name only – second names, he said, were nobody's business – and shortly afterwards the men were outside on the sidewalk of

25th Street. "Well, Bob, dare we share a cab?" joked Downs as he turned to the man beside him – his friend Robert Low, a fellow newspaper correspondent he himself had recruited for COI.

But the joking soon stopped and Downs was to get a foretaste of the more serious side of security quickly enough on his mystery journey to the north. Killing time in New York between trains, he spent too long with his literary agent discussing cancellation of a contract to write a book, and faced the first bad moment of his new assignment when he realized he had missed the train to Toronto and had no idea of what to do once he arrived. Reporting back to Garland Williams was out of the question. The only solution was to beat the train to Toronto.

But despite all his ingenuity the problem defeated him. There were no scheduled flights out of New York to Toronto that night and he was unable to charter a private plane. So he resigned himself to looking a fool on his very first mission, and did the next best thing he could think of. He sent a telegram to Low explaining that he would follow at the same time twenty-four hours later, and instructed Western Union to page Low after every stop until the telegram was delivered. But his friend had taken Garland Williams's indoctrination about secrecy to heart. When the conductor went through the train after the first stop, paging, "Mr. Robert Low for a telegram", he decided that it must be an initiation test and sat silent until the train left. The same thing happened at the second and third stops, while Downs in New York became increasingly frantic waiting for an acknowledgement that the telegram had been delivered. Finally, during the fourth attempt at delivery, Low decided that it must be genuine and furtively snatched the telegram from the hands of the agent.

When Downs arrived at Union Station in Toronto on the next day's train, he was rather relieved to be met by a man who could see the funny side of the story. It was Roper-Caldbeck. But as the two men drove eastward from Toronto towards Whitby and Camp X, it was neither the kilt nor the accent of his new commanding officer that Downs noticed. Although he had never been to Canada before, he had grown up in Montana where the winters were as cold and hard as those in Ontario. The snow on the ground and the nip in the air provided an unexpected and welcome reminder of home. For Kenneth

Downs and his American companions, Camp X was to be home for the next four weeks.[7]

Fifteen of Donovan's men had been through Camp X courses by the time the first SOE inspection team from London arrived in mid-March to check up on progress. "Some of these will be instructors in the schools [Donovan] intends to set up," the two inspectors reported to London, "and the others are going into the field."[8]

At about the time that this news reached London, a new instructor from the SOE schools in Scotland joined Brooker and company at Camp X. Destined to move on very quickly to work directly with Donovan's men in the United States, he became a legend to many OSS agents and is now a cult hero to contemporary soldiers of fortune.

Captain William Ewart Fairbairn – known variously as "Fearless Dan" or "The Shanghai Buster" – was a pioneer in early SWAT techniques, a co-inventor of the famous double-edged Fairbairn-Sykes commando knife now widely used by special forces throughout the world, and the founder of the basic principles of combat pistol-craft and close-combat techniques used in all SOE and OSS training schools.

He was in his late fifties by the time he arrived at Camp X in late March 1942, fresh from having established, with his fellow knife expert Sykes, the silent-killing course at the combined operations special training school at Lochailort on the western coast of Inverness in the Scottish Highlands – even more bleak and isolated than the winter shore of Lake Ontario. George Langelaan, one SOE agent who passed through Fairbairn's hands in Scotland, later wrote in his memoirs *Knights of the Floating Silk*:

> Off duty, his conversation was limited to two words: yes and no. I never once saw him pick up a newspaper or a book. All his interest, all his knowledge, all his intelligence – and he was intelligent – concentrated on one subject and one subject only – fighting. His knowledge of anatomy was surprising though, apart from the main organs of the human body, he had never attempted to find out the names of the various bones or muscles, and throughout his short, jerky explanations, he would

merely refer to "this bone" or "that muscle" and point it out or touch it with his finger.

Bickham Sweet-Escott once observed him working with Sykes at an SOE training school north of London, and noted drily that they had many methods to impart. "They were all long, complicated, and hard to remember," he recalled, "but each of them ended with the phrase: 'and then kick him in the testicles'."

Fairbairn's fighting methods had been learned in the service of the British Empire in China, and his real achievement was to introduce the martial arts of the East to the special forces of the West. One of fourteen children from a London working-class family, he was christened after the great nineteenth-century Liberal prime minister William Ewart Gladstone. His love affair with the East had begun two years after Queen Victoria's death, when, as an eighteen-year-old Londoner enlisted in the Royal Marine Light Infantry, he was shipped out to Korea to help guard the British Legation in Seoul. A few years later he bought his way out of the army, and in 1907 enlisted as a constable in the Municipal Police at Shanghai.

Shanghai in those days was one of the most violent cities of the world. Every night those citizens too poor to pay for a proper funeral slipped down the funeral piers below the Nantao shipyard, and launched their dead on a final journey. On the top of the flimsy coffins were paper flowers, and while the swelling bodies eventually disappeared, the paper flowers floated in and out, in and out, on the tide. So, too, the living debris of Shanghai floated out each morning and night into the streets: the conjurers and their apprentices, the professional executioners, the beggars and thieves of all sorts, the whores and their overlords, the gamblers and the opium dealers. Upon this sublime chaos the Shanghai Municipal Police sought to impose some sort of order. For Fairbairn, this was to be home for thirty years.

An incident shortly after his arrival in China proved a turning point in "Fearless Dan's" life, transforming him from a conventional imperial policeman into a leading expert on the subject of the Eastern martial arts. One night, while policing the notoriously violent brothel district, he was attacked by several assailants and woke up the next morning to find himself in hospital. Placed strategically beside the bed was a sign advertising the skills of a jiu-jitsu instructor. He got the message and over the next few years, with the help of a Japanese instructor, progressed towards the black belt, which he finally received in 1926. According to his biographer, William Cassidy, he was the first Caucasian honoured with the distinction. In the same year he published what he had learned in a small handbook with the title *Defendu: Scientific Self-defence*, which soon became an official text for the police forces of Hong Kong and Singapore as well as of Shanghai. Only the previous year he had developed the unique and specially equipped mobile Shanghai Riot Squad to deal with civil disorder in the city. By the time he retired as assistant commissioner and chief instructor in 1940, he was widely regarded as the leading expert in British imperial policing throughout the Far East.

The former Shanghai policeman, needless to say, was a specialized taste. Not everyone liked or could even tolerate him, and although he impressed a number of the recruits he also made enemies among his colleagues at Camp X. Brooker found him vain, domineering, and egotistical, and was not sorry when after a few weeks Fairbairn was loaned by SOE to train COI recruits in the United States. Fairbairn caught the American imagination, however, and he became one of the most popular members of the OSS training staff. He left an indelible impression on the hundreds of OSS students who passed through his deadly hands with their mastery of silent killing and other dirty tricks. The slight and elderly figure with the gentlemanly manner, and what the official OSS training history describes as "mature charm", put aside all pretence when it came to fighting.

Richard Dunlop, who later served with the OSS in Burma, was trained by "The Shanghai Buster". "All of us who were taught by Major Fairbairn," he wrote later, "soon realized that he had an honest dislike of anything that smacked of decency in fighting."[9] Richard Helms, director of Central Intelligence at the time of the Watergate scandal, was one of the many CIA men – including five directors – who began their careers in OSS. He, too, received training in unarmed combat from Fairbairn. Although he never had to use the skills that "Fearless Dan" taught him, he found the experience helpful in his later career. "It put a man in the right frame of mind," Helms's biographer Thomas Powers reported in *The Man Who Kept the*

Secrets, "it gave him a bearing of confidence, and it let him know the nature of the business in which he was engaged, which, office routine at one end, was treason, betrayal, and violence at the other."

Fairbairn's particular form of ungentlemanly warfare seems also to have exercised its mesmerizing effect on the president of the United States. One of the OSS schools, known as Area B, was established some sixty miles northwest of Washington, D.C., in Maryland, in the Catoctin Mountains. Practically next door was "Shangri-La", President Roosevelt's weekend retreat, now better known as Camp David. It was at Area B that Fairbairn spent most of his time with the Americans. Here, with his opposite number in the OSS, Rex Applegate – who had been trained at Lochailort and was the author of *Kill or Get Killed*, one of the most complete studies of close combat ever written – he established the basic silent-killing course. In the summer of 1943 Donovan and James Byrnes, then head of the Office of War Mobilization and later to become secretary of state, went down to spend a weekend with the president. Donovan and Byrnes went over to Area B and watched Fairbairn give a demonstration of his skills. They then invited Fairbairn back to meet the president. Here – in the words of Byrnes – he enthralled Roosevelt with his "repertoire of stunts and stories, and by his assortment of trick weapons". When SOE officially seconded Fairbairn to the OSS with the rank of major, it was, according to one source, at the personal request of the president.

The night of April 9, 1942, was bitterly cold with a strong east wind sweeping across the darkened huts at Camp X. Sometime before dawn, a fire, caused by either a faulty stove or careless smoking, broke out in the kitchen of the officers' mess. Within minutes the hut was in flames, rapidly fuelled by the wooden construction and driven hungrily by the wind. Futile efforts were made to put the fire out by throwing buckets of water on it, but within half an hour all that was left of the officers' quarters, the visitors' accommodation, and the two dining rooms was a pile of smoking ruins. Several of the staff lost their personal possessions, and during the temporary sleeping arrangements that followed, many of the students found themselves sleeping in the cold old farmhouse or else in tents provided by the

Canadian Army. There was only one casualty: a Dalmatian, the personal pet of Commandant Roper-Caldbeck.

Roper-Caldbeck had arrived at Camp X to find that the Canadians had got everything working. The real job of keeping it running smoothly and efficiently for the rest of its life was in the competent hands of Art Bushell, the silver-haired and bushy-browed adjutant and quartermaster and a veteran of Canada's campaigns on the Western Front in the First World War. He did a great deal to smooth the way with local military headquarters, which provided what was needed and did not ask too many questions. The Canadians also went out of their way to get the best possible cooks for Camp X. Roper-Caldbeck was determined, in the words of General Constantine, "that the selected candidates...at the school shall leave with the highest regard for the Administration in every detail."[10]

"They have all treated me like an old friend," he told Constantine at Christmas in thanking him for the assistance of his staff.[11] Milner, the demolitions expert, got generous help in purchasing ordnance equipment from such firms as Canadian Industries Ltd., and his constant demand for explosives helped to provide the Camp with its solid cover as an explosives testing ground. The press, briefed by Brooker and given a demonstration of Milner's skills, accepted the story quite happily.

But Roper-Caldbeck ran into problems. His relatively brief stay at Camp X was marked by several unfortunate incidents, not all of them his fault, although he had no one to blame but himself for an early mistake: On a courtesy call to BSC in New York he fell badly afoul of Stephenson when he failed to turn up for a Sunday morning appointment after a lively night on the town. Stephenson was furious and refused to see him after that.

The one real tragedy to occur while he was commandant happened when one of his junior officers collapsed and died of a cerebral haemorrhage. Captain Howard Burgess was a twenty-six-year-old instructor working at Beaulieu when Brooker requested his services to replace Fairbairn, who had left for the United States. Burgess arrived at Camp X in mid-May and had been lecturing only a few days when, in the middle of a class on security, he suddenly paused, asked if anybody had noticed "the lightning", and collapsed on the floor. He died in hospital from the effects of his stroke five days later and was buried in the Oshawa cemetery.

This sobering reminder of personal mortality came on top of constant disciplinary problems. Roper-Caldbeck found dealing with the Camp's inevitable teething problems something of a strain. He felt that some of the locally recruited Canadian staff were unreliable and undisciplined, and on one occasion in requesting the withdrawal of two of them had complained plaintively to Constantine that "they are all drinkers of cheap wine".[12] Such lack of discrimination in their drinking was obviously hard to take, and suggested that the gentlemanly background of Harrow and Sandhurst was not the best preparation for the robust social climate of the Canadian soldiery. Constantine comforted him with the thought that some few "odd personnel" were inevitable. "The latter I fear one cannot be sure of this side of the grave," he wrote to Roper-Caldbeck two days before Christmas; "there are the human frailties and nature to contend with." After he had returned to the gentler landscape of his home in the fox-hunting region of Leicestershire, Roper-Caldbeck wrote to thank Constantine for all his help and expressed the hope that he might one day return to Canada. "I hope that when I do return life will have reverted to normal and that the Nazis and Japs will have been destroyed once and for all. If that has happened," he continued, "I will seek your advice once more, but *not* on military matters. I shall be keen to find out about the best place for hunting the duck and geese!"[13]

It is hardly surprising that Roper-Caldbeck made little long-term impression on the Camp. Far more influential was the Camp's first chief instructor, Bill Brooker. When Roper-Caldbeck was recalled to Britain in August 1942, Brooker, now promoted from major to lieutenant-colonel, succeeded him as commandant. For the first fifteen months, Camp X bore the imprint of Brooker's personality.

"The key to the whole success of Camp X was to make a first-rate impression on the Americans," said Brooker, recalling his SOE mission in North America some forty years later. He pursued this strategy with relentless determination as chief instructor and commandant of Camp X from the time he arrived in Canada in December 1941 until he returned to Britain in March 1943. It provided the dominant theme of the Camp's operations in this early period, and was outstandingly successful. When the Anglo-American Alliance in secret warfare was finally achieved and the OSS could stand as an equal partner to SOE, a great deal of the credit was due to Brooker and Camp X.

Bickham Sweet-Escott was sent to Washington as part of a high-level SOE mission to North America in 1942, and he visited Camp X while Brooker was in charge. "Oshawa was organized with a real Knightsbridge Barracks efficiency," he recalled. "There was a great deal of spit and polish, saluting, and sharp words of command. Knowing only the somewhat happy-go-lucky, lackadaisical atmosphere of military establishments in the United States at this stage of the war, most of Bill's visitors from OSS were immensely impressed."

As soon as Brooker arrived at Camp X as chief instructor, he devised one way to impress the visiting Americans before they reached Whitby. As Kenneth Downs found out, the chief instructor insisted that as part of the performance they turn the journey itself into a mission and come to the Camp by different routes, using various forms of cover. Later on, when post-war myths about Camp X began to flourish, there would be talk about the Americans coming soundlessly across Lake Ontario by moonlight. This was not true. But there were several other ways to reach Whitby and Oshawa from the United States without being too obvious, and they all gave Brooker the opportunity to impress Americans with British expertise in the cloak-and-dagger world of espionage. Men would take the train from Buffalo to Toronto and be met at a downtown rendezvous, where pre-arranged recognition signals would be exchanged. Or they would arrive in Montreal and take a train to Oshawa, where they would be met discreetly by a member of the instructional staff. They could also fly into Toronto and be driven up Highway 2 at night to the Camp. The main point was to make the journey itself part of the experience, and to instil security-mindedness into the Americans even before the spit and polish began.

Once there, most *were* impressed. Downs thought Brooker "a very clever choice of person" to run courses for the Americans, with his theatrical and demonstrative skills, his deadpan quips, and his ability to convince them – at least temporarily – that he had actually been a secret agent in Occupied Europe. "We knew by the end that it was phony," Downs admitted, "but it was impressive and opened up a whole new world for us. It turned our values upside down and we wondered about making a world fit for terrorists. But we went along with it because it was war and the enemy was doing the same thing."

John Bross, another of Donovan's men who went up to Camp X in the summer of 1942 for a four-week course, was equally impressed. In his case the lessons carried over into the CIA, where he eventually ended up as an assistant to Richard Helms, the "Man Who Kept the Secrets" as CIA chief from 1966 to 1973. Bross was one of the "three Bs" at the CIA in the 1960s, the trio consisting of himself, Richard Bissell, and Tracy Barnes, who during the great inquests of the 1970s came under attack for many CIA covert action disasters, such as the Bay of Pigs invasion of Cuba in 1961. Underlying these operations was a powerful faith in the ability of the United States to detonate popular explosions against unfriendly regimes.

It was a strategy that went back to the Office of Policy Co-ordination (OPC), created under President Truman in 1948 to set the Soviet Union ablaze by covert action; Bross had been the head of its East European division in the 1950s. Many of the ideas espoused by the OPC and CIA can be traced back to the SOE training syllabus and indoctrination given at Camp X.

Bross considered, correctly, that by the time he got to the Camp its main purpose was to indoctrinate COI-OSS leaders and future instructors in the philosophy of secret war rather than to train operatives for secret missions. "It was of tremendous value to OSS," he remembered, "because it gave you a picture of the problem and told people who would have decision-making authority of the potential for such work, what would and would not work. It was a *sine qua non*, really, for everything OSS did."

Bross, too, was almost mesmerized by Brooker's personality, and impressed by the Camp's efficiency. "He held us spellbound and could tell us fantastic stories in French as well as English. He reminded me of Henry the Eighth in his youth. As for the Camp, it was wonderful. I was one of a mixed bag of no more than twelve or so. There was a Marine Corps lieutenant and at least one British civilian among the group. Time was well allocated, the weather was magnificent, the courses were interesting and challenging, and we got on well with our British colleagues." Sufficiently well, indeed, that after spending some time as an OSS instructor in the United States Bross went on to work with SOE at the OSS liaison office in London and, in 1944, was put in charge of the three-nation (British-American-French) paramilitary teams (known as Jedburghs) parachuted into France before and after D-Day to co-ordinate local resistance.[14]

Anglo-American harmony at Camp X was not always the rule, however, and there were some predictable cultural clashes. One American operational group that went to Camp X that summer of 1942 showed that the two English-speaking nations were still far from being kissing cousins. One of the first of Donovan's groups to go into the field, it was sent to fight behind enemy lines in Burma and was led by Carl Eifler, a forty-six-year-old American once described as a "mastodon incarnate".

Eifler was made for conflict. He had been a policeman in Los Angeles, a patrolman on the Mexican border, and a customs inspector in Honolulu before being recruited by Donovan in February 1942 to help roll back the Japanese tide in the Far East by taking saboteurs behind enemy lines in China – the beginnings of Detachment 101, one of OSS's most famous units. Eifler commanded it for over two years in a career that was marked by tempestuous controversy.

"Vinegar Joe" Stilwell, who commanded American forces in China and had good reason to know Eifler well, once described him as the U.S. Army's "Number One thug". There is little to suggest that he was wrong. Even in Eifler's biography, *The Deadliest Colonel*, he is described as "one of the most individually devastating and apparently indestructible men who ever lived." The hard-drinking, barrel-chested, two-hundred-and-fifty-pound Eifler embodied the buccaneering side of OSS so beloved by Donovan. One of the colonel's favourite ways to impress new recruits was to order them to punch him in the stomach as hard as they could while he took the blows without flinching. Another was to casually drive a stiletto a couple of inches into the top of his desk while interviewing a recruit and see how he reacted. He drove both himself and his men hard, and frequently went into elephantine rages, at which point his normally stentorian voice would rise to hurricane pitch. It was no wonder that he made enemies along the way and became known throughout the OSS as "Colonel Thundercloud".

Brooker was certainly no friend after Eifler had visited Canada. He and six of his men made their way from Washington to Whitby in the now-time-honoured method of travelling incognito and separately. Each had been given an individual rendezvous with a driver once they reached Canada by train, but Eifler found himself waiting longer than he cared to – thirty minutes, he decided, was too much. So he telephoned the secret number he had been given (an innovation since Downs's misadventure in February) and another driver was sent out to pick him up. "Damned sloppy methods," Eifler complained bitterly when he finally arrived.

Things got no better. Eifler's group debagged one of the British instructors and hung his trousers from the top of the flagpole. Later, no doubt accidentally, another British instructor broke one of the Americans' eardrums by firing a .45 automatic too close to his ear. Eifler himself became a training casualty. One day an instructor demonstrated the power of a Magnum weapon by firing at an old piece of farm equipment, and fragments of steel flew into Eifler's leg. Typically, Eifler tried to dig them out himself with a penknife, but in the end he had to make a visit to Oshawa Hospital to have the leg tended by a surgeon.

The Anglo-American Alliance was further strained when Eifler turned the tables on his instructors during a training exercise. The field assignment began with the would-be saboteurs sneaking past "enemy" sentries to place a (dummy) charge on the railway line that formed the northern perimeter of the Camp. After "ambushing" the imaginary freight train, they were to blow up a cliff-top "fortress", in reality just a tower. But Eifler, whose antennae were unusually attuned, sensed a trap.

Determined not to allow his unit to be ambushed, he outfoxed the hounds by delaying the attack on the fort for fifteen minutes, giving himself time to scale the cliff. Making a crude "bomb" with gun cotton and a primer, he crawled as silently as any German sapper up behind the Brits. Lighting the tiny fuse, he hurled his thunderbolt, bellowing, "Jump, you bastards, jump!" As some of Camp X's most seasoned veterans of the secret war did just that and then streamed down the hill in full flight, Eifler collapsed at the foot of the tower unable to stop laughing.

Despite this display of initiative and the successful defence of his mission, or perhaps because of such exploits, there was relief all round when the course was over and the Americans returned to Washington. "Eifler himself and those he personally recruited did not appear to be particularly suitable as organizers for special operations," laconically noted a BSC report.[15]

Nonetheless he was spectacularly successful in organizing the first COI combat group to go into the field. The unit was conceived in the spring of 1942, as the Japanese were advancing in Southeast Asia, hoping to cut off Allied overland connections with China. Eifler, with a lack of imagination uncharacteristic of his later exploits, suggested that they call themselves Detachment 1. But Garland Williams, Goodfellow's aide, thought this too revealing – the British would see how truly small-scale the American operations were. He named the unit, with admirable panache, Detachment 101.

Although Detachment 101 was the first of Donovan's special operations groups to take to the field, it was not sent into the field that Eifler had first envisioned; he had hoped to set up an intelligence network inside China. But for a variety of reasons this original plan fell through. The defeat of Japan was a secondary goal in Washington's Eurocentric strategy. No one wanted to embarrass Generalissimo Chiang Kai-shek, who had his own intelligence operations under the mysterious and probably murderous General Tai Li, described in OSS reports as "The Heinrich Himmler of China". Stilwell himself, although said to prefer the regular infantry and to consider guerrilla warfare "shadow boxing", decided that Eifler's men might be useful in support of his efforts to retake northern Burma and reopen a land route to China. Giving Eifler ninety days to establish an intelligence and guerrilla campaign behind Japanese lines, Vinegar Joe sent him off with a curt "All I want to hear are booms from the Burma jungle."

That jungle, Winston Churchill once said, was "the most formidable fighting country imaginable". Most of the booms were eventually provided by the Kachin, one of the hill tribes of whom Sir Reginald Dorman-Smith, governor of Burma from 1941 to 1946, said, "Those Hill peoples were the rocks against which the tide of invasion by the 'invincible' Japanese army broke."

Launched as an experiment, Detachment 101 was based at a tea plantation near Nazira, in Assam Province, inside India. Its operations followed what Kermit Roosevelt in his *War Report of the OSS* called a model approach to paramilitary action.

> After the establishment of a main operations headquarters, a supply base near the combat zone, and the installation of training and communications facilities small teams of trained intelligence agents were parachuted or infiltrated overland into the target area. Wherever possible, the agents were equipped with radio sets and maintained close communication with headquarters. Their function was not only to reconnoiter but also to make cautious contact with reliable natives and prepare the way for the arrival of combat nuclei. When conditions were reported favorable, combat nuclei of eight or ten Americans each were parachuted to receptions arranged by the agents. The nuclei had the dual function of recruiting and training agents on the spot into guerrilla bands, and beginning operations to harass the enemy. Supplies were to be delivered regularly by air drop, or, in some cases, by small planes landing on secret airfields cleared and maintained behind enemy lines.[16]

If the techniques were by the book, the results were singularly unorthodox, primarily due to the invasions of the Kachin. Regarded by their lowland neighbours as barbarous savages, the Kachin had in fact done nothing more than evolve their own particular cultural strategies for survival in the fluid political arena of the Golden Triangle. They had for generations supplemented their subsistence economy, based on rice cultivation and hunting, with opium smuggling and mercenary service to local warlords. They had been in the service of the British Burmese Police Force for decades and entered the service of the OSS early in 1943.

While the tribesmen learned how to operate a radio and took in the rudiments of cryptography, the men of the OSS learned from the Kachin survival skills for jungle warfare. One innovation, which particularly impressed the Americans, was meant to ensure as few Japanese as possible survived any ambush. The Kachin had observed that the Japanese tended to dive into the underbrush on each side of the trail when fired upon. Careful hunters that they were, the Kachin whittled bamboo poles into sharp stakes, hardening the ends in the fire. These they planted just off the trail in the inviting vegetation that offered the only cover. The Japanese soldiers impaled themselves, of course. Eventually, however, they were instructed to fall flat, in the centre of the trail, when attacked. Not to be deprived of their prey, the Kachin laid another snare. They booby-trapped the path with anti-personnel mines, each spiked with a .03-calibre bullet on the mine spring, waiting to be released by the weight of a soldier as he threw himself down on the path out of reach, he thought, of Kachin fire.

If the Kachins made colourful allies, "Colonel Thundercloud" could certainly match them. He occasionally charmed snakes and kissed cobras on the top of the head and often wrestled with a pet bear. Eventually, however, he struck his head on a rocky shore during an abortive attack on Ramree Island, and was placed on the invalid list, and command of Detachment 101 passed to John Coughlin, another Camp X graduate.

Burma has often been called the forgotten front. The campaign has been variously seen as a romanticized but still sordid adventure, a wasted effort, and an important and integral part of the war against Japan. Perhaps we might return to the measured prose of Kermit Roosevelt:

> While in general, the record of OSS activity in Europe emphasized the role of a clandestine operation in preparing for large-scale amphibious landing operations in major theaters of war, the achievements of OSS [in Asia] illustrated – among other things – how clandestine activity in a secondary theater could, to some degree, substitute for the direct commitment of front-line military forces, fulfilling the same strategic purpose at much smaller cost.[17]

And it was at Camp X that Eifler and the original members of Detachment 101 got their first taste of that clandestine warfare and covert operations.

The names of individual Americans trained at Camp X are now difficult to trace. Files in Washington either have been lost or still remain classified, and the Camp X records themselves carefully omit such details. But most of the Americans trained at Camp X were staff officers of one kind or another, and many of them only went to Canada for the weekend. Brooker's short briefing courses, beginning on a Friday and ending on a Sunday, taught visitors just the basic elements of secret war. These courses were popular, Bickham-Sweet noted, because "...it was extraordinary what you could get into a couple of days. But there was another attraction. Most OSS officers had been commissioned in the U.S. Army, some directly into high ranks, and many were self-conscious about their so-called 'cellophane commissions' (you can see through them, but they keep the Draft off). A trip to Canada earned an American soldier a campaign medal, and this removed some of their self-consciousness."[18]

Camp X also provided a taste of the legendary Brooker. Most officers returned from a weekend there with a better idea of what secret operations involved. "Too much credit cannot be given to the aid received from British SOE at this stage of the game," recorded the official history of OSS training, which the CIA partially declassified in 1978. "British SOE played a great part if not the greatest in the planning of the new [sabotage] schools [in the United States]."[19]

The fundamental long-term influence of the Camp X courses on the Americans was in affecting the very way COI-OSS conceived of special operations and in indoctrinating those who provided the instructional core at OSS schools in the United States. In the first group that went to Camp X with Kenneth Downs, at least three became important in the training of OSS agents, and almost all early OSS instructors were trained at Camp X at some point. Downs himself was slated to be an instructor, but left on an army assignment shortly afterwards; by 1943 he was back in OSS, escorted Donovan through the Sicily and Normandy landings, and became the commander of a secret intelligence field detachment during the liberation of Paris.

But three of his colleagues on the first northern trip that winter of 1942, Philip Strong, George White, and Louis Cohen, left their mark on the history of OSS training. Strong became head of its Special Operations Division in August 1942. Cohen went on to become chief instructor at Areas B and E, opened up by OSS in the Washington area, where he used courses adapted from the Camp lecture syllabus provided by SOE. Before the end of the war he, too, like Bross, served as a liaison officer with SOE in London. George White, a veteran officer of the Bureau of Narcotics, worked as chief instructor at Area A and then became commandant of A-2 in July 1942 before passing on to become director of all OSS counter-espionage training.

But White's best-known contribution to OSS was the famous field test he administered to the New York gangster August Del Gaizo, otherwise known as "Little Augie". White, who later became a special investigator for the post-war Kefauver Committee's inquiry into organized crime, was already exploring with Del Gaizo how OSS might benefit from Mafia assistance in Italy when he administered the test. It was all part of a drug experimentation program to see whether truth drugs could be used in interrogations.

Initially begun in the fall of 1941, the programme had been abandoned but then revived again in September 1942 by Dr. Stanley Lovell, Donovan's chief scientist in charge of research and development. Lovell, wrote Corey Ford in *Donovan of OSS*, "was a sunny little nihilist, his spectacles twinkling and his chubby face creasing with merriment as he displayed his latest diabolic devices." These were normally of a physically explosive character – one of his favourites being a powdered form of TNT resembling wheat flour that he christened "Aunt Jemima" – but Lovell now wanted White to test a more subtle substance: tetrahydrocannabinole acetate. OSS was looking for an unwitting subject, and White suggested Little Augie, a well-known drug smuggler, king of the Lower East Side, and opium user.

During two visits to White's apartment, and once during a car ride, Little Augie smoked several cigarettes laced with the new drug. White later reported that on all three occasions the gangster became garrulous and indiscreet, and on one visit generously offered his services to the American government as a hit man willing to dispose of the militant labour leader John L. Lewis, president of the United Mine Workers. It is therefore something of an understatement that, as White noted in one report, the information he had got from Little Augie "could be damaging to the subject and is a class of information that subject would never give under ordinary circumstances. There is no question," he concluded, "but that the administration of the drug is responsible for loosening the subject's tongue."[20]

Shortly afterwards, Donovan terminated this promising but alarming drug-induced probe, and White had to revert to the more conventional methods of interrogation taught at Camp X.

The colourful and the improbable figures like White and Eifler, the solid and respectable like Cohen and Downs, the influential like Bross – Camp X witnessed all these types in the Americans it welcomed. But the most important of all for the story of Camp X was one who made the journey to Whitby in the spring of 1942: Kenneth Baker.

Shortly after Pearl Harbor, Donovan summoned two men to his office. One was a former vice-governor of the Philippines and professor of political science at the University of Michigan, Dr. Joseph Hayden; the other was a social psychologist, Kenneth Baker. Both were working in Donovan's Research and Analysis Branch. Donovan came quickly to the point. According to the OSS training history, the following exchange took place:

"I want you to start the schools."

"What schools?"

"Our spy training schools."

"But we don't know anything about spying."

"Who does?"

Thus put in charge of secret intelligence training, Hayden and Baker quickly realized, like others before them, that the solution to the problem that Donovan had posed lay with the British. One of the first things they did was visit Stephenson's men in Washington, Dick Ellis and Colonel "Barty" Pleydell-Bouverie. This was the first step to a full-scale adoption by the OSS of British training methods.

Baker had taught psychology at Ohio State University before joining up with Donovan. Now he was back in the classroom – this time teaching a small handful of COI recruits how to be secret intelligence agents – and he soon realized that he lacked direct experience. During a trip to Washington, Brooker suggested to him that a visit to Camp X would be beneficial. Shortly before the fire, and at about the same time as Fairbairn, the American arrived at Camp X. In two intensive weeks he learned everything he could about SOE training and almost memorized the syllabus. Deeply impressed, he returned to

Washington that spring, taking back with him three things that were to have a profound effect on the Americans' approach to secret warfare. First was an immense faith in Brooker and his training methods. Second was a promise by Brooker to act as an adviser in setting up the American training schools. And third was a copy of what became known as "The Bible" – the entire SOE training syllabus from Camp X. In the growing faith of shadow warfare, Baker had returned from his pilgrimage carrying the works of the prophet.

Within days of his promise to act as adviser to the Americans, Brooker arrived in Washington bringing with him a man who knew even more than he did about SOE training: Jimmy Munn, the head of the Beaulieu SOE school in Britain. Later to become commander of Massingham, the SOE base in Algeria, and then head of training for SIS, Munn had crossed the Atlantic to inspect Camp X as well as to meet the Americans. Philby, who knew Munn well from Beaulieu days, remembered him as "a young colonel of the sensible military type, as opposed to the no-nonsense military, the mystical military, and the plain-silly military. He neither barked nor advocated Yoga [and] held together a shoal of pretty odd fish in a net of personal authority." More prosaically, Americans described him as "matter-of-fact".[21]

Brooker and Munn soon realized that Donovan's men were already facing a severe crisis. Their newly established training programme was in considerable chaos. As mentioned earlier, Donovan had created separate divisions of COI to deal with special operations and secret intelligence. The former was known at this stage as "Special Activities, Goodfellow", or SA/G, because Preston Goodfellow was in charge; and the latter was known as "Special Activities/Bruce", or SA/B, its head being David Bruce, later to be OSS chief in London and, after the war, American ambassador to France, Germany, and Britain. Baker and Hayden (who soon dropped out of the picture) were in Bruce's division. Garland Williams was in Goodfellow's. When Brooker and Munn arrived in Washington, it was to find that SA/G and SA/B had set up their own schools. But the arrangement was causing problems and there was a great deal of useless duplication of effort. What, the Americans asked the SOE experts, could they advise on the basis of their own experience?

In a succession of meetings in Washington that spring, the two SOE experts made a few trenchant suggestions that carried considerable weight and set the American programme on the path toward rationalization and centralization. First, they said that *all* agents needed extensive training, and even secret intelligence agents benefited considerably from some elementary special operations training. Physical exercises and fieldcraft training helped instil self-confidence. So, in their view, combined training made far more sense than the existing arrangements. Second, Brooker stressed, SOE knew from experience that agents should keep in close and continuous touch with their geographical desks: the man or woman going behind enemy lines was isolated and alone, and needed to know that one person at home base was fully familiar with everything about the mission. To be effective, the agent had to give his or her personal allegiance to real people, individuals who stayed with the mission from beginning to end. This applied during training, too, Brooker emphasized, so the Americans should quickly reorganize their set-up to take this into account.

Brooker's advice was more than theoretical, however. He also helped in the selection of individual agents recruited by COI. One such case involved "Gerhard", the code-name of a recruit who had taken part in one of the first training courses organized by Baker. Picked to establish a network of American secret intelligence agents in India and Ceylon, he had quickly turned out to be unsuitable. His instructors described him as "arrogant, boastful, talkative, uncooperative, and unadaptable".[22] Furthermore, they said, he lacked personal courage. What should they do with him? Baker turned to Brooker for help. Brooker's advice was simple and forthright. "Gerhard" should not go into the field at all, anywhere, and he should be got rid of immediately. But this should be done in such a way as to protect security, and therefore "Gerhard" should be talked to frankly and told that he would be closely watched after his departure to ensure that he told no one of any details of his training. Baker followed the advice and there was no more trouble from "Gerhard".

By the summer of 1942 Brooker was deeply involved in helping the Americans. On frequent weekend visits to Washington from Camp X, he became a close ally of Baker. The American's visit to

Canada had set him on a course that seemed irreversible. When Donovan agreed to follow Brooker's advice and set up a combined training programme that got rid of the distinction between secret intelligence and special operations training in September 1942, Baker became its first director. He took over at a crisis point. Too many people had been recruited too quickly, training had been too decentralized and uncoordinated, and a lot of potential agents were either unsuitable or else were kicking their heels impatiently waiting to go on missions that had not been planned or set up. The fall of 1942 saw a huge cleaning-up. There were large-scale changes in personnel and methods, and for a while all the OSS training schools were closed down. There was one exception: "The Farm".

After his return from Camp X, Baker had modified "The Bible" to suit his own needs. Inspired by his Canadian experience, he had established his first special training centre for secret intelligence operations, and under the new combined training system it handled advanced training for those undertaking both intelligence and special operations missions.

RTU-11, to give the school its official title, was, in the words of one OSS report, "a highly secret, small, extremely select school".[23] Like its Canadian prototype, it was conveniently located yet sufficiently isolated to be secure. Hidden in the Maryland countryside just twenty miles from Washington, it was set up in an inconspicuous country home leased from a wealthy Pittsburgh industrialist. The hundred-acre estate continued to be actively farmed through the war, and RTU-11's official cover was as an army gadget-testing centre. With its comfortable and spacious rooms, its broad manicured lawns, and its small swimming pool, the American Farm was more luxurious than its Canadian cousin. It eventually developed into the advanced training school for OSS secret intelligence agents, who were individually prepared for their special missions. "Here," records one recently declassified wartime OSS report, "students are given personal instruction in reporting, battle order, personal cipher, target geography. They do much individual study and research.... They are urged to work hard at their individual problems and then to relax, take walks, swim in the outdoor pool (in warm weather) or play games.... It is the instructors' aim to send the students away from 'The Farm' full of pep and eager to get at their work overseas."[24] In all, over eight hundred men and women trained there for missions in Europe. It became known for its small but intensive classes, its unique ability to provide training facilities for OSS female agents, and its field exercises including undercover trips to nearby cities such as Baltimore and Philadelphia.

Not the least of its attractions was "the populist" Brooker himself, a frequent guest lecturer who arrived from Camp X for weekends armed with his repertoire of stories illustrating the principles and practice of undercover work. Most OSS men and women who graduated from The Farm found him inspirational, even if they knew there was a great deal of fantasy in his claims to have been an agent himself. Sweet-Escott, while he was working for SOE in Washington, also spent weekends there in 1942. "Bill's lectures were, I thought, exactly what was needed. From what he told us, it seemed that he had had an exceedingly exciting war." (It was on one of these weekends that an American colleague solemnly asked Sweet-Escott if Brooker was head of the British Secret Service.)

Americans seem to have either loved him or loathed him. The strong but ambiguous response to the commandant of Camp X within the OSS, as well as fascinating insights into his teaching method, can be read in the history of OSS training, the full version of which was only released by the CIA in 1985.

Lt. Col. Brooker was, perhaps, the most colorful of the British officers loaned to [Schools and Training] [it began], he was very aggressive and sometimes not too diplomatic, and he gained many supporters as well as many detractors within OSS. It was not beneath him to employ bluff in "getting across" his lecture material by casting himself in the role of leading character in his spy thriller stories borrowed, probably, from many sources. *He* was the one responsible for the capture of this German agent in Canada. *He* was the one who interrogated this recalcitrant German prisoner. *He* was the one who briefed and dispatched this British agent to Germany – and the story would be complete with touching and intimate details. He himself would no doubt have been the first to admit that he was a big bluff (for he actually had little if any operational experience) but his argument would have been that any method was justified if it conveyed the necessary lesson to the students. This, however, did not make him any the better loved in some quarters of OSS.[25]

But Brooker got things done.

Many others benefited from yet another Brooker innovation: the weekend course for OSS executives and desk officers. This was designed to improve relationships between the agents and the geographic desks that were responsible for defining and planning missions. Occasionally these events would be enlivened by a demonstration from Fairbairn, but essentially the short course was Brooker's own show – one that he had first rehearsed and perfected at Camp X.

Brooker spent most of the late summer and fall of 1942 in and around Washington or teaching at The Farm. So important did his role become, and so dependent was OSS on his advice, that when Baker was put in charge of OSS training Brooker was his counsellor and adviser. Between devising and then running the weekend courses for busy OSS executives and helping Baker sort out administrative problems, he also found time to prepare a new syllabus for special operations training. Baker modified it slightly to suit the needs of intelligence trainees, and it became the basis of an entirely new OSS training programme that was put into place that fall under the centralized directorate. The new programme, Brooker told a meeting of the heads of OSS geographical desks in Washington early in September, was a service department that could be adapted to the practical requirements of each geographic desk. It would allow the needs of each individual agent to be discussed on its own merits, Brooker told the OSS men, and "where absolutely necessary an individual agent will be given whatever training time allows".[26]

Brooker and Baker between them now formed the OSS Training Directorate. Three months later, and almost exactly a year after Brooker's arrival at Camp X, the two men had a lengthy meeting with Donovan. At the end of it they agreed that training was so important that it should be set up as a separate branch of OSS, with Baker directly responsible to no one but Donovan himself. That same day – December 14, 1942 – Brooker sat down and wrote a lengthy document setting out Baker's mandate as head of the new branch. "I have written a draft of what I have called Directive Number One, to the

Commandants of all schools," Brooker also informed Baker that same day. "I think it would be a good thing...to send [it] out...thus striking while the iron is still hot."[27] When Baker was finally confirmed as its chief by Donovan's official order on January 3, 1943, Brooker could pride himself with the thought that in all its essentials OSS had adopted the SOE principles and methods he had first put into place at Camp X.

Donovan himself was deeply aware of the OSS debt to Brooker during the twelve months since the Englishman had arrived in North America. In a personal letter to him on December 27, 1942, he wrote: "I am convinced that our training program, due in large measure to your inspiration and guidance, has made rapid strides, and am confident that it will show most satisfactory results.... It is my hope that our association may continue not only for its already proven worth but for your aid in the problems of both war and peace which lie ahead."[28]

CHAPTER 4

"All This Stuff":
Agent Training at Camp X

One of the primary objects of the instructor is to make his students attack-minded, and dangerously so.... No instructor should be satisfied unless his students become thoroughly proficient in the performance of the few simple things enumerated in the syllabus. Dull as it may become, constant repetition is the only road to proficiency and constant repetition there must be, no matter how much students may complain of boredom. Their business is to learn, at any cost. By proficiency is meant the ability to execute all the requirements of the syllabus swiftly, effectively and neatly, without having to stop to think.[1]

"It turned our values upside down and we wondered about making a world fit for terrorists," Kenneth Downs said about his training at Camp X as one of Donovan's first Canadian-trained recruits. "For the first time I really got a picture of what being a secret agent might be like," remarked CIA official John Bross when he looked back with forty years' hindsight on his training at Whitby. For these Americans, as for the Canadians trained there, Camp X was a radical departure from the past and an eye opener to a future world of danger and violence. For Donovan and Gubbins, the training syllabus helped to ensure a unity of doctrine and effort between OSS and SOE. So before picking up the threads of the story to see what happened at Camp X after the summer of 1942, let us look at the training its agents received.

Camp X was only one part of a world-wide network of training schools run by SOE – but it was the only one in the Western Hemisphere. Its three-digit designation of Special Training School 103 meant that it was located overseas rather than in Britain. Its two immediate numerical predecessors were STS 101 in Singapore, which fell to the Japanese in February 1942, and STS 102, based at Haifa in Palestine, which ironically and incidentally was to train future leaders of the Haganah who fought against the British for the establishment of the Israeli state. Other overseas schools were to be found in North Africa, Australia, Ceylon, and India. All of them were different, specializing in different levels of training, emphasizing different skills, and operating in sometimes radically different fields of operation. But at the core of each lay the same body of doctrine and experience that SOE ensured was taught wherever the school was based. There were certain universals in the art of secret war that all agents, whatever their origins or destinations, had to know.

The SOE training system was largely built from scratch at the beginning of the war, and was constantly being revised and improved in the light of experience. From the vantage point of the 1980s it is hardly surprising that some of it appears elementary or even amateur. Few of those who devised it had much prior experience in the arts of ungentlemanly warfare. Still less had they much initial conception of the ruthlessness of the opponents against whom they were sending their trainees. Nonetheless, by the end of the war they had evolved a system capable of producing agents whose skills would rival those of the most sophisticated contemporary urban terrorists. Camp X played a role in this melancholy evolution, but it also had its own unique contribution to make.

For all their relative inexperience, the British at least had the advantage of having maintained an Empire by often unorthodox methods. Their secret intelligence service existed largely to preserve its influence, and they had learned much about sabotage and guerrilla warfare, some of it from the anti-colonial resistance movements dedicated to its destruction. Lawrence of Arabia's successful campaigns behind Turkish lines in the Middle East exercised a powerful hold on the British imagination; while some army officers – Gubbins among them – became convinced by their experience fighting Michael Collins and his Irish nationalists that future wars would place a premium on special and irregular operations. The Americans on the other hand were novices. The OSS set up its own Training Directorate in September 1942, but the crucial dimension taught by experience in the field was still lacking. Thus throughout 1943 the OSS was, in the words of its own post-war history, "forced to lean heavily on the British for assistance". In practical terms this meant relying on the expertise that lay closest at hand within the carefully guarded confines of Camp X.

In contrast to SOE training in Britain, the average training period at Camp X lasted no more than three or four weeks. Thus the course obviously could not give more than an introduction to the universal SOE skills. For the most part, Camp X approximated a Group A school, where the emphasis was on paramilitary training. But the Camp X syllabus also covered important elements from the Group B schools' experience, including enemy identification and the recruiting of sub-agents, and the three chief instructors at the Camp all came directly from the advanced schools at Beaulieu. Camp X, in short, compressed elements from across the spectrum of the SOE syllabus. It was more than a preliminary, but less than a finishing, school. For SOE's needs in North America, and for the purposes of BSC, it was exactly what was needed.

The Camp X training programme provided a basic map for the wide variety of travellers who began their journey into secret warfare on the shores of Lake Ontario. The courses differed according to the needs of each recruit or group of recruits, because their destinations were widely (and often wildly) different, ranging from the exotic to the banal and from the secure to the most dangerously unpredictable. Some became secret agents in France or North Africa, or guerrilla fighters in the hills of Burma, Bosnia, or northern Italy. Others monitored clandestine German wireless transmissions in South America, or became experts in operational propaganda at Allied headquarters in various fields of command. Still others were destined for the often tedious but nonetheless vital routine tasks of filing security reports in Washington, New York, or Ottawa. Some were destined to become instructors at OSS training schools, where they would take up the burden of training other recruits. Others merely returned to their regular jobs at Stephenson's headquarters in

New York or Donovan's in Washington. But however different their destinations, the terrain they crossed was similar for all and the landscape varied only with the different angles from which it was viewed.

Brooker described the syllabus as an *à la carte* menu from which the training staff selected the dishes appropriate to the tastes of the clientele. For the FBI they would heavily flavour the course with security. But for the others they would whet the palate with a heavy stress on the basic elements of foreign propaganda, and for OSS and SOE they would provide a solid dish of basic agent training. But for all, there was the *hors-d'oeuvre* consisting of the basic "Brooker treatment" – which meant a strict attention to spit and polish and a careful respect for discipline.

In part, Brooker designed the treatment to impress the Americans. He was appalled at the slackness and casual approach to military affairs that he encountered during his first visit to the United States, and was determined that, as a British showcase in North America, Camp X would convey a message of seriousness and high purpose. So his emphasis on discipline – not always appreciated by North American recruits – had a PR component. But it also reflected his own opinions about the survival skills needed in security and intelligence work. "It appealed to me enormously," he said. "It gave me scope to do the things I believed in." One of his strongest beliefs was that – as he put it forcefully in retrospect – "if there's anything loose in the intelligence business, you're dead." An agent had to acquire an almost photographic memory and to internalize the order of everything; only then would he know when something was out of place, lost, abnormal, and hence suspicious. So when Brooker insisted that most recruits keep themselves and their quarters tidy and immaculate, it was not for appearance's sake. It was an integral part of the training itself.[2]

Of all the Camp X instructors, we have already briefly encountered the most colourful and the most notorious. This was Major Dan Fairbairn, the former Shanghai policeman, who passed through Camp X for several weeks in 1942 on his way from Scotland to more or less permanent loan to the OSS. Described by his biographer William Cassidy as "a quiet man, with the manners of a priest",

Fairbairn was known for a specialty, silent killing, although as an instructor he taught other skills, too, and was an expert in knives and pistols. He taught his students how to board and leave a train travelling at high speed, how to enter a house from the second storey, and how to walk up the face of a cliff using a rope. Recruits regarded him with awe, and he left an enduring mark on SOE by developing the basic syllabus on close combat. Subsequently used by all SOE training schools, it was a standard course from which other instructors were allowed to deviate only with express permission.

"Close combat" was a misnomer. The purpose of the course was to teach the arts of fighting and killing without firearms, although it included the use of a knife. "Silent killing" was a far better description because it defined with clinical precision the principal object of the course: to kill, and to kill silently. This was made abundantly clear in the introductory talk given by every instructor at the beginning of each new course. Close combat was a skill that every agent in the field required, Fairbairn and his successors told their students, because there would always be a moment when the agent would either be without a firearm or unable to use it for fear of raising an alarm. The German sentry guarding the bridge, the railway line, or the factory had to be dispatched quickly and quietly. At this point the agent had to forget any dimly held notions of fair play: "This is *war*, not sport. Your aim is to kill your opponent as soon as possible. A prisoner is generally a handicap and a source of danger, particularly if you are without weapons. So forget the term 'foul methods'...'Foul methods' so-called, help you to kill quickly. Attack your opponent's weakest points, therefore. He will attack yours if he gets a chance." It was a lesson repeated time and time again until the students remembered it even in their sleep. Silent killing was not just a technique; it was a state of mind. Only when the instructor had instilled this thoroughly in his charges could the course be considered complete.

CLOSE COMBAT

SYLLABUS

1st PERIOD: 1. Introduction to C.C.
                    Objects and Explanation of system.

2. Blows with the side of the hand.
   Practise with dummies.

2nd PERIOD: *Other Blows.*

1. How to kick.
2. Boxing blows.
3. The open hand chin jab.
4. The use of the knee.
5. Use of head and elbows.
6. Fingertip jabs.

3rd PERIOD: *Release from Holds.*

1. Wrist.
2. Throat.

   With One or Both Hands.

3. Body holds.
4. Having released, show subsequent attack.

4th PERIOD: *Crowd Fighting.*

1. Technique.
2. Practise with dummies.
3. "Mad" 1/2 minute.

5th PERIOD: *Knife Fighting.*

1. Practise with dummy.

6th PERIOD: *Special Occasions.*

1. Killing a sentry.
   a) If you are armed with a knife.
   b) If unarmed.

c) Spinal dislocator.

NOTE: This last exercise requires great care when practising.

2. Disarming.

Method A.
Method B.

3. Searching a prisoner.
4. Taking a prisoner away.
5. Securing a prisoner.
6. Defence against downwards or sideways blow.
7. Gagging a prisoner.

As at other SOE schools, students at Camp X practised their newly acquired skills on dummies, some of them straw-filled for practice with the knife, and on each other. In the latter case the instructor stressed the extreme danger of ignoring standard submission signals. "Your object here is to learn how to kill," the students were told, "but it is quite unnecessary to kill or damage your sparring partner, you will get no credit if you do so." As mentioned earlier, one of Fairbairn's deadliest inventions was the double-edged knife honed to razor sharpness. First developed from Boer War bayonets in the armoury of the Shanghai Municipal Police, it was too dangerous to use in training; instead, the students had to use dummy knives. But for the holds and techniques, they learned that even wood was too dangerous a substitute for steel. Rubber being unobtainable, they resorted to short pieces of suitably thick rope. There was no shortage, however, of German helmets, invaluable for use in practising sentry attacks. These became more complicated as the war progressed. Through bitter experience of attacks conducted in the Fairbairn method, the Germans instructed sentries to carry their rifles slung in a way that hindered the attacker and made silent killing almost an impossibility. New counter-measures were devised by SOE and taught at Camp X by which, if one agent acting alone could not achieve silence, a team of two could.

By the time students graduated, they had perfected a certain number of skills, to be used in a wide range of situations; thus they were well prepared for their inevitable encounters with armed opponents. They had learned how to kill using the side of the hand or a well-aimed kick to the head ("always the side or back, never the top"). They had been taught the use of the knee, of the head, of the elbows, and of the fingertips, and above all they had been told never to stop just because an opponent was crippled. "If you've broken his arm," they learned, "it's of value only because it makes it easier to kill him." They had practised how to escape from seemingly impossible holds and how to fight in crowds, where the object was not to kill but to escape as quickly as possible. They had learned about knives: how to hold one, how to thrust, how to parry. What part of the body to aim for – the abdominal area being the principal target – and what to do once you got there. They had been taught how to break a man's neck with a simple hold, and how to search a prisoner. The latter was chillingly simple: "Kill him first" was the advice. "If that is inconvenient, make him lie face to the ground, hands out in front of him. Knock him out, with rifle butt, side, or butt of the pistol or with your boot. Then search him."

Such promising holds as the Japanese Strangle, the Rock-Crusher, the Flying Mare, and the Cross-Buttock were spoken of, but none of them was taught. It was obviously not because SOE had scruples. Rather the contrary. Each of these methods had shortcomings that made the agent vulnerable to counter-attack. But more to the point, if an agent was in a position to apply them, he was then equally in a position to make a killing attack. So why not do so? Even in the methods rejected, the Camp X close-combat course emphasized once again that its primary purpose was the silent death of those who put obstacles in the path of the agents.

As well as being suitably trained for silent killing and unarmed combat, the recruits might also have occasion to use weapons, so Camp X gave them weapons training. Sharing the language of the OK Corral, SOE was interested in *gunfighting*. Since an agent's life might very well depend on how well he had been taught, instructors would not let a bad shot out of the Camp. They instilled in the student mind the impression that he was actually killing the target and to shoot as though his life depended on it. "As with every sport, providing the

principles taught are sound, practice makes perfect." The principles
so diligently instilled and practised had as their goal, within the con-
straints imposed by time and the supply of ammunition, "to turn out
good, fast, plain shots". Whether in the use of machine carbines like
the Tommy gun or in action with a pistol, the principle was the same:
"tremendous speed in attack with sufficient accuracy to hit the vital
parts of a man's body, for killing at close quarters demands aggres-
sion and extreme concentration."

There were certain obstacles in producing these good, fast, and
plain shots. One was the recruits' previous experience. Instructors
presumed that many of their students had some "revolver training in
the old style" and, while being careful not to denigrate such skills as
might have already been acquired in skeet shooting, had to impart the
innovative "instinctive method" of firing.

The first point was that a pistol was not a weapon of self-defence
but of *attack* – it was a combat weapon. Armed with the weapon under
consideration, usually a .22 Hi-Standard or .32 Colt, the instructor
conjured up a dramatic encounter while on a mission:

Picture in your mind the circumstances under which you
might be using the pistol. Take as an example a raid on an enemy occupied house in darkness. Firstly consider your approach. You will never walk boldly up to the house and stroll
in as though you were paying a social call. On the contrary,
your approach will be stealthy. You will be keyed up and excited, nervously alert for danger from whichever direction.
You will find yourself *instinctively* crouching; your body
balanced on the balls of your feet in a position from which
you can move swiftly in any direction. You make your entry
into the house and start searching for the enemy moving along
passages, perhaps up or down stairs, listening and feeling for
any signs of danger. Suddenly on turning a corner, you come
face to face with the enemy. Without a second's hesitation you
must fire and kill him before he has a chance to kill you.

This method of course meant that an agent would never fire standing straight up, nor in any of the "fancy stances" common to competi-

tion shooting, and never have time to use the sights. Since recruits under such conditions might be worried about the accuracy of their aim, they practised "instinctive pointing", "the natural way that any man points at an object when he is concentrating". Students stood directly in front of each other and pointed, at the instructor's commands, to such targets as the exact centre of each other's stomach, or left foot or right eye. When doing so, no one actually looked down his finger. Rather, "instinctively", the arm, with the finger extended, came in to the centre of the body. Here the finger, and of course its extension the gun, was in position right down the line of eyesight. Such pointing gave the shooter a natural control over direction and elevation when firing.

After demonstrations and practice in holding the pistol or crouching in the firing position, the recruits were ready for some of the more elaborate target exercises using live ammunition. For example, using the .22, students were to imagine they were outside a German beer cellar, automatics loaded and drawn. In the old style of attack, in order to position themselves for firing, they would have to rely on a totally silent approach. This, of course, was not only dangerous but impossible. SOE felt their method was much superior: "You have reached the doorway of the cellar by a stealthy approach, making no sound whatever. Very quietly turn the handle of the door as far as it will go, and then, preparing yourself for the effort, you kick the door open and kill your targets before they have a chance to realize what has happened."

If this all sounds rather like a B-grade movie, or reads like a spy novel, or looks like a TV SWAT team in action, it is because SOE instinctive firing was so successful that after the war this innovation swept through commando schools, boot camps, and police academies alike, replacing forever the older shooting style.

SOE and its agents were also unusual in their preference for the ugly Sten gun over the Thompson sub-machine-gun. Recruits were warned not to be put off by the Sten gun's "rough appearance". It was acknowledged that the short-barrelled .45-calibre Tommy gun, firing seven hundred rounds a minute, was a valuable weapon for close combat. But the Sten gun was the favourite. Light, weighing only seven pounds, it fired 9mm Luger ammunition readily available on the Continent, it was easily and quickly disassembled and hidden, and

could be fired dry since the working parts did not have to be regularly oiled. And, finally, slogging through a swamp, crawling up a
beach, or fording a stream was unlikely to render the Sten gun useless, since water, mud, and sand did not affect its operation. Firing
five hundred rounds a minute, accurate up to a hundred and seventy-
five yards when fired from the shoulder, it was the ideal weapon,
SOE told its students, "for the type of work with which we are concerned".

Since that type of work often involved agents being parachuted
into enemy-held territory, recruits when possible were given training
in foreign weapons, particularly those in use in the various cogs of the
German war machine: everything from the German Imperial Service
Revolver to army rifles like the Mauser *Einheitsgewehr* and the
Spandau Maxim machine-guns. Weapons from those countries most
likely to be the target of SOE missions – Belgium, France, Holland,
Spain, Poland, the Balkans and Greece, Italy, and Japan – were available in special collections.

As a last note, there were the assorted "hints" and final
instructions designed to let the recruits know that, while they had
been trained by the book, individual initiative and talent would still be
of utmost importance in actual combat. "The methods you have been
taught during the course have been proved to be the best in
gunfighting. But it is impossible to give a ready-made solution to
every problem which is likely to arise." Still, with the rudimentary
weapons training they did receive, SOE attempted to give all its students at least "a sporting chance" against their enemies in the deadly
game of secret warfare.

Most of the people trained as SOE agents did not function as lonely
outriders; many worked with the irregulars of anti-Fascist partisan
armies. Whether operating in the fertile plains of Croatia, the mountains of Montenegro, the forests of eastern Bosnia, or the jungles of
Burma, the basic principles of guerrilla warfare were the same.
Recruits were taught at least some of these at Camp X.

For example, they learned through lectures and exercises how to
move across open countryside at night, avoiding not only German
patrols but suspicious peasants and their dogs. Over and over they
were told that "nine times out of ten the direct route is a bad one" and

to "avoid the most obvious route of approach – this is where the defence will be strongest." Since the primary aim was to move as silently as possible, certain features of the landscape were to be avoided: "any farmyard or place where domestic animals are confined is a deathtrap." Dark-coloured ground, the product of a large number of small shadows cast by rocks and vegetation, was to be avoided. When they could not get around noisy ground, they were to wait for a "counter-noise" such as a gust of wind or a train, to disguise the sound of their own passage.

Not only could a barking dog or rocky ground alert an enemy sentry, but the guerrillas could give themselves away as well. Hence there were to be "no squeaking shoes, creaking leather braces or crackling mackintoshes". Prior to moving out the whole party was to jump up and down on a floor, listening for any keys or loose change in partisan pockets. Agents were told to lift their feet higher at night than during the day, and steps were to be shortened to avoid the noise made by boots brushing against long grass. Partisans, instructors noted, should keep their feet pointed straight ahead and never walk "like Charlie Chaplin, which presents a larger area of frontal surface and is noisy".

Not only must they not be heard; they must not be seen. Collectively, they were never to move in front of a body of water or the unbroken skyline, which would present perfect silhouettes for waiting snipers. The moon should always be in front of the partisan and behind the enemy. Individually, each man was to blacken his hands and face and wear clothing which was neither very light nor too dark, but neutral in tone. His personal equipment was to include a walking stick wrapped in an old bicycle tube; a pocket torch wrapped in rags to muffle any jingling; a watch with a luminous dial, worn with the face next to the wrist; a compass with a similar dial; and a handful of sweets or cough drops to keep the throat moistened and prevent coughing.

When on the move, an estimate of fifty yards a minute was a safe one. It was very important, instructors would stress, to make frequent stops to listen intently, although, as recruits were reminded, "human ears are badly placed for hearing". Slightly opening the mouth improved this. Students who absorbed all this information did well in exercises such as "night stalk on a house", in which those who reached their target rooms undetected were rewarded with cases of beer. Beer would undoubtedly be in short supply in the partisan camps of Yugoslavia and northern Italy, for which many of the men trained at STS 103 were bound, but it made Oshawa by moonlight a little more palatable.

Not all agents were meant to be single operatives or act as part of a partisan army. Some were recruited and trained to organize spy rings, intelligence networks, saboteur units, and underground cells. For such an important mission, a spymaster, "whatever his previous walk of life, must be a man of the world, capable of talking easily to comparative strangers, and better still, of handling men."

Since these operations were of relatively permanent nature and extremely vulnerable to betrayal by informers and double agents, the importance of picking the *right* people, or "helpers" as they were called, was paramount. "Recruiting," students were told, "is the most dangerous part of subversive activity." There were three basic principles to follow. First, "quality must come before quantity." Particularly in the early stages of setting up networks, when the agent's principal assistants would be chosen, the importance of totally reliable individuals was paramount. Second, people who volunteered their services were to be regarded as probable *agents-provocateurs.* Rather, the spymaster should always retain the initiative and recruit the man for the job. And third, people should not be recruited until there was work for them to do. "Otherwise," it was pointed out, "there will be a dangerous period of hanging about."

But what made a man, at great risk to himself and family, help SOE agents in their dangerous and illicit games? A hierarchy of motives existed, according to Camp instructors. The most desirable motivation from their point of view was patriotism, followed by religious or political opposition to the regime, "need" (not to be confused with bribery), a hatred of Germans, and a love of adventure. These were all good motives for an active and committed agent.

Occasionally all spymasters have need of other helpers, some less than willing, for special short-term services that require less than full commitment. In such cases certain other levers could be used. Personal sympathy worked well with women, the students were told; they might consider presenting themselves as hungry, persecuted victims of the Germans. Nonetheless, timeless fears about *la femme fatale* found their way into the lectures. "In recruiting women, information about their personal attachments is most useful. These may prove dangerous," instructors cautioned, "and on no account should a woman be recruited who is motivated solely by sentiment." Then there was "greed", although of course "a man who is bribed is untrustworthy." Sex could be a powerful motivation, or, as it was more prosaically put, "procuration in one form or another may be useful in some cases."

The minor sins of everyday life could also be put to use in securing helpers. Some people could be recruited on the basis of flattery and an appeal to their sense of self-importance; local officials chafing under Nazi supervision were thought particularly susceptible here. For others, snobs and social climbers, the suggestion that titled people were in the organization might be sufficient inducement. And finally there was fear. Instructors warned their pupils that "although it is wisest to avoid blackmail as far as possible, it may be useful in an emergency, and for that reason any information about people's private lives and weaknesses should be remembered."

Recruiters were to seek out their helpers in a variety of places: these would depend on the area in which the agent was operating, but might typically include ex-soldiers' groups, trade unions, the professions, religious communities, and fraternal organizations such as the Freemasons. If the potential agent survived his first encounter with the recruiter, whose opening conversational gambit might be a casual "I wonder how they organize these sabotage attacks around here", and passed a simple test such as delivering a harmless message, he was ready for work. In some cases, students were advised, "Some kind of initiating ceremony may have a useful effect on the recruit's attitude and conduct (e.g. oath of secrecy)." It was important to impress recruits with their responsibilities, although the agent always had to be careful not to employ the technique on people who would be unimpressed by it.

What work would these sub-agents do? In part, this was dictated by the primary function of the organization. Propaganda, passive resistance, major sabotage, and paramilitary activities all made different demands on the spymaster and his agents. Regardless of actual function, however, any organization had to divide itself into a num-

ber of units, each with a specific responsibility. For example, the security section had to keep watch on enemy counter-espionage efforts;
the reception committee met agents parachuted in from abroad; the
finance section made sure that agents were paid and their expenses
covered; and the emergency-measures people were in charge of safe
houses, hide-outs, and escape routes.

Whether the organization used a large number of agents or only a
handful to fulfil its mission, the organizer always had to bear in mind
a number of basic rules, based on popular psychology and good
office-management techniques, meant to ensure an easy alliance between security and efficiency.

No more than five or six "staff officers" in charge of sections, and
the organizer, made up the nucleus of the ring. They were to be supported by a larger number of individual agents, but for optimum
security in all cases, these people were to have a minimum number of
contacts inside and as little information as possible about the organization itself. Thus the maximum use was to be made of "cut-outs", or
intermediaries linking two or more agents or an agent and the outside
world.

Most businessmen in that wider world would have recognized the
more mundane personnel problems and management techniques
taught at Camp X. The spymaster was to institute regular salary
scales; no agent was to know how much another was being paid.
Indeed, it was said that "the organizer should look after his agents in
the same way that a good employer looks after his employees."

Finally, the organizer was to assure his agents that, in case of
illness or arrest, every assistance would be given to him and his
dependents. The ringleader was to "impress upon each agent the
power of the organization to protect those who were loyal and to pun-
ish those who betrayed it." Those agents who did, however, "double-
cross" SOE and its missions were to be frightened into co-operation,
paid off, or preferably, because it involved the least risk, killed. But it
was best to *prevent* betrayal and treachery in the first place by
"stressing the ruthlessness and the long arm of the organization. Although the agent only knows a few people that he can betray," SOE
instruction pointed out, "his superiors are well aware of his activities
and can always take vengeance."

*

On the plane of everyday reality, we all maintain some distinction between the self and the other. But in the extraordinary world of espionage there is sometimes a need for what SOE called "the other self", that persona which exists only for a particular mission. SOE taught its agents how to create their own covers, how to invent a new identity with both a past and a present.

That past could be the agent's own, which had the advantage of being easily remembered, mainly true, and fully supported by documentation. Or the agent's past could be appropriated from a real person, usually dead, but always "distant". This cover story also had the advantage of being real and hence consistent, but there was always the chance that people acquainted with the dead man would be startled by his sudden reappearance. Finally, a totally fictitious past could be invented, free of entanglements but also of confirming records, the documents that provide the "proof" of our continued existence. Whatever past was chosen, it had to be plausible and as factual as possible while merging with the agent's undercover present. His "ostensible present must be consistent with his alleged past."

Recruits were given helpful hints on maintaining the fictions of the other self: always respond to the new name immediately, avoid foreign slang, choose friends consistent with the personality and social class of the new persona.

To disguise the subversive nature of his activities an agent should have a cover occupation that not only accounted for his presence in a particular place and for the source of his income but presented opportunities for observation, travel, and voluminous correspondence. For example, that of stamp dealer was considered ideal.

The creation, "on paper", of this new identity was matched by a new physical persona. The recruits at Camp X were treated to courses in make-up and disguise worthy of any theatrical master. But lest images of the stage obscure the real talents of the make-up artist, students were reminded that "disguise does *not* mean covering your face with greasepaint." Rather, it "must have as its basis the art of being and living mentally as well as physically in the new role." Thus, remembering what instructors called the golden rule, students were never to come out of character: "a workman should not have clean hands and behave like an educated man", "a merchant seaman doesn't wear suede shoes".

Sometimes short-term disguises were needed on an emergency basis – an escape from the Gestapo or exit from a building under surveillance. The SOE handbooks were full of tips here, beginning with the general one that an agent should imagine the basic description of himself that a witness might give to a policeman, and then work to change that description.

Since clothes were more easily changed than the features of the face, agents were urged to keep several changes, from "rough gardening clothes to a good lounge suit", and reminded that "stripes downwards with a single-breasted suit make a man look taller". Hair should habitually be worn longer than normal so that an abrupt cutting would dramatically alter the face. If an agent had an hour to wait before boarding the Orient Express, SOE recommended Max Factor hair whitener for imparting distinguished greying temples. Although little could be done to change the shape of the head, a variety of hats and caps would help. In addition, the agent could, using duo-liquid adhesive, ensure that his ears would be pinned to his skull for a full twenty-four hours. For the more adventurous, the nose could be altered by inserting in the nostrils two small round nuts through which holes had been carefully drilled with the end of a fountain pen inner tube. "This will give a very squashed tipped nose and it is possible to breathe quite freely." Teeth could be stained with iodine; charcoal or black pencil applied to facial lines could age a face; whereas a very close shave followed by hot towels, alum, and talcum powder tightened the skin and gave a fresh, young appearance.

Graduates of the course, equipped with a new past, present, and physical presence, were warned, however, that "good background cover is hard to build up and easily destroyed. Always therefore avoid trouble with the authorities. Be inconspicuous. Vary your appearance, habits and haunts." Submerge the real self in the underground other.

A course in police methods and counter-measures was of value both to secret agents working behind enemy lines and to FBI or RCMP security officers. It taught students about surveillance techniques, house and personal searches, burglary, and interrogation. The students learned about them from both the defensive and the offensive angle. Brooker emphasized that "the best way to be a good security officer is to know the tricks of the enemy." This meant that trainees would not only know when they were being followed and how to shake off their pursuers, but would also be able to carry out successful surveillance themselves.

Also important was instruction in communications, which taught the principal methods by which an agent in the field communicated with his external base as well as with those he might use within his network, and were therefore fundamental to all special operations. Carelessness in setting up clandestine rendezvous was a prime cause of successful German penetration of SOE networks in Occupied Europe, and instructors were always looking for lessons to be learned from experience. In this case SOE found that underground Communist cells had much to teach them. In July 1943 a clandestine Communist newspaper in Belgium, *L'Organisateur*, warned members of the Party that the high number of arrests it had been suffering was due almost entirely to members' failure to observe basic security rules in their internal communications. It spelled out some fundamental guidelines that were based on hard experience about arranging meetings, and recognition signs, using train stations ("main railway stations must never be used, only suburban or small town stops"), and setting up meeting places. A copy of the instructions fell into SOE hands; it was passed on to London, and from there found its way into the basic Camp X syllabus.

Most students also learned about codes and ciphers. A code, agents were told, "is a method of concealing a message in such a way as to make it appear innocent". A cipher, on the other hand, "is a method of converting a message into symbols that do not appear innocent, and have no meaning to a person not possessing the key". Instruction, however, meant more than mastering a particular method or cipher. It had to beat the often stringent German censorship. Not only did a message have to fulfil the basic requirement of being understood only by the addressee and not by the enemy, but the enemy also had to be unaware that a secret message was being passed. This meant that, for the agent in the field communicating within a network, codes and secret inks were of greater value than ciphers. Nonetheless, there would be some circumstances in which a cipher would be useful to an agent. Therefore Camp X taught a course in two basic ciphers, the Playfair and the Double Transposition, both of which were secure, provided that certain precautions were taken. This skill helped both those destined for offensive missions and those involved in counter-espionage. Many a German spy ring in the United States was broken because security agents learned how to look for coded messages in apparently innocent letters and telegrams.

The Playfair cipher was essentially a revival of the British Army's field cipher from the First World War, so called after Sir John Playfair, who had recommended the system for use in the Crimean War. It turned out to have certain disadvantages, and in the course of 1942 SOE first restricted its use to communications within networks and then eventually replaced it with Double Transposition.

Playfair required the agent to memorize a short line of verse – let us say "April is the cruellest month". The line would then be written out horizontally into a square grid of five letters across and five lines down, with no letters ever being repeated. The grid would be completed by listing all the letters not used, in alphabetical order (I and J being combined). Thus we get:

```
A  P  R  IJ  L
S  T  H  E   C
U  M  O  N   B
D  F  G  K   Q
V  W  X  Y   Z
```

With this basic grid in hand, the agent could encipher every message. Let us suppose the word to be enciphered was "Danger". First of all, it would be broken into bigrams: DA NG ER. Taking the first bigram, DA, the agent would then draw a straight line joining the two letters, thus:

```
↑A   P  R  IJ  L
Ⓢ   T  H  E   C
U   M  O  N   B
D   F  G  K   Q
Ⓥ   W  X  Y   Z
```

In this case, as the two letters stand in a column, the letters would be replaced by the letters *below* each one, to give the enciphered bigram VS. If the letters had been joined by a *horizontal* line, each one would have been replaced by the one to its right. Thus the plain bigram UN would become MB. Finally, if the plain bigram formed a *diagonal*, then the cipher bigram would be created from the other diagonal of the same rectangle. Hence, the second bigram in the word DANGER, NG, becomes OK, as follows:

```
A  P  R  IJ  L
S  T  H  E   C
U  M (O) N   B
D  F  G(K)  Q
V  W  X  Y   Z
```

The third bigram, ER, would become HI:

```
A  P  R (IJ) L
S  T (H) E   C
U  M  O  N   B
D  F  G  K   Q
V  W  X  Y   Z
```

Thus, the enciphered text for the word DANGER becomes VSOKHI.

The system had the advantage of requiring an agent to carry a memorized verse; therefore he or she possessed no incriminating message. But experience with early SOE missions showed that unless the verses were changed frequently, the cipher could be broken once the enemy had intercepted a number of messages. Hence it was phased out beginning in 1942 and replaced by Double Transposition. This cipher was safer, but much more complicated, and like all systems it had its disadvantages. Not the least was that most agents detested it because it took inordinate time and was prone to error. More important, however, was that, with the development of sophisticated crypt-analysis machines, Double Transposition could be broken fairly quickly. When the Allies began to realize this in the course of 1942, they slowly phased out this system, too, and eventually replaced it with the "one-time pad" – a cipher that, in the words of one expert, Pierre Lorain, represents "the pinnacle of development in the field of cryptography."

The principle of the one-time pad was simple. Essentially, it meant using a key only once. The agent took into the field a personal table provided by Baker Street printed out on a silk handkerchief. The letters of the alphabet were listed along the top and under each of them, listed vertically, the same alphabet letters with, next to each one, the cipher alphabet letter, randomly determined. For example:

A	B	C	D	E	F	G	(etc. to Z)
Ax	Am	Ao	Ad	Az	Aq	Av	
Bm	Bz	Bx	Be	Ba	Bu	Bz	
Cx	Co	Cm	Cf	Cb	Cv	Cl	
Dc	Dn	Do	Dg	Dx	Dg	Ds	
Ey	Ec	Ec	Ey	Ek	Ey	Ey	
Fn	Fg	Fb	Fz	Fs	Fl	Ft	

(etc. to Z)

The agent also took a ten-page microfilm booklet in which were listed hundreds of incoherent keys in five-letter groups, such as GCHQA FANYB LMNXZ UPLOF. Let us then suppose that the agent wanted to send the message DROP MEDICAL SUPPLIES. Broken down into five-letter groups, the message would be rendered as DROPM EDICA LSUPP LIESX. (This is referred to as the plaintext.) If there were only four letters in the final group, an X was used. The first four keys would then be entered above the five groups, thus:

Key   GCHQA FANYB LMNXZ UPLOF
Plaintext   DROPM EDICA LSUPP LIESX

The ciphertext was determined from the printed table on the silk handkerchief. Taking the first letter of the key groups, in this case G in the horizontal column, the agent would vertically scan the column headed G down to D, and find the small letter "s" next to the D. That "s" became the cipher letter. The process was repeated for every letter of the message. Once the agent had enciphered the message, he or she then destroyed the key immediately by cutting it from the microfilm and burning, dissolving, or swallowing it. When all the key groups were used up, Baker Street would provide another ten-page set. Provided that the key did not fall into enemy hands, the system was foolproof, mathematically unbreakable, and relatively easy to use. From mid-1943 onwards SOE used it for its European networks, and agents coming to Camp X towards the end of its life learned something about its principles.

Camp X trainees also learned something about secret inks – another practice borrowed from the Beaulieu schools. The advantage of secret ink over a message in code or cipher, of course, was that the latter, if found, was immediately suspect, whereas a secret-ink message concealed in an innocent letter aroused no suspicion. The problem, though, was to find secret inks that were difficult to detect. Broadly speaking, the Camp X trainee was told, there were two main groups. First there were the "natural fluids", such as animal secretions, saliva, urine, semen, fruit juices; these were the oldest and the simplest, but for that reason also the most easily detected. They all showed up under either ultra-violet light or heat, and hence were not to be used where any form of censorship was in existence – which meant most of Europe. So the agent would have to rely on the second group, the chemicals, of which the agent learned the main types with their degrees of susceptibility to detection. All these, the instructor emphasized, should be used at maximum dilution and never before a sample had been developed to ensure the correct strength was being used. Almost as important as the ink, though, was the paper. It should never be glazed, coated, or lined. Best of all was newsprint because of its poor sizing, and the ink should always be applied by a brass nib held level at the smallest angle to the paper. Thus prepared, the agent had a fair chance that his secret message would get through.

"Propaganda is the art of persuasion with a view to producing action. Today it is useless for our propaganda merely to persuade Frenchmen that the Boche is a swine. It must also instruct Frenchmen how to kick the Boche out of France." In such tones began the many courses given at Camp X on operational propaganda, the main type of propaganda carried out in Occupied Europe by underground agents. There were five main steps a potential agent had to learn. These involved fact-finding, policy, composition, reproduction, and distribution. But first of all, what was propaganda and what could it achieve?

The most basic lesson the agent quickly learned was that propaganda was never an isolated thing, but merely one weapon in the whole armoury of underground warfare. "Passive resistance, sabotage, guerrilla warfare, and internal revolution are other weapons, which, with propaganda, must be knitted into a whole." As passive resistance plus propaganda led to sabotage, and sabotage plus passive resistance led to guerrilla warfare, and so on, propaganda could be described as the oil in the machinery of subversion, and therefore an essential component in the whole Allied war effort. It was, as Goebbels had said, "the Fourth Arm of Warfare".

The course thus took the agent through the various steps of the propaganda process. It began with "the raw material", which was provided by the facts of the political situation in the occupied country. But these facts, the agent was told, should never be thought of as static. The picture of the local political scene that the agent created in his mind should not be like a chart or a map or a photograph. Instead, "it should be imagined like a moving film at a cinema – where the frame remains fixed but the contents are mobile."

Politics, moreover, was far more than party politics, but involved every factor affecting the self-interest of each group, class, and organization within the agent's field of operation. The agent had to quickly determine which specific groups he or she could profitably attack, and then determine the chosen group's opinion on a given political fact – the fact-finding stage of an operation. Camp X lectures placed strong emphasis on the importance of accurate methods, and favoured random sampling. But how was random sampling to be carried out in underground conditions? Methods would have to be different from those in peacetime, but the basic principles remained the same: people should never be prompted, and actions could often be more reliable than words. If security made direct questioning impossible, the agent could often elicit information indirectly, without appearing to ask for it, listen to gossip in cafés and bars, and observe behaviour.

Once the agent had determined facts about his target group, the time was ripe for presentation, the writing of the propaganda. It was a skilled job, requiring the application of set principles: "Good advertising," the agent learned, "is based on set principles; good writing on deep feeling. Good propaganda needs both; and the good propagandist will use the latter to mask the former." But, instructors warned, "the principles must never be allowed to 'show through'. We are not sending men back to Occupied Europe to sell soap." A leaflet, for example, should present one General Idea supported by particular ideas written in simple and concrete language. Never say "hunger" when you can say "empty bellies", the agent learned, or use the word "patriotism" when you can say "love of France". Try whenever possible to appeal to self-interest. Before actually writing a leaflet, the agent was told to write down on paper answers to the following questions: What General Idea am I selling? To whom am I selling it? Where am I sending the message? When must it be delivered? Against what opposition? From whom is it supposed to come? How do I link all these together? Above all, does the message contain the three vital elements of stating a grievance, giving a message of hope, and providing a call to action?

Much of the instruction on propaganda at Camp X would have been familiar to an advertising executive in any large company and, indeed, operational propaganda ran largely parallel to modern advertising techniques – but with one difference. The reader of the advertisement selling soap *knows* that it is an advertisement he or she is reading. The recipient of underground operational propaganda should never suspect that propaganda was involved. Hence the need for careful campaigns skilfully attuned to local requirements and disguised as the product of local organizations. For that reason, the agent had to be familiar with the technical aspects of reproduction and distribution, and know where to go to find reliable printers. Ironically enough, the agent learned, the best pro-Allied work in Europe often was done by printers working inside the print shops of German-controlled newspapers. The reasons for this were fairly obvious. These men were under less surveillance, they had a more ample supply of newsprint, and, whereas anti-collaborationist writers had been fired from the press, the Germans could not afford to get rid of printers, especially when it took seven years to train a master printer in the technology of the era.

When a leaflet was ready, how should it be distributed? The obvious way was the best: by post. It was safe for the recipient because usually the receipt of propaganda, as opposed to its retention or distribution, was not an offence. And for the agent, provided that precautions were taken, it was also secure. In the country, mail was never to be posted in large batches, and was always to be broken up in appearance. In cities, the opposite rule applied. One of the best covers an agent could use was that of an office clerk delivering bundles of mail at commercial mailing time.

Camp X taught its recruits the rudimentary arts of secret war both by the book and on the ground. Lectures were combined with practical exercises, the mix varying according to the needs of the individual or the group. Some parts of the syllabus lent themselves more obviously to one form than to another. All students were given an introductory lecture by the chief instructor on the objects and methods of irregular warfare. This stressed the contribution to be made by Allied espionage and propaganda, and by the encouragement and support of passive resistance, sabotage, and secret armies. "You will be a cog in a very large machine," the recruits were told, "and its smooth functioning depends on each separate cog carrying out its part efficiently. It's the object of this course to clarify the part you will play."

That part, it was suggested, at least in the first year at Camp X, might eventually come to be much larger than any of the recruits could possibly imagine. The American Carl Eifler remembered a British colonel terrifying the student class at Camp X by pointing out that if Fortress Britain fell and the Allies lost the war, then the last defence of democracy must be waged by them, the New World warriors, underground. Adding that "the politicians got us into this mess and now it's up to the military to get us out," the colonel went on to suggest that "when this thing is over, if ever those politicians get us into a similar mess, maybe we should turn our talents on them." Unsure whether this was a touch of the wry humour for which the British were famed, the Americans nonetheless swore a personal oath never to lay down arms if democracy was trampled under German jackboots or strangled by Italian blackshirts.

On a more mundane level, the particular courses varied according to the part to be played. This applied not only to *what* was learned but also to *how* it was taught. Information about the Nazi Party and the German armed forces, as well as basic indoctrination about the goals

of the Allied war effort, could only be taught by the book. In addition
to lectures, therefore, the Camp provided a small library filled with
what Brooker described as "mood pieces". The student with time on
his hands – difficult when the day began with breakfast at eight-fif-
teen and ended with supper at seven o'clock – might choose among
several biographies or autobiographies of secret agents and escapees
such as von Rintelen's account of his work as a German agent during
the First World War, *Dark Invader,* or George Hill's memoirs of his
work for British espionage in Russia in 1917-18, *Go Spy the Land.*
(By 1941 Hill was once again in Russia, this time with a radically different mission: he was sent back to Moscow as chief SOE liaison man
with the NKVD.)

Available, too, was a selection of purely instructional books on
such subjects as aircraft recognition, codes and ciphers, guerrilla
warfare, and combined operations and, for the student who wished to
digest in a more tranquil setting the lessons in silent killing, there was
a copy of Fairbairn's handbook *Get Tough.* It was to be found nest-
ling somewhat incongruously next to that innocent product of an
earlier age, Baden-Powell's handbook based on his Boer War experiences and eagerly devoured by many a twelve-year-old, *Scouting for
Boys.* The large number of books on the political background to the
war included William L. Shirer's *Berlin Diary*, Edgar Snow's classic
Red Star Over China, and the ex-Nazi Hermann Rauschning's denunciation of his former creed, *Revolution of Nihilism.*

Last and certainly not least was a small fictional section dealing
with spies and partisan war. It included Steinbeck's story of resistance
in Norway, *The Moon Is Down*, a book that, when published in 1942,
much moved Winston Churchill; Hemingway's account of the Spanish
Civil War, *For Whom the Bell Tolls* ; and the classic British spy tales
by John Buchan and Somerset Maugham, *The Thirty-Nine Steps* and
Ashenden. The latter was based on Maugham's own experience in the
First World War as a British secret agent, and was reputed to be of
such realism that it was recommended reading for all British secret
intelligence officers. "Never before has it been so categorically demonstrated," the *Times Literary Supplement* had said on its publication
in 1926, "that counter-intelligence consists of morally indefensible
jobs not to be undertaken by the squeamish or conscience-stricken."
And anyone reading it at Camp X in anticipation of a field mission

might have been forgiven for lingering rather pensively over Maugham's portrait of "R", Ashenden's superior. A tall, lean man "with a yellow, deeply-lined face"; hard, cruel eyes; and a pleasant and cordial manner; his philosophy is brutally frank. "Of course," "R" says to Ashenden at one point, "a lot of nonsense is talked about the value of human life. You might just as well say that the counters you use at poker have an intrinsic value. Their value is what you like to make it; for a general giving battle, men are merely counters and he's a fool if he allows himself for sentimental reasons to look upon them as human beings."[3]

It was not, perhaps, the mood Brooker would have stressed to his students.

CHAPTER 5

"Oh So Subversive":
Cloak-and-Dagger Operations

Critics of the OSS, then and now, have argued that many of its missions were ill considered and owed more to the boys'-adventure-story tradition than to the needs of twentieth-century warfare. OSS, they claimed, stood for "Oh So Silly" – or, more ironically, "Oh So Subversive". If the critics needed ammunition, they could probably have found it in the mission of one of the first American agents to go to Camp X, Ilia Tolstoy.

For some 3,000 years, millions of Buddhists, Jains, and Hindus believed that the navel of the earth and the axis of the universe lay somewhere between China and India, somewhere in the holy kingdom of Tibet. For a very short time in 1942, Donovan and a few other people in the Office of Strategic Services seem to have shared that belief. A multitude of myths and sacred tales supported the faith of the religious, but OSS thinking seems to have been based on some far-fetched strategic assessments.

The scenario went something like this: what if Japan, driving relentlessly through the jungles of Indo-China and Siam and overland through China towards British India, were to meet up with her Axis partner somewhere in Middle Asia as the German juggernaut rolled eastward to Suez? The State Department decided that the Dalai Lama should be made aware of America's friendly feelings towards his tiny theocracy. The War Department thought a feasibility study on the use of the old caravan route between India and China for military supplies would be of interest.

Launched onto a secular pilgrimage to the Forbidden City of Lhasa in pursuit of these rather nebulous objectives was Captain Ilia Tolstoy. A professional adventurer, sometime explorer, and grandson of the famous Russian novelist, he had been in the first graduating class sent by COI to Camp X in the winter of 1942.

By all accounts it was an unhappy experience. Tolstoy, then in his forties, with experience fighting in the Russian Army during the First World War, was older than most of his fellow Americans isolated together in the wintry confines of Camp X. When not in training, they treated the Camp X mess like a student fraternity house, with lengthy drinking sessions and the occasional hazing expedition. Tolstoy seems to have regarded these antics with quiet middle-aged resignation, but on one occasion his stoicism gave way. During a more than usually lively evening Tolstoy was seen by the others to be sitting stiffly apart, his back rigidly upright, "as though," remembered one of them, "tortured by the stupidity of it all." As events moved to their climax, Tolstoy pushed himself back from the table. When his head came within range of a window, a hand reached through and deposited the contents of a large garbage can all over him. For several seconds Tolstoy sat still and stared at the men around the table. Then, rising slowly, he walked stiffly to his room, garbage still draped around his shoulders. As he sat down on his bed, it gave way with a resounding crash, the victim of a careful piece of sabotage carried out by another of the American putative secret agents. At that point Tolstoy snapped. In a frenzy of cool and deadly rage he reduced the bed to a neatly piled heap of wood within five minutes, and was beginning on the rest of his room when Roper-Caldbeck, who had been happily joining in the celebration, finally calmed him down. After that, his mission in the field that summer of 1942 must have seemed like a holiday.

Accompanied by fellow thrill-seeker and OSS officer Lieutenant Brooke Dolan, Tolstoy left Washington in July, seen off by "Wild Bill" Donovan himself with a cheery "Keep in touch if you can". In New Delhi they reported to "Vinegar Joe" Stilwell's headquarters in the Imperial Hotel while British government offices in India arranged the final details for their trip. Wished godspeed, in perfect Chinese, by General Stilwell, and carrying two hundred and ninety pounds of

camera equipment and "scientific instruments", they were on the road
to Shangri-La by September 1942.

They followed trails that were little more than yak tracks, en-
countering caravans of mules and donkeys labouring up and down the
Himalayan passes under huge loads of grain, wool, and marmot hides.
"At 14,000 feet," Tolstoy recalled in an article written in 1946 for the
National Geographic Magazine, "we sometimes felt the effect of the
altitude and would wake up in the night gasping for breath. We found
that propping ourselves in a semi-sitting position was best for sleeping." Wealthy armed merchants, mounted on sure-footed ponies,
passed them by, their faces hidden by painted masks and goggles
against the sun, sand, and dry winds. Their way was eased by the Red
Arrow Letter, a piece of red cotton cloth about sixteen inches wide
and two feet long, from the Dalai Lama, carried in the bosom or on a
staff by an outrider in advance of the travellers, informing village
headmen that they were to accommodate the two American officers
and supply them transport at reasonable rates. In spite of this hospitality, however, Dolan was overcome by pneumonia. While waiting for
him to recover, Tolstoy amused himself by playing polo and giving
cavalry drills. "To my long experience as a horseman and my skill in
caring for animals," Tolstoy wrote, "I attribute the ease with which I
made friends with the horse-loving Tibetans."

A month later, with Dolan recovered, they resumed their trek,
stopping to take in the major sights on the way. They visited the village of the Porus, the untouchables of Tibet and buriers of the dead.
In Tibet, Tolstoy wrote later, "people are not usually buried. The
Porus carry bodies to a hilltop where, with the skill of a surgeon, they
cut them into portions small enough to be devoured by vultures. The
Porus are paid for this task and also inherit certain silver decorations
from the dead. Those we saw," he added, "were well bedecked in
silver."

At the famous Samden Gompa monastery, headed by a five-year-
old abbess known as the "Diamond Sow", Dolan impressed the monks
with his scholarly skills in recognizing Buddhist images. In turn, the
two men were impressed by the story of the origins of the Diamond
Sow. The first one dated back to 1717, when the monastery – then a
nunnery – was besieged by Mongols. After a long siege the abbess was

said to have opened the monastery gates and at the same time turned her nuns into sows. Impressed by the miracle, the Mongols retreated.

Both men were presented with magic seeds wrapped in prayer-covered Tibetan papers. Luckily, they had done their anthropological homework, for they were equipped with a large number of gifts for presentation at such times. Thoughtfully, as well, they had packed their dress uniforms. They donned them before meeting local dignitaries, discarding the combat gear they normally wore.

On another continent Tolstoy might have been a real "safari bwana", a big-game hunter, but in Tibet the Dalai Lama discouraged the killing of wild animals. Therefore Tolstoy had to content himself with photographing them and taking notes on the location for possible sabotage operations, should the Japanese occupy Tibet.

Eventually, after many more adventures, the party reached the gates of the City of Mystery. Lhasa, with her sister city of Timbuktu, the most tantalizing of travellers' prizes, lay before them. Here, in a roadside park, the Americans were ushered into a tent, seated in the place of honour behind a small table laden with dried fruit and candy, and served buttered tea from large copper teapots. After throwing rice over their shoulders to appease the spirits, the two men were presented with letters of welcome and ceremonial scarves from the various functionaries of the elaborate Tibetan court. They inspected a detachment of the Trapchi regiment serving as a bodyguard to the Dalai Lama, and then followed their escort to their temporary headquarters – the house of Frank Low, the "Additional British Political Officer for Sikkim, Bhutan, and Tibet". Here they waited for the court astrologer to discern the most auspicious date for their meeting with the king.

The audience was set for 9:20 A.M. on December 20, 1942, in the Potala Palace, splendidly isolated on a huge rock high above the town. At the appointed hour "Mud" and "Slug", as they were known to their OSS colleagues, ascended to the roof of the palace and then to a single room used for official receptions. They stood for a few minutes surrounded by rows of monks before a heavy curtain was drawn aside and the two explorers were ushered into the throne room.

The Dalai Lama sat cross-legged on his square throne chair of teakwood inlaid with gold, a high-peaked yellow hat on his head. The regent, who exercised all civil and ecclesiastical powers until the king attained his majority, sat on a lower throne to the right.

Tolstoy and Dolan had carried with them, all the way from America, gifts sure to please the ten-year-old boy "with healthily pink cheeks" whose people seemed to Tolstoy to be still living in the fourteenth century. They brought a signed photograph of Franklin Delano Roosevelt in a silver frame, a presidential letter in a cylindrical casket, a gold chronograph that informed its wearer of the hour, day, month, year, and current phase of the lunar cycle, and a small model galleon in silver, a personal gift from "Mud" and "Slug" to His Holiness.

These objects were presented to the Dalai Lama on a scarf, according to Tibetan custom. After a round of tea-drinking and rice-throwing, the king entertained other pilgrims seeking his blessing. Through an interpreter he inquired after the state of Roosevelt's health, and Tolstoy assured him that the president was "quite well". This ended the formal reception, but in a private informal meeting immediately afterwards Tolstoy was pleased to see His Holiness trying on the elaborate wristwatch. Feeling it was an historic moment, he was moved to write, "So far as we could learn, this was the first time in history that direct communication had been made by a President of the United States with the Dalai Lama of Tibet."

Undoubtedly true. But what was really accomplished during this mission by one of Camp X's earliest trainees? Surely the "King of the United States" was delighted with the Tibetan stamps, three rare coins, four pieces of gold brocade, a presentation scarf, and a framed picture of the Dalai Lama sent in return. Just as surely, Tolstoy and Dolan must have been delighted with the Legion of Merit that Donovan pressed upon them.

The monthly report of the OSS for the period ending October 1942 had outlined the goals of the mission: "to observe the 'Attitudes of the peoples of Tibet'; to seek allies and discover enemies, locate strategic targets and survey the territory as a possible field for future activities."[1] "Mud" and "Slug" fulfilled these limited objectives. Reporting in the *National Geographic*, Tolstoy noted, "We soon realized that Tibetans who knew of the United States were interested in the outcome of the war and had a sympathetic feeling toward us.

They had, however, great doubt as to our ability to defeat Japan, since at the time Japan was almost at their border."

For their part, the Tibetans seem to have charmed the two American officers. Tolstoy informed Washington about the loss of important revenue since the outbreak of war as Tibetan wool merchants became unable to sell their materials to U.S. automobile rug manufacturers. He also passed on their request for a powerful radio transmitter and pressed Donovan to respond positively, reminding the OSS chief that "We were treated by everyone very well and I hope that we have laid a good foundation here. I know they like the U.S.A. better now and know more about it."

However, the State Department objected. Granting such a request would be "politically embarrassing and cause irritation and offense to the Chinese".[2] Indeed, Tibet had been in the Chinese sphere of influence since the reign of the Manchu emperors of the early eighteenth century. Chiang Kai-shek did not look favourably upon an independent radio communications network in Lhasa over which he would have no control. Nonetheless, "Wild Bill" persevered and the Tibetans eventually received their transmitter, setting off diplomatic alarm bells in both Britain and China, who began to suspect that America had political designs on the navel of the world.

And what of "Mud" and "Slug"? Captain Dolan, sent as an OSS agent to the Chinese Communists, was killed soon after V-J Day. Ilia Tolstoy, dabbling in the movie business and sponge cultivation in the Bahamas, became a noted ichthyologist and managed an aquarium in Florida before dying in New York in 1970.

Obsession with secrecy put an abrupt end to the mission of another – although very different – American visitor to Camp X that year, Ed Coffey, one of several FBI men who took the route north to Canada.

The visit was the result of an arrangement that Brooker himself made with FBI director J. Edgar Hoover, and was more a gesture of friendship than a practical necessity. The G-men had their own training centres in the United States, and at the FBI Academy, located in the huge reservation of the U.S. Marine Corps at Quantico, Virginia, they could learn practically everything they needed to know about close combat, self-defence, pistol shooting, interrogation, and other security techniques. But Stephenson badly needed to mend some fences with the FBI.

Back in April 1940, SIS chief Sir Stewart Menzies had sent him to Washington to meet Hoover and discuss methods that the British and Americans could adopt for fighting German activities in the Western Hemisphere. After his appointment as SIS station chief in New York, Stephenson had made relations with Hoover a top priority. Co-operation had been good. BSC helped the FBI in a number of areas, providing technical help in the arcane skill of clandestine mail opening, for example, and providing it with valuable leads in counter-espionage cases: thirty-six of the forty-two German agents arrested by the FBI in 1941 and 1942 were identified with the help of information from Rockefeller Center. In return, Hoover let BSC use the FBI's radio transmitter to send its top-secret messages to London – the only radio link Stephenson enjoyed with London until HYDRA, a new communications system, opened at Camp X in the spring of 1942. But Hoover was a jealous guardian of the empire he had controlled since 1924. He insisted that security operations on American soil were his business alone and no one else's, and that BSC's job was purely one of liaison: it should not run operations of its own in the United States. After Pearl Harbor, Hoover became more adamant. Although he had agreed to provide BSC with its radio communications link to Britain, the FBI did not have the codes and were suspicious of the large amounts of traffic being sent, which suggested a scale of operations that made Hoover uneasy – especially as BSC was now involved with Donovan, a personal *bête noire* of Hoover.

Relations did not improve when, early in 1942, the FBI uncovered a clumsy scheme by a member of BSC, Denis Paine, to find discrediting material to be spread around about Adolf Berle, an assistant secretary in the State Department who was determined to curtail Stephenson's power in the United States. Berle, a Harvard-educated lawyer from a well-established New England family, had been taking the lead among those Americans who felt that the United States should exert more control over security and intelligence activities now that America was in the war. On New Year's Eve, 1941, Berle chaired a top-level Anglo-American-Canadian conference at FBI headquarters in Washington to discuss improved co-ordination on these matters. "It was clear from the outset," Harford Montgomery Hyde wrote later in his book *Secret Intelligence Agent*, "that Berle's principal target was BSC, whose activities he plainly resented." Once the FBI had conclusive proof of Paine's misdemeanour, they called in Stephenson and told him they wanted Paine out of the country before midnight. The only "dirt" he had got, it appears from a note in Berle's diary, was that Berle and his wife had twin tubs in their bathroom. "This would be amusing," Berle noted, "if it did not illustrate the danger which is run from having these foreigners operate."

It was hardly surprising that in March 1942, as the first of Donovan's men returned from their training at Camp X, Hoover announced – in the bureaucratic prose of an internal BSC history – that "he did not feel the FBI were on terms of such confidence with BSC or with Mr. Stephenson to make close working relations possible."[3] Shortly after that, and despite a personal meeting between the quiet Canadian and the American prima donna, the FBI terminated the radio agreement and BSC was forced to rely on HYDRA and other means of telecommunication.

Another source of friction in this period was the FBI's handling of the famous double agent Dusko Popov, code-named "Tricycle". Popov, a Yugoslav, had volunteered to become a German spy for the *Abwehr* in Belgrade in 1940, but had almost immediately got in touch with British Intelligence, who then proceeded to run him as a double agent in their massive wartime deception game against the Germans known as the "double-cross system". "Tricycle" operated in Britain for a while, but then in 1941 his German controller instructed him to go to the United States to obtain items of strategic information. In order to keep up the pretence that he was still loyal to Berlin, the British arranged his journey to America where, on his arrival in New York, he came under the auspices of BSC. The FBI, however, insisted that because he was on American soil *they* should control him.

Popov's stay was an unhappy experience. After the war he would claim that he had told Hoover about Pearl Harbor in advance and that his warning had been ignored. This was a self-promoting myth. More to the point was that Hoover disliked and mistrusted Popov, and refused to run him as a high-level double-cross agent. Hoover had a puritanical and unsophisticated view of the world of espionage, and for him the fact that Popov had once volunteered to work for the

Nazis was enough to damn him. Popov's FBI controllers took a strong dislike to his liberal and high-rolling life-style in New York, and failed to give him top-grade information to pass on to the Germans so that they would keep him in play. Stephenson at one point protested strongly to Hoover about FBI conduct of the case, but to little effect. Finally, in August 1942, the FBI refused to have any further dealings with the case and Popov returned to Britain, where he resumed his successful career as a top-grade double agent. "FBI incompetence" was the BSC assessment of the whole affair.

At this juncture in BSC-FBI relations, Brooker happened to be conferring with Stephenson in New York on a quite different matter. The director of BSC regarded Camp X as being in many ways "his", and he was alarmed by the growing relations between the Camp X staff and Donovan and the OSS. Stephenson told Brooker that he wanted a greater say in the running of the Camp, and arranged for him to fly to London to discuss the whole question personally with Gubbins. However, on arrival in London after a long and uncomfortable flight, Brooker sided with Gubbins, who was determined that Camp X should remain under SOE control and not fall into the hands of Stephenson "and the civilians" at BSC. In any case, he pointed out to Brooker, Camp X was only one of SOE's world-wide network of schools, and central direction had to be maintained. Brooker carried the message back to Stephenson, but wondered how he could sweeten the pill. Stephenson himself provided the answer when he began to tell Brooker of his problems with Hoover.

"I think I can help," said Brooker.

"How?" asked Stephenson.

"What if I offered the FBI use of Camp X?" replied Brooker.

"Go ahead and fix it," came the reply.

Brooker did. In a personal meeting with Hoover, the born salesman quickly piqued Hoover's curiosity and a deal was struck.

Shortly afterwards Coffey arrived at Camp X from the Washington FBI office, where he worked in the technical section. But he was no sooner there than all the deeply ingrained G-man security and undercover techniques he had absorbed were violated by an unexpected phone call. "Message for Mr. Coffey," a voice said at the other end of the phone. Convinced that his cover had been blown and that German spies had followed him to Canada, Coffey took instant fright.

The next day he took a flight back to Washington and never returned.[4]

A more successful visit was made by another FBI man, Percy J. Foxworth, head of the FBI's New York Bureau. Foxworth, a man in his mid-thirties known to everyone as "Sam", had been the principal American contact for the SIS station chief in New York, Captain Sir James Paget, even before Stephenson had arrived on the scene in the spring of 1940. Stephenson then encouraged the relationship by helping Foxworth as much as he could. The first major opportunity for showing goodwill came in the fall of 1940, when Hoover sent Foxworth on a South American tour as an undercover member of a trade development mission headed by Nelson Rockefeller, to establish an FBI secret intelligence service throughout South America. Stephenson went out of his way to give the New York Bureau chief introductions to all the British SIS chiefs in the area so that they could advise him on co-operative measures.

After that, relations between Foxworth and BSC officials were good, even when those between their masters were less than harmonious. Harford Montgomery Hyde, who worked in the SIS section of BSC, described his relations with Sam as particularly friendly. Foxworth and a number of other FBI agents from the New York branch went up to Camp X shortly after the Hoover-Brooker agreement. Here, under Brooker's personal guidance, they received the standard courses in secret agent techniques. The visit might have helped Foxworth to learn some of the subtleties of the game that BSC thought the FBI lacked in operating double agents, for, ironically, Foxworth as a regional FBI chief had been in charge of Popov during "Tricycle's" free-wheeling stay in the Big Apple. However, Foxworth had little time to demonstrate any skill he might have acquired at Camp X. While on a special FBI mission to North Africa in January 1943 he was killed in an air crash in Dutch Guyana.

Casablanca, on the Atlantic shore of Morocco, had been Foxworth's destination. Firmly in Allied hands following the North African landings, it was shortly to witness the historic meeting between Roosevelt and Churchill at which they pledged themselves to fight until the unconditional surrender of Germany. But to the east, German forces were still bitterly resisting the Allies in Tunisia, and North Africa had become a major base for American and British special forces. In their midst roamed the eccentric figure of Carleton S. Coon.

Eager to make himself useful in unorthodox warfare, Coon had first approached U.S. Army Intelligence but had been rebuffed. In desperation he had then contacted a Major Sinclair, a British SIS agent in New York, who had already been in touch with Coon's old friend and Morocco specialist Gordon Browne, a businessman, to see if he would work for the British. Sinclair told Colonel Robert Solborg, Donovan's special operations man, about Coon, and in December 1941 Solborg recruited both Coon and Browne into COI. Their mission was "to go to Morocco, make contact with the Riffian tribes, and hide out in the mountains when the Germans came."

This was all part of Donovan's ambitious plans for COI in Northwest Africa, the one area in which he believed he could make a quick and decisive impression that would ensure COI's credibility and survival. Most of the region was controlled by Vichy France, and the rest by the Spanish. It was crucial to the Allies that the entrance to the Mediterranean be prevented from falling into German hands. German influence was strong, and there were constant fears that they might occupy the area either by an advance through neutral but friendly Spain or by Rommel's westward advance from his foothold in the North African desert. Since relations between Vichy France and Britain were hostile, the Americans, who still maintained official relations at Vichy, were in the best position to find out exactly what was happening. In early 1941 twelve State Department vice-consuls – known as "The Twelve Apostles" – were carefully placed throughout North Africa to keep an eye on German activities. Then, shortly before Coon's recruitment, Roosevelt had agreed that Donovan should take control of all undercover intelligence operations there.

Churchill's lengthy and crucial visit to Washington with his chiefs of staff that December further highlighted the region. The British argued that it should be the first target of an invasion. Although the Americans disagreed – they only came round to the British view in the spring of 1942 – the discussions raised the question of what they might usefully do in the area to promote Allied strategic goals. Donovan seized the opportunity. Before the month was out, he had drafted a plan for Northwest Africa that involved establishing contact with native chiefs, cultivating pro-Allied sentiments among the

French communities, organizing small guerrilla groups, and establishing secret arms and ammunitions caches. To implement the plan he appointed Colonel William Eddy, a First World War Marine hero, expert on the Middle East, and former head of the English Department at the American University in Cairo.

Eddy additionally briefed Coon and Browne on the mission given them by Solborg, and then left the United States to establish his base in Tangier, the international port on the coast of Spanish Morocco and a notorious centre of espionage and intrigue. Shortly after Eddy arrived in the Mediterranean in late January, Coon travelled secretly to Camp X.

He followed the normal procedure. "I was told to go to a city in Canada," Coon wrote discreetly in *Adventures and Discoveries* in 1981, "where I would meet others of my kind in a hotel lobby. We were to identify ourselves by secret gestures and apparently innocent greetings." Once in Toronto, Coon was driven with the others from the King Edward Hotel to Whitby, where he was given a Canadian Army uniform and assigned a false name, which he had a tendency to forget. It was "Ben". But his fellow recruits always thought of the retiring college professor as "the man who invented the disappearing donkey". While there was a noted shortage of small Arab boys and even donkeys on the shores of Lake Ontario, "Ben" was nonetheless able to outline the basics of a surprise package that foreshadowed his later successes as an OSS agent in the desert wars of North Africa. A compliant and unsuspecting donkey would be loaded with a timing device and a whopping seventy-five pounds of the new plastic explosive, "composition C". A child would tether this Trojan horse to the nearest tent full of German officers and then slip quietly away. At the preordained moment, donkey, tent, and the *Wehrmacht's* best and brightest would all disappear in a thunderous explosion and terrible flash of light. Or so it was hoped.

When not pursuing such special interests, Coon took the usual courses in unarmed combat, street fighting, and demolition, and, like Ilia Tolstoy before him, came in for some practical jokes. One of his fellow students, described by Coon as a "beefy braggart and bully", threatened to shave off his moustache by force. "If you do, I'll kill you," replied Coon. A few days later the same student invited Coon to join him for a few minutes' chat on a small mound of earth, and then left, saying he would be back in a minute or two. Rather than wait, Coon also left, and before he had gone very far the mound was blown up with a buried charge on a timing device left by the bully braggart. It was a rigorous ten days. When he returned to the United States and was waiting transport to Morocco, he visited the Harvard Faculty Club, only to have his colleagues tell him how much weight he had lost.

Coon arrived in Tangier in late May via Bermuda and Lisbon, and immediately reported to Eddy in the U.S. naval attaché's office in the Calle de America. Shortly afterwards he was joined by Gordon Browne, who had preceded him by a month, and they were soon in liaison with their British opposite numbers in SOE and SIS. The local SOE man was a mining engineer, Edward Wharton-Tigar, and one of the first things they did was to agree that Coon would focus on Moslems while SOE concentrated on Christians, the object in both cases being to organize subversive groups that would prevent or subvert a German takeover.

Coon also received firsthand evidence of SOE technical know-how in the field of dirty tricks. Requested by Wharton-Tigar to drive around French Morocco looking for stones in the road ballast to serve as models for explosives to hold up a German advance, Coon and Browne with difficulty rounded up a tankful of gasoline and set off up-country. "We discovered," reported Coon in a personal narrative later written for OSS at Colonel Eddy's Algiers headquarters, the Villa Rosa ("a small but sumptuous residence next to Eisenhower's HQ"), "that there were very few stones along the roads, but that mule turds were to be found in great abundance." Describing them later as "large enough for our purpose, uniform in size, and fat and greenish brown", Coon and Browne furtively collected several samples and smuggled them back to Tangiers. From there they went by diplomatic pouch to London. "We took care to explain," Coon reported to Donovan, "that the full, rich horse dung of the British countryside would not do in Morocco; it was the more watery, smaller-bunned mule type that would pass there without suspicion." Eventually the turds came back in plastic facsimile and were used, Coon noted with pleasure, "to good effect later in Tunisia."[5]

Coon had other things to do than collect turds for the British. His main mission was to contact native leaders and establish pro-American resistance and intelligence groups. He did this through two main contacts. The first was a man he code-named "Tassels", a former general in the rebel army of the Riff leader Abd-el-Krim and a now prominent and influential business leader in Tetuán. The second was a man code-named "Strings", leader of the most powerful religious brotherhood in northern Morocco, an organization as formidable, Coon reported to OSS, "as the medieval Assassins". Fifty thousand francs changed hands, and "Strings" became America's man. Coon had taken a risk. At Camp X, Brooker in his lectures on subversive organizations had said never to link up with a pre-existing organization because it could be too easily penetrated by the enemy. In Coon's view, his experience with "Strings" offered an exception to the rule.

At nocturnal meetings in villas, mosques, and the back seat of their official car, Coon and Browne laid detailed plans for a revolt of the Riffs. Dealing with "Tassels" presented security problems because he was a prominent man and could not risk being seen with the OSS men. Therefore they would pick him up at night in their car at some pre-arranged spot and get him quickly into the back seat. "Once in the car," Coon reported, "we would transform him. Sometimes we would turn him into a Fatma, or Arab woman, with a veil. Other times we would turn him into a *shaush,* with a tall fez on his head garnished with the U.S. seal in gold metal, or the naval attaché's seal – thus we were merely taking one of our servants to a villa to wait on a cocktail party." Seldom inaccurate, "Tassels" would report on battle order and troop movements "in great detail". Thus armed, Coon and Browne plotted the landing of parachutists, the delivery of guns, and the cutting of roads and collected a huge amount of local intelligence through other agents with such esoteric names as "Mr. Fish", "The Neanderthal", and "Big Moh".

Coon also acted as a courier for the British, smuggling .45 pistols, Sten guns, ammunition, and flares from the SOE station in Gibraltar across to Tangier and then down to Casablanca in the diplomatic pouch. Potentially this was a highly dangerous job. In March 1942 a courier doing the same thing had been blown to pieces, along with over thirty innocent civilians, when the package he was carrying exploded and sank the Gibraltar ferry in Tangier harbour. But the

worst Coon suffered was aggravation when the British Foreign
Office lost its nerve and ordered operations to stop.

There was worse to come. Seeing himself as America's answer to
Lawrence of Arabia, Coon had brought with him from the United
States a complete Riffian warrior's costume, which he had planned to
wear as he was parachuted in to join a Riff uprising. A black woollen
ajjab, or cloak, would fall over his shoulders, covering short cotton
trousers that ended at the knee and were held up by a string. A yellow
kerchief or white cotton square would serve as a turban. Riffian men
never appeared in public without a belt and pouch; therefore a leather
cartridge belt and a green and white leather bag, a scrip, which in
former times would have housed powder for a flintlock, lead balls,
and assorted knives, were required to complete the ensemble.
Lawrence of Morocco would at least look the part.

But such romantic fantasies collided harshly with reality. Once
Allied invasion plans were under way, it became obvious that the best
local support would be given by the French colonists, provided that
they could be persuaded to change their loyalty to Vichy. But the
French in Morocco and Algeria had no desire to see agitation among
the natives, least of all when encouraged by the Americans. The
British, with their own natives to worry about, agreed. Coon's and
Browne's well-laid plans came to nothing. Plans to bring the famous
Abd-el-Krim, leader of the 1925 Riff insurrection, back to Morocco
from his French-imposed exile on Réunion Island to lead a revolt in
Spanish Morocco if General Franco opposed the Allied landings were
quickly scotched. Coon never got to wear his costume, and instead observed the Allied landings from the nearby safety of Gibraltar.

Darlan's assassination occurred while Coon was filling in time
between missions, "a messy and chopped up" period in his OSS
career. Shortly before the murder, SOE instructors, including Captain Michael Gubbins, General Gubbins's son, withdrew from the
training camp at Ain Taya, leaving Coon wearing British battle dress
with a blue *Corps France* cap alone there with the French. How much,
if anything, he knew in advance of Bonnier de la Chapelle's plan remains a mystery. Talk of assassination was in the air, countless
French groups in Algiers were determined to rid themselves of
Darlan, and the admiral himself told the Americans that he believed

he was on a hit list. After his death, and once Bonnier was out of the way, the new French regime blocked further investigations into what historians now agree was certainly an essentially French conspiracy. Coon's1943 report merely refers to Darlan's death in one line, and he told Donovan that he knew nothing about it. Nor did he claim any credit for it. In *A North Africa Story*, in fact, he suggested that while an OSS man must be prepared to die in the performance of his duties, those duties are "intelligence, antitransport, anticommunication, and antimorale. His job is not antipersonnel." Not political assassination, except, or unless, as Coon put it, "the personnel in question be the top of a hierarchy, like Mussolini or Hitler or Franco, or someone else in a high post whose death will cause confusion and disaster to the enemy."[6] His proximity to the *Palais d'Eté* on the afternoon of Christmas Eve can easily be explained by the visit he was paying to see his boss, Colonel Eddy, that afternoon.

Nevertheless, Eddy, anxious not to have his operative involved in even a routine police investigation, thought it best to get him out of Algiers. Within hours of Darlan's death Coon was on his way to link up with an SOE detachment on the Tunisian border. Allied troops, advancing along the North African coast from both east and west, were shortly to squeeze the Germans from their North African foothold. The task of the BRANDON Mission, which Coon now joined, was to infiltrate enemy lines for demolition and sabotage of enemy communications and transport, as well as to collect tactical intelligence.

"Pig Hill" was the name that SOE gave to its desert base at Djebel Hallouf, a lead-mining centre requisitioned by Allied forces. From here Coon got another chance to play out some of his Lawrence of Arabia fantasies. Driving around the countryside in his old Studebaker, he built networks of Arabs who provided him with local intelligence and occasionally helped the SOE men – including Michael Gubbins – to carry out sabotage against German or Italian troops. While temporarily in charge of a lighthouse on the Mediterranean coast at Cap Serrat, Coon was almost defeated by his own ingenuity. To protect his lighthouse, he set booby traps every night and then had to spring them again every morning. "Remembering where they all were," he later complained, "taxed my memory, and I acquired a phobia against taking my trousers down and defecating in the woods lest I hoist myself on one of my own petards."

One effective method of gaining intelligence, he discovered, was to take hostages. "We found that when we entered a distant village where loyalty was wavering," he subsequently reported, "we could take the eldest son of the most important man and hold him pending his father's arrival. The old man inevitably came, with gifts, demanding his son. He was sent back to get good information of enemy positions, and when he came the second time his son would be released if the information were satisfactory.... This use of hostages was our chief source of intelligence aside from the work of our own patrols."

Shortly after Coon's arrival at Djebel Hallouf, Colin Gubbins himself arrived to look around and inspect SOE operations in North Africa. "He was very friendly," Coon wrote, "and took me with him to dine and spend a night at a shooting lodge in a cork forest full of wild boars." At the dinner Coon found himself sitting two places away from Randolph Churchill, the prime minister's son. Churchill announced that he had a truckload of explosives outside which he planned to drive to Bizerta and leave next to a German ammunition dump. A timing device would do the rest. But, Coon recalled, "in the early morning hours we were wakened by an explosion. A large hole gaped in the earth where Randolph's truck had been parked."

The need for intelligence ended soon after the battle of the Kasserine Pass in February 1943. General Jurgin von Arnim, the German commander in Tunisia, attacked American positions at Kasserine and inflicted a sharp and humiliating defeat on them before being held. From then on, Allied forces advanced towards Tunis from the south, west, and southwest until all German and Italian forces in North Africa, about 250,000 men, capitulated on May 12. Coon returned to Morocco, where he once again worked with native groups, this time to protect the rear of General Mark Clark's Fifth Army against possible infiltration, sabotage, and even invasion from the Spanish zone, which harboured numerous German agents. Once again, however, Coon's Lawrence of Arabia fantasy came to naught. It "received its *coup de grâce*," he wrote in *Adventures and Discoveries*, "when Hamid, a known German agent, admitted to one of our group that the rumour of a German invasion was being spread to keep

us busy and to sap our manpower, which was needed on other fronts."
Soon after, Coon found himself assisting with the liberation of
Corsica in May 1943, where he was chagrined to have the use of his
plastic mule turds banned by the French general in command of the
operation. He had misadvisedly used the word "*merde*" while briefing
the general on his intentions.

Coon's final mission for the OSS was to patch up relations with
SOE over an incident involving aid to Tito's partisans in the fall of
1943. Major Louis Huot, OSS chief of operations in Cairo, had established a base at Bari, in southern Italy, following the Italian surrender
and Allied occupation. From there he launched Operation AUDREY,
a massive scheme to provide Tito with arms and ammunition. But
AUDREY angered the British because the Mediterranean was a
British theatre of war and Churchill had just appointed Brigadier
Fitzroy Maclean to take charge of SOE operations in Yugoslavia. The
OSS scheme was a direct challenge to the British, and threatened seriously to damage SOE-OSS relations. Coon was sent to Bari to sort
out the mess.

Scarcely had he arrived, however, when he fell seriously ill with
nervous exhaustion and had to be evacuated back to the United States.
His sentiments would have made him an ideal conciliator. Coon's
entire wartime career was a testimony to the close co-operation that
had existed between OSS and SOE. From his SOE training at Camp
X, he had taken part in joint SOE-OSS operations in North Africa. He
had worked with SOE in Gibraltar; his work at Algiers on the eve of
Darlan's assassination had been at an SOE base; and in the Tunisian
desert he had been under local SOE command. It was with genuine
enthusiasm that he wrote, shortly after his return to America, that
"Probably one of the happiest unions in the history of international
relations was that which existed and still exists between OSS and our
British counterpart the SOE.... I have never met anywhere a finer
group of men than the SOE outfit, and I would consider it a privilege
and a pleasure to go anywhere and take on any job with them."[7]

History does not tell us if Coon's SOE colleagues felt the same about
working with him. But it is a matter of record that SOE-OSS co-
operation at the official level was formalized in top-level secret

arrangements reached in London in the summer of 1942 while Coon was flitting about in the souks of Morocco and Brooker was fascinating Americans with his tales of derring-do at The Farm in Maryland.

On June 10, 1942, six days after the Americans had decisively halted the Japanese advance in the Pacific at the Battle of Midway, ten days after the RAF's thousand-bomber raid on Cologne, and while Rommel's Afrika Korps was punching holes in British defences before Tobruk, Donovan left Washington by plane for New York. Aboard were three top members of his staff: James Murphy, a personal assistant and long-time acquaintance since Donovan's days as U.S. assistant attorney general; Preston Goodfellow, head of Donovan's Special Operations Division; and Garland Williams, who had moved on from training to taking care of Donovan's supply and procurement. Also aboard was Stephenson's chief liaison man with Donovan and head of BSC's Washington office, Colonel "Barty" Pleydell-Bouverie. In New York they picked up Stephenson himself and on June 11, in a British plane, they flew from Montreal to London.

There, on June 16, Donovan met the British War Cabinet and briefed its members on the nature and scope of the organization he headed. Since his departure from Washington, this had changed. Roosevelt had signed an executive order in Washington only three days before, transforming COI into the OSS (Office of Strategic Services). Apart from transferring the Foreign Information Service from Donovan's control to that of the newly formed Office of War Information (OWI), this decision, in Bradley Smith's words in *The Shadow Warriors*, "merely froze into reality the various activities and branches that the colonel's busy mind had generated up to that moment." In the long term, however, it meant that the Joint Chiefs of Staff exercised more control over the OSS and now restrained some of the more enthusiastically buccaneering adventures of Donovan's men.

Meanwhile, in the SOE headquarters at 64 Baker Street, Goodfellow and Williams were hammering out an OSS-SOE agreement, the full details of which were only finally declassified by the CIA in 1982.

The main reason for Donovan's visit to London was an urgent plea from Sir Charles Hambro, the new executive head of SOE who had recently replaced Sir Frank Nelson. Donovan's organization and SOE were expanding so rapidly, Hambro wrote in notes he prepared for the meeting, that it was essential for them to meet and work out arrangements so that they did not get "thoroughly tangled up". Co-ordination at headquarters level in both Washington and London had to be accompanied by co-operation in the field. "It is essential," he wrote, "to avoid the situation where there will be two completely in-dependent organisations working in the field, with all the consequent dangers of crossing lines, competition for agents and material etc." In some cases, the SOE chief went on to suggest, "the problem could be dealt with by assigning the given region exclusively either to the American or British organisation." But he recognized that there would be few such simple cases and that, in most areas, sharing as-signments would be necessary. Furthermore, sharing would be mutu-ally beneficial in the areas of technical and operational intelligence, training, and finance.[8]

Discussions lasted several days, and on June 26, 1942, Donovan and Hambro signed a wide-ranging agreement on co-operation that became known as the London Agreement. In William Corson's words in *The Armies of Ignorance*, "in one sense [it] may be described as a global version of the Parker Brothers' game of 'Monopoly', wherein the two teams divided up control of the world between themselves and made arrangements for 'joint tenancy' in some countries with one or the other acting as the landlord/coordinator for a wide range of subversive secret activities." Tommy Davies and Barty Pleydell-Bouverie won agreement in principle from Goodfellow on the pool-ing of research and production resources and on the termination of all cash transactions between the OSS and SOE. Instead, "each side should finance their own production and...there will be no payment, or financial obligations as between the two organisations or their res-pective governments" – a considerable boon to the cash-starved British.

On the geographical zones of influence, the British also did well. SOE was to have primacy in India, East and West Africa, and, at least until the American strategic role in Europe was better defined, in Western Europe. The OSS was to have primacy in China, Australia,

THE CANADIAN CONNECTION

Charles Vining, journalist and businessman, chosen by William Stephenson as BSC's first representative in Canada. Later he was to be head of the Wartime Information Board.

oronto stockbroker Tommy Drew-Brook replaced ning as local troubleshooter for BSC. "The Little amo" had flown as a pilot with Stephenson in the First World War.

Mrs. Barbara Harris and the Camp X Museum, Oshawa

The megalithic George B. McClellan, now remembered as the father of Canada's modern security service. As head of the RCMP in Toronto, he worked closely with the Camp X staff.

THE CANADIAN CONNECTION

The main personality in the wartime Departmen
External Affairs concerned with intelligence affe
Tommy Stone ended his diplomatic career as Ca
ambassador to The Hague.

"Man of Influence" Norman Robertson. As
Undersecretary of State for Foreign Affairs in Ottawa,
he gave the green light for a handful of his top officials
to help the British in running Camp X and other intelligence operations. Ottawa Parliament buildings can
be seen in the background.

Colonel Layton Ralston, the Minister of
Defence whose consent guaranteed Cana
military co-operation over Camp X. He v
probably the only member of the Canadi.
Cabinet to know about it, with the possib
ception of the Prime Minister, Mackenzi
Here, he is seen, right, with King.

THE STAFF

senior Camp X staff, 1942–43. Centre, Lieutenant-Colonel R.M. ("Bill") Brooker, British Army, Comman-
Far left, Bill Ross-Smith, an Australian-born member of BSC New York; left, Major Art Bushell, Canadian
ny, Adjutant; right, Major Cuthbert Skilbeck, British Army, Chief Instructor and successor to Brooker; far
right, Captain Fred Milner, British Army, demolitions instructor.

group photograph of the Camp X staff in 1943, the year that saw most of the training for action behind
enemy lines.

THE CLOAK-AND-DAGGER TEAM

Bill Brooker

Bill Brooker, chief instructor and second comma▮ of Camp X, 1942–43. Kim Philby remembered h▮ from Beaulieu days as "the dynamic salesman ty▮ while some in the American OSS believed he wa▮ of the British Secret Service. Brooker later worke▮ closely with the OSS in Britain.

Brooker's successor was Cuthbert Skilbeck, who had also worked at the British SOE School at Beaulieu. After the closing of the training school the Canadians asked him to help with the interrogation of German POWs. Eventually he returned to the family trade of drysalting in the City of London, and he is now honorary archivist of the Dyers' Guild.

National Archives, Washington

"The Shanghai Buster", William Ewart Fairbairn, ▮ vented the famous double-edged commando knife ▮ taught Camp X recruits the arts of silent killing. Se▮ onded to the OSS, he became a legendary figure in America's first modern spy agency.

THE CLOAK-AND-DAGGER TEAM

or Paul Dehn, poet, musician, and
st, who as chief instructor at Camp
1943–44 put his talents to use as a
ropagandist. Using his wartime experience, he went on to write the
creenplays of such famous films as
e Spy Who Came In from the Cold
and *Goldfinger.*

"Fun with Hamish was always a noisy affair." Hamish Pelham-Burn, the Scots demolitions
instructor whose ingenuity sometimes had unpredictable results. Formerly a pilot in the Royal
Air Force, he later led an expedition to the Selkirk Mountains in western Canada.

Canapress

"The Quiet Canadian", William Stephenson. As head of British Security Co-ordination in New York he regarded Camp X as a "showroom" for the Americans and provided SOE's principal liaison with Washington.

THE AMERICAN LINKS

Founder of the OSS, precursor of the CIA, General William ("Wild Bill") Donovan. Camp X was created with Donovan's needs principally in mind, and American agents were among the camp's most important recruits. "The British," Donovan later said, "taught us everything we knew."

zer prizewinning dramatist Robert E. Sher-
ood, confidant of Franklin D. Roosevelt and
of Donovan's Foreign Information Service.
ny of his propaganda experts were trained at
Camp X.

TRAINING EXERCISES

The assault course. Agents needed to be in physical shape.

Haycart passing a road check; eight "partisans" lie beneath the straw.

Many an agent behind enemy lines failed a simple identity check.

the South and Southwest Pacific, North Africa, Finland, and the Atlantic islands. To be shared "fifty-fifty" were Burma, Siam, Malaya, Sumatra, Germany, Italy, Sweden, Switzerland, Portugal, and Spain. Liaison missions in both Washington and London were to be strengthened. But if the agreement seemed in many ways to favour the British, the Americans gained something back in the vital area of training. On the last day of the talks, June 23, Goodfellow asked SOE to accept OSS officers at its specialized training schools in Britain. "In the past three months," he stated in a memorandum handed to the British, "several officers of the S.O. organisation have been permitted to attend the British SOE training school at Toronto, Canada, where the training was carried on along the lines of the paramilitary and advanced schools. It is now considered extremely desirable that a large number of American officers be permitted to attend the various specialized training schools in Great Britain, and particularly is it considered essential that American S.O. officers be detailed for short periods of time to the various operational stations and offices in England." Such an arrangement would not just help the individuals involved, the OSS suggested, "it would also be a most powerful factor in insuring unity of doctrine and effort in the future operations of the two national organizations." Gubbins agreed. Soon over sixty OSS officers were receiving training throughout Britain.

For Camp X, as well as for Stephenson and BSC, the London Agreement marked the end of one phase and the beginning of another. So far as BSC was concerned, it meant that its Special Operations Division had to be enlarged and strengthened with the infusion of experts from London who could give Donovan expert advice based on SOE experience. Within three weeks of Donovan's address to the War Cabinet, Hambro had sent out a top-level mission from Baker Street to establish itself both at BSC headquarters in Rockefeller Center and at its Washington liaison office to advise the OSS on special operations activities in the Balkans and Middle East, Africa, South America, the Far East, and Western Europe. In overall charge was Louis Franck. So far as Camp X was concerned, the London Agreement emphasized what Brooker's presence as *de facto* chief adviser to the OSS schools had already demonstrated. Many OSS needs could now be met by its own schools in America, and those that could not received the required expertise at the specialized SOE schools in Britain.

The successful conclusion of a full and formal relationship between American and British special forces meant that for SOE's school in Canada the period of the Americans was essentially over. Significantly, none of the sixty OSS officers whom Gubbins agreed to take on as a result of the London Agreement was assigned to Camp X. It now had other tasks to perform.

CHAPTER 6

Policemen of the Airwaves:
HYDRA and the Radio Game

Wreaths of smoke from the expensive Havana curling up to the ceiling, a giant Great Dane at his feet, and a generous glass of Napoleon brandy in his hand, the handsome grey-haired Englishman, wearing an impeccably tailored tweed suit, gestured to the young man to join him beside the old stone fireplace. The offices of the British Uruguayan Railway Company in the Montevideo central railway station were palatial, and the company's leading director, H.H. Grindley, was a member of the large and influential Anglo-Uruguayan community that ran many of the most important businesses in the country. H.H. not only liked his brandy and cigars but flourished in the power and influence of his position.

The young man was Norman Delahunty, a Canadian wireless operator who had spent several weeks training at Camp X. Newly arrived early in 1943 after several months of monitoring for signs of Japanese interest in the Panama Canal region from Quito, 10,000 feet up in the Ecuadorian Andes, he had already learned of H.H.'s political pull in the sophisticated Uruguayan capital. More important, he also knew that from the spacious upstairs office where he now sat nervously sipping Grindley's brandy, the Englishman acted out a clandestine role as local BSC station chief running covert operations against Nazi interests in the country.

He had also heard that H.H. revelled in the cloak-and-dagger part of the job and was a formidable disciplinarian. He affected a brusque, no-nonsense manner and had a reputation for dealing decisively with people who rubbed him the wrong way. It made him a feared and respected figure among other Camp X wireless operators in the region. One of the less worldly of them had made the bad mistake of writing to New York to complain about some aspect of H.H.'s behaviour that had offended him. Within days he had found himself out of a job. Another, naïvely assuming that personal letters transmitted through the diplomatic pouch would pass uncensored, had quickly found himself hauled over the coals for using what he was solemnly told was "inappropriate language" (it was, in fact, the robust phraseology learned from his English instructors at Camp X).

H.H. ran a tight ship, but his horizons were broad. Montevideo was at the centre of a highly sensitive area crucial to Allied interests in the South Atlantic. Lying at the mouth of the River Plate, which formed the frontier with Argentina, the Uruguayan capital was an ideal monitoring post. Both countries were important sources of food for the Allies, and U-boats prowled off the coast waiting for the kill. Uruguay was a friendly neutral, but across the river, Argentina was a right-wing dictatorship harbouring sympathies for Nazi Germany, and there were several German agents and networks operating in the country.

But any speculation as to why H.H. had summoned him to share his cigars was quickly ended as the Englishman came directly to the point. In the double-cross system, one of the most successful and closely guarded secrets of the Second World War, captured German agents were being "turned around" to help the Allied cause by supplying their former German masters with information carefully devised and controlled by Allied intelligence. The system enjoyed the greatest success in fooling the Germans in Europe, particularly about details and timing of the Normandy invasion. But on a lesser scale the game was also played out in South America. Delahunty, H.H. explained, was to be one of the players.[1]

A Nazi spy on his way to Uruguay had been spotted by British counter-intelligence *en route* from Germany via Lisbon. Given an offer he could not refuse, he had agreed to co-operate with the British by transmitting back to Hamburg under control. Delahunty's job would be to supervise his transmissions and ensure that he sent only the messages he was given. He was also to help the man set up his radio in a house about ten miles from Montevideo.

A week later Delahunty met the Nazi agent for the first time. It was to be the beginning of a curious relationship that lasted until the end of the war, when the Hamburg station signed off in the last days of March 1945 with a "*Heil Hitler!*" and a promise to be back on the air shortly from another location. The spy turned out to be a Spaniard who had fought as an officer with Franco's forces in the Spanish Civil War and had then been trained for radio work by the Germans in Hamburg. Known to Delahunty simply as "Luis", he was a handsome and polished man in his mid-thirties, who, with his dark wavy hair, struck Delahunty as "typically Latin". But he spoke no English and as a result his Camp X watchdog quickly had to fine-tune his Spanish.

The house from which "Luis" was to transmit the carefully scripted messages prepared by H.H. and BSC in New York was out in the countryside. It was kept meticulously clean and its unseen guardians had thoughtfully provided it with a grand piano and an icebox kept amply supplied with beer. Every week the two men would go out to the house, driven in an old Model A Ford by "Vignoles", a clerk from H.H.'s office, and there methodically set up the equipment and wait for Hamburg to come through on the 31-metre band. "Luis", a relative novice who could not transmit too well, would painstakingly follow the text in front of him under the watchful eyes of Delahunty. The information he passed on was deliberately selected to convince the Germans that they were dealing with a valuable and genuine agent. The messages were usually harmless compilations of military information that was either public knowledge or known from other sources to be familiar to the Germans, such as the length of the Montevideo runway or the previous month's figures for U.S. aircraft production. In between these genuine items would be carefully selected pieces of misinformation, planted to deceive the Germans about sensitive matters such as Allied shipping movements and supplies. Regrettably, however, "Luis" was never able to provide his German masters with information about the one thing they seemed most interested in: details of the Allies' sonar submarine detection system.

Suddenly, just as Delahunty had begun to fall comfortably into the routine and was beginning to enjoy his weekly sessions with the Spaniard, an incident occurred that reminded him dramatically that the game of double agents could be a serious and deadly one. One night, after they had established contact with Germany, "Luis" unexpectedly made a small deviation from procedure. Instead of using the normal radio abbreviation in giving Hamburg the number of his message – "nr" – he used the abbreviation "no". Delahunty, well aware that this might be a crucial security signal that "Luis" was using to tell Hamburg that he was operating under enemy control, immediately informed H.H.

The next week when the two men turned up at the country house, H.H. himself was there to greet them. Wearing a fedora pulled low over his eyes and a trench coat turned up at the collar, and with the side pockets of his coat bulging ominously, H.H. was in a rough and belligerent mood. Before he allowed the agent to make his weekly transmission, he took him into a darkened back room for interrogation from which "Luis" emerged looking less than his usual ebullient self. The next day H.H. told Delahunty to begin learning the Spaniard's "fist" – the unique set of characteristics of every telegraph operator as he formulates and weighs the dots and dashes of the Morse code. It was a clear and ominous sign that Delahunty was being prepared to take over, should H.H. decide to remove "Luis" from the scene.

Delahunty never knew whether the Spaniard's slip had been deliberate or accidental, and in the end H.H. agreed to let "Luis" go on transmitting in the regular way. Despite the strain of knowing that if he ever made a mistake again, he might – as he once cheerfully admitted to his Camp X chaperone – be "*liquidado pronto*", "Luis" seems to have kept a sense of humour. Delahunty never forgot the night several months later when the Spaniard had finished a particularly good radio contact with Hamburg. The two men had kept their relationship purely professional, each knowing that the link between the double agent and his guardian was fraught with the possibility of betrayal. But each was also human, and in the months they had been working together, they had reached some unspoken understanding about the greater game in which they were playing their parts. Tonight, as if in celebration, the Spaniard sighed with relief, fetched a beer from the icebox, and sat himself down at the grand piano. After gracefully and skilfully playing a selection of classical and Andalusian music, he suddenly stopped, turned to Delahunty, and said with a smile, "This is the way it is in the movies when the police break in."

*

Delahunty was only one of several radio operators trained at Camp X and sent to South America by BSC. Originally, BSC (acting as agent for SIS) had envisaged these men carrying out two tasks: first, handling an extensive secret communications network that the British planned to set up throughout South America in case the Germans gained control in the region and second, monitoring or intercepting clandestine transmissions between German agents working for the *Abwehr* and their home base in Hamburg. So far as the first task was concerned, Pearl Harbor altered the situation dramatically. American entry into the war as a full-fledged ally changed the picture in South America and made a large British secret communications network unnecessary. Equally to the point, the Americans were strongly opposed to the plan, regarding it as interference in a region they considered their own zone of influence. Thus BSC abandoned the first plan and concentrated on the second by establishing, in 1942, monitoring posts – mainly under diplomatic cover – at San José (Costa Rica), Barranquilla (Colombia), Caracas, Montevideo, Lima, Quito, Santiago, Trinidad, and São Paulo.

Recruitment of the men to run these monitoring posts began almost as soon as Camp X became operational. Tommy Drew-Brook first approached the Canadian military authorities early in the New Year of 1942 for help in finding wireless personnel. He was quickly informed that this would not be easy. There was a high demand for skilled operators within the armed forces themselves, and the civilian field was practically exhausted. Undaunted, Drew-Brook began to trawl on his own among the civilian amateur operators ("hams") in Ontario. At the outbreak of the war most radio amateurs had been ordered to suspend operations immediately as a basic national security measure. They had also been instructed to dismantle their equipment, and the government sent out official inspectors to ensure compliance. Some had then been re-activated in 1940 in order to help the Canadian military monitor German propaganda, U.S. amateurs across the border, and possible illegal transmissions. But few of the remaining hams expected to be back on the air before the war was over, and none of them had any idea that his expertise would be needed in the way that Drew-Brook now required.

For assistance, Drew-Brook relied heavily on the services of an Englishman called Eric Curwain, recruited by SIS in 1938 to work as a wireless operator in Europe. Curwain had been in the British Embassy in Warsaw when the German invasion had started the Second World War. And like the other British personnel, he had eventually made his way home via Romania. Once in Toronto to help Drew-Brook in the early spring of 1942, Curwain set to work. "Armed with permission from the Royal Canadian Mounted Police," he wrote later, "I contacted the Department of Transport Inspector in charge of radio regulation for Ontario and asked him the names of the best hams."[2] Using the pseudonym Bill Simpson, Curwain would then talk to the men he contacted in small cafés or in hotel lobbies in downtown Toronto and find out whether they were interested in undertaking special war work. If they seemed suitable, he informed Drew-Brook, who after interviewing them passed their names to BSC in New York.

In due course each received a letter from BSC headquarters accepting the "application for employment" and stating salary and other terms of employment. These included the provision that employment could be terminated on thirty days' notice. Unlike recruits for the SOE training courses, the wireless operators were not enlisted in the armed forces but were employed directly by BSC itself on civilian contracts.

Curwain clearly relished his role as a cloak-and-dagger operative in Toronto. Perhaps frustrated by years as a lowly radio operator hidden away in the communications rooms of British embassies while his superiors plotted the overthrow of governments and purloined the secret war plans of His Majesty's enemies, he applied his full creative energies to impressing his raw Canadian recruits with the importance and mystery of the world into which they were being initiated. The ritual he devised for Norman Delahunty was typical.

Delahunty was just a teenage amateur radio enthusiast working with the Toronto radio firm of Rogers-Majestic, living peaceably at home with his parents while waiting to join the Signals Section of the Royal Canadian Air Force, for which he had volunteered some months before. One morning, out of the blue, he received a telegram offering no hint of its origin and bearing the simple and cryptic message "CAN OFFER INTERESTING APPOINTMENT IN CONNEC-

TION WITH WAR EFFORT", followed by a telephone number that he was to call at eight o'clock that evening. Consumed by curiosity and overcoming the natural caution of his mother, who was convinced that it presaged an overture from no less than the Nazi secret service itself, Delahunty followed instructions and soon found that he had an appointment to meet a man "aged about 40, wearing a red tie and with no cuffs on his trousers", near the house telephones in the lobby of the Royal York Hotel at noon the next day.

Skipping out of work early, Delahunty spent several nervous minutes in the lobby of the British Empire's largest and newest hotel trying to look inconspicuous while he carefully examined the trouser cuffs and ties of all those who passed by. This stressful exercise was mercifully terminated when he heard himself being paged over the hotel loudspeaker. At the reception desk he was handed a message regretting that plans had changed and asking him instead to go to a house in North Toronto at eight o'clock that evening. By coincidence, it happened to be the night of Toronto's first wartime test blackout. Driving through the darkened streets. Delahunty felt that he was starring in an old movie he had seen long ago but that, instead of being in staid old Toronto, he should be in Berlin or Lisbon. The feeling intensified when his tentative knock on the door of the house was answered by a man holding a lighted candle who beckoned him inside without a word. It was Curwain. There was some brief small talk, and then the Englishman showed Delahunty into a study where he was placed in front of a telegraph key and oscillator and given a test in Morse code. Having passed the test and some other inscrutable proof of acceptability, he was then told that he was being considered for work that might take him to Central or South America.

Delahunty was hooked. Curwain now orchestrated several more clandestine meetings in the same style. Terse messages such as "PROCEED IMMEDIATELY ROOM 1134 ROYAL YORK HOTEL" would be changed at the last minute to "ROOM 343 KING EDWARD HOTEL" or some other downtown Toronto location, until Delahunty thought that the whole thing was degenerating into cliché. Eventually he was told that he would be going with several others like himself to a top-secret training camp for three weeks and should therefore immediately quit his job without explanation. Feeling somewhat badly about this, he did as he was told and soon found himself bound for

Oshawa. Cloak and dagger accompanied him to the gates of Camp X. He and three or four others were instructed to take a scheduled bus to Oshawa, get off at a particular stop, and wait at the street corner. When a car stopped beside them, he was to ask, "Is this Mrs. Campbell's car?" Still feeling as though he were in a movie, he followed instructions and all went according to plan. By the late spring of 1942 he found himself safely ensconced at Camp X preparing for what was to be one of the highlights of his life as a radio ham: a top-secret mission to intercept clandestine German transmissions to and from South America.

Delahunty and his group were not the first of the radio hams to reach Camp X in 1942. One who had arrived earlier was another Torontonian, Eric Adams,* whose tasks once he arrived in South America provide a typical example of the work these radio outfits did. After an unsuccessful start in Caracas, Adams eventually ended up in Santiago, where the streets were safe at three o'clock in the morning, people did not dine until nine, and everybody drank wine. To Adams, a young man from Toronto where they rolled up the sidewalks at night and where, in 1941, "wine" meant a furtive bottle of cheap sherry tippled in a downtown alley, it was an eye-opener. But for the most part he had a conventional and typical wartime career as a policeman of the airwaves in the mostly middle-class and cosmopolitan capital of Chile. There were few discomforts and rarely any danger, only occasional jibes from British expatriates about why he was not at the front. He was more likely to be called upon to fix Madame Ambassador's hearing aid than to blow up Gestapo headquarters. The tedium, however, could be almost deadly.

Adams was particularly irritated by continuous requests to check out voice broadcasts that over-eager colleagues in the embassy thought suspicious. Most of these were of no interest, although a few provided comic relief, as when an "expert" in Oriental languages mistook the "sing-song" tones of scrambled commercial messages for high-level Japanese intelligence.

But however tedious and routine, the work that Adams was doing was vital to Allied intelligence, for the Second World War was the first real "radio war". Agents and networks were scattered over many

* This Eric Adams is not to be confused with the Eric Adams later arrested during the Gouzenko affair.

fronts, across many international frontiers, and between various continents, far from their control centres. It was imperative that intelligence reach a home station at optimum speed for analysis. While an agent with a false-bottomed suitcase full of purloined dispatches and a cyanide pill in case of capture remains firmly planted in the public imagination, strategic and often tactical planning was much more frequently informed by burgeoning radio-telecommunications technology.

Such systems relied, at the local level, on a person like Adams, quietly sitting in his small room in the chancellery of the British Embassy in Santiago, patiently "prowling" the airways listening for clandestine radio transmissions, which he then sent on to the New York headquarters of BSC for decoding and discussions on further action. "My receiving equipment consisted of two National HRO receivers," Adams recalled later. "[The messages I intercepted] were in Morse and were always encoded in five-letter groups so that the contents were actually never known to me. My job was just to intercept them, copy them, and make them available to BSC in New York."[3] Depending on the urgency, Adams would send them either by coded cable or by the more routine method of typing them out and sending them in the weekly diplomatic bag.

These short-wave messages were routinely identified by their letter call-names and five-letter-group codes. Sometimes he would receive tips from New York on where to "look"; at other times he was curtly informed where *not* to listen. He managed to pick up many oddities, particularly from the Soviet Union, where "every second Russian must have had a radio". And once he excitedly intercepted what seemed to be an enemy code, only to be told that it was merely a routine communication being tapped out from inside a British tank in the North African desert. Such transmissions he was simply instructed to "drop".

Others, he was assured by BSC, were "covered elsewhere", for this sort of intelligence-gathering was conducted not only separately by all the Allied powers but also simultaneously by several different organizations for each country. A bit of Anglo-American rivalry, however one-sided, seems to emerge from Adams's account of his monthly courtesy call on a group of Coast Guard radio operators also engaged in intelligence-gathering. The differences in manpower and *matériel* so common in the comparisons of the British and American war machines were clearly in evidence. The American Coast Guard contingent, twelve strong and only thinly disguised as weathermen, were operating the latest in radio equipment, supplied, if not with all the comforts of home, at least with a Coca-Cola machine. They thought that one man in Santiago, on duty twenty-four hours a day, seven days a week, was a bit of a joke – or so Adams always imagined.

Whether such an elaborate outfit ever monitored anything more interesting than did BSC's South American network remains unclear. The list of what Adams did *not* monitor is certainly interesting: no military intelligence, no enemy commercial services, no propaganda broadcasts such as those by Tokyo Rose and Lord Haw-Haw. These were not the concern of the BSC operators. Rather, they intercepted the coded messages of clandestine radio stations, typically Axis agents or sympathizers using illegal transmitters to send reports from enemy or neutral territory back to a control centre. Many of these were not only small-scale but even amateurish, but the case that provided the most excitement for our man in Santiago was the semi-professional circuit known as 13/43. It was most likely a group of "rebel" Argentine Army officers, possibly operating with semi-official immunity, who broadcast to a "home station", Number 13, in Hamburg, headquarters of the *Abwehr*. The Buenos Aires group, probably using a series of vans or trucks, was the forty-third clandestine station reporting back to Hamburg.

At 5:30 P.M., local time, Adams would tune in 13/43 on one of his two HRO receivers, handy for listening at other times to Vera Lynn on the BBC. Never knowing what was actually being said, he recorded the coded messages and then put them into a simple transposition cipher to disguise the original message. He then cabled them to New York for action. Adams believed that most of the information sent by 13/43 was quite banal, just information easily available from open sources; but it was his most important catch. One day it inexplicably disappeared from the airways.

This same circuit, 13/43, also provided a target for Delahunty in Uruguay, where he operated secretly from offices on the fifth floor of the Montevideo stock exchange. The signals came in strong from across the River Plate and for a week Delahunty was kept on his toes following its constantly changing frequencies. Then, just as Adams remembered, it went dead. New York thanked him for a job well done and told him to forget all about it. 13/43 never came back on the air and Delahunty could only speculate on what had happened. Perhaps, he thought, his boss H.H. had had an even more decisive colleague in Buenos Aires.

Occasionally, but only occasionally, Adams received an electrifying message from BSC. "I was once tipped off that there was 'information that' a man by the name of Kurtzmuller was on a boat bound for Chile and would probably be setting up a clandestine radio station in Santiago...and that he would be using such and such a call-sign. Obviously they'd got some very precise information on this gentleman. Well, all this came to pass, and I reported it, and after two or three weeks I got another cryptic message, 'information that' this gentleman would not be heard from further, which is precisely what occurred." Adams, too, wondered if this was an example of the British secret service in action.

Equally untypical but exciting was a "most urgent" message from New York directing him to a low-frequency short-range transmission that only he would be able to pick up since it was meant to be sent and received locally, probably by an agent signalling an Axis submarine lying in shallow waters off the Argentinian coast. Dropping everything else, Adams tuned in to the frequency he had been given and listened around the clock. "I got the thrill of a lifetime," Adams now remembers, "when at some such hour like three o'clock in the morning I actually heard this guy – I just about fell off my chair – he went into an *en clair* message, or plain English, and sent the phrase 'I have lost my code book'. It was one of the more exciting moments of my career." This speaking *en clair* was meant both as an emergency signal and as a deception technique to fool an Allied monitor.

Needless to say, it did not fool any of the Camp X "piano players", as the W/T operators were familiarly known, and indeed the Germans seem to have betrayed some remarkable naïvety in thinking that the use of English ham lingo would camouflage their operations. For example, to start a transmission, as they sometimes did, with "GE DR OB, TNS FOR CALL," which, translated, meant "Good evening dear old boy, thanks for the call," was a dead give-away since no Allied operators ever used plain language of this kind. The Germans also used another evasive technique that likewise rebounded: the daily changing of call-signs. The same station coming up on the same frequency with a different call-sign immediately alerted the Camp X graduates that something was wrong. Only neophytes would have been fooled.

Adams was no neophyte, for he had been an amateur operator since 1936, when he was nineteen years old. Trying to join up as an RCAF wireless air gunner, an occupation with a notoriously high casualty rate, Adams fortunately miscalculated the labyrinths of the military mind. He was told that what the air force really needed – that day at least – were cooks. He had tentatively accepted a position with his second choice, the Ferry Command out of Gander, flying aircraft across the Atlantic to Great Britain, when he was called by an instructor from the Radio College of Canada. This man mentioned something about "a security mission", but Adams's real introduction to BSC came through Eric Curwain, who, in the routine that soon became familiar to many others, set up an informal interview in the lobby of Toronto's King Edward Hotel. Here Curwain quizzed the young man on his radio knowledge and asked him about his general health, hinting that he might be needed for some secret duties in some other part of the world. "He never mentioned South America," Adams recalls, "but he did suggest that the Middle or Far East could be involved." After thirty or forty minutes Curwain closed the conversation on a noncommittal note.

Adams came away with no clear understanding of either an assignment or an organization, but with a very vivid impression of the soft-spoken Curwain, who he thought resembled the suave English actor David Niven. "I realized after it was all over," said Adams, "that he'd learned a great deal about me, but I knew nothing about him. The interview was left on the basis 'don't call us, we'll call you' and I had no means of contacting him."

In the intervening two weeks the RCMP ran a check for a criminal record and then, after a couple more interviews at the house owned by Tommy Drew-Brook where Norman Delahunty had first encountered the ghostly, candle-lit face of Eric Curwain, Adams was accepted. Rather quaintly asked in typical BSC fashion how much money he would need, he made a conscientious and cautious reply, only to hear later that others had "needed" twice the salary he requested. Fringe benefits, in the form of medical and dental work, were minimal, and the pay remained unchanged for three years. But such considerations were of minor interest to a single young man who had been living with his parents and was now eager to join the fray.

Shortly after breakfast on April 9, 1942, Adams joined about five others, each clutching a single suitcase, in a suite at the Royal York Hotel. One of the others was Bill Hardcastle, also a Torontonian. The journey out to Camp X remained clearly etched in his memory some four decades later. "We started out in an army station wagon and travelled east on old Highway Two," Hardcastle recalled. "The driver kept looking in his rear-view mirror to see if we were being followed." At the top of Thornton Road, which led south from the highway to Camp X, the driver suddenly stopped the car, got out, walked around it, kicked the tires, and glanced around in all directions, and then jumped back in. "We went down Thornton Road," Hardcastle said, "like a bat out of hell." For Adams, "it was all a bit of a movie-like thing. We didn't know where we were going and there was no conversation between ourselves and the driver."

Camp X left a less than electrifying first impression: "Muddy duckboard everywhere," noted Adams. "What the hell are we doing here out in the middle of this field?" wondered Hardcastle. These first unfavourable reactions soon gave way to relief that the reception was friendly and their living quarters comfortable. Housed in a newly constructed single-storey building, each man was assigned a small private room with closet and dresser. "Our rooms were really nice – no cheap stuff – nice furniture, a desk, bed, lamp, and chair," recalled Hardcastle. "Quite a nice little set-up," said Adams. It all seemed rather mundane, but the initial induction lectures were anything but ordinary. "We were told that this was a very vital mission and that we were not to talk or tell anybody, including wives and parents, where we were, where the Camp was located, or anything else. The standard spy school thing. Then we had a lecture about how it didn't matter what happened to us, God and the Empire was all that mattered" – all of which, Adams recalled, "was quite hair-raising for a Toronto boy who was feeling quite nervous."

It was soon followed by another alarming event. Warned in the lectures that their lives would constantly be in danger, the trainees were in fact burned out of their beds on the very first night by the fire that killed Roper-Caldbeck's dog. Adams at first thought that this was carrying realism too far. "All I can remember was a voice outside shouting to me to jump, and being impressed by how fast a room can fill with smoke. By the time I jumped, I was already beginning to lose my sense of direction. The fire was probably caused by careless smoking, but it was a very dramatic introduction for people who had been told only hours before that someone might try to get rid of them."

Things then settled down into a more routine pattern that was generally observed over the three-month course. The training time-table divided the day into a number of periods, most on clandestine radio techniques, including recognition and interception. A number of "schemes" or exercises featured the old farmhouse as a home station, which the recruits, their transmitters set up on the lakeshore under the trees, practised contacting. "We imitated clandestine radio activities," Adams recalled; "we were playing the role of the agent in enemy territory."

Life was not always easy. Relations between the young Canadian civilian recruits and their British military instructors provided potent material for cultural misunderstanding. The officer in charge of the radio instruction team was Lieutenant James Adams, an Irishman, in-evitably known as "Paddy", who had an accent as thick as his head of black hair. Some of the recruits found him humourless, and he had the reputation of operating on a short-fuse temper. It was not im-proved by his accent, which often caused his observations and commands to go unnoticed. "He might have been talking to me in Hindustani," Eric Adams said.

But the closest day-to-day contact was with the British non-commissioned staff who provided them with practical instruction in everything from Morse code transmission to unarmed combat. George de Rewelyskow, the sergeant-major, impressed many of these peaceable recruits with his chilling instructions on how to incapacitate an opponent. "You push their eyes in with your fingers," he once told a new recruit, a nervous bank clerk from Toronto. "I couldn't do that," protested the trainee in horror. "If you don't," replied the champion wrestler, "you might get yours pushed in."

Adams was the recipient of equally alarming remarks during pistol instruction in the shooting range. "I remember one of my in-structors telling me very cheerfully that if anybody armed me with a hand-gun I should be sure not to get a .45 because my hand was too small.... We used to get jolly lectures about how, if you have to shoot somebody, shoot him in the stomach because he won't spend much time worrying about you after that. And we learned that you stand back from a man before shooting him because the bullet doesn't mind travelling three feet farther."

If all this was rather remote from the prospects that Eric Curwain held out to the radio hams, Sergeant Court, in charge of explosives instruction, seemed to belong to another race altogether from the gentlemanly Drew-Brook. Court revelled in disturbing the recruits. He had an unpopular habit of creeping up behind unsuspecting trainees and firing a pistol close to their ears to see how far they would jump. And on one occasion, to surprise some outside workmen, he arranged for an explosion that sent a piece of shrapnel spinning only a few inches past their heads. Hardcastle, standing close by, recalled that the red-hot piece of metal sounded like a buzz bomb as it passed by. Eventually, in 1943, Court left Camp X unmourned by most.

As for the corporals from the Royal Signals Corps, they were hard-bitten veterans of Britain's imperial outposts who could transmit at speeds and for lengths of time that left Adams and the others open-mouthed. These NCOs also had some difficulty in adjusting to the problem of disciplining civilian charges in Canada after handling the natives of the Middle East, China, and Singapore. Wedded to concepts of spit and polish, which most of the hams regarded with contempt, they were fond of reminiscing about how much easier life had been, with Chinamen to bring them cups of tea on command.

Practical demonstrations were interspersed with lectures and exercises on codes and ciphers – "standard spy school stuff," Adams thought – to which were added a course on map reading, lectures on global time zones and Greenwich Mean Time, upon which all radio operations ran, and discussions of German activities during the Great War. Recruits acquired only "modest skills" in these areas, and were instructed in firearms and unarmed combat at an even more superficial level. "It wasn't of much practical value," Adams said, "but it alerted us to what the real world could be like if we were unlucky."

Only once in his Santiago assignment did Adams fear that he might have to put into practice the doubtful skills he had acquired at Camp X. He awoke late one night to watch with growing horror the door of his bedroom being slowly pushed open. Not wanting to die in bed, he dutifully and manfully arose to meet his fate. Boldly flipping on the light, he was astonished to see a bashful private in the Chilean Army who had lost his way after visiting the upstairs maid.

Not all of the radio hams recruited in the late winter and spring of 1942 ended up in South America. BSC's abandonment of its plans for an extensive South American network meant that some of those first recruited for this work were disappointed. Bill Hardcastle was one. The prospect of going to South America, probably to Buenos Aires, had helped him endure some of the more mundane moments of training at the Camp. "I was pretty excited, since I was told that Buenos Aires was a hotbed of German agents," he recalled in an interview many years later.[4] Like Delahunty, Hardcastle had been intrigued from the moment he had first been approached by Eric Curwain. What particularly grabbed him was an interview with Tommy Drew-Brook in the Royal York Hotel. The quiet stockbroker, who was careful not to identify himself, reassured the apprehensive Hardcastle that he should not worry about his parents, who would be looked after if anything happened to him, and that he would receive a decent salary for what was absolutely crucial war work. "Obviously," said Hardcastle, "these people had the means to run a pretty sophisticated operation. They could talk cash. He had a whole suite in the Royal York. That was a pretty prestigious sign in those days."

Alas for Hardcastle, eager to escape the dreary routine of the advertising department of the *Toronto Daily Star,* where he had been working when Curwain first tracked him down, Anglo-American rivalries and the fortunes of war meant that the Buenos Aires operation was cancelled at the last minute. Instead of spending the war keeping an eye on German spies in Argentina, he remained confined to the more familiar surroundings of Camp X. His job was the equally important one of helping maintain HYDRA, the linchpin of British secret radio communications in North America.

*

The story of HYDRA goes back to the summer of 1941 and the intensifying co-operation between Donovan and Stephenson. This collaboration extended far beyond the discussion on special operations that led to the creation of Camp X and other COI-SOE arrangements, and went deeply into the realm of secret intelligence. SIS in London was particularly interested in the creation of a transatlantic secret communications network that would facilitate not only American-British co-operation in general but in particular a joint intercept campaign against enemy communications. As the war progressed, BSC played an increasingly important and until now little-appreciated role in the creation of this transatlantic intelligence community. With the help of previously unexamined internal BSC documents, however, the broad features of the picture can be sketched.

BSC had begun life as a counter-espionage and intelligence agency for the British in North America. As the FBI and OSS steadily took over these functions, BSC's role during the course of the war increasingly became that of acting as the channel through which intelligence was passed between the FBI and London. More important, however, was its role in SIGINT (Signals Intelligence). As the 1981 official history of British Intelligence in the Second World War has recently indicated, "BSC, from being the channel by which Sigint items were occasionally brought to the attention of US authorities, developed the important additional function of providing in North America the security arrangements and the communications facilities that were required for the passing of intercepts between London and Washington."[5]

Early in the war the Americans knew that the British were reading top-level German codes. It has been widely claimed that Stephenson was personally responsible for passing on information from ULTRA between Churchill and Roosevelt. This is possible, although it is unlikely that any material was actually identified as being derived from ULTRA since this would have been too risky. Instead, it would have been identified as coming from "a secret source". The Americans were given ULTRA-derived intelligence in only an oblique and most general form for the first two years of the war. In the spring of 1941, when Britain faced a major crisis because of German victories in the Battle of the Atlantic, Churchill began to insist, over the objections of "C", his secret intelligence chief, Sir Stewart Menzies, that more information from ULTRA should be passed to the Americans to help them fight the U-boats in the Atlantic.

By this time the Americans *had* been given some harder information but they by no means knew the full story. Early in 1941, two U.S. Navy and two U.S. Army representatives visited Bletchley Park, where they were told something about the breaking of the Enigma cipher. In return, they gave the British a copy of the PURPLE machine, which was used for the breaking of the Japanese diplomatic cipher and represented a major triumph for the American code-breakers under the brilliant cryptanalyst, Colonel William Friedmann. At about the same time the Americans and British exchanged experts and information at their respective intercept stations in the Far East, and were soon working closely together on breaking a variety of Japanese communications. It was, as Ronald Lewin, the historian of ULTRA and MAGIC (Japanese material), has written, "an extraordinary coming together. Months before Pearl Harbor a basis had been laid for Anglo-American collaboration in the most sensitive areas of signals intelligence."6

Donovan himself had been given an inkling of the scale of British successes in the intercept war when he visited Britain with Stephenson in June 1941. Here, according to Nigel West, he "was indoctrinated into some (but by no means all) of the secrets of ULTRA." Later on, after the war, Stephenson himself told Whitney Shephardson, the first wartime head of OSS secret intelligence in London, that Donovan had been excluded from a great deal. "The only routine material that I was specifically barred [by London] from passing to Donovan was the high-level cryptographic product [ULTRA].... I endeavoured to the end to get the Combined Chiefs of Staff to authorize [this]...but it was never agreed."7 For the first time, too, Donovan met a man who was to play a crucial behind-the-scenes part in the HYDRA story.

Brigadier Richard Gambier-Parry was head of Section VIII of SIS, its communications division. A former member of the Royal Welsh Fusiliers, a veteran of the Royal Flying Corps, and an old Etonian, he had been recruited by SIS from the Pye electronics firm in 1938, and he had very quickly modernized and expanded its wireless facilities to create a world-wide independent SIS network. Junior officers regarded Gambier-Parry as a genial paternalist and referred to him as "Pop". Rival British agencies took a less benevolent view of him. SOE resented SIS control over their communications, which Gambier-Parry only reluctantly relinquished in 1942; while M.I.5 lost out to "Pop" in a bitter battle for control of the Radio Security Service (RSS), responsible for tracking down enemy agents in Britain and thus an essential underpinning of the double-cross system. Based in Hanslope Park, a mansion close to the code-breakers at Bletchley, the RSS shortly afterwards became "Special Communications Unit No. 3" and was responsible for enemy agents' communications world-wide. Gambier-Parry then further added to his empire by acquiring radio transmitters for black propaganda campaigns. One of these schemes was ASPIDISTRA. This was the name assigned to a huge 500-kilowatt transmitter to be built for the purpose of beaming British propaganda to Occupied Europe. But for that he needed Donovan's help in acquiring a huge RCA transmitter that he had located in the United States. When the two men met during Donovan's visit, the American agreed to help with ASPIDISTRA and also discussed many other issues of wireless communications where they could help each other. Shortly afterwards Gambier-Parry decided to make a visit of his own to the United States to pursue all this more closely.

"In October 1941," Stephenson told Shephardson later, "I arranged for the lecturers in communications in [SIS] to come to Washington to assist in the establishment of a world-wide system of clandestine communications for COI." This was gilding the lily because Stephenson was merely following instructions from London and acting in his role as facilitator. But as usual he did this superbly and Gambier-Parry was deeply impressed. He reported back to SIS in London that behind a diffident and unemotional exterior Stephenson was one of the most able men he had met, and that during his visit the BSC head had been "extremely helpful". That visit had covered a wide agenda, including preparation of a general plan for secret communications in South America (the plan subsequently abandoned), arranging for the training of W/T agents and the production of equipment for them, and securing radio supplies in the United States, including ASPIDISTRA. Gambier-Parry also reached an agreement with Harford Montgomery Hyde in BSC's SIS division on the pooling and distribution to London of all intercept material coming to BSC from Canadian and American sources.

There had also been discussion about co-operation with Donovan (referred to throughout BSC documents as 48917; Stephenson was 48000), as well as other U.S. departments. Most important of all for HYDRA and Camp X, however, was the successful recruitment of the man to establish and run the separate communications division now needed by BSC. That same man was also to act as communications adviser to Donovan.

At the time Stephenson appointed him head of BSC commun- ications, Benjamin (Pat) deForest Bayly was a ruddy-faced, stocky professor of engineering at the University of Toronto. One of the leading post-war Canadian experts in communications intelligence re- members Bayly as "genial", while technicians who worked on the HYDRA installation at Camp X describe him as a gregarious man who liked to play the piano on his off hours. Elizabeth Wood, one of the Canadian women recruited to work in the Washington BSC office where Bayly was a frequent visitor, remembers him as "a great guy, easygoing, but a hard worker."[8] Hard work and ability took Bayly far in the Anglo-American-Canadian wartime communications intelli- gence community, and it meant that he ended up with intimate know- ledge of some of the war's most closely guarded secrets.

It was all a far cry from the small provincial world of London, Ontario, into which Bayly was born in 1903. His father was a doctor who for thirty years was medical health officer in Moose Jaw, Sas- katchewan, and later served as medical officer of the 46th Battalion of the Canadian Expeditionary Force in France during the First World War. Bayly junior showed an early and enthusiastic interest in the exciting new technology of radio communications as it developed in the 1920s. Determined to master the subject, he paid his own way through college, at least according to one story, by playing the piano in movie theatres. He was only a second-year student at the University of Toronto when he was appointed a special instructor in radio com- munications. Later on, he was to give public lectures for the Royal Canadian Institute on the basic principles of receiving and transmit- ting. As soon as he graduated with his BA in Science in 1930 he joined the Department of Electrical Engineering at Toronto as assistant professor specializing in radio technology. Apart from the war years, when he was given an extended leave of absence, he remained a professor in the department until he resigned in 1950 to establish the Bayly Engineering Works outside Toronto. Eventually the company was sold to a German consortium at considerable profit to its original investors, and Bayly and his wife retired to California.

Bayly's business success relatively late in life was built on the secure foundation of his wartime career with British Security Coordination. Stephenson, who had built much of his wealth on the patenting of wireless photography, depended completely on Bayly in everything to do with communications.

Bayly's first task was to build the communications system discussed during Gambier-Parry's visit to New York and to find out as much as possible about SIS requirements. Early in November 1941 he flew to Britain for three weeks of intensive briefing by the SIS communications chief, who later told Stephenson in a hand-delivered "private and personal" letter that he was more convinced than ever that Bayly was the right man for the job.[9] Bayly's meetings with SIS officials, including Sir Stewart Menzies, covered the creation of communications channels in South America, the manufacturing of specialized radio equipment in Canada, the possibility of permitting the OSS to use SIS radio channels, and the appointment of a top SIS specialist in intercepts to be attached to BSC. The reason for this was that Gambier-Parry had decided the time had come for the division of intercept activities into zones of operation in order to avoid duplication of effort, and for the pooling of the intelligence end product into a central point so as to be widely available to all links in the Allied chain. The SIS intercept specialist at BSC would be responsible for achieving this program in North America through arrangements with the Canadians and the Americans. Eventually just such an arrangement with the Canadians guaranteed that material intercepted by the Examination Unit in Ottawa was passed on to BSC and fed into the greater Allied pool of joint intelligence.

But the most important issue for Bayly to deal with was to do with secret transatlantic communications by radio. With the volume of material to be passed from North America growing rapidly, a South American SIS network still anticipated, and the need to send ULTRA across the ocean by the most secure and rapid means possible, SIS needed a new radio channel of its own.

Up to then, it had been helped by the FBI, which permitted BSC to use its Maryland-based radio system for the transmission of material to Britain. But, as we have seen earlier, the British kept the ciphers to themselves and Hoover was increasingly unhappy that he had no idea what was in the two or three hundred messages a week passing from BSC to London. In July he had asked Stephenson for the cipher and had been refused. It was not hard for Gambier-Parry to conclude that he could probably not depend on this channel for long, so he told Stephenson on November 19, 1941, that he intended to open a circuit that terminated in Toronto. It would be furnished with high-speed, high-powered equipment and would carry, not just normal SIS telegraphic traffic, but top-grade cryptographic material. Thus was born HYDRA, the main wartime trunk station for SIS (and SOE) communications between North America and Britain.

The planning of this radio communications network had, of course, coincided with the discussions between BSC and SOE that fall over the training school in Canada. Intelligence experts such as Gambier-Parry had quickly realized that the obvious solution was to establish the two projects on the same site. Therefore, when the original SOE training staff arrived in Whitby in early December 1941, three of the party were members of the Royal Signal Corps – corporals and sergeants with long experience working for British Army communications in the Far East. They were followed within less than a month by Lieutenant "Paddy" Adams, also of the Royal Corps of Signals, recruited by SOE in November specifically for service at Camp X. His job was to be principal wireless instructor, to teach ciphers, and to erect the radio station.

"One day a big van came into the Camp and unloaded crates of communications equipment. When it was unloaded, someone yelled, 'Go to it, fellows!' We proceeded to build it from a photograph. We hooked it up, and away she went."[10]

This was how Bill Hardcastle remembered the beginnings of HYDRA, which was eventually to become an even larger operation within Camp X than the SOE training school. "HYDRA was always expanding," the Camp's third and last commandant, Cuthbert Skilbeck, remembered forty years later. When he and the SOE training staff left Camp X in 1944, HYDRA remained behind, even more expanded in size, and survived into the 1960s as an operation run by the Canadian Army.

HYDRA – so called because like the mythical beast from Greek legend it was many-headed with its three sets of rhomboid, or diamond-shaped, antennae – was an improvised station constructed from radio parts acquired somewhat haphazardly from all over North America. With the closing down of amateur transmissions, Pat Bayly scoured the continent for spare equipment, which BSC bought up and then arranged for shipment to Canada. The first transmitter was a 2500-watt machine that had been operated by hams in Toronto. Collected early in May 1942 by a panel truck from a private house in downtown Toronto, it soon became known as "the little rig" to distinguish it from the larger transmitter that was taken apart and shipped up in crates from Philadelphia a few months later. WCAU had been a popular radio station in the City of Brotherly Love, operating from a 10-kilowatt, high-frequency, water-cooled transmitter. At Camp X, as Hardcastle remembered, Bayly had thoughtfully provided his technicians with a comprehensive photographic "map" of the WCAU transmitter *in situ*. With its help, and with Bayly himself occasionally coming up from New York to lend a hand, they carefully reconstructed the machine that was to become the most powerful of Camp X's wartime transmitters.

Messages passed between HYDRA and the BSC office in New York by way of telex lines, using a Western Union commercial cable between New York and Buffalo, and then a Canadian National cable from Fort Erie. Cable was also used to link New York with Ottawa and Washington. To protect the security of this network, Bayly developed the telekrypton, an on-line cipher machine capable of handling the enormous volume of teletype communications needed by BSC. Based on Western Union equipment extensively modified by Bayly, it marked a considerable improvement on earlier systems for handling teletype traffic and dramatically speeded up the transmission rate.

Sir Edward Travis, head of Bletchley Park, coined its name, the Rockex, while on a visit to Stephenson from Britain. Having looked over Bayly's workshop, where the prototype machine lay awaiting final approval before it went into mass production, Travis glanced out of the window of Stephenson's office on the thirty-sixth floor of Rockefeller Center. Below, he saw members of the famous Rockettes, long-legged precision dancers belonging to one of America's most famous institutions, sunning themselves on a flat roof next to Radio City Music Hall. The standard British cipher machine was known as the Typex. The name "Rockex" for Bayly's machine sprang spontaneously to Travis's lips. And so it remained, a name spawned by commercial pop culture counterpoised to the prosaic Typex of the British and the classically derived Enigma of the Germans.

BSC technicians installed Rockex machines at Camp X as soon as they became available, and from there they provided BSC with a rapid, sophisticated, and efficient communications system. Soon, all communications between BSC and SIS in England were enciphered using this system, including the transatlantic cable system, which from 1943 also linked BSC with SIS in London.

The installation of the Rockex at Camp X involved another change: the arrival of the first women. The first one to arrive was Cecily Gates. Working as a bank clerk in the same Toronto office as Tommy Drew-Brook, and with a friend whose sister had been taken on board for BSC by the quiet stockbroker, she took courage into her hands one day, went up to the eleventh floor of the building, and volunteered her services. In mid-June 1942 she arrived to operate the first Rockex machine, transferring messages coming in from Britain over HYDRA onto tape for transmission to New York, and vice versa. There being no accommodation for women at Camp X, she was billetted with a discreet couple in Oshawa who asked no questions. "I was picked up every morning at eight-thirty and driven to the Camp," she now recalls. "I remember a string of beautiful pine trees. I had a busy job. Once inside the Camp I never went anywhere.... I was in the HYDRA building and never saw any of the men being trained."[11]

To instruct her in the use of the Rockex, Pat Bayly sent a trained operator from BSC in New York, Bobbie Griffiths. Later to become wife of Kevin O'Neill, the head of Canada's top-secret post-war communications intelligence agency, the Communications Security Establishment, Bobbie Griffiths spent two weeks at Camp X introducing the Rockex. In her spare time she was taken in hand by some visiting OSS men. "They tried to tell me to shoot from the hip into the lake," she remembers, "but I wasn't very good at it." Afterwards she returned to New York and then, before the end of the war, joined the code-breakers at Bletchley Park in Britain as executive assistant to Travis.[12] By the time Cecily Gates herself left Camp X for BSC that September, two more female operators had arrived, and their numbers were to increase as HYDRA expanded.

Bayly's major achievement as head of BSC communications was to develop a mechanism that overcame the technical problems caused by the interface between radio and cable transmissions. The Rockex was a cipher machine for use with tape, the letters being represented by the combination of the presence or absence of holes in the tape. This meant that messages from New York arriving at HYDRA and destined for SIS in Britain still had to be converted by hand into Morse before they could be transmitted – a slow process of about twenty-five words a minute. Bayly solved the problem by developing mechanical keyers that "read" the tape and then automatically keyed the transmitter.

This machine, developed early in 1943, increased transmission speed up to one hundred words a minute; the introduction later of a photo-electric keyer increased the rate to three hundred words a minute. It was a major contribution to Anglo-American intelligence-sharing arrangements. While a lot of top-secret material could be sent by transatlantic cable, HYDRA offered an alternative and faster route. "Bletchley Park," wrote Gordon Welchman, one of its greatest wartime experts, "depended heavily on supplies of American equipment, and on ways of achieving compatibility between British and American practice.... One of our chief concerns was the interface between British long-distance radio communications using Morse code and the radio teletype preferred by the Americans." The system devised by Bayly also possessed, he noted, "a very attractive feature. The speed of transmission [from HYDRA] was adjustable according to atmospheric conditions, so that at any time information could be passed at the highest rate that the conditions would allow."[13]

Welchman's observations on Bayly's work at BSC and HYDRA were based on thorough familiarity with the technical aspects of ULTRA. For the first three years of the war he had headed Hut Six at Bletchley Park, responsible for breaking most of the German Army and Air Force material, and in 1943 he found himself appointed assistant director of mechanization, or A.D. (Mech), by Travis. By this time the operation had become a massive and sophisticated transatlantic effort.

American entry into the war placed joint intelligence arrangements on a more formal basis. Two high-level British delegations visited Washington in early 1942 and agreed on the co-ordination of intercept programs, the exchange of intelligence information, and full co-operation in the field of cryptography. Co-operation became even closer, and by the spring of 1943 a formal agreement on SIGINT (known as BRUSA) was reached whereby the Allies agreed to exchange personnel, implement joint rules for handling intelligence, and use agreed-upon methods for its distribution.

In August 1943 American army cryptanalytic teams arrived at the Victorian mansion where the code-breakers worked, to join the British experts. At the same time the mechanization of procedures for handling the huge volume of material, transmitting it across the Atlantic to Washington, and protecting its security became a major task.

Bayly, as head of BSC communications, had by this time become the on-site liaison man in Washington in charge of mechanization procedures for handling ULTRA material passing between the two Allies. Welchman came to know Bayly well. "My first assignment," he recalled in his book, *The Hut Six Story* , "was to work closely with the Canadian Colonel B. deF. Bayly, always known as Pat...fortunately we liked each other from the start. Indeed, it would have been hard not to like Pat. He was an exuberant person with infectious enthusiasm." Welchman got a quick taste of this when Bayly paid his first visit to Bletchley Park to be fully initiated into its secrets. After Travis had introduced the two men, Bayly asked to be taken to the teleprinter room. From here he contacted BSC in New York directly on one of the machines and asked them to request his wife, who was in their downtown Manhattan apartment, to be in the office half an hour later. "Sure enough," Welchman remembered, "she was on the line, and, since they were both proficient teletype operators, I witnessed a husband-and-wife conversation via transatlantic cable. It was my first introduction to the actual operation of teletype equipment, an area in which Pat and I would do a great deal of work later on."

For the time being, however, Bayly's work with Welchman dealt with the security aspects of the machinery involved in the ULTRA operation as well as the broad field of Anglo-American technological liaison on ULTRA. "Pat and I," wrote Welchman, "concentrated on two areas of activity in which Bletchley Park depended heavily on supplies of American equipment and on ways of achieving compatibility between British and American practice; cryptographic application of punched-card technology and the handling of government communications."

The work was extremely sensitive, and the veil of secrecy that surrounded it was only partially lifted when Welchman published his book in 1982. For his part, Bayly still refuses to talk about his work for BSC, perhaps because he continued to work for the British on intelligence communications after the war. "The Quiet Canadian", the sobriquet given to William Stephenson by Robert Sherwood, more correctly applies to Benjamin deForest Bayly.

HYDRA was not in itself a coding or code-breaking centre, nor was it designed to intercept German or Japanese communications. On occasion, however, it *did* intercept. This happened because the peculiarities of radio transmission sometimes meant that intercept stations in Britain could not find signals coming from Occupied Europe, while receivers in eastern Canada could. At such times, London would instruct HYDRA to carry out search-and-intercept operations. It would also happen – very occasionally – that SIS London would have HYDRA search for signals from a British agent in Europe, again because of peculiarities in wireless propagation conditions. So far as the handling and transmission of intercept material were concerned, HYDRA was a crucial part of the Anglo-American-Canadian system constructed to ensure a co-ordinated intelligence effort.

George Carruthers, another of those 1942 recruits who never made it to South America, eventually became head of operations in the Camp X communications room. He later recalled that "Most of the traffic consisted of messages picked up by operators listening to Japanese ship-to-ship or ship-to-shore transmission."[14] This material, intercepted in the Far East, was then relayed on British channels via Ceylon to London, and then from London it passed via HYDRA for transmission by BSC to Canadian and American authorities for analysis. In the reverse direction, material intercepted in North America was transmitted to London, making HYDRA an integral part of a system in which there was fully developed Allied co-operation in signals intelligence. It was a harbinger of things to come.

The post-war Allies continued to operate closely on intelligence matters and this co-operation intensified in the Cold War. In 1947 the three governments extended the 1943 BRUSA agreement and signed the UKUSA agreement on the sharing of communications intelligence, "the most secret agreement ever entered into by the English-speaking world", in the words of James Bamford, author of *The Puzzle Palace*. Under UKUSA, the United States, Great Britain, Canada, Australia, and New Zealand divided the globe into spheres of cryptographic influence, with each country assigned to specific targets. They also standardized procedures and indoctrination practices. BSC and HYDRA had a small but important role in the evolution towards this historic agreement. Although BSC no longer existed when UKUSA was signed, HYDRA, as a unit within the Canadian Army's radio network, continued to play a part in Allied communications intelligence for the next twenty years.

CHAPTER 7

"Rackets and Balls":
Casting the Global Net

Midsummer's Day, 1942, was swelteringly hot in Washington. Winston Churchill, on his second wartime visit to the American capital to discuss Allied strategy and TUBE ALLOYS, the code-name given to the atomic bomb project, luxuriated in the air-conditioned comfort of the White House, took a leisurely breakfast while reading his morning cables, and then joined Roosevelt in his study. While the two men were standing talking beside the president's desk, General George Marshall brought in a telegram addressed to the prime minister. Thus Churchill learned of the fall of Tobruk and the surrender of its garrison of 30,000 men to the triumphant forces of Rommel's Afrika Korps. This was one of the heaviest blows that Churchill was to receive during the war. "Defeat is one thing, disgrace is another," he wrote later, linking the defeat in North Africa to the surrender of another British garrison at Singapore only four months before. The fall of Tobruk opened the gateway to Egypt and Cairo, headquarters of the British forces in the Middle East. Within three days of the catastrophic news reaching Churchill, Rommel had crossed the Egyptian border and was speeding towards Cairo. The British Army took up defensive lines around El Alamein, just forty miles to the west of Alexandria, and throughout the city of Cairo smoke began to rise from the chimneys and back gardens of British political and military offices as documents were burned and preparations made for the evacuation to Jerusalem.

Cairo was not just the headquarters of British forces in North Africa and the Middle East. It was also the site of SOE's major base outside London, and the Cairo offices periodically would be purged as SOE London attempted to assert its authority over what it saw as inefficiency or insubordination. SOE Cairo was responsible for operations into the Balkans as well as the Middle East, but co-ordination with both London and the local military command provided fertile ground for misunderstanding and muddle. The Cairo headquarters were in a block of flats known as the Rustem Buildings, and as Rommel's forces threatened Britain's hold on Egypt, SOE London took the opportunity to carry out yet another purge of personnel. One of the newly appointed SOE officers was Basil Davidson, in pre-war life a journalist, but since 1940 an SOE agent who had operated first in Hungary and then in Istanbul. As the battle in the Western Desert reached its climax, Davidson found himself placed in operational command of the SOE Yugoslav section at the Rustem Buildings.

"After the provincial quiet of Istanbul," Davidson wrote many years later in *Special Operations Europe*, his wartime memoir, "Cairo had all the bustle of a strange and various metropolis. Forceful characters abounded." One of them was Maurice Oldfield, of the Secret Intelligence Service, later destined to become its head ("C") and reputed to be the model for John le Carré's fictional hero, George Smiley. Another was the historian Hugh Seton-Watson, an expert on Balkan affairs, who enjoyed a somewhat dubious local reputation as inventor of the unofficial and irreverent emblem of SOE: a tasteful design of tennis equipment entitled "Rackets and Balls". But by far the most forceful set of characters was a group of men Davidson encountered out on the edge of the desert.

Close to the luxurious Mena House Hotel, in the shadow of the Great Pyramids of Gizeh, was a small, square-built villa that had once served the distinctly unmilitary needs of local gentlemen. Lushly decorated in pink, its lampshades made out of watered silk, it now served the more robust purposes of SOE and provided a retreat from the bustle of the Rustem Buildings. Behind its high stone wall, hidden from the outside world, the villa that fall also sheltered a group of men impatiently waiting for the beginning of the mission for which they had already received extensive training and preparation. Stubbornly argumentative and increasingly restive, the men impressed Davidson with the depth of their feelings about the war. Forty years

CAMP LIFE

The comforts of the commandant's pa
provided a welcome relief from the da
cares of running STS 103.

Nothing here to reveal that Camp X was more than an ordinary army camp. BSC called it "The I
The local population thought it was a demolitions-testing centre.

Purpose-built in the fall of 1941, Camp X provided comfortable housing for its staff and students on the
grounds of an old lakeside farm.

CAMP LIFE

Officers' mess, scene of Ilia Tolstoy's hazing and Paul Dehn's impromptu piano concerts.

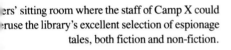

ers' sitting room where the staff of Camp X could ruse the library's excellent selection of espionage tales, both fiction and non-fiction.

Hamish Pelham-Burn

"The best bar (and barman) between Montreal and Toronto." Now the site of the largest liquor warehouse in the province of Ontario.

TRAINING EXERCISES

American "clients" on a summertin
exercise on the shores of Lake Ontar

R-and-R on manoeuvres.

"Map Reading", Camp X, summer
of 1942.

TRAINING EXERCISES

Tiger Moth practises quick landing-and-takeoff operations, one of the exercises introduced at Camp X by Hamish Pelham-Burn.

f Pelham-Burn's spectacular shows.

Hamish Pelham-Burn

Canadian Yugoslav recruits, in uniform, on patrol. Most ended up fighting alongside Tito's partisans.

CAMP LIFE

...ain Fred Milner, demolitions instructor and one of ...arliest of the British-trained staff to arrive at Camp X, poses by the lake. He was later posted to SOE ...iers and ended the war as an SOE agent in Burma.

Cuthbert Skilbeck

Cuthbert Skilbeck

...estler by profession and Camp X instructor in unarmed combat, Sergeant-Major George de Rewelyskow gazes at the frozen lakeshore in the winter of 1942.

"HYDRA"

HYDRA, Camp X's top-secret telecommunications centre, made use of the talents of many amateur radio hams under Toronto professor Pat Bayly, Stephenson's communications chief in New York.

This innocent-looking building shields HYDRA's receivers a transmitters. Tent to the right housed recruits burned out of th quarters by the fire of April 1942.

HYDRA's operations room. Radio equipment now looks dated, b in fact it did a sophisticated and important job, linking Ottawa, Washington, New York, and London.

HYDRA equipment was obtained wherever it could be found. This letter reveals one of the methods used by the Camp X team.

CONFIDENTIAL

File: 12P 1-1-X

DEPARTMENT OF NATIONAL DEFENCE
(Army)

No. 12 Coy., Cdn. Pro. C.,
280 Lansdowne Ave., Toronto, Ont.

12th May/1942.

D.A.P.M.,
Headquarters, M.D. 2,
159 Bay Street,
Toronto, Ontario.

Army Truck parked at
Parkwood Rd. Toronto.

        Reference your telephone conversation
re the m/n on 11th May/42. This matter was investigated by
a detail of this Unit and the following information obtained:

2.   The occupant of the m/n premises, one
Harry Livingston, was interviewed. He stated that he was
an amateur radio operator and that he had a very valuable
Radio Transmittor which was adaptable to Army purposes and
which at the present time was not available in sufficient
quantities. Consequently, he had been requested to sell
same to the British Gov't.

3.   On Sunday, 10th May/42, a Capt. Adams,
who is described as a British Army Officer, (no further
information available) and two other soldiers with documents identifying themselves, reported to Livingston and
proceeded to dismantle the transmittor. This took approximately the time mentioned, 13 hrs., as the men had to be very
careful. The Army Truck remained in front of Livingston's
house during this period. Livingston was unable to tell
our detail the destination of the apparatus but he overheard the
Officer instruct the men to pack the equipment carefully as
the last few miles was very bad road.

4.   L/Cpl. Clark, who investigated this matter
has been cautioned that no details of his investigation
should be further disclosed.

                (F.E. McMahon) Capt.,
                A/O.C. No. 12 Cdn. Pro. Coy.

MAY 13 1942

D23
41-2

(131)

T.S. 25-1-1
(DAAGII).

SECRET   CANCELLED

Headquarters, Military District No. 2,
159 Bay Street, Toronto, Ontario.
24th November   2.

Dear Colonel Chesley: COOKS - Special 25-1-1

        The Officer Commanding Special 25-1-1 is
desperately in need of first class cooks, as he
considered it most important that the selected candidates arrive at the school, should leave with the
highest regard for the Administration in every detail.

2.   With the above in view, it is requested
that steps be taken to ascertain whether the under-
mentioned cooks, who were given particularly good
reports at the Cooking School while at Camp Borden,
could be made available:-

        G.46579 Sgt. Melton, F.C.
        No. 21 Coy. V.G.C., St. John, N.B.

This N.C.O. passed head of his class. Cooked for his
own Restaurant for ten years and has had considerable
experience in Army Cooking. Dependable, and co-operative.

        C.57635 Pte. Gagne, J.P.
        No. 33 C.A.(B) T.C., Lansdown Park.

Good report at Cooking School. Two years army cooking,
dependable, energetic and slightly bi-lingual (mostly english)

3.   It is readily understood that this is an unusual
request but it is considered extremely important.

4.   May I be informed accordingly, please.

                Yours sincerely,   D23

                (C.F. CONSTANTINE),
                MAJOR-GENERAL
                D.O.C.   M.D. No. 2.

Colonel L.M. Chesley,
Director Staff Duties,
Department National Defence,
Ottawa, Ontario.

(31)

Secret armies, too, march on their stomachs. A request for first-class Canadian cooks to be sent to Camp X.

DOCUMENTS

Among the strongest critics of the "Intrepid" myth are those who worked closely with BSC and other secret wartime agencies. In this letter to the London *Times*, Cuthbert Skilbeck, Camp X commandant 1943–44, protests against the film version of *A Man Called Intrepid*.

'A Man Called Intrepid'

From Mr Cuthbert Skilbeck

Sir, As I commanded the so-cal Camp X in the film *A Man Cal Intrepid* for some two years 1 fo the wholly fictional handling n distasteful, if not ludicrous.

I join Colonel Buckmaster (A 9) in deploring such a mixture fiction with real history.

By all means let us have stories of fiction, but to trad history so flagrantly and to real names in a fictional story n be unacceptable.

Yours faithfully,
CUTHBERT SKILBECK.
c/o Dyers Hall,
11-13 Dowgate Hill, EC4.
April 9. 1958

CAMP X
1941 – 1946

ON THIS SITE BRITISH SECURITY
CO-ORDINATION OPERATED SPECIAL
TRAINING SCHOOL No. 103 AND HYDRA.

S.T.S. 103 TRAINED ALLIED AGENTS
IN THE TECHNIQUES OF SECRET
WARFARE FOR THE SPECIAL OPERATIONS
EXECUTIVE (SOE) BRANCH OF THE
BRITISH INTELLIGENCE SERVICE.

HYDRA NETWORK COMMUNICATED
VITAL MESSAGES BETWEEN CANADA, THE
UNITED STATES AND GREAT BRITAIN.

THIS COMMEMORATION IS DEDICATED
TO THE SERVICE OF THE MEN AND
WOMEN WHO TOOK PART IN THESE
OPERATIONS.

Author's photograph

The memorial plaque at the Camp X site on the shore of Lake Ontario at Whitby.

later, the impact they made on him can still be felt. "Craggy men with huge shoulders," he described them, "hard of face, their hands clawed with toil, and as stubbornly powerful in their convictions."

These were the Yugoslav Canadians, the first group of ethnic Canadians to have been trained at Camp X, and also the largest and most successful. What path took them from Whitby to Cairo? From where had they begun, and what was their ultimate destination? And in what greater game of international chess were they the pieces?

Hitler's forces had attacked Yugoslavia in April 1941 with seven Panzer divisions and devastating aerial attacks on Belgrade, the capital, which had left 17,000 dead. Within days the royalist government had fled to London and Yugoslavia had vanished from the map. The twenty-year-old state of the South Slavs lay divided between the puppet government in the Serb capital of Belgrade and the separatist pro-Fascist state of Croatia, while Italian, German, Hungarian, and Bulgarian troops occupied its soil. Resistance to occupation sprang up almost immediately, fuelled by savage German retaliation that took fifty civilian lives for every German soldier killed. By August 1941 rumours of fighting and revolt in the mountains of Yugoslavia began to reach the outside world. In London, this news quickly seized the romantic imagination of Winston Churchill. While Mackenzie King was touring Canadian troops in England on his first British visit, and while Tommy Davies was preparing for the vital discussions in the United States with Stephenson and Donovan about Camp X, Churchill pressed SOE for word of its plans to assist the Yugoslav revolt. Three weeks later, on September 20, the Royal Navy submarine *HMS Triumph* landed a small four-man mission by night on the Montenegrin coast.

Mission BULLSEYE, as it was code-named, was led by Captain D.T. ("Bill") Hudson of SOE, and was the first step in what was to become massive British involvement in wartime Yugoslavia. Soon Hudson's mission was established at the headquarters of General Mihailovich, the royalist officer fighting in the mountains. Before long the BBC was projecting an image of Mihailovich that cast him not only as the leader of Yugoslav revolt but also as a symbol of European resistance to counterpoise that of the Norwegian Quisling, symbol of collaboration.

If the job of SOE was to set Europe ablaze, then it should fan the flames of revolt in Yugoslavia. That much seemed obvious. But as time passed and the British peered more deeply into the fire, the picture began to transform itself into a forest blaze whose direction shifted with bewildering speed. Top-secret intercepts of German communications read by the British in Cairo and London soon began to reveal that Mihailovich was on occasion prepared to make local truces with the enemy, and that the most bitter and extensive fighting with the occupiers, especially in Croatia, was being led by a quite different resistance force, that of the Communist partisans led by Tito. The war in Yugoslavia was a civil and ethnic as well as a military struggle. As the bitterness of civil strife was added to the savagery of the German occupiers, the British found themselves faced with a dilemma. Should they continue to support Mihailovich, representative of the royalist Yugoslav government and best guarantor of a conservative and non-Communist post-war Yugoslavia? Or should they support the partisans who were more willing to fight the Germans? What were British priorities, and which resistance group was the most useful? The high-level policy debate raged between London and Cairo throughout 1942 as the Foreign Office, SOE, Churchill, and the Chiefs of Staff tried to reach agreement. Finally, at a meeting of SOE, SIS, and Foreign Office officials on August 8, it was agreed that the possibility of sending a British mission to the Communists in Croatia – with whom up to then SOE had had no direct contact – should be explored.

Even before this policy decision, however, SOE had taken steps to recruit men suitable for contact with the partisans. While officials were moving towards tentative agreement in London, the fruits of a recruiting drive for men of Yugoslav origin were being harvested in Canada.

Canada was fertile ground for recruiting such men. In the 1920s Yugoslavs had immigrated to Canada, driven by hunger and hardship rather than any permanent desire to turn their backs on their native land. Many were still Yugoslav citizens, had strong links with Croatia, and most were active in left-wing, labour, and Communist movements. They were to be found scattered across the country and throughout the diligently kept files maintained by the RCMP on "subversives" and "agitators". For all their geographical dispersal they were not too difficult to find.

Early in 1942 – long before doubts about Mihailovich began to surface officially – SOE London requested BSC in New York to facilitate a recruiting mission to Canada to find a hundred Yugoslav Canadians suitable as agents in their homeland. BSC in turn mobilized its Canadian contacts in External Affairs, National Defence, and, as soon as Drew-Brook had cleared the matter, with RCMP Inspector McClellan. The latter provided names from secret RCMP files, and to supplement their efforts Drew-Brook advertised for volunteers in *Novosti*, a left-wing Serbo-Croat newspaper. He also used the services of Eric Curwain. In return for a generous living allowance and considerable latitude in his job, Curwain was to do most of the legwork for Drew-Brook's recruiting and, in the case of the Yugoslavs and other left-wing or Communist recruits, act as a cut-out in order to keep the stockbroker's identity concealed. Before long, potential recruits had been located from across Canada. Prior to being sent to Camp X for training they were interviewed by the SOE recruiting mission, which spent several weeks travelling across the country from Quebec to British Columbia.

The head of the mission was Colonel S.W. ("Bill") Bailey, a major figure in SOE's relations with Yugoslavia. Before the war Bailey had worked in Serbia for a British metallurgical company, and he spoke fluent Serbo-Croat as well as a number of other languages. He joined SOE in 1940 and became one of its leading experts on Yugoslavia and the Balkans. After serving as SOE representative in Istanbul, he worked on Greek affairs before going to Canada on his recruiting mission. Later he was parachuted into Yugoslavia on Christmas Eve, 1942, as the senior British liaison officer at General Mihailovich's headquarters. His job was to clarify exactly how much Mihailovich was actually fighting the enemy and to what degree British support should be continued. He then stayed with Mihailovich until British assistance was finally withdrawn from the doomed royalist leader in 1944.

Accompanying Bailey to Canada was a more intriguing figure: Captain William Stuart, who was recruiting not for SOE but for SIS. Stuart's background made him a natural for any intelligence agency. He was born in Bosnia and educated in Yugoslavia and Hungary. His father was Scottish and his mother Hungarian, and he spoke fluent Serbo-Croat, German, and Hungarian. He had immigrated to Canada in the 1920s and become a citizen in 1933. He was quickly recruited to work for the Immigration Department of the Canadian Pacific Railway, screening immigrants from Central and Eastern Europe, and worked for some time in both Prague and Zagreb. After the outbreak of war Stuart was recruited by the British Foreign Office to be vice-consul in Zagreb. Here, with his background and expertise, he specialized in intelligence and security work. When Yugoslavia was occupied in 1941, he stayed behind to destroy files, was briefly detained by the Italians, and then made his way back to Britain. He was obviously extremely well qualified for the task of identifying likely recruits in Canada, as well as for undertaking secret work himself in Yugoslavia.

Like Bailey, Stuart was subsequently parachuted back into Yugoslavia. He took part in the historic first drop by British officers into Tito's headquarters in Montenegro, in May 1943, where his companion was SOE Captain William Deakin. Tragically for Stuart, however, his mission came to an abrupt end. Within days of his arrival the Germans launched an aerial attack on Tito's forces, already dispersing in the face of a major ground offensive. Caught on an exposed mountainside, Deakin and Stuart sheltered with Tito and his staff as best they could behind rocks and in depressions on the ground. A bomb splinter wounded both Deakin and Tito, but another killed Stuart instantly as he took cover by a large beech tree. Only a few minutes earlier he had persuaded the British party to cut into their meagre rations by opening a tin of sardines instead of saving it for the next day. "It's better to open it and die with a full stomach," he had joked.[1]

One obvious place to look for the Yugoslavs was in the Canadian Communist Party, where sections of individual ethnic and national groups were attached to the Party's Central Committee. At the head of the Yugoslav group was a man called Nikola Kovacevich, a grey-haired stalwart in his mid-fifties who had been sent out by the Yugoslav Communist Party in 1937 to establish contact with *émigrés* in the United States and Canada. Settled in Canada illegally, Kovacevich went under the name of Karko Sikich, the name of a legal resident who had died earlier in an accident. Kovacevich and other

Yugoslav members of the Canadian Party deliberated the issue of collaboration with the British in lengthy discussions with the Party leadership.

Several meetings were also held between Bailey and top leaders of the quasi-legal Communist Party at which Bailey explained the background to Britain's needs. According to one source, he was quite frank about these. At his first meeting he was asked point-blank by Kovacevich why he was seeking only Communists when there were plenty of pro-royalist Yugoslavs to be found. Bailey replied that the royalists were collaborating in Yugoslavia and only the Communists were really fighting.[2] This answer may, of course, have been designed merely to please his audience, but it seems unlikely. A noticeable feature about the mission was that SOE told neither the royal Yugoslav government in London nor the Yugoslav consul-general in Montreal about it. This casts an intriguing light on the evolution of British policy and SOE's role in its development, because at this time – before the meeting of August 8 in London – no official sanction appears to have been given for any contact with the partisans, and British policy to all outward appearances was full support for Mihailovich.

Eventually the Communist Party agreed to help and suitable volunteers were found across the country. As soon as Bailey and Stuart had selected the men they wanted, they were assembled in the barracks of Military District 2 in the fairgrounds of the Canadian National Exhibition. There was more screening, and then between thirty and forty men were finally chosen for training. Many, like Kovacevich, were illegal residents, and only a minority had Canadian citizenship. Shortly afterwards, military transport vehicles drove them out along Highway 2 to Whitby, turned down Thornton Road, and took them past the closely guarded gatehouse into Camp X. It was July 22, 1942. They had arrived for four weeks' preliminary training in the skills they would refine in SOE schools overseas and then apply in the mountains of Yugoslavia.

In Canada, Brooker and Skilbeck, the new chief instructor at Camp X, were as impressed by the Yugoslavs as Davidson was to be in Cairo. "They had motivation and seemed to be fearless," Skilbeck now remembers, "but of course we never knew how any of our students fared once they had left us."[3] Brooker recalls them as rough men accustomed to harsh conditions and undoubtedly among the fittest of all the Camp X trainees during the war. Three things about them stuck in Brooker's mind: "They hated the RCMP and its local chief George McClellan; they drank slivovitz like water and liked to roast sheep on a spit; and they could not wait to get to Yugoslavia to fight the Germans."

When the time came for the first group to depart for the long journey overseas, Eric Curwain was equally struck by their strong commitment to the fight. Invited to join them in a banquet, he later described it as an emotional affair. Pacific coast fishermen, Ontario miners, woodsmen, trappers, and craftsmen from across the prairies celebrated with a moving dignity, and when the evening was over the departing members of the group embraced their friends. "The Yugoslavs told us frankly they were not going to fight for Canada or Britain; they were at war with the Nazis and the Fascists," Curwain recalled in "Almost Top Secret", the unpublished memoir that he completed shortly before his death.

Stevan Serdar, a veteran miner from Quebec who had fought on the Republican side in the Spanish Civil War, told a Yugoslav journalist in 1980 that before departure they also met with Tim Buck, secretary-general of the Communist Party, who told them that they were on the way to fight fascism, the common enemy of the Soviet Union and the Western allies, and that they should do everything they could to further the cause. But not, he went on, anything that would be "against the interests of the Party and the progressive movement." They should resist any attempts to abuse their commitment to goals contrary to their beliefs and, just in case, they were given the names of Party contacts in Cairo.

Buck's reminiscences, published under the title *Yours in the Struggle* in 1977, provided a different version. Improbably, he claimed that Donovan personally went to Toronto to recruit the Yugoslavs and approached the editor of the Communist newspaper, the *Canadian Tribune*, for help. Donovan could certainly be impulsive and indiscreet, but the story seems unlikely and there is no other evidence to support it. More convincingly, Buck referred to a meeting with the volunteers at a farm outside Toronto where "I told them exactly what it was they must expect and that there was still time for any man to withdraw." None of them did, Buck noted, "because they were all working fellows who were giving everything they had for the movement at that time." They also gave Buck a souvenir: a tweed jacket they had arranged to have made by a tailor. "Why a jacket?" Buck asked. "Well, you have only two and one of them is very old, so better give you this than a medal," came the answer.

For some of the Yugoslav trainees, getting to Cairo proved as dangerous as guerrilla warfare in the mountains of Bosnia. In early September, eight of the Camp X graduates boarded an old Greek cargo ship, the *Andreas*, out of St. John's, Newfoundland, which then joined up with a convoy out of New York destined to take the South Atlantic route across from Brazil to the east coast of Africa and up to Suez. A few weeks later, off the coast of Trinidad, the escorting ships left the convoy, which then broke up to let each ship make its way down to the south coast of Brazil before making its dash to the Cape of Good Hope. On November 4, 1942, the day the British Eighth Army made the decisive breakthrough at El Alamein and irrevocably turned the tide of war in North Africa, a German U-boat hit the *Andreas* with two torpedoes. Crippled, the cargo ship and its passengers took to the lifeboats. The U-boat surfaced and attacked with cannon and machine-gun fire. Two of the Camp X trainees were killed, along with the ship's captain and several crew members. Two others of the Yugoslavs, including Nikola Kovacevich, were severely wounded, and two more were slightly injured. For three nights, three of the survivors drifted in an open lifeboat before being rescued and shipped back to Trinidad. For the others, the ordeal was longer: they were eleven days at sea before being picked up and taken back to the West Indies.

Kovacevich, too seriously wounded to continue the journey, returned to Canada, where he stayed until the end of the war before being appointed Yugoslav representative to the International Labour Organization. Curwain was instructed to offer him compensation when he got back to Toronto, but Kovacevich declined on the grounds that he had not accomplished his mission. To the suggestion that his family might need the money, he dismissively replied that since they were all in Yugoslavia and he did not know whose side they were fighting on, they were none of his concern. But in the end he agreed to accept a portable typewriter.

But the remaining five agents eventually made it safely across the Atlantic in the luxury liner *El Nil*, finally arriving in Cairo early in February 1943. Here they were joined by the second group of recruits from Canada who had crossed on *The Star of Alexandria*, and by five American Yugoslavs working for OSS. Joined by Stuart, the SIS agent who had accompanied Bailey on his Canadian recruiting mission, the Camp X men undertook extensive parachute training at Camp X's numerical predecessor, Special Training School 102, established at Ramat David, close to Haifa in Palestine. But for much of the time they were kept in seclusion in the SOE villa out by the pyramids.

The Rustem Buildings headquarters had become a microcosm of the huge debate still raging among the British about the merits and demerits of Tito's partisans and Mihailovich's Chetniks. Since the previous summer nothing had yet been done to contact the partisans, and British policy was still to support Mihailovich, despite growing evidence that he was not prepared to fight the Germans in the kind of conflict the British desired. Bitter disputes broke out within SOE itself about what to do. Basil Davidson's recollections of the political whirlwinds that swept around the craggy partisans from Canada are amply borne out by those of members of the group themselves and of others who worked with SOE Cairo at this time. "Soon," Davidson remembered, "the opposing sides began to face each other with all the passion that set the Children of Light against the Children of Darkness. Fighting alliances were made, recruits were sought, morality wavered, truth lowered her head. Squadrons of memoranda were loaded up and launched...confusion seemed to reign."[4]

Caught in the whirlwinds, the Camp X recruits knew where their loyalties lay. Refugees from royalist Yugoslavia, they had no intention of fighting for Mihailovich. Stevan Serdar, who became a colonel in Tito's post-war Yugoslav Army, remembered one occasion when a British officer visited the villa out by the pyramids and told them that, since the partisans had been virtually annihilated, their best bet was to join up with Mihailovich, who was the man getting British support. But other British officers, including Davidson himself, told them the opposite. Another was James Klugmann.

Klugmann has long been a figure of controversy. An owlishlooking intellectual who was a former secretary of the Cambridge University Communist Party, Klugmann had come into SOE from the British Army without disguising his enthusiastic support for Britain's Soviet Ally in the struggle against fascism. After the war he joined the Central Committee of the Communist Party of Great Britain and began to write its never-completed official history. Ever since, some historians seeking to explain Britain's switch in 1943 from Mihailovich to support for Tito have singled Klugmann out as a key to the mystery. That view is simplistic. British policy shifted for major reasons of strategy far beyond the power of a single junior officer in Cairo to manipulate. But Klugmann certainly had a powerful impact on the Yugoslav Canadians. Ideologically committed to the fight against fascism already, they provided Klugmann with a captive audience for his rousing lectures about the historical inevitability of their victory in Yugoslavia. Davidson described him "choking from the smoke of the cigarette between his lips, raising sympathetic laughs, interrupting himself to wipe his spectacles, blinking encouragement at questions, fielding all disputes and continually adding to his edifice of explanation."

By March 1943, however, talk was wearing thin and the Camp X men were becoming restless. But Klugmann reminded them that history was on their side: its dialectics would make them victorious.

Klugmann was right. Unknown to the men isolated in the pink-toned interior of their villa in the desert, events behind the scenes were moving rapidly. Three things finally crumbled the wall of resistance to an SOE approach to the partisans. First was the appearance on the Cairo scene in late 1942 of a legendary figure in the annals of SOE, Colonel C.M. ("Bolo") Keble. He was, wrote former SOE agent Patrick Howarth, "a peppery little man with a marked physical resemblance to a beetroot."[5] Davidson described him as a "small and rather bouncy man" with a large round head mounted directly on broad shoulders whose "manner of reigning combined the quick in-out of a commando raid with the onward drone of a brigade of tanks." The campaign to which Keble devoted himself on being posted to SOE in late 1942 was to get a mission to the partisans. Far from being a Communist or even left-wing, Keble was a dyed-in-the-wool conservative from an impeccable British Army regiment. But he had both a secret and a burning ambition.

The secret was that in a previous position at army headquarters in Cairo he had been a privileged recipient of top-secret intercepts of German communications in the Balkans – ULTRA information. These intercepts had not been given to SOE, but Keble, still on the distribution list and reading them daily, learned from messages sent by the *Sicherheitsdienst,* or SD, the security wing of the SS, that partisan units in Bosnia and Croatia were causing considerable trouble. This was Keble's secret and his trump card. Combined with his ambition for promotion, it added up to an almost irresistible force.

Keble rationed his intercept material with care, as Davidson quickly found out. "I became aware of Keble's move soon after New Year's Day of 1943," he recalled. "During a lunch hour...[Keble] rushed in and locked the door behind him. With what seemed to be a more than usually hectic air, he advanced to my desk and put down several slips of paper.

"Tensely, he said: 'Enemy traffic. From now on you will receive them every few days. You will treat them as most secret. You will study them. You will await my orders'."[6]

Davidson did. A few days later the second new factor in the equation came into play: the arrival at SOE headquarters in Cairo of the young SOE captain, William Deakin. Deakin had just spent several months working with Stephenson in New York on various abortive South American schemes; but more important was that as a young professional historian in peacetime he had worked as a research assistant for Winston Churchill on his life of Marlborough. Keble instructed Davidson to tell Deakin about the picture emerging from the intercepts, and together they carefully prepared the case for sending a mission to Tito.

The third factor was the visit of Churchill himself to Cairo early in 1943. No one could accuse Churchill of being a Communist, an agent of influence, or a Communist dupe. A deep-dyed Tory of the bluest colours, with impeccable anti-Bolshevist credentials, Churchill was nonetheless a pragmatist who had immediately seen the need to extend support to the Soviet Union in order to defeat the Nazis. Deakin, with his personal access to the prime minister, painted the picture as revealed by the intercepts, and argued that the British should contact the partisans in Bosnia and Croatia. Churchill was convinced, and his weight threw the balance in favour of those in London and Cairo who had been arguing since at least August 1942 for such a decision. Early in the spring of 1943 the decision was made: attempts would be made to reach the partisans.

Those chosen for the task were the Camp X Yugoslavs. Out in the desert villa Klugmann told them of the decision early in April and asked for volunteers. All of them elected to go, but only six were chosen for the first two drops to be made into the mountains. Their targets were areas that from the intercepts were known to have partisan groups and were familiar to the Camp X agents.

"One evening in April 1943," Deakin later wrote in *The Embattled Mountain*, "I went to the villa outside Cairo where the Croat groups were isolated and tense. After briefing them on the details of our planning and on the latest picture which had been pieced together, I gave them a firm assurance that our headquarters would only issue final technical instructions if it was considered that the realistic chances of success were high. I remember," Deakin added, "using the phrase '60-40'."

On the night of April 20, 1943, two groups of the men briefed by Deakin took off in Halifax bombers from a British airfield at Derna in the Libyan desert. In the early nighttime hours of the next day, and some 1500 kilometres from their desert base, the Canadian Yugoslavs parachuted back to their homeland in blind drops to eastern Bosnia and western Croatia.

Both groups were successful. The group that parachuted into eastern Bosnia, code-named HOATLEY 1, was led by Stevan Serdar and consisted of two other miners from Quebec. One of them, George Diclich, had also fought in Spain with Serdar. Landing close to an area of hard fighting between the Germans and the partisans, they quickly reached local partisan headquarters and were welcomed with great enthusiasm as representatives of the Allies. The next day the partisans launched an attack on a nearby German stronghold in their honour.

But the new arrivals were also greeted with great suspicion. The partisans, wary of German ploys to trick them, at first refused to take the group at face value. Only when a partisan who had fought with Serdar in Spain arrived to identify him some ten days later was the group permitted to use its radio. And it was only after Tito's main headquarters, well to the south in Montenegro, had confirmed by messenger that all was acceptable that the local partisan group fully accepted them.

The second group, code-named FUNGUS, was led by Petar Erdeljach, a stonemason, and consisted of two other men. One was Paul Pavlich, another Camp X graduate, a worker from the shipyards of Vancouver; the third member of the group, Alexander Simich, was a Serb who had been living in England. FUNGUS had been told by Cairo to contact the partisan headquarters for Croatia and to see if reports that members of the Croatian Peasant Party were fighting in the hills were true. Within twenty-four hours of landing, the FUNGUS group had been taken to the headquarters of the Croatian command. Like their compatriots in Bosnia, however, the partisans regarded the group with suspicion. "The commander recounted to me after the war," Deakin wrote, "that his first reaction was to shoot the party out of hand as disguised German agents. They carried two W/T sets, and no written instructions. But, as we had gambled, they succeeded in confirming their identity and local connections."

The local commander also took the precaution of radioing a message to Tito's supreme headquarters. Tito sent back the following message: "Radio set must not be taken away from mission. You can ask them, if they do not need two sets, to lend us one. But I underline – only if they give it to you freely and without pressure. You can let them contact England [sic]. Give them necessary information about Chetnik treachery and/or enemy forces but no information about our forces ... until we give you the details." In Cairo, a few days later, a radio operator on the roof of the Rustem Buildings heard the first messages to reach the British from behind partisan lines. "The... establishment of radio contact between the Croat party and its British base," wrote Deakin, "was of marked psychological importance...at last the British, whatever their motives, were deliberately seeking to establish exploratory relations with the Partisan command."7

For the next few weeks the FUNGUS mission provided the only link between the British and Tito. On the night of May 18-19, FUNGUS was supplemented by two British officers dropped by parachute. One of them, Major William Jones, a man with a passion for beekeeping, was not a Camp X graduate, having been recruited by SOE in Britain. "SOE sent many unlikely agents into occupied Europe," writes Roy MacLaren in his book *Canadians Behind Enemy Lines*. "But few were more unlikely than...Jones." A fifty-year-old badly wounded Canadian veteran of the First World War, Jones had won the MC and now enjoyed the use of only one eye. When the Second World War came along, Jones, eager to fight again, tried first to join the Canadian Army, but was rejected. Then the Royal Air Force turned him down when he applied to become a pilot. Nothing daunted, the gallant and eccentric Jones somehow succeeded in being selected for a Balkan mission. Thus he came to land in Croatia, where he became an enthusiastic and uncritical supporter of the partisans. His long and rambling radio dispatches to Cairo, full of what Deakin later described as "wild and irresponsible enthusiasm" for the partisans, were sufficiently devoid of military significance that the cryptographers learned to ignore them, including those which the passionate Jones addressed "For Churchill's and Roosevelt's eyes only". Eventually he moved north to Slovenia and fought for several months with local partisans against the Germans. As one of the most popular Allied officers in Yugoslavia, Jones, who died in 1969, now prominently features in the museum of the resistance in Ljubljana.

Now that preliminary contact had been made and the partisans had indicated their willingness to accept contact with the British, the way was open for the dispatch of the first British liaison officer to Tito himself at central partisan headquarters. Through a radio message sent from Montenegro to Croatia, and then transmitted by the SOE mission to Cairo, Tito signalled that the British should send this mission to Durmitor in Montenegro.

Thus it happened that Captains Bill Deakin and William Stuart, accompanied by four others, parachuted down to Tito's headquarters on Durmitor Mountain on May 28, 1943, after another dusk departure from the aerodrome at Derna. Stuart and Deakin each had a separate W/T set and operator, and their own ciphers. Stuart's mission was to report on the military situation, whereas Deakin's was to consult with Tito on joint operational missions: "to arrange for the Partisan forces to attack specific targets on enemy lines of communication," his official instructions read, "...and to convey the wishes of GHQ, Middle East, to the Partisan GHQ and to report the point of view maintained by them."

Of the party of six, Ivan Starkevich, who was attached to Deakin as an interpreter, was one of the Camp X group. They arrived at the climax of the so-called "fifth offensive" launched by German forces to wipe out the partisans. Over 100,000 German and other Axis troops had Tito surrounded and were also attacking them from the air. As we have seen, Stuart, the Canadian SIS man, was killed in such an attack shortly after his arrival. But Tito, accompanied by the surviving members of Deakin's mission (code-named TYPICAL), broke out of the German encirclement and his partisans moved north into Bosnia. Within days the British chiefs of staff finally recognized that the partisans represented the most formidable anti-Axis fighting force outside Serbia.

With the dispatch of these missions in the spring of 1943, British policy had opened the door to a radical realignment of its policy towards the Yugoslav resistance. Missions still continued to be sent to Mihailovich and the Chetniks, but by the end of the year the British decided to cut their links with him. Early in 1944 they began to withdraw their missions, and by the end of the year Mihailovich was on his own.

Two years later, with Tito's Communists in complete control of post-war Yugoslavia, Mihailovich was captured in the Serbian hills where he and a few remnants of his Chetniks had taken refuge. Tried and found guilty of high treason, he was shot by a firing squad on July 17, 1946, and buried in an unmarked grave. "Destiny was merciless towards me," he told the court that condemned him, "when it threw me into the most difficult whirlwinds. I wanted much, I began much, but the whirlwind, the world whirlwind, carried me and my work away."[8]

More Camp-X-trained Canadian Yugoslavs were sent to the partisans in the summer of 1943. One of those who parachuted in that summer was Nikola Kombol, a middle-aged lumberjack from Vancouver. Between July 1943 and May 1944 he served as an interpreter to a number of the British teams operating in Bosnia and Serbia before being evacuated to Cairo because of ill health. But Kombol, a confirmed Communist, was determined to return. In September 1944 he parachuted back into his homeland, this time into Macedonia. After several months he found himself back at the SOE base in Bari, in southern Italy, and from there once again returned, this time by a motor gunboat across the Adriatic. Eventually he was recommended for the British Military Medal.

The HOATLEY group led by Serdar fought in Bosnia with the partisans until the end of the war. Here, in eastern Bosnia, Basil Davidson encountered them once again. He had been parachuted in during the summer of 1943 to link up with partisans in the Vojvodina, close to the Hungarian border, and was eventually to find himself crossing the Danube back into Hungary itself. He described Serdar and his friend George Diclich as tougher, more decisive, and thinner than when he had known them in Cairo, their battle dress uniform in rags. But both were immensely strong and muscle-bound. Having fought in Spain, they were radicals who knew exactly why they were there. "For them," Davidson remarked, "there were no degrees between black and white."

Five of the Camp X Yugoslav recruits died in the partisan war, either killed in battle or shot by their captors. Of the survivors, nearly all of whom parachuted into Yugoslavia as planned, most remained loyal to the cause for which they had volunteered in the first place. In the sparse language of a secret Canadian post-war report, "the British authorities encountered immense difficulties when operations drew to a close in withdrawing the Canadian Yugoslav agents...some of them...flatly refused to return either to their original pioneer units or, for that matter, to Canada."[9] Instead, they remained in post-war Yugoslavia to help build the society whose foundations they had helped to create in the bitter hills of their homeland.

At almost exactly the same time as these men had begun their missions at Camp X in the summer of 1942, there had been some significant changes in the running of the Camp. As noted earlier, Brooker's guiding belief during his time as commandant was that the key to its whole success lay in making a first-rate impression on the Americans. But what was to happen when this job was over and the Americans had absorbed basic SOE doctrine and had set up their own schools in America? With Brooker spending more and more time in Washington helping Ken Baker with his OSS schools, what was to happen at Camp X?

Neither the commandant nor the instructors had any direct responsibility for recruiting. This work was carried out by a specialized recruiting section set up at BSC headquarters in early 1942 which guaranteed continuity in the task of contacting, recruiting, training, and transporting trainees. It also provided liaison between BSC and the OSS and between the training needs of SOE and those of SIS, and it depended heavily on the work done by its agents in Canada, the United States, and Latin America.

From the beginning, Stephenson's organization faced a paradox in its search for recruits, especially where those assigned to become secret agents fighting behind enemy lines were concerned. The United States with its large heterogeneous population was potentially the most fruitful source of recruits; but so long as it remained neutral, it was reluctant to have any of its citizens or its resident aliens recruited by another nation, however friendly, for active service overseas. For that reason BSC found it difficult, if not impossible, before 1942, to get permission for the recruitment of Americans. After Pearl Harbor and the active entry of the United States into the war, the paradox changed shape but the problem remained. Now the Americans wanted recruits for their own organizations, and Stephenson was obliged to promise that he would not poach on American territory. In exchange for the valuable gifts he was able to give the OSS, the latter occasionally agreed to recruit for SOE in the United States. But this arrangement was limited and fell far short of meeting BSC requirements. After all, the OSS needed as many people as it could find for itself. By force of circumstance, therefore, BSC eyes turned elsewhere – to Canada and Latin America. Coincidental with this shift of emphasis away from the United States came the first major change in the Camp's leadership.

When Roper-Caldbeck returned with some relief to Britain in August 1942 to take over command of Audley End House, an SOE school for the training of Polish agents located south of Cambridge, Brooker's first job as the new commandant was to find a chief instructor and, predictably, his eyes turned to the advanced SOE school at Beaulieu. The chief instructor there was a man with whom Brooker had worked before, and, like himself, was a former field security officer trained in counter-intelligence work. While Canada was still absorbing some of the terrible losses of the Canadian troops at Dieppe, where almost 20 per cent of the Second Division were killed and almost 2,000 taken prisoner, Major Cuthbert Skilbeck arrived at Camp X to take over training.

At the outbreak of the war Skilbeck had answered an advertisement in *The Times* asking for people who spoke French and German. He had lived briefly in both Dresden and Paris in his late teens, and his working knowledge of both languages was sufficient to see him commissioned by March 1940 as a second lieutenant serving as field security officer in Marseilles. When France fell, he was evacuated from Marseilles to Gibraltar.

Once back in the United Kingdom, Skilbeck was posted to the Intelligence Corps and became an instructor in security at the Intelligence Training Centre at Matlock. He was recruited by SOE at almost the same time as Brooker, in March 1941, and as a captain worked closely with his future Camp X colleague at Beaulieu. "Having started the war in field security [counter-intelligence]," Skilbeck recalled, "it was a natural step to become an instructor in the reverse operations. Rightly, from a security point of view, each area of operations was kept secret from the other. Students at Beaulieu, and at other 'schools', had *noms de plume* and we had no concern with their ultimate work, though we had certain facts of their background to be able to assess their general value."[10]

Shortly before Brooker left for Canada, Skilbeck was promoted to major and became chief instructor to the finishing schools. In 1942 it was at Brooker's specific request that he was then sent out to Camp X as chief instructor. The two men knew each other well. They had had similar backgrounds since joining the army in 1939, they had both served in the Intelligence Corps, and both had helped to establish SOE training courses at Beaulieu, where they had shared a room.

Skilbeck, who had worked for the family firm, a City of London merchant company dealing in dye-stuffs, possessed personality and skills different from those of Brooker. But the two men got on well together, and if Skilbeck brought different assets to the job, they were complementary ones perfectly suited to the needs of Camp X in its middle and later life, when the emphasis shifted from giving priority to American needs to the training of recruits in Canada itself.

This was only a relative, not an absolute, shift. Under Skilbeck the Camp X staff continued to work closely with American agencies;

Skilbeck himself spent much time in the United States, and OSS men were being trained at the Camp as late as the fall of 1943. But the vital public relations work with the Americans had been done under Brooker. Now, the emphasis was on hard work and training within the Camp, and on letting the variety of instructors get on with their work in their own ways. Relations with the Canadians needed to be intensified, and at this Skilbeck was eminently successful – so successful, indeed, that when Camp X closed down the Canadian government asked him to help with the de-Nazification programme among German prisoners of war held in Canada.

"I spent some ten months in Ottawa and London on this fruitless job," he recalls, before eventually returning to civilian life in London at the end of the war.

Scarcely had Skilbeck established himself at Camp X in August 1942 than he was faced with his first major challenge. "I remember the evening when at dinner a telex arrived ordering us to prepare a two-week course of security training and to send the syllabus and details back to the UK then and there." He stayed up with Brooker all that night devising a special syllabus, and the two men sent it back to London via HYDRA the next day for approval.

But what was it all about? Where was the emergency that created such a panic demand? As Skilbeck soon learned, it was a response to the situation in South America. From the beginning of the war until the tide turned in the Allies' favour, there was substantial anxiety, particularly in the United States, about German activity and influence there. Memories of German efforts to involve Mexico in the First World War still lingered, and as early as October 1939 the Americans had stage-managed an inter-American conference at Panama to insulate the New World from the conflicts of the Old by establishing a security zone that extended in places as far as 1,000 miles from the eastern coastline.

But the nightmare that really haunted the Americans was the spectre of the fifth column. Mesmerized by extravagant reports about German fifth-column successes in the collapse of France and Western Europe in the spring of 1940, Americans projected their fears onto the large German populations of the South American republics, which in total amounted to about 1,750,000 people of German origin. These fears led in 1940 to a major marketing campaign to sell the image of a benevolent Uncle Sam throughout Latin America – a cultural and political offensive dubbed by one cynic "Pattin' the Latin".

Brazil was a special source of anxiety. Strategically it dominated the Atlantic coast of South America, and its German minority amounted to almost a million people. There were strong commercial links with Germany, the government was a right-wing dictatorship, and the *Abwehr* had constructed an extensive espionage network in the country. German agents were relaying information about Allied raw materials and Atlantic convoys, as well as intelligence transmitted by agents in the United States, Canada, and other Latin American countries. Americans were particularly afraid that the Germans might acquire military bases in the region and give the Third Reich a foothold in the Western Hemisphere. Fifth-column fears escalated after the fall of France. J. Edgar Hoover declared that "the best way to control Nazi espionage in the United States [is] to wipe out the spy nests in Latin America", and in June 1940 the FBI set up a Special Intelligence Service to cover Latin America.

BSC also gave the region high priority. Stephenson, his ear acutely tuned to American sensitivities on the one hand and, on the other, to London's desire to impress on the Americans the common dangers they faced from the Nazis, made sure that he kept the Americans supplied with information about the region. When Roosevelt appointed Nelson A. Rockefeller as Co-ordinator of Inter-American Affairs in August 1940 with a mandate to strengthen American and undermine German economic influence throughout Latin America, BSC provided much of the basic intelligence with which Rockefeller's organization worked. Stephenson also established a Ships' Observers Scheme by which British agents were placed on all neutral ships sailing from South American ports to report on anti-Allied behaviour – a scheme that eventually employed over four hundred people. A special section in BSC kept a close eye on all Latin American strategic raw materials, and BSC agents throughout the region helped to protect supplies destined for Allied use.

Churchill was particularly concerned about Latin America because of his obsessive awareness that Britain's lifeline lay across the Atlantic to the Western Hemisphere. Throughout 1941, as he desperately worked to create an effective alliance with the neutral United States, he urged on everyone the dangers to strategic raw materials in

South America through espionage and enemy subversion. After the United States entered the war, the situation worsened. The Battle of the Atlantic became an unrestricted war, and although many South American states, responding to U.S. pressure, cut their official links with Germany early in 1942, vital raw materials from the Western Hemisphere were more vulnerable than ever. In Chile and Argentina, which did not break off diplomatic relations, German espionage continued undisturbed.

Throughout the winter and spring of 1942, Allied shipping losses in the Atlantic mounted daily. This was what the German Navy came to know as "the happy time", when Admiral Karl Doenitz's U-boats, with an almost free run of the American seaboard, devastated Allied vessels. Operation PAUKENSCHLUG (KETTLEDRUM-ROLL), launched by Doenitz against American shipping two days after Pearl Harbor, exploited the hopeless unpreparedness of the U.S. Navy for submarine warfare. Convoys were massacred off the American, Caribbean, and South American coasts, and by March Churchill was demanding to Roosevelt that urgent action be taken. He even offered, in a telling reversal of roles, to provide the Americans with some Royal Navy corvettes. By June, General Marshall told Admiral Ernest King, who was in charge of the U.S. Navy, that "the losses by submarines off our Atlantic seaboard and in the Caribbean now threaten our entire war effort." Three million tons of Allied shipping and over five hundred ships had been sunk in the Atlantic since Pearl Harbor, and the summer of 1942 witnessed anxious discussions in London about the crucial issue of raw material supplies.

In early June, Britain's top intelligence experts in the Joint Intelligence Committee took an intensive look at the threat to supplies from Latin America by enemy organizations active in the region. "Enemy power and influence in Latin America," they concluded, "though unlikely to be used immediately in a major attack on Allied supplies, constitute a serious danger which may at any time become critical. This danger would be greatly reduced by the destruction of enemy organizations both German and Japanese."[11] The threat was not only to Allied supplies, the Joint Intelligence Committee concluded: it lay also in the help that Axis sympathizers might give to enemy raiders and submarines off the coast of South America, and in the vulnerability to subversive action of many South American governments.

Immediate action to destroy German organizations throughout Latin America was urgently needed.

This was easier to recommend than to put into practice. As we have seen, the Americans jealously guarded South America as being in their own sphere of influence, and if Allied relations were to remain harmonious, it would have to be the Americans who took the lead. But as the Joint Planning Staff of the British Chiefs quickly pointed out, American reliance on conventional diplomacy in Latin America, even with all the economic power the United States could exert, would not accomplish the desired goal. Donovan and the OSS had been forbidden to operate in the region, and J. Edgar Hoover, who had rigidly kept the FBI's monopoly of security control over Latin America, was concerned with American, not British, interests. Stephenson and BSC had been able to take very little direct counter-action of their own to protect these British interests against Axis subversive activity. The only successful step had been the Ships' Observers Scheme. And even though the gravity of the situation had now prompted Roosevelt himself to ask the British for full details about SIS and SOE methods, he was not prepared to give them a free hand in America's backyard. "Neither our own nor the United States policy at present goes nearly far enough," the Joint Planners concluded. "In fact the enemy is having almost a free run."

So what could the British do? The Chiefs of Staff decided on June 8 that one thing was to develop as fully as possible an efficient SIS and communications system throughout Latin America. With better information about Axis activity, there would be a greater chance of convincing the Americans to act decisively. Another step would be to intensify SOE activity in the region. This would not necessarily be through violent means, the Chiefs of Staff concluded, but "by financial and economic attack on enemy individuals and organizations with a view to discrediting or disrupting their activities." Finally, and perhaps most effectively of all in the circumstances, the British communities throughout South America should be organized to join in the effort. "British Security Co-ordination," the Chiefs noted, "can also assist by extending the present overt measures at South American ports to warehouses, mines, and depots further inland."

. These high-level decisions in London to expand the security effort throughout South America quickly made themselves felt at Camp X in the summer of 1942. For if BSC was to train large numbers of people from the area in counter-sabotage and security, where better to do this than at Brooker's school at Whitby? Within days of the London meeting, Stephenson had received his orders and had given the issue top priority in New York. The man he placed in charge was Mostyn Davies, a former British civil servant who had just arrived in New York with Louis Franck's mission from SOE headquarters in London. Like others who came from London on a recruiting mission, Davies was eventually himself sent overseas on a secret mission, once his work at BSC was finished, to contact Bulgarian partisans about whom SOE knew very little. Tragically, neither Davies nor his second-in-command was to survive. Both were caught and shot by the Germans in 1944. But in New York in 1942 Davies and the others worked hard on the South American scheme.

It was an exceptionally delicate issue, the enemy being almost as much the American FBI director as the Germans or Japanese. SOE's presence in South America had been steadily built up from the time that BSC set up its special operations division in early 1941. By June 1942 SOE claimed, according to the most recent information from SOE archives in London, to have fourteen chief agents employing two hundred and nine sub-agents in place. But these efforts were hampered in general by American sensitivities about unilateral British intervention in South America, and in particular by Hoover's jealousy.

One SOE officer who had suffered from this was none other than Bill Deakin, the man later parachuted to Tito. In the early summer of 1941 Deakin was suddenly ordered by Baker Street to join BSC in New York, where his task would be to set up a Latin American SOE section. This began, Deakin now remembers, "an eccentric interlude in my service with SOE."12 Knowing neither Spanish nor Portuguese, and ignorant of Latin America, Deakin found himself working with Ivar Bryce under the command of Richard Coit. The Latin American scheme involved establishing a network of agents to identify and disrupt Nazi, Italian, and – after Pearl Harbor – Japanese anti-Allied activities. Lists of names were drawn up, consisting mostly of members of the local British communities, and, Deakin remembered, "we did draw some splendid maps." But little or no sabotage was carried out, and the whole operation was suddenly cut short in the spring of 1942 when Hoover, as part of his campaign to bring Stephenson to heel, forced BSC radically to curtail its operations in South America.

Even in the face of the crisis that summer the American Chiefs of Staff showed as great a possessiveness about the region as did Hoover, and the British initiative was smothered. "The U.S. attitude," the British Joint Staff Mission in Washington reported back to London on September 21, "showed clearly that they consider security matters in Latin America to be a matter concerning U.S. alone."[13]

The American Joint Chiefs of Staff, indeed, insisted that American programmes in the area were adequate, even if they were not all yet in full effect. "It is [the] firm conviction of Joint US Chiefs of Staff," British officials in Washington were told, "that [the] status quo should be maintained [in] Latin America." In the long term, this put a veto on SOE operations in South America altogether. On November 20, 1942, Louis Franck recommended to London that SOE should withdraw from the region on the grounds that, in the words of an SOE document, "at this stage of the war, the usefulness of SO in Latin America is virtually at an end." SOE London accepted the inevitable. Its archives reveal that by April 1943 its organization had been reduced from three hundred and four people to nine (six "observers" and three secretaries). Eighteen months later, even this skeleton structure had disappeared.[14]

In the short term, however, the British persisted with their plan to increase security. The project to use Camp X to train members of SOE's Latin American network earlier identified by Bryce and Deakin, therefore, had to be carried out with considerable care. Bickham Sweet-Escott, newly arrived in Washington that summer, remembered how these men "were told to be exceptionally discreet in Washington and New York about the object of their journey."[15]

The first recruits from Latin America completed their training in August 1942, and thereafter for several months Camp X witnessed the arrival by air of a steady stream of men every two weeks. By early 1943 a network of agents – known as industrial security officers – covered South America. For the most part they were senior personnel from British-owned or -controlled companies. "Railwaymen from Argentina, Peru, Chile, Venezuela and Colombia," Skilbeck remembered, "managers from the great meat-packing firms of

Argentina and from the hydroelectric undertakings – all started by British money and under British management." Some of them were quite elderly, and for those in the later groups, going up to Canada during the Ontario winter was as challenging as the two-week course. "We had some fifteen-twenty senior men arriving by air every two weeks in deep winter. As many had lived most of their lives in places where they hadn't seen snow since they were children in England, Ontario in winter was quite an experience." But in Skilbeck's view the recruits from Latin America were excellent. They were keen, they were highly motivated, and Camp X gave them a real sense of actively assisting in the British war effort.

SOE London felt the same way. Sir Charles Hambro reported in November 1942 to Lord Selborne that by the end of January 1943 "thirty-nine Industrial Security Officers will be at work in South America. Much credit," he added, "must go to STS 103...instructors have shown unending patience with difficult students and all of these return with a new outlook and as keen as mustard to get on with a job they have already done well in the field."[16]

After leaving Whitby, trainees discussed with specialists at BSC in New York specially prepared reports on the security of their particular enterprises. These then formed the basis of their preliminary instructions in anti-sabotage and security techniques that they introduced throughout Latin America. With only small exceptions, an internal BSC report noted in March 1943, all British railways, power companies, oilfields, *frigorificos*, essential mineral undertakings, and merchant houses had been brought into the scheme, which encompassed six administrative zones throughout the continent.[17] The scheme provides a useful reminder that BSC was as interested in security as it was in offensive intelligence, that it trained people in counter-espionage as well as sabotage, and that its field of operational responsibility lay in the Americas, not Europe.

Norman Delahunty, on his way down to South America later in 1942, was an unwitting beneficiary of the vigilance of the British industrial security officers. Finding himself in some difficulty while being interrogated by an American customs official in Panama over the passport given to him by BSC in New York, he suddenly felt a tap on his shoulder.

"I say, didn't we meet in Washington last week, old chap?" said a British voice, which then firmly addressed its attention to the customs officer and vouched for Delahunty's identity. There were no more questions and Delahunty quickly found himself shepherded through formalities by the owner of the voice, a man he had certainly never seen before in Washington or anywhere else. The man identified himself as a soft-drinks salesman working in La Paz, Bolivia, who had simply "wanted to help a chap out". He then offered to show him around Panama City, and Delahunty, with twenty-four hours to kill, agreed. He never learned the man's name and, with Brooker's lectures at Camp X on security firmly in mind, was careful not to give anything away. Caution turned to suspicion when his guide dropped a reference to Oshawa and asked if he knew a man named "Busty". Since this was the nickname of one of the wireless instructors at the Camp, Delahunty quickly changed the subject. Was the man a German spy? he wondered.

That night, doubling up with the man in a hotel room because of a shortage of rooms in the city, he slept with his passport under the pillow. He need not have worried. His guide was one of the Camp-X-trained South American security officers who had been commissioned by New York to keep an eye on the young man in transit.[18]

Camp X served the needs of BSC headquarters as well as those of the recruits destined for Europe and South America. Like the OSS Farm in Maryland, the SOE Farm in Canada helped to indoctrinate the men who were to handle and train the field operatives. Like Donovan at OSS and Brooker at Camp X, Stephenson firmly believed that those involved at BSC headquarters in security and the running of agents of various kinds should have some flavour of the job their recruits were going to undertake. Hence many a senior BSC executive, accustomed to a more comfortable New York or Washington lifestyle, would find himself on the train to Toronto bound for a one- or two-week course at Camp X. At the very least this would remove a few inches from his waist. At the most it might give him an insight into what life in the field was really like.

Tom Hill was typical of the many BSC staff from New York who spent some time at Camp X. Hill had been doing editorial work for trade journals in Toronto when he was recruited by Stephenson for

BSC. Within a short while he was compiling intelligence reports for SIS and acting as a personal assistant to Stephenson at his New York headquarters.

One of his major jobs was to produce the *Western Hemisphere Weekly Intelligence Bulletin.* Stephenson conceived the idea, Hill now remembers, because "it could be useful to people in the field who might be able to relate a development in another country with something going on in their own [and] to boost their morale."[19] Based on all incoming reports to BSC – with the exception only of material likely to blow an agent's cover – the report ran to ten or twelve single-spaced mimeographed pages and was sent, not just to BSC people in the field, but also to London and to the British Embassy in Washington. Stephenson later described it as "a model of the way in which vital information should be selected and set out. It enriched our 'shop window' whose viewers, as you know, are privileged and few."

In 1942 Stephenson decided that Hill and several other head-quarters staff should take a course at Camp X. Most were people with journalistic background working on intelligence or propaganda, but there was also a former RCMP officer, Ernest Bavin, who took care of many of the Camp X trainees passing through New York on their way to Europe. Bavin, indeed, had resigned his position as a super-intendent in the RCMP to join BSC, but remained in close liaison with Canadian authorities on all security issues. "Nobody told us why we were being sent," Hill now says, "but I rather assumed it was partly for morale purposes and partly to give us a feel of how things were done in intelligence jobs other than those done at typewriters."[20]

Hill's impression of the Camp was of a bustling place with an important job to do, and in the week that he and the others spent there he had little time to relax. Like all students he wore army fatigues to help maintain the Camp's cover as a regular military operation and, like them, he learned something about the full range of SOE agent training. "We took lectures about codes and ciphers and techniques of tailing, and sessions about how to use a revolver or other hand-gun and shoot quickly and effectively without pausing to take aim, and how to do the same sort of thing with a Tommy gun."

The BSC staff also learned about silent killing and demolitions. But since these skills were unlikely to be needed within the safe confines of Rockefeller Center, they were observed rather than learned.

There was some limited practice in close combat, but not enough for them to make use of, and when it came to explosives they merely received a lecture and were then treated to one of Milner's or his successor's spectacular demonstrations. Unlike those chosen for work behind enemy lines, they neither handled explosives nor learned about wireless transmission; nor did they have to take part in extensive daytime and nighttime exercises outside the Camp. Neither did they do a great deal of physical training, although to deskbound journalists even the most moderate course at Camp X must have seemed like arduous exercise. And they rose early. "A batman brought me tea at six o'clock in the morning," Hill remembers.

Hill journeyed to the Camp with a colleague, Cedric Belfrage, whose post-war career was to take a highly controversial turn. A journalist and a British subject, he was to be expelled from the United States in 1953 during the McCarthy witch hunts because of his alleged Communist sympathies. Within BSC he was one of a small group of left-wing idealists who saw the war principally as a fight against fascism. Belfrage was working in the intelligence side of BSC when Stephenson sent him to Camp X. "We were all looking out for possible recruits for parachute missions and were supposed to get acquainted with what we were recruiting for", is how Belfrage now recalls the experience. "At the same time we were necessarily security-minded and expected to forget the details. For my part, I've forgotten them anyway."[21]

Another BSC executive who took the trip to Canada was David Ogilvy, who later made his post-war reputation as one of Madison Avenue's most successful advertising men, founding the huge agency of Ogilvy and Mather. One of the most well-known and highly successful campaigns he initiated was "The Man in the Hathaway Shirt" series, which featured photographs of an elegant man sporting an eye patch. "At sixty miles an hour the loudest noise in this new Rolls-Royce comes from the electric clock" was another of his inventive advertising headlines. The trick, Ogilvy wrote recently in his *Confessions of an Advertising Man*, was to give the ads "a strong dose of 'story appeal' [that] would make readers stop and take notice."

There was plenty in Ogilvy's own life to provide a good story-line. A Briton who immigrated to the United States at the outbreak of the war after working for a London ad agency, Ogilvy joined forces

with Dr. George Gallup and quickly learned the value of public-opin-
ion sampling in developing marketing skills. Soon he was putting
these at Stephenson's disposal as well as working as a junior intelligence officer at the British Embassy in Washington. "Here," he wrote
in the memoirs he called *Blood, Brains and Beer*, "the game was to
see how many telegrams I could get approved by the hypercritical
levels above me; my record was forty-two in four weeks.... I marvel
at my ability to write with the austerity that was required, and to
master the complexity of the subjects."

For Stephenson, Ogilvy collected and manipulated economic
intelligence from Latin America. "Our primary function," he recalls,
"was to ruin businessmen whom we knew to be working against the
Allies, and to prevent Hitler laying his hands on strategic materials –
industrial diamonds, tungsten, vanadium, antimony, etc. I came to
know more about these matters than anyone in Washington, and was
able to give OSS an average of forty reports a day."

But it was the rugged and dangerous life of a secret agent in
Occupied Europe that caught Ogilvy's imagination when he joined
BSC, and the course at Camp X was his first assignment. It was a far
cry from the world of the Rolls-Royce and the button-down shirt.
"Here," he wrote, "I was taught the tricks of the trade. How do you
follow people without arousing their suspicion? Walk in *front* of
them; if you also push a pram this will disarm their suspicions still
further. I was taught to use a revolver, to blow up bridges and power
lines with plastic, to cripple police dogs by grabbing their front feet
and tearing their chests apart, and to kill a man with my bare hands."

Accompanying Ogilvy was Jean-Paul Evans, a counter-
intelligence expert whom we shall meet again later for his part in the
Gouzenko affair. For Evans, Camp X was "certainly extremely
interesting and I think gave us a good idea of the kind of training
through which agents were put."22 Yet another of the BSC visitors to
Camp X was Bill Ross-Smith, an Australian-born businessman, who
was principally responsible for building up the Ships' Observers
Scheme. Ross-Smith spent at least two interludes at Camp X, and once
stayed three or four months helping the instructional staff.

One of those sent to Camp X while Ross-Smith was there was
Daniel Hadekel, a member of a Russian *émigré* family that had settled

in Canada just before the outbreak of war. Recruited into BSC from naval work at Halifax, Hadekel was assigned to its counter-espionage section, where he worked on Latin American cases. In the summer of 1942 he was sent to Camp X for a two-week course of basic training. The full ritual of clandestine rendezvous was impressed upon him when he received his instructions in New York. He was to take the train to Oshawa where he would be met by a maroon-coloured Mercury. He was to confirm his identity to the driver by asking, "Is this Campbell's car?" The driver would then answer, "Yes, he sent me for you." But Hadekel, like many an initiate into the mysteries of secret service, was soon to discover that theory often differed markedly from practice. On arrival at Oshawa station he found himself with five or six others self-consciously trying to look inconspicuous. To add to their embarrassment, no maroon-coloured vehicle was visible. They tried to look purposeful while the other passengers left the station. Eventually, only an old Ford station wagon was left. After several minutes Hadekel finally went up to it and asked the driver, "Is this it?" "Sure," came the reply, "hop in." But if the rendezvous was less polished than it might have been, the course was "well run and tough." Hadekel learned about small arms and silent killing, and experienced security from the offensive end by penetrating guarded factories and warehouses on exercises.[23]

None of these men served overseas. But the training they received at Oshawa helped to emphasize the need for the most careful training in security, and gave them an insight into the intricacies of clandestine life.

At about the time the first group of Camp-X-trained Yugoslav Canadians finally arrived in Cairo, and while the unstoppable Colonel Keble was launching his campaign to send a mission to the partisans in Bosnia and Croatia, SOE in London realized that the expansion of its activities in Yugoslavia would require many more recruits able to speak Serbo-Croat. Bailey and Stuart had hoped to find a hundred volunteers during their summer recruiting mission in Canada, but in the end only about forty had been suitable even for Camp X. SOE, hoping to find more, once again informed BSC of its needs, and in turn BSC contacted Drew-Brook, who then discussed the request in

Ottawa. In mid-January 1943 he was able to tell Stephenson that the path had once again been cleared.

By now Bailey had been parachuted to Mihailovich's head-quarters, and Stuart was with the first Yugoslav group training in the Middle East, so SOE sent out yet another of the Yugoslav experts to interview Canadian recruits. Major R.F. Lethbridge arrived in Toronto by mid-January and remained in Canada until the end of March 1943. Like Bailey and Stuart, Lethbridge had worked in Yugoslavia before the war, and as a mining engineer had been involved with some of Stephenson's pre-war business interests in the area.

In the course of Lethbridge's recruitment drive, he and Drew-Brook had worked out an arrangement with the National Defence Headquarters whereby all recruits for Camp X would in the first instance be enlisted into the Canadian Army. This had the immediate advantage of placing them under military discipline and of increasing the security of the operation. Each man had to sign a declaration that he also agreed to transfer to the British Army when requested. Once enlisted, and having passed Canadian Army medical tests, the recruit was posted to Military District 2 and then transferred to Camp X. After training, the recruit was discharged from the Canadian Army and transferred to the British Army as soon as he arrived at a British port. If he proved unsuitable for special duties, he was transferred back to the Canadian Army and Military District 2. All financial commitments from the moment of enlistment were ultimately covered by the British. Drew-Brook was able to inform Ottawa on January 13, 1943, that SOE London had agreed to this plan. From then on, this procedure applied to practically all recruits who volunteered for special duty and were trained at Camp X. The only exceptions in 1942 were the large group of wireless operators who retained civilian status and were employed directly by BSC itself.[24]

Drew-Brook's arrangements in the winter of 1943 to have all Camp X recruits enlisted in the Canadian military reflected a much broader change taking place in SOE and OSS that was to put an end to what has been described as "the Brooker era".

Throughout the previous months, pressure had been mounting for SOE and the OSS to bring their command, doctrine, and operations into line with the needs of the military. Donovan and the OSS were now operating under directives from the American Chiefs of Staff, and SOE, initially regarded by the British military with profound distrust as an amateurish and dangerous outfit, was itself becoming more military. Gubbins, now a major-general, became the deputy head of SOE in December 1942 and finally replaced the banker Sir Charles Hambro as its head in the following summer. So far as training was concerned, these trends had a profound effect. Schools designed for small and specialized groups of individuals with well-defined tasks known in advance, or for individual secret agents engaged in undercover operations behind enemy lines, were all very well. But as the Allies moved over to the offensive after the North African landings and the desert victories against Rommel, needs changed. The British and the Americans in general, and Donovan and Gubbins in particular, began to envisage major operations in partisan warfare in places such as Yugoslavia, Greece, and North Italy, not to mention the eventual D-Day landings. It was obvious that SOE-OSS training would have to become both more paramilitary and better geared to training large numbers of men. In short, the "cloak-and-dagger" era was coming to an end. Those who found themselves out of step would have to go.

Kenneth Baker was forced to take a commission in the U.S. Army in the spring of 1943 in order to help solve many of the problems of supply and the handling of military recruits. But he did so reluctantly. He was even more resistant to changing the OSS syllabus away from the one he had so carefully learned, and then refined, from Brooker and the SOE curriculum at Camp X. His differences with the military slowly built up over the early months of 1943 and came to a crisis in July when the chief instructor at his Maryland Farm, an ex-newspaperman called Knox Chandler, committed suicide. Baker, who had already taken a short leave of absence to attend the staff school at Fort Leavenworth, was now relieved of all control of OSS training. As for Brooker, Baker's ally in many a struggle to get OSS training on its feet in the pioneer days, he had already left Camp X. In March 1943 SOE had transferred him first to Beaulieu, then to the joint SOE-OSS school in Algiers. Although he was to keep a strong con - nection with the OSS until the end of the war – Brooker ended up escorting OSS students through the British schools – his days at Camp

X were over. Skilbeck now took his place, and remained commandant until the Camp closed down. Brooker's transfer was routine – he had been at Camp X since December 1941 and all the British staff were regularly rotated – but it was also true that he found himself out of sympathy with the growing paramilitary nature of secret operations and never disguised his views about this. In any case, by that time he had more than accomplished his original mission. "The school is really well run," two observers from London had reported to SOE during an inspection in March 1942, "and all credit should be given to those responsible, especially to the Chief Instructor, Major Brooker, in whom the Americans have full confidence." Later, on New Year's Eve, 1942, Sir Charles Hambro himself wrote to Brooker expressing his appreciation of the work of the staff at Camp X. "You have all done a splendid bit of work in 1942," he said, "and you can all congratulate yourselves on the fact that the school in Canada is one of the best advertisements that we have got in America and has done a very great deal to cement the good feelings between SOE and OSS."[25]

The same month that Brooker left Camp X, Major H.A. Benson, SOE's number-two man at BSC in New York, went up to Camp X for a personal inspection tour. In a report now to be found in the SOE archives, he reported that "The spirit of STS 103 is good and the discipline is high. The Camp is well kept and it compares favourably with training establishments of a similar character in England."[26] BSC itself now drew up a secret balance sheet on the Camp's achievements since its opening sixteen months before. Two hundred and seventy-three students in thirty courses had graduated from Camp X. Of these, the largest single group, fifty-eight, consisted of those trained for special operations in the field, and of these twenty-two were Yugoslavs. The next largest group was formed of the South American security officers, of whom there were fifty-three. There followed forty Americans trained for the OSS, including fourteen instructors, and then an additional twenty-seven trained for the Office of War Information, the propaganda agency. A further six Americans had been trained for the psychological warfare branch of the U.S. Army, and the FBI had sent up ten of its men. Four RCMP men had received Camp X training, and twenty-one of BSC's own staff on the special operations side from New York had taken courses there. Nineteen W/T operators had been trained at the HYDRA facility.

The Secret Intelligence Service had also benefited from the STS 103 facilities. Thirteen of its field agents had attended courses, two fewer than the number of SIS office staff from New York and Washington. More important than the numbers was the judgement of BSC's own report on its training achievement. Although designed to boost its own position with London, it nonetheless aptly described the Camp's principal achievements: "The school has fulfilled a usefulness which cannot be underestimated in creating and developing friendly feelings towards Britain by those American organizations which have made use of it."[27]

CHAPTER 8

"Blood and Tears":
Missions Behind Enemy Lines

By the summer of 1943 the tide of war had turned decisively in favour of the Allies. The Germans had surrendered at Stalingrad in February and in North Africa in May. Within the space of four weeks, between June 29 and July 25, American forces landed in New Guinea, the Russians defeated the Germans at Kursk in the greatest tank battle of the war, Sicily was invaded, and Mussolini was deposed as Italian dictator. In September, Allied forces landed on the Italian mainland, and within a month the Italians had changed sides to help close the ring around Hitler's diminishing Reich.

For SOE and the OSS, these developments opened up vast new opportunities and also brought much of their long-range planning substantially closer to fruition. In the West, D-Day was now in sight and SOE-OSS plans for mobilizing the French resistance had to be carefully integrated with the strategic and tactical planning of the Allied high command. The occupation of Italy gave new strength and urgency to special operations in the Balkans and Central Europe. From bases in southern Italy, SOE and OSS were now in a far stronger position than before to wage war behind enemy lines.

Camp X was directly affected by these developments, which that summer led SOE to comb the New World once again for recruits suitable for operations into France, northern Italy, the Balkans, and Central Europe. From Brooker's departure in March 1943 until the end of the year, a varied assortment of recruits for these areas passed through the Camp.

*

There were also some major changes in the training staff at this time. Skilbeck, as the new commandant, was faced with the same problem that Brooker had been. Where was he to find a suitable chief instructor? And, as before, the answer lay at Beaulieu. Its chief propaganda instructor, Paul Dehn, soon found himself following the well-trodden path to Camp X.

Paul Dehn's career with SOE formed a brief and intriguing interlude in the life of a man whose work is familiar to millions but whose name remains largely unknown. Dehn was a highly successful post-war screen writer, producing screenplays for such films as *Seven Days to Noon*, Zeffirelli's version of *The Taming of the Shrew*, Anthony Asquith's *Orders to Kill*, and – just two years before his death from lung cancer in 1976 – *Murder on the Orient Express*. Appropriately enough for a man whose last SOE mission during the war was to write a handbook called *Agent Techniques in the Field,* he also wrote screenplays for three of the best-known post-war spy films: *Goldfinger*, from Ian Fleming's James Bond novel of the same title, and two films based on John le Carré best sellers, *The Deadly Affair* and *The Spy Who Came In from the Cold.*

Dehn's knowledge of both spying and the cold was based on personal experience, much of it gained in Canada. It was a bitter winter night in 1943 when he arrived in Toronto to be met by Skilbeck. As they drove to Camp X through the deserted streets of what was then widely known as "Toronto the Good", memories of stern North Country nonconformity stirred in Dehn's Jewish soul. "My God," he said, "it reminds me of Manchester on a Sunday." He quickly set out to dispel any Presbyterian gloom that might affect the Camp. At Beaulieu he had shown a remarkable talent for entertainment. Kim Philby thought he was the star of the team and described him as a man "who bubbled and frothed like a trout stream [and whose] tomfoolery at the piano shortened the long summer evenings."[1] Many a long night at Camp X was similarly enlivened.

George Glazebrook, the Canadian official in the Department of External Affairs who by this time was in charge of BSC liaison, went to Camp X for a weekend briefing course as part of a group that included the directors of Canadian Intelligence and Tommy Drew-Brook. One of the strongest memories he retained was of an evening in the mess with Dehn at the piano singing a song he had just composed entitled "Love Me Three Times a Day, After Meals". If at Beaulieu Dehn had shown what the official history of SOE has described as a "vivid imagination and a rollicking sense of humour", at Camp X he was, in the words of one of his colleagues, "a bloody good night-club act."

But there was far more to Dehn than a quick wit, a piano, and a pack of cigarettes. He was a first-rate instructor who had been classified at Beaulieu, in the words of official SOE records, as "outstandingly good".[2] For all his surface froth, he was, to use Philby's words again, "a serious man with a warm and generous strain of romanticism". Like his two predecessors he had enjoyed the privilege of a private education (Shrewsbury and Oxford), and had also spent time in the Intelligence Corps before being recruited into SOE where, before moving to Beaulieu, he had been a personal assistant to Gubbins.

His parents were prosperous Manchester cotton merchants; his godfather was the prominent drama critic James Agate. It was Agate's example that had inspired Dehn to become a writer, and from Agate he had learned the basic lessons about this deceptively easy skill, the eventual mastery of which not only turned him into an expert writer of screenplays but also an accomplished librettist, poet, and lyricist. The combination of a powerful imagination, great sensitivity, and a strongly developed linguistic gift made Dehn a highly effective instructor. Skilbeck thought his greatest strength was as "a good thinker and a clear talker".

SOE evidently thought the same. After Camp X closed down, they sent him to London and to liberated France to work on political warfare techniques. When Germany surrendered, he undertook an SOE interrogation mission in Norway. Finally, he completed his SOE work by compiling the agent handbook in which he distilled the experience he had garnered both at Beaulieu and at Camp X. It was hard for some of his wartime colleagues to reconcile this man with the bachelor who in later life became an ardent ornithologist. But Dehn had merely transferred his acute perceptive skills to a less harmful species.

Dehn also received high marks from the Americans. Despite their gradual emancipation from reliance on the British, they still occasionally made use of the expertise available at Camp X. During the crisis of that summer caused by Ken Baker's departure as head of OSS training, they turned once again to the British. Cuthbert Skilbeck spent most of July and August 1943 in Washington as special adviser on training, filling in the gap between Baker and his successor. Dehn went with him and immediately impressed the Americans with his chosen field of expertise in black propaganda, which the OSS described as Morale Operations (MO).

"Black" – as distinct from "white" – propaganda was both subversive and disguised in origin. Its methods included false rumours; leaflets and documents; the running of "freedom stations", which were radio broadcasts pretending to be operating from behind enemy lines but which were in fact run by the Allies; and the support of fifth-column activities. In 1943, OSS Morale Operations – regarded by many field officers as a form of rear-echelon insanity – was under the control of Fred Oeschner, a former bureau chief of the United Press Agency office in Berlin who would later be the first to approach future CIA director Richard Helms – whom he had sent as a rookie correspondent to cover the Nuremberg Rally in 1936 – about joining the OSS. Oeschner was so impressed by Dehn's abilities that he tried unsuccessfully to have him transferred permanently from Camp X to the OSS.

But that summer Dehn spent most of his time in the United States lecturing on propaganda to the main OSS basic training school at Area E, a site in Maryland some thirty miles from Baltimore consisting of three country houses on an isolated estate. He also helped Skilbeck, who had temporarily taken charge of the short briefing course at The Farm. During the special weekend course for several OSS officers in August, the two of them put on an impressive show, with practical demonstrations from Fairbairn. The three of them covered the entire range of subjects from recruiting to morale operations in the field.

Dehn surpassed even Brooker as a raconteur who could hold and entertain his audience. Post-war OSS historians described him as "one of the finest lecturers to grace a classroom.... Listening to one of Major Dehn's lectures," they said, "was better than reading the most exciting of spy thrillers."[3]

Millions of movie goers would undoubtedly agree. Indeed, the *International Encyclopedia of Film* suggests that his *best* screenplays drew upon his experiences as a major in the SOE. This is most immediately apparent in his 1958 award-winning screenplay of *Orders to Kill*. Bosley Crowther, writing for the *New York Times*, gives us its flavour. "The point is made very clearly that only the toughest, most cold-blooded and emotionally stable people were used to perform the critical assignments of counter-espionage in World War II. Then it goes right ahead to show us a completely soft and unstable guy being given the task of destroying a treacherous member of the French underground."[4]

The hero is identified as an American airman, "played in a conspicuously delicate fashion by Paul Massie [*sic*], a young Canadian", trained by a character called Major MacMahon, not unlike our Major Fairbairn of Camp X. And what did he learn? "Our chap is drilled intensively, schooled in the techniques of killing a man commando-fashion and taught to have no pity at all." These scenes must have been very graphic, for Dehn's brother now recalls some trouble with the censor over the documentary detail on the "how to kill" sequences. Having made his way to occupied Paris, 1944, however, the young flyer is appalled to discover that he actually likes his victim, a gentle little man who likes cats, and, even worse, he believes the Frenchman to be innocent. Urged on by a woman in the underground, he does the deed but, eventually, pays a high price. He becomes a guilt-ridden alcoholic.

The reviewer concludes that "this promising melodrama loses steam and credibility and ends in a sad heap of sentiment that should make an old cloak and dagger boy turn gray." The current edition of Halliwell's *Film Guide* has kinder words: "Strong, hard to take but well-made war story about the effects of war on conscience."

Dehn's screenplays often had such an undercurrent, for he continued throughout his career to suggest that our chosen political and ecological paths will lead us to our destruction. The most popular forum for these views is his screenplays for the *Planet of the Apes* film series of the 1970s. As well as being fascinating science fiction, they are political allegories about our collective extinction after a nuclear holocaust.

This same message is clear in his *Seven Days to Noon*, for which, with his co-author James Bernard, he won an Oscar in 1952. Here an atomic scientist, realizing the ultimate madness of pursuing his ex-

periments, breaks under the strain and threatens to blow up London
unless all research on atomic weapons, world-wide, is immediately
scrapped. Two years after the atomic attacks on Hiroshima and
Nagasaki, three years after his departure from Camp X, and "on the
middle night of my life", his thirty-fifth birthday, Dehn penned the
following lines in his poem, "Thirty Five":

And men shall die, knowing a new grief:
That the world may die, in which their works should live,
Making the life void and the works vain;
As I know now, who stand
Under bare trees on the middle night of my life
With the white moonlight worming at my brain
And the shadow of Black Rock across the land.
Mankind shall weep upon the latter day,
Under the mushroom cloud, not for their own
Death; but because their children and their town
Died the same night as they.[5]

Helping OSS during its 1943 training crisis was not the only
contribution the Camp X staff made to the American shadow warriors that year. Skilbeck and Camp X did a great deal to help one of the
president's closest advisers, Robert Sherwood, in setting up the
Foreign Information Service (FIS).

A former editor of *Life* and a four-time Pulitzer Prize winner,
Sherwood was typical of many writers and intellectuals mobilized for
the American war effort. One of the earliest recruits to Donovan's
organization, the six-foot-seven-inch Irishman was an ardent Demo-
crat and occasional speech-writer for Roosevelt. His plays had mir-
rored the changing attitudes of his generation to war. Badly wounded
in France while serving in the Canadian Black Watch, Sherwood had
returned from the First World War disillusioned and wedded to pacifism. The triumph of European dictatorships in the 1930s saw him
reluctantly revise his views. *There Shall Be No Night*, his successful
Broadway play of 1940 inspired by the Soviet attack on Finland,
proclaimed the message that pacifism was not enough and that liberty
had to be defended. From then on, Sherwood became an ardent interventionist. He broadcast widely, and one of his most vigorous efforts,

a denunciation of American isolationists such as Lindbergh, was broadcast to Canada in August of 1940 with the purpose of convincing Canadians that they were not isolated in their struggle. His views made him a natural candidate for Donovan. The two men had first met at the play's première in New York, and shortly afterwards Donovan put him in charge of the Foreign Information Service, responsible for foreign-propaganda broadcasting.

Based in New York and staffed by New Dealers, liberal journalists, and major figures of the American literary scene, the FIS formed one of the two first branches of the COI. Sherwood prepared guidelines for broadcasters and later on acquired broadcasting times of his own on short-wave radio stations. At the same time he found himself struggling with many conservatives who had found their way into Donovan's organization. Still, in the view of one historian of OSS, Bradley Smith, its operations were far and away the most successful of those launched by Donovan at this time.

But Donovan and Sherwood were not to stay together for long. Sherwood was jealous of his close relationship to Roosevelt, and he came to resent Donovan's easy access to the president. "Shy and abnormally sentimental," wrote Corey Ford in his biography of Donovan, "he was capable of fierce loyalties and equally intense dislikes. The depth of emotion which made his dramas so memorable...was an integral part of his own somber and sensitive nature." More important, however, was a profound philosophical split between the two men. Donovan believed that American foreign propaganda should become exclusively a weapon of subversive war, "a judicious mixture of rumour and deception, with truth as a bait, to foster disunity and confusion in support of military operations," he told Roosevelt early in 1942.[6] Sherwood strongly disagreed, believing that propaganda should stick to the truth and that resorting to the methods of the enemy could only damage American interests. The conflict was resolved only when, during the transition from COI to OSS, Sherwood's Foreign Information Service was transferred from Donovan's control to that of the Office of War Information. Donovan was then able to pursue his own philosophy of foreign propaganda as "an arrow of penetration" through the OSS Morale Operations Branch. Sherwood, for his part, continued to enjoy a close relationship with the White House, and after the war wrote his

Roosevelt and Hopkins, one of the standard reference books on FDR's wartime leadership and his relationship with his close political confidant, Harry Hopkins.

As the FIS expanded, it needed help in learning about aspects of foreign propaganda work, especially operational tasks carried out by agents in the field. Sherwood, like his rival Donovan, turned to the British, and Stephenson, conscious as ever of the political importance of doing everything he could to help Americans fight the shadow war, lent him Sidney Morrell, one of his own experts. A former journalist who had been with BSC since it began in 1940, Morrell soon arranged for several of Sherwood's men to go to Camp X for training. A group of ten men went there in November 1942, followed by three more groups over the next five months. "Some of them, destined to become agents in the field," Skilbeck recalls, "had full training including weapons and explosives." Others received abbreviated instruction designed merely to familiarize them with the basic principles about propaganda taught at Beaulieu and distilled into concentrated form by Brooker and Skilbeck. Ironically, many of these had been formulated by Philby, who had been recruited into SOE on the strength of his reputation as a journalist and had painstakingly developed the basic Beaulieu syllabus on the subject. Among the Americans who benefited from Camp X training in operational propaganda, Morrell reported in April 1943, were "the chiefs of the [OWI] outposts at Stockholm, Cairo, Istanbul, New Delhi and Chungking". Sherwood himself visited Camp X during the first course for OWI men in November 1942. Morrell, who accompanied him, felt that the American "was greatly impressed both by the nature of the training and by the impression it had made on the students".[7]

As happened with Donovan, once Sherwood had acquired some basic expertise, he set up his own training programme in the United States. Its main school was based in the former Marshall Field mansion at Huntington on Long Island. The head of the school, Spike Field, a man who had lived by his wits in various endeavours and had good connections but was no relation to Marshall Field, had gone up to Camp X for some basic training in 1942. There he mobilized Skilbeck, Morrell, and Brooker to help him develop the syllabus on Long Island. Skilbeck had no particular claim to expertise on the subject, but as commandant of Camp X he seems to have impressed both

Sherwood and Field. He became a frequent visitor to the Long Island mansion and to Sherwood's office in downtown Manhattan. At times he found the burden of being assumed to be an expert rather onerous. "Sherwood had a quite unjustifiable admiration of my ability," Skilbeck recalled recently, "for I recollect a Sunday morning session with him and his aides when he asked me to expound my policy for propaganda in the Far East. My ability to kick for touch had its full rein!"[8]

Sherwood was nonetheless impressed. He said in a personal letter to Brooker in January 1943, "how grateful we are in this office for the inestimably valuable help that you are giving us. The course is a masterpiece of well-considered concentration."[9]

The most difficult test of Skilbeck's relations with Sherwood came, however, in the early summer of 1943 when Camp X was laying on yet another of its courses for OWI recruits. Training as well as operations had its dangers, as SOE always recognized. "A one per cent casualty rate was considered acceptable," said one of the instructors after the war when reflecting on his SOE experience both in Canada and in Britain. Camp X never suffered from such a high rate, but it did have its casualties. One of these was fatal.

The accident occurred during a tactical exercise on the afternoon of June 23, 1943, when a group of the OWI recruits were practising advancing under fire. Artillery fire was simulated by various charges of dynamite wrapped around with detonating fuse, but the small-arms fire was real, being fired from Thompson sub-machine-guns by members of the training staff above the heads of the advancing recruits. Some hundred and seventy-five yards from the firing line one of the students, Fred Boissevain, suddenly collapsed, killed instantly when a bullet entered the top of his skull about two inches behind the forehead and lodged in the base of his skull. A court of enquiry chaired by an official from the Ontario Attorney-General's office subsequently found the death to have been caused either by defective ammunition or by the freak collision of two bullets, one of which then ricocheted downwards into the unfortunate American. The instructor in charge of firearms training at the Camp was Captain Hamish Pelham-Burn, although he had not been present on the day of the accident. Asked by the court if he considered such training to be desirable, he replied as follows: "On such an exercise as this owing to the extreme shortness of the range…[a] sub-machinegun with the sights at 500 yards would be perfectly safe…on previous schemes…all bullets fired finished up several hundred yards out in the lake."

Tragic though this was, it had little or no effect on Camp X's relations with OWI. Both Drew-Brook and Skilbeck assured the Canadian military authorities that "insofar as the American end is concerned… everything is under control and…there will be no repercussions." "Sherwood was fantastic about it," Skilbeck still remembers, "but then he'd been in the British Army in the First World War and understood."[10]

Captain Hamish Pelham-Burn was a new paramilitary instructor who had arrived at Camp X with Paul Dehn that March. In an earlier age he would have been one of those Victorian explorers of the empire who left their names on countless maps of distant frontiers and forbidding mountain ranges. A tall, dark, blue-eyed romantic from the Scottish Highlands who after the war was to lead a two-man expedition to the Selkirk Mountains in Western Canada, Pelham-Burn had been sent to take charge of sabotage, weapons training, and general fieldcraft exercises.

He was the perfect complement to Dehn. For while the latter brought to Camp X an urbane sophistication enriched by the Beaulieu tradition, Pelham-Burn came straight from the SOE training centre at Arisaig in the Western Highlands. Pelham-Burn knew at first hand something about survival. Educated at Harrow and Sandhurst, he had narrowly escaped capture with the Seaforth Highlanders during the collapse of France. Back in Britain, he had joined the Royal Air Force, and completed his training as a fighter pilot just before the end of the Battle of Britain. He flew Hurricanes until he was grounded by a minor medical ailment. In July 1942 he wangled his way into SOE through family connections, and within a short while became an instructor at Arisaig, where he briefly commanded a school in which Vietnamese agents were being trained.

Pelham-Burn brought vigour, energy, and enthusiasm to his job at Camp X. His first love was explosives, and he seemed eager to blow up anything at the slightest notice. Brooker described him as "a bit wild", and George Glazebrook vividly recalled him over forty years later as "a wild Highlander".

Given his first two contributions to Camp X, this seems an apt description. A few days after his arrival, he decided to construct a new pistol range where recruits would learn to fire quickly and at short range in the dark. Inside an old Dutch barn left standing from the original farm buildings, he carefully constructed a maze of passageways out of straw bales. As the recruit passed by, targets hidden behind the bales would be set moving by wires manipulated by an instructor following along behind. It was a good idea that worked as long as only automatic pistols were used. But Pelham-Burn wanted something more dramatic. He decided to try out the exercise using a Tommy gun. It was a disastrous move. At the first burst the straw caught fire, and within minutes the entire barn burned to the ground.

Not content with this first rush of enthusiasm, Pelham-Burn then decided to impress a group of high-ranking visitors from New York and Ottawa with a display of pyrotechnics. Still glorying in the ready availability of explosives, which contrasted sharply with the strict rationing at SOE schools in Britain, he prepared his demonstration with a generous hand. The resulting explosion smashed windows in Oshawa. It was good for the Camp's cover as an explosives testing site, but it left the commanding officers with a lot of apologizing to do. As Skilbeck later recalled, "fun with Hamish was always a noisy affair." Nonetheless, the commandant considered him a first-rate instructor.

Of course, as with Paul Dehn, there was a serious side to Pelham-Burn, and he made an important contribution to the Camp's syllabus. He brought imagination and initiative to the job, and considerably extended the number and variety of fieldcraft exercises both inside and outside the Camp. In addition to night exercises, he introduced several involving aircraft. A local RCAF station lent three Tiger Moths for basic pick-up exercises in which putative agents wearing full gear learned how to leave and board aircraft as quickly as possible – the kind of thing they might have to do in a country like France, where pick-up and drop-off operations using Lysander aircraft from England were quite common. Pelham-Burn was also the first instructor to see the potential of some of the local Canadian staff, and recruited and trained two of them to help him. Pelham-Burn thought Camp X better than any of the SOE Arisaig schools.[11]

Of a quite different ilk was Captain Ramsay Rainsford Hannay, a Scot from a wealthy landed family who had both inherited and married well, and is now chief of the clan Hannay. A pre-war barrister and assistant legal adviser to the Scottish Board of Trade, Hannay worked for SOE at the BSC offices in New York and Washington in 1942 before being sent to Camp X in January 1943. Here he received some basic training and then helped to drill the civilian staff working at the HYDRA installation and worked on map-reading exercises. Hannay himself is remembered by colleagues for his unbarrister-like contributions to mess life, and in particular his enthusiastic imitations of Harry Lauder, the great Scots music hall singer of the 1920s. His recollections of Camp X now are somewhat vague, but he retains a vivid memory of one incident that took place during his training of some French Canadians. One night in the mess, discussion turned to hypnotism. One of the trainees said he knew how to do it, so he gave a demonstration using one of his fellow students stretched out across several chairs. "There was a nasty few minutes, though," Hannay recalled, "when he couldn't get the man back." But most memories were pleasant: hospitality at the McLaughlin home in Oshawa, friendly Americans from OSS, and peaceful afternoons map-reading in the Ontario summer landscape.[12]

There was one notable fact about Hannay that few people knew and even fewer would have guessed. Not only was he a namesake of the secret-agent hero of John Buchan's classic spy novel *The Thirty-Nine Steps*, Richard Hannay; he was related by marriage to one of the great British spymasters of the century. His father-in-law was Sir William Wiseman, who had headed the British Secret Service in North America during the First World War and was a precursor of Stephenson. At the time, Wiseman was living in New York, where he was deeply involved in business and high finance, and as a friend of Stephenson, he kept in close touch with BSC affairs. But although Hannay was a frequent visitor to New York during the war, his high-powered connections there left little or no mark on the daily life of the Camp.

*

One of the earliest recruits to pass through Camp X with the new team of Skilbeck, Pelham-Burn, and Paul Dehn in charge was Jan van Schelle, a Dutchman who was living in Brazil when he was recruited by Ivar Bryce in his campaign to find suitable secret agents from among the immigrant communities in South America. He is mentioned fleetingly in Camp X records as having left Canada following training "on or about 28 May 1943, through the port of Halifax". In Britain he underwent paramilitary and advanced training, and some time later that year was parachuted into Europe. Bryce, writing his memoirs in 1970, told of the sequel. "He landed among a reception committee composed of Gestapo, and was never seen again. His life in Brazil had been useful and happy, and it was I who suggested to him what he might exchange it for."13

Bryce was referring here to SOE's major wartime catastrophe, which overtook its Dutch section. For almost two years, from early 1942, the Germans, by skilfully playing back the radio of a captured SOE Dutch agent, had deceived SOE into thinking its networks in Holland were secure. A model operation of its kind, known by H.J. Giskes, the *Abwehr* officer who ran it, as Operation NORTH POLE (NORDPOL), it ensured that all SOE agents parachuted into Holland in this period fell directly into German hands. Shocked and traumatized by the experience, many told their captors more than they wanted. By the fall of 1942 the Germans "knew not only the names and appearances of every officer in N section, and of every instructor at all the schools their captured SOE agents had attended," in M.R.D. Foot's words, "but which brand of cigarette or pipe tobacco each of them preferred, which one was married and which a bachelor, which one had a moustache and which was clean-shaven." Giskes reported directly back to Hitler through Admiral Wilhelm Canaris, head of the *Abwehr*. All SOE supplies fell into German hands, and several RAF planes were shot down either shortly before or after completing SOE drops. "Operation NORDPOL," wrote Giskes in his post-war memoirs, "was no more than a drop in the ocean of blood and tears, of the suffering and destruction of the Second World War. It remains nonetheless a noteworthy page in the chequered and adventurous story of Secret Service, a story which is as old as humanity and as war itself."14 The fault for the disaster lay with SOE's N (Dutch) Section in London, which inexplicably failed to notice warning signals included in messages sent by the captured wireless operator. Most of the agents paid for the mistake with their lives. Of the fifty-one SOE agents involved, practically all were shot.

Ivar Bryce died in England in April 1985 without learning of the results of investigations into the SOE files on van Schelle. Therefore he never knew that van Schelle had not only been touched by NORDPOL but that he had been an unwitting actor in a German deception game that extended far beyond Holland and threatened a major SOE network in France; and, more important from van Schelle's standpoint, that the young Dutchman had not been shot but had made it safely back to England, and then after the war had returned to his home in Brazil.

Jan David Anton van Schelle, to give him his full name, was initially recruited by Bryce in Brazil for SOE work in and around São Paulo. Some time early in 1942 he went to Camp X for training, where, his SOE file records, "He made an exceptionally good impression".[15] By June of that year he was at work in São Paulo. "Passing as a disgruntled Dutchman who has made every effort to join his country's forces," his file reveals, "only to be met with rude and ungrateful indifference on the part of the authorities, he has gradually become involved with members of the NSB [*Nationalsozialistische Bund*, the principal Nazi organization] and is now successfully infiltrating the German organization." Van Schelle paid a high price for this role as a supposed Nazi sympathizer. During a clamp-down by Brazilian authorities early in 1943 he was rounded up and spent six or eight weeks in a Brazilian prison associating with the Germans imprisoned on suspicion of espionage. By the time he was released, SOE's decision to reduce drastically its networks in South America made him redundant. So on March 17, 1943, BSC offered him for possible service with SOE's N Section, and shortly after it accepted him for European service van Schelle returned briefly to Camp X *en route* for advanced training in Britain.

By the time he had completed the finishing courses at Beaulieu in the autumn of 1943, SOE had finally begun to have serious doubts about the security of its networks in Holland. Already in June it had halted all operations there while it attempted to find out what was going on, and the RAF banned all SOE operational flights. Partially reassured by parallel investigations by SIS, SOE carried out two trial

RAF sorties to Holland in October. They failed, and by mid-November SOE had reluctantly admitted that its organization in Holland was under total German control.

Van Schelle's drop behind enemy lines occurred just as British suspicions reached their climax. So, instead of finding himself parachuted into Holland, the young Dutchman (code-named "Apollo") was dropped along with another Dutch agent (code-named "Brutus") on the night of October 18-19, 1943, from an RAF bomber into Belgium on Operation BADMINTON RUGGER. His mission was to deliver money to those operating escape lines in Belgium and Holland, and "to follow and report on an escape line in Belgium." He had the additional tasks of reconnoitring the German defences along the line of the Ysel River and making plans for supplying the civil population of Holland with food when the Allied invasion of Europe began.

Escape lines were the essential arteries of SOE networks in Europe. It was relatively easy to get agents into Europe by parachute, but how to get them out? Only a few, mainly from France, could be taken out on pick-up operations by small Lysander planes, which could quickly land and take off before being spotted by the Germans. For the rest, it was a question of making their way carefully and slowly through unfamiliar territory to a neutral state, such as Spain or Switzerland, and from there back to London. By 1944 SOE's escape lines throughout Europe were handling about an agent a day.

But escape lines were exceptionally vulnerable to German penetration. The successful ones demanded tight security, careful organization, and the most reliable of members. They worked, as M.R.D. Foot said in *SOE in France*, "With the usual appurtenances of secret service in fiction, except for the excitement, the gunplay, and the easy women; most of the time most of the agents led an extremely dull life, existing as calmly and discreetly as they could, busied with their cover employment as commercial travellers, booksellers, doctors, laundresses, or whatever it might be."

The basis of all escape lines was the existence of safe houses, where agents being exfiltrated could rest undetected between stages of their journey; and cut-outs, a system preserving anonymity between members of the chain in the escape line. One member would escort escapees to a prearranged point and leave them there. Fifteen minutes later the guide for the next stage of the journey would arrive, exchange an agreed-upon password, and conduct them to the next point, and so on down the line until they were escorted across the Pyrenees into Spain (the usual way out). Ideally, the system meant that members of an escape line knew only the two rendezvous at each end of their link in the chain. If the system worked according to plan, the only danger of penetration came at the very beginning. Because while no member of the line knew another (even telephone communications were on a cut-out system), the passengers came into contact with every link in the chain. If an enemy penetration agent entered the line, chaos could follow.

SOE's biggest and most successful escape line in Occupied Europe was the VIC line, which operated in France. Unwittingly, van Schelle came close to being an agent of its destruction, and only the courage and care of its organizer, Victor Gerson, saved it. Gerson was in his mid-forties, a quiet, discreet, and wealthy textile manufacturer who had been born into the Anglo-Jewish community in Southport, Lancashire in 1898. After the First World War and service in the British Army on the Western Front, he had settled in Paris, where for the next twenty years he led a respectable bourgeois life as a dealer in fine rugs and carpets. When Paris fell to the Germans in June 1940, he and his second wife, a young Chilean actress called Giliana Balmaceda, fled to Britain.

Both were soon recruited by SOE, and Giliana, who owned a Chilean passport with a valid visa for Vichy France, was the first woman SOE agent to be dispatched into France. Victor Gerson followed soon after, and on a second mission to France in 1942 he set up the VIC line. He formed its core from friends in the Lyonnais Jewish community, "choosing those who were Jewish by descent," writes M.R.D. Foot in *Six Faces of Courage*, "because they would already have had some practice in keeping themselves discreetly apart from the mainstream of ordinary life around them, but avoiding those who were ostentatiously Jewish in manner, appearance, or religion, because they would be too conspicuous." The three main "junctions" of the line were in Paris, Lyons, and Perpignan. To get passengers from there into Spain over the Pyrenees, Gerson made a lucky find in securing the services of a young Spanish anarchist from the Spanish Civil War who used the cover name "Martin". In Paris and Lyons he relied on two close personal friends, Jacques Mitterand and George Levin. Constantly travelling through France by train – invariably by first class, under his genuine cover as a textile merchant – Gerson carefully supervised operations and kept a vigilant eye on the circuit's security. In the fall of 1943 van Schelle and VIC crossed paths.

Van Schelle's mission almost came to an abrupt end even before it started when the RAF plane carrying him and "Brutus" was shot down by flak east of Antwerp. Fortunately the pilot made a successful crash landing and the two agents managed to jump from the burning aircraft. But they had to abandon all their equipment and radio sets, and became separated from each other in the darkness and confusion.

More obscurity was to follow as the two men became enmeshed in yet another of Giskes' schemes to penetrate SOE. Several months earlier, in January 1943, SOE had dropped a group into Holland with the code-name GOLF, whose mission was to prepare escape routes through Belgium and France into Spain and Switzerland. Immediately captured by Giskes' men, who had prepared the reception, the GOLF group's radio was played back to London. Over the following months the *Abwehr* gained valuable knowledge of several SOE escape lines. Giskes' chief agent in charge of these operations was his deputy, Richard Christmann.

Christmann, who one anonymous post-war American interrogator said "looks and behaves like a waiter", had been deported by the French from his native city of Metz after Alsace was returned to France in 1919. After service with the French Foreign Legion and as a Gestapo spy, he had joined Giskes in Holland running NORDPOL, where he used the code-name "Arno." In May 1943 he had helped penetrate one of SOE's major French resistance circuits, PROSPER, by means of an escape line.

For their successes in Holland Giskes and Christmann relied heavily on a Dutch informer who went under the name of Ridderhof. Besides the road-haulage business he owned, he was also engaged in a variety of black-market activities. "A large, fat, bloated sort of fellow" in the words of one of Giskes' assistants, Ridderhof had volunteered his services to the Germans as a "V-Mann", or *Vertrauensmann* (a trusted informer), telling them that he could provide information about two English secret agents operating in The Hague and at Arnhem. Indeed he could, for he worked for them. Once Giskes had established Ridderhof's *bona fides* as a reliable informant, he gave him a number – F2087 – and a cover name, "George". When London instructed the GOLF team in the summer of 1943 to prepare for the arrival of "Brutus" and "Apollo" by setting up a safe house for them in Brussels, Giskes decided to use F2087. The Dutchman had a *pied à terre* there, and Giskes thought he would be ideal in fooling the two new SOE arrivals into believing that they were in safe hands. Once they arrived, the *Abwehr* officer would wait for an opportunity to exploit the SOE agents in whatever way seemed best. So, having sent F2087's address to London, he sat back and waited.

"One early morning," he recalled, "a severely shaken and bedraggled individual appeared at the house in Brussels...clearly most relieved to be once again safe among friends." The man was "Brutus", van Schelle's companion on the ill-fated flight from Britain. Twenty-four hours later, van Schelle himself turned up, "as tattered," Giskes remembered, "and as woebegone as his friend."[16]

Giskes was aware by this time that London had deep suspicions about the Dutch networks. Two captured SOE agents had escaped in August and Giskes knew that they would attempt to alert London. Time was running out for NORDPOL. But, he calculated at this point, if he could not salvage everything, perhaps he could at least convince London that the GOLF radio link was secure. Van Schelle provided him with an opportunity. If he could arrange for van Schelle's safe return to Britain, and use the GOLF radio link to make the arrangements, then London would conclude that GOLF was a genuine and secure network. "Apollo," wrote Giskes, "might have been the first genuine NORDPOL agent to return to England to report his experiences, and we certainly banked a lot on him."

Van Schelle seems to have walked straight into the plot. Suspicion apparently was the last thing on his mind as he told F2087 all about his mission in Holland, and he quickly fell into line with the carefully planted suggestion that, since he had lost all his equipment, he should immediately make his way back to Britain. For Giskes, the plan would also have a bonus. If he could convince London of the need to exfiltrate van Schelle, then SOE would provide him with a contact address in Paris. With any luck, this would open up entry to a new escape line. If Giskes then made sure that van Schelle was accompanied by one of his own men, another escape line would be blown.

All went according to plan. After hesitating for two weeks, London finally agreed that van Schelle should return to London, and duly provided him with a contact address in Paris for the VIC line. Giskes then chose van Schelle's companion to accompany him all the way to Spain: his faithful lieutenant Christmann, who by this time was masquerading as a Dutch resistance agent under the code-name "Arnaud".

Van Schelle seems to have remained innocent of the double play going on around him, and to have believed he was part of a genuine SOE operation. He talked fully and freely to F2087, and when he received the orders to head for Spain, he set off in Christmann's company apparently oblivious of danger. The two men arrived in Paris, stayed several days at a safe house, and then were taken by courier to Lyons. But if van Schelle was not suspicious of Christmann, Gerson's deputy in Lyons, George Levin, was. He quickly separated the two men and closely cross-questioned "Arnaud" who, after making an excuse that he had to return to Holland to supervise a diamond-smuggling operation, vanished. This was none too soon for Christmann. Gerson, who had been visiting Barcelona at the time, had received a message there from Lyons warning him about Christmann. But it was too late for the VIC line. Eight weeks later the *Abwehr* collected its harvest. On January 21, 1944, ten of the French people who had sheltered Christmann and van Schelle in Paris and Lyons were arrested, along with the courier who had guided them between the two cities. Levin, Mitterand, and Gerson themselves escaped because they had already moved on.

But Gerson's security precautions and rigid operational rules now proved their worth. The arrests scarcely damaged the VIC line at all, and they had minimal impact on its operations. None of the ten arrested could tell the Germans much of value about anything other than their own small section of the circuit. And Gerson had very carefully, and unknown to any of those involved in the first escape line, set up second and third parallel escape lines, "dormant alternative lines," M.R.D. Foot writes, "ready to spring into action, without notice, at the sound of a telephone delivering a code word." The crucial links across the Pyrenees remained untouched, and with new safe houses and a new courier VIC was operating again at full capacity within a matter of days.

And what of Jan van Schelle? Separated from Christmann in Lyons, he made his way safely down the VIC line through Perpignan to Spain, and from there returned to England, which he reached on December 16, 1943. By this time SOE had learned the full scale of their Dutch disaster and were in desperate need of new agents for Holland. But from van Schelle's debriefings and the suspicions about Christmann, SOE quickly realized not only that GOLF was under German control but that van Schelle himself was blown and therefore useless for a further mission. According to the SOE archives, he was "sent on extended leave which lasted until after 'Overlord' ". This is undoubtedly a euphemism for action taken by the disposal section of SOE's security and intelligence directorate. Commanded by Air Commodore Archie Boyle, who had worked in air intelligence for some two decades, the disposal section's task was to provide cover for SOE agents exiting from the service and to ensure that they were not security risks. For that purpose, it maintained what was known as "the cooler", a country house in the remote Scottish Highlands where SOE agents could be detained for long periods of time. This is undoubtedly what happened to van Schelle, who knew far too much for comfort about SOE plans in Holland and its overall role in the impending liberation.

He was luckier than the two compatriots whose escape from the Germans in August had presaged the end of Giskes' operation. They reached the Dutch legation in Switzerland in November and were able to warn SOE of Giskes' success in NORDPOL, thus providing the final devastating proof of the scale of the *Englandspiel* disaster. But before they reached Britain, Giskes, still playing the radio game, had managed to sow doubts about their loyalty in London's mind. Playing for safety, SOE had them shut up in British prisons until the success of OVERLORD was assured.

Van Schelle was signed off from SOE on June 21, 1944, and transferred to the Dutch headquarters in London for sabotage and underground armed resistance in Holland. After this, his wartime career is impossible to trace. But eventually, when peace came to Europe, he ended up back in Brazil.

On the same day that van Schelle left Halifax, the military authorities in Ottawa notified General Constantine at military headquarters in

Toronto that arrangements were under way for the transport via New
York of a group of sixteen recruits who had completed training at
Camp X. These were the Yugoslav Canadians who had been found by
Major Lethbridge on his follow-up recruiting drive to supplement the
job done by Stuart and Bailey the previous summer. Nothing, however, is known about these men or the missions they undertook with
the partisans in Yugoslavia, and their fates remain hidden in the files
still held secret in London and Ottawa.

More is known about the Italian Canadians who followed hard on
their heels through Camp X. Early in the year BSC, on London's
instructions, had launched a recruitment drive, and by April Drew-
Brook was arranging interviews for possible candidates already serving in the Canadian armed forces. In May, seven men were sent to
Camp X for preliminary training. A month later, in mid-June, Drew-
Brook arranged their transfer to Halifax for embarkation to Britain,
where they passed through the standard SOE training before being
sent to SOE's major Mediterranean base at Bari.

The Italian situation had changed radically in the few weeks
between the agents' training at Camp X and their arrival at Bari.
Mussolini was removed from office in late July, shortly after the
Allies had captured Sicily, and early in September the Italian government of Marshal Pietro Badoglio negotiated a surrender. But the
Germans quickly moved to occupy most of northern Italy, and after
SS officer Otto Skorzeny led a daring operation to rescue Mussolini
from his imprisonment in the Gran Sasso, the former dictator was
installed as head of a new Fascist government in the north.

Partisan warfare and resistance against this puppet government
grew rapidly over the next few months. Once again SOE found itself
faced with another political conundrum. The partisans were a heterogeneous force of republicans, liberals, socialists, Communists, and
left-wing Catholics who were determined to see a complete renewal
of Italy's political and social fabric at the end of the war. They were
popular, and by the time the Allies occupied Rome in June 1944 the
partisans numbered over 100,000. But this very strength and radical-
ism alarmed the Allies, who wanted neither a civil war nor the loss of
Italy to a Communist-dominated government. For Churchill, an
avowed conservative monarchist with an acute sense of Italy's importance to British imperial requirements in the Mediterranean, the

choice in Italy seemed to lie between the king and the Communists. As the Communists formed the most militant edge of the partisan movement, this posed a familiar problem for SOE. Were they to ignore such a useful tool against the Germans? The answer was no and yes. The partisans would be assisted, SOE decided, but not in a way that would encourage their political objectives.

Italy was given a high priority in 1944, and during August alone over sixty agents and some nineteen W/T sets were infiltrated to the partisans in the north. But SOE carefully instructed its liaison officers to keep a close eye on the partisans, and took care not to provide large-scale deliveries of rifles, small arms, or ammunition that might be used to assist insurrection. And as the Germans retreated, anti-sabotage and law-and-order tasks played an increasing role in many of its missions.

Most of the Camp X Italian recruits spent their time in northern Italy involved in important but fairly anonymous routine tasks as interpreters or wireless operators. Most survived the war. But one who did not, and whose short time as an SOE operative in his native country illustrated SOE's concern with counter-sabotage, was Giovanni di Lucia. Born in Ortona just before the outbreak of the First World War, di Lucia moved with his parents to Niagara Falls, Canada, in the late 1920s. He took a degree in Romance languages at the University of Rochester and was at the University of Western Ontario in London, Ontario, in 1942 on an officers' training course when he was approached about volunteering for special duty in Italy. After training at Camp X and at Bari, he was parachuted into a group of partisans operating north of Verona in early 1944. SOE had instructed them to help protect bridges and hydroelectric installations from destruction by the retreating Germans, part of the general Allied strategy to ensure that Italy did not fall into chaos and revolution after the war.

For several weeks di Lucia operated with this group, which was only too ready to harass the Germans in any way it could. It was while fighting with the partisans in a skirmish with German troops that di Lucia was captured in May 1944, and suffered the usual fate meted out to European partisans captured by the enemy. After being permitted to write a short note to his family, he was shot by a firing squad virtually on the anniversary of his arrival at Camp X.

*

The next major group to arrive at Camp X in the summer of 1943 were the Hungarian Canadians. Like the Yugoslavs, they had been approached in the summer of 1942 and asked to volunteer for special duty. For the most part they, too, were Communists or left-wing, and twenty-two of them came forward at the promptings of the Communist Party. Even in the case of non-Communists, the RCMP could help to identify them, for several were not Canadian citizens and had to report as enemy aliens following the declaration of war between Hungary and Britain in December 1941.

Unlike the Yugoslavs, however, they were interviewed or recruited not by a mission sent out from London but by Eric Curwain. There followed a long silence that was finally broken in mid-June 1943, almost a year later, when seven of the volunteers were asked to report to Military District 2. Here they followed the procedure agreed upon with Major Lethbridge a few months earlier, and the two members of the group not already in the army were enlisted. From there, they took the route of the Yugoslavs and were driven out to Camp X for their preliminary training. They were officially transferred to STS 103 on August 2, and by the end of the month Drew-Brook was pressing Ottawa to provide transport to Britain for the first of the Hungarian recruits who had completed their training. In September they sailed from Halifax to Greenock on the *Queen Elizabeth*.

Among them was Andre Durovecz, a Hungarian Canadian journalist in his early thirties who worked for a small left-wing newspaper in Toronto. On arrival in Britain, Durovecz – who took the cover name "Daniels" – spent several weeks training at Arisaig and then was flown out to Cairo for further specialized instruction. Then, after several weeks at the SOE base at Bari, he was parachuted with three others into Slovakia in September 1944. Their goal was to cross over into Hungary and make contact with the resistance.

Durovecz found his training at Camp X intensive and rough. "Every minute of every day was filled," he later recalled in an interview. "We were not given a minute's rest. We were either running or crawling all the time...it was pounded into us so that it became part of our nervous system. It became part of our senses." He and his fellow Hungarian recruits spent hours on ropes scaling the cliffs along the shoreline of Camp X, and at night went on lengthy exercises devised by Hamish Pelham-Burn in the countryside north of the Camp. "They were bloody awful," Durovecz remembered; "they would give us a map and a compass, tell us our target, and then when we got there hours later tell us new targets had been chosen. Somehow, we'd stagger off in all directions."[17]

There were also simulated demolitions exercises against nearby targets such as the General Motors plant in Oshawa, the port of Toronto, and the Montreal-Toronto railway line. To block a railway line, Pelham-Burn thought it was more effective to destroy a bridge or viaduct than simply to cut the line, which could be repaired within hours.

If these exercises toughened them physically, Durovecz also found that the small-arms exercises conducted with live ammunition introduced him to a whole new range of emotions. "It made you cool, but at the same time you were angry and determined." And in the underground firing range where practice was carried out under Pelham-Burn's direction virtually in the dark, Durovecz thought that recruits were "almost tortured mentally" until they hit the target. Still, he sensed that Pelham-Burn had some respect for him and his group. "He really liked the Hungarian lads. I think he felt that we shared a peasant background which made us able to get close to people...all that sort of thing really counted...the kind of people we were, our political beliefs, our determination and our stamina."

Pelham-Burn also fired them up. "I'm going to go to Churchill," he once told Durovecz and the other Hungarians, "and tell him to give us 100 Hungarians and 100 Scots and together we are going to —— Hitler."

For all this, however, Durovecz found that little of his training either at Camp X or in Britain really equipped him for the experience of being in the field. Despite extensive parachute training at Bari, he was not prepared for the almost unbearable tension of the actual night flight and jump into Slovakia – "You either had to be crazy or drunk to jump out of an aircraft at that altitude" – and when he finally made it into Hungary, little of his training was of use in overcoming the political maelstrom in which he found himself.

Hungary by this time was stony ground for SOE. For most of the war, this essentially feudal country ruled by a powerful and reactionary land-owning aristocracy had been a half-hearted ally of the Germans. Although it had declared war on the Russians and the Western Allies in 1941 and Hungarian units were fighting on the Eastern Front, Admiral Miklos Horthy, the septuagenarian regent, was keen to extricate his country from the forthcoming débâcle, and like most of his countrymen feared the prospect of Russian liberation.

Shortly after the Italian surrender in September 1943, the Hungarian government under Prime Minister Miklos Kallay, a member of one of Hungary's oldest families, had sent out peace feelers to the British, and discussions through SOE channels in Istanbul continued for several months. The Hungarians also continued to resist many German demands. They refused to expel the large Jewish population – some 800,000 – and thus the Jews were temporarily sheltered from Hitler's Final Solution. The Hungarians also refused to take action against the Allied aircraft flying over Hungarian territory bound for the Reich, and resisted German requests to install their own anti-aircraft batteries.

For Hitler, faced with the now remorseless advance of the Red Army on the Eastern Front, this became intolerable. On March 19, 1944, he ordered German troops to occupy Hungary and that same day a new government under a more amenable prime minister was installed in Budapest. Special SS forces under the dreaded Adolf Eichmann arrived at the same time. Within a month Jewish deportation to the death camps in Poland had begun and Hungary became yet another country open to full-scale Nazi repression, sometimes eagerly helped by local native Fascists.

In September Durovecz found that these conditions made his mission almost impossible. Leaving the rest of his group to shelter with Slovak partisans near Banská Bystrica, he made his way to Budapest by train, expecting to make contact with resistance groups there who had wireless contacts to the partisans in Slovakia. But the initial contact name given to him by SOE in Bari proved to have been dead for several months, and he was unable to find genuine identity papers to replace the forged and unconvincing ones handed to him before departure.

Deciding that he should report back to his group in person, and not knowing that they had been captured and killed soon after he left them, Durovecz made his way back to the frontier, but was arrested as he tried to cross it in mid-October. Several weeks of brutal interrogation at the hands of German and Hungarian police followed before he was transferred to the Zugliget prison camp just outside Budapest. Here he met up with Joseph Gelleny, one of his fellow Canadians who had also been captured, and after four days the two of them managed to escape and hide out in the city.

By this time the capital was in chaos. On the same day that Durovecz had attempted to cross back into Slovakia, October 15, Horthy revealed to the Germans that he planned to surrender to the Allies. The Nazis' reaction was swift. German troops occupied strategic points in the city, including the radio stations; Horthy was arrested and deported to Germany; and Ferenc Szalassi and his Fascist movement, the Arrow Cross, seized power.

Meanwhile the Red Army entered the country, captured the city of Debrecen, and then laid siege to the capital, where street fighting broke out in Pest in the last days of December 1944. The Arrow Cross government mobilized the population and publicly executed hundreds of deserters and resisters. Hitler ordered his SS generals to defend every house in the city and forbade them to leave. Bitter street fighting followed and the city was quickly reduced to rubble. By early January the Red Army units had reached the centre of Pest and the Nazis retreated across the Danube, destroying the bridges as they went. In February, the beleaguered German garrison surrendered.

During this time Durovecz and Gelleny remained hidden in Budapest, sheltering in the cellars of churches and houses controlled by the resistance, and assisting Red Army units in their hand-to-hand fights with the Germans. As soon as the Russians were in control, Durovecz and Gelleny turned themselves in and were transferred to Debrecen. From there they were flown by the U.S. Air Force to Bari and then on to Britain. By July 1945 Durovecz was back in Toronto.

His mission was only one of several failed attempts to stimulate Hungarian resistance following the German occupation. Bickham Sweet-Escott, who was posted to Cairo following his liaison work with OSS in Washington, found himself briefly in charge of SOE

Hungarian operations. He had little faith that much could be achieved, both because the Hungarian police were so vigilant and because the one SOE agent with the best chance of getting results in Hungary had concluded that things were hopeless. This was Basil Davidson. After his experience with the Canadian Yugoslavs and the partisans in Bosnia, he had taken on the mission of crossing into Hungary and making resistance contacts. He was an ideal candidate for the job, having worked in Budapest for SOE in 1940-41. Descending from the Bosnian hills to the plains of Vojvodina, Davidson did his best in 1944 to link up with armed resistance across the Danube. "In due course I went over the midnight Danube," he recorded, "and sojourned in enemy-held towns and listened for a sign from the north. But no sign ever came."[18]

Despite this, SOE in Bari went ahead. Although the missions of two of the Hungarian Canadians were cancelled because their operational areas had already fallen into the hands of the Red Army, the remaining Camp X alumni were parachuted into their homeland over the summer of 1944. As Sweet-Escott had virtually predicted, all were arrested.

The first to go was Gustav Bodo, a farmer already in his forties who had lived in Canada for some twenty years. His task was to pave the way for a larger team, which would enter Hungary from partisan-controlled territory in Yugoslavia and work with resistance forces in the city of Pécs. He parachuted into Croatia just three days before the D-Day landings in Normandy and made his way as planned across the Hungarian border. Once in Pécs, however, he was almost immediately arrested by the Hungarian police – probably as the result of an informer's denunciation – and then handed over to the Gestapo. Before he disappeared from the air he was able to transmit radio messages omitting the agreed security checks, thus alerting the base in Bari. SOE was able to recall the remaining members of the group who had already parachuted into Croatia.

Once again, however, anxiety to achieve results overrode caution. The leader of the group, a British officer called John Coates, convinced his superiors in Bari that despite Bodo's fate the industrial population of Pécs offered fertile ground for stimulating resistance. Therefore in September 1944 he and two more of the Hungarian

Canadians, Michael Turk and Joseph Gelleny, parachuted directly into Hungary. Almost immediately they were arrested and soon found themselves incarcerated in prisons in and around Budapest. (It was at this point that Gelleny met up with Durovecz.)

The fourth unsuccessful mission to be sent into Hungary that summer included another Camp X student, Alexander Vass. The youngest of all the Hungarian Canadians, he had worked for several years in Toronto as a linotype operator and his methodical and careful approach to problems had given him high marks from his instructors. Under the cover name of "Lieutenant Vincent", Vass returned to his homeland as a translator in a mission code-named DEERHURST, headed by Lieutenant-Colonel Peter Boughey, who had worked for almost the entire war in the Balkan section at SOE headquarters in Baker Street, and whose earlier request to be sent into Hungary had been turned down by Sweet-Escott and SOE Cairo. In order to hide his importance and seniority, Boughey went into Hungary disguised as "Sergeant Connor" of the Black Watch.

The group parachuted into Hungary early in July but landed several miles from the designated drop zone. Within twenty-four hours of landing they were arrested by units of the Hungarian Army. Shortly afterwards they were moved to Budapest and, after being unsuccessfully interrogated by the Hungarian secret police, were handed over to the Gestapo. More interrogation followed until they were moved northwards to Vienna in October. Here they were transferred from Gestapo to *Luftwaffe* control and shipped westwards to various interrogation centres in Germany itself. At a POW centre at Limburg they were caught in an RAF bombing raid on the local railroad. Boughey survived, but Vass, along with the nominal leader of their group, was killed. It seemed emblematic of SOE operations into Hungary as a whole, and in particular of the abortive missions of those who had begun their journeys scarcely a year before at Camp X.

While the Hungarian Canadians were being trained at Camp X, London had been informed that attempts to recruit from another ethnic group in Canada had largely failed. In the event, only two Canadians of Romanian background completed training at the Camp, although a third was enlisted and began the course. He, however, deserted.

The Romanians were recruited by Alfred Gardyne de Chastelain, a businessman-turned-secret-agent typical of so many men who worked for SOE. A former sales manager in the 1930s for a British-owned petroleum company in Romania, de Chastelain had also done undercover work for SIS. He was involved in attempts by Section D of SIS to sabotage the Romanian oilfields in 1939-40 when Romania slid into the Axis empire. He then worked for SOE in London, and in June 1943 was sent to Canada to recruit Romanians for SOE operations aimed at organizing an Allied *coup d'état* . After returning from Canada, de Chastelain himself was parachuted into Romania just before Christmas, 1943. His mission, code-named AUTONOMOUS, was controversial from the beginning and almost led to the demise of SOE itself.

It was already clear that Romania would be occupied by the Red Army at the end of the war and that the Soviet Union regarded Romania as falling within its own sphere of influence. The presence of an SOE mission in the country in touch with pro-Western factions angered the Russians, who argued that there was an implicit Anglo-Soviet understanding about Romania's future that guaranteed predominant Soviet influence. They lodged a strong protest with Churchill, who in turn complained strongly that SOE had over-stepped the mark.

"It does seem to me," he commented bitterly in May 1944, "that SOE barges in in an ignorant manner into all sorts of delicate situations...it is a very dangerous thing that the relations of the two mighty forces like the British Empire and the USSR should be disturbed by these little pinpricks interchanged by obscure persons playing the fool far below the surface."[19]

Churchill, the prime mover in creating SOE, had on more than one occasion intervened to save it from enemies in Whitehall; this time, however, he joined its enemies, and for a while it seemed as though SOE would be disbanded. But Churchill's temper was short-lived in the light of its impending tasks at D-Day, and he quickly returned to his view that SOE's relations with resistance in Europe were too important to be lightly disrupted.

For de Chastelain personally, the AUTONOMOUS mission also seemed to promise disaster. The party was dropped blind, and within twenty-four hours had been picked up by the Romanian secret police.

They were thoroughly interrogated both by the Romanians and by a German intelligence officer but were not, in the end, handed over to the Germans. The Romanian dictator Ion Antonescu decided to use the cipher communications that de Chastelain had brought with him to contact the British in order to take soundings about negotiations to remove Romania from the Axis alliance. The contretemps with the Russians put an end to that, and eventually de Chastelain was allowed to fly to Istanbul – but only after King Michael had launched a successful *coup d'état* against the Antonescu government in August 1944.

Churchill's angry intervention forced SOE to put a stop to further missions to Romania. This, ironically, put a premature end to the SOE careers of the two men recruited by de Chastelain himself. Both had trained at Camp X and then at SOE schools in the Middle East. Neither George Georgescu, a petrochemist from Sarnia, nor Victor Moldovan, a machinist from Windsor, who completed their advanced training in Egypt, carried out the missions for which they had been recruited.

De Chastelain had taken a liking to Canada during his largely futile recruiting attempts in the summer. Drew-Brook had entertained him with his usual generosity while he toured Ontario interviewing potential candidates. The night before de Chastelain left Toronto Drew-Brook took him to see the popular patriotic film *In Which We Serve*. Eric Curwain, who accompanied him on his recruiting drive, described him as an excellent mimic and conversationalist, and one young woman who met him at the Drew-Brooks' found him both charming and good-looking. When de Chastelain left SOE, it was to Canada and a successful post-war career in the Western Canadian oil industry that he returned.

At a quarter past nine on the night of June 5, 1944, immediately following the nine o'clock BBC news broadcast to France, the announcer began to read out a stream of apparently meaningless and disconnected lines of poetry. Those in France who regularly listened at considerable personal risk to the BBC found nothing unusual in a few lines of poetry at this hour. Practically everyone, including the German SD, knew they were *messages personnels*, coded messages, for resistance circuits throughout the country. But tonight the list was considerably longer than usual.

The reason was simple. At the same time only four nights before, the BBC had transmitted a similar series. To the leaders of underground circuits who knew their meaning, the messages gave a warning that the Allied invasion was imminent. Now, the second half of the message – usually the second half of a couplet of verse – meant that the resistance throughout the country should move into action and begin the campaign of sabotage and harassment of German forces for which it had been preparing for months. Even before the first Allied troops waded ashore on the Normandy beaches at dawn the next morning, forty-five SOE-controlled circuits and one hundred and forty-five SOE-trained officers launched the offensive that marked the culmination of Baker Street's planning for France since it had sent the first agents across the Channel in 1941. That night, almost 1,000 attacks were launched against French railroads by SOE circuits.

One of the circuits mobilized that night was known by the codeword DITCHER. Led by an Anglo-Spanish agent called Albert Browne-Bartoli – whose sister, Elaine Plewman, an SOE courier, was to be executed at Dachau along with the well-known SOE agent Noor Inayat Khan ("Madeleine") – DITCHER operated in Burgundy and had a number of contact houses in Lyons.

Not only was France's second-largest city frequently referred to as the "capital" of the French resistance; it was also the headquarters of the infamous Klaus Barbie, head of the local Gestapo. Barbie's victims among the resistance and the local Jewish population were imprisoned in Fort Montluc, an old military prison in the city where, in a deliberately stage-managed act of poetic justice, Barbie himself was to be briefly interned some forty years later after his extradition from Bolivia. When Allied advances up the Rhône Valley later that summer forced the Germans to withdraw, Barbie began to execute *en masse* the prisoners who still remained.

Of the many massacres, that at Saint-Genis-Laval, a southwest suburb of the city, was the worst. On Sunday morning, August 20, 1944, one hundred and twenty resistance prisoners, bound together in pairs, were driven in two buses to an old unused fort in the suburb. Two by two, the prisoners were taken out of the bus, led to an upstairs room, and machine-gunned to death. As the bodies mounted, new victims had to clamber on top of them. Eventually, with blood pouring through the ceiling of the room below, the Germans soaked the corpses with petrol, set the building alight, and then dynamited it.

One of Barbie's victims that day was a young French Canadian, André Beauregard, who had worked as a wireless operator for DITCHER. Transmitting overtime in order to keep up with the flow of messages required by D-Day, he had been caught by a German direction-finding team and taken to Gestapo headquarters. The clinically sparse words of a post-war Canadian report by Colonel Felix Walter, Canada's liaison officer with SOE London, tell us all we need to know about what happened next: "His reason is believed to have been unhinged by the tortures to which he was subject."

Beauregard was not the only French Canadian to work for DITCHER. Two months after he arrived in France by a Lysander aircraft, Jean-Paul Archambault parachuted in to organize and train sabotage groups throughout the region in preparation for D-Day. Within three weeks of his arrival a third French Canadian, Lionel Guy d'Artois, parachuted in from a Halifax bomber to join him.

Both d'Artois and Archambault were graduates of Camp X. Unlike Beauregard, who had been recruited from the Canadian forces in Britain and therefore trained at SOE domestic schools, they had been recruited in Canada. Along with Leonard Taschereau, another French Canadian working for a resistance circuit near Troyes, in Champagne, they were the only success stories from a major effort in 1943 to recruit French Canadians for the shadow war.

In September 1943 SOE, through the normal BSC-Drew-Brook channel, asked the Canadian military authorities if they could supply twenty-five French-speaking officers for special duties. With a growing surplus of infantry officers in Canada in 1943, the SOE request came at an opportune time, enabling the Canadian Army to unload some of the older ones. Indeed, so enthusiastic was the army that it had already taken steps to find thirteen volunteers, who were ready for training at Camp X. The army had even offered to change the arrangement by which the recruits were paid by the British. In this case, the Canadians were prepared to cover all costs, including pay, allowances, and pensions. The minister of national defence, Layton Ralston, approved the proposal. He also approved BSC's second request for twenty-five more officers, made only a month later.

In all, forty-nine French-speaking volunteers were found, making this the second-largest group of Canadian trainees at Camp X. But, unlike the Yugoslavs, this group proved a failure. Although it produced three of the best Canadian agents ever provided to SOE, these three were the only ones who proved suitable or willing to go on missions at all when the moment arrived. All forty-nine were sent for two weeks' initial training at Camp X. The training staff was not impressed, and at the end of the course recommended that thirty were unfit for the physical or psychological strains of clandestine war. Even this was too generous. Of the remaining nineteen, twelve were sent over to Britain for advanced training in late October, and of these only two were up to SOE standards. Six chose the option of withdrawing between their final briefing and departure on mission and were then held – as was normal – incommunicado in Scotland for several weeks so as not to jeopardize the mission for which they had been trained.

Why were so many unsuitable? At first glance it might seem a question of age. But a number of agents who had already successfully trained at SOE schools were also in the over-thirty-five category. A more likely explanation is that, in the haste to unload older officers, Ottawa chose volunteers without close scrutiny. Since they were initially screened by the Canadian Intelligence Corps before being told to report to Military District 2, they avoided the more rigorous screening by experienced SOE officers that the Yugoslavs had undergone at the hands of Bailey, Stuart, and Lethbridge. It was a time-consuming and costly mistake, and created extra work for Camp X.[20]

Guy d'Artois, the last of the three Canadians to arrive in France to work for the DITCHER circuit, left the strongest impression on SOE. "Major d'Artois," noted Felix Walter's official post-war account, "impressed his training officers as being the perfect example of a soldier of fortune."

D'Artois arrived at Camp X in the fall of 1943 almost by accident. He had been stationed for nearly two years in Britain with the famous Vingt-Deux Regiment from Montreal before being posted to North America in 1942 to take parachute and commando training with the Canadian-American Special Service Force in the United States. SOE's drive to find suitable French Canadians coincided with a leave that d'Artois was taking at the time in Montreal, and soon he found himself at Camp X being assessed for suitability as an underground leader.

In the advanced training that followed in Scotland and England, d'Artois made his mark in more than the paramilitary skills of a soldier of fortune. On the same training course was Sonia Butt, a young teenage blonde, the youngest female agent SOE sent to France during the entire war. Within weeks she and d'Artois decided to marry, and talked of going on a mission together to France. SOE headquarters, all too aware of the Germans' habit of torturing married couples in each other's presence, quickly forbade the idea. Nonetheless, the two young agents got married in London in April 1944 and there was little that Baker Street could do about it except ensure that they went on different missions and were kept well apart, their whereabouts unknown to each other.

D'Artois parachuted into Burgundy on the night of May 1, 1944, and showed considerable energy and initiative in his work for the DITCHER circuit. Not content to organize, equip, and command two underground battalions that successfully blocked German access through the area in the days following D-Day – an operation that earned d'Artois a DSO and which Maurice Buckmaster, the head of SOE's French Section, described as "outstandingly successful" – he also devised an ingenious underground telephone system that gave advance warning of German troop movements and guaranteed considerable success in sabotage and ambush attacks. To finance these operations, d'Artois hit on the bright idea of capturing a wealthy local collaborator and holding him to ransom. Indeed, one of his most successful campaigns was in terrorizing local collaborationists. Mobilizing a special security squad, he arrested over a hundred such people, including members of the collaborationist *Milice* and German informers.

Later on, after he had left France and returned to Canada, d'Artois boasted in a newspaper interview how his group had responded to the German habit of shooting wounded prisoners captured in fighting against the resistance. "We retaliated by lining up fifty-two of their men and shooting them one by one. They killed a total of fifty-nine of my men.... Their favourite method was to club them to death with their rifle butts." Such exploits gave d'Artois a colourful reputation. Felix Walter noted that of d'Artois' security group some thirty were women "who appear to have been devoted to the dashing commander whom they knew as 'Michel le canadien'."[21]

D'Artois, like the other French Canadians who returned to London after their service in France, volunteered for further duty with SOE in Asia. But his enthusiasm for the life of a soldier of fortune got the better of him. Reunited with his wife in Paris, he returned with her to Canada on a month's leave during Christmas 1944. Unable to resist the lure of publicity, he gave the newspaper interview, quoted above, about their adventures behind enemy lines. SOE was not amused, least of all by the headline, "SHE ATE WITH THE GESTAPO. KILLED SOME? WHY, SURE." Such loose lips led SOE to decide that this time d'Artois had gone too far. The other French Canadians sailed back to London early in January to join their troopship to Bombay. D'Artois returned to civilian life.

Jean-Paul Archambault was the second Canadian to parachute into France before D-Day to work for DITCHER. Archambault was serving in the Canadian Army Postal Corps when he volunteered for training at Camp X in the fall of 1943. A postal worker from Montreal in his mid-thirties, he operated in the hill country around Lyons where his work was typical of many of the steady, unspectacular, but essential tasks carried out by SOE circuits both before and after D-Day. He helped to form and train three groups of saboteurs who focused on the railway network in and around Lyons and contributed to the delay and harassment of Germans attempting to reinforce the front in Normandy. Eventually, in October, units of the American Seventh Army reached the region and Archambault's work for DITCHER, for which he was awarded the Military Cross, was over.

It was not, however, the end of his SOE career. Like many others who had served in Europe, Archambault was asked when he got back to London if he was willing to take part in special operations in Asia. Shortly afterwards he left for Bombay, and by mid-February he was preparing for jungle warfare at SOE's Eastern Warfare Training School at Kharakvasla, near Poona, in India.

Force 136, as SOE in the Far East was known, faced far different and more daunting tasks than SOE in Europe. Its area of operations included Burma, Siam, China, Indo-China, Malaya, and Indonesia, its vastness creating enormous communications and logistics problems. While its basic mandate was the same as in Europe, it had to encourage and support resistance amid a population either cowed into submission by the Japanese, hostile to a return to colonialism and therefore unwilling to help, or even antagonistic. Moreover, behind enemy lines in Asia, white men were a distinctly visible minority. To vanish into the local population, as secret agents did in Europe, was impossible. Inevitably, therefore, paramilitary warfare took on greater importance for SOE in Asia, where agents parachuted into the jungle had to remain hidden from the Japanese while concentrating on organizing local populations into guerrilla bands. Even then, patterns of secrecy more suitable for SOE in Europe persisted, and Force 136 was never fully integrated with the regular forces. Charles Cruikshank, writing its official history, *SOE in the Far East* in 1983, concluded that South-East Asia Command under Mountbatten, along with SOE headquarters, failed "to use Force 136 for what it was – a straight paramilitary force – [and] to remove it from the inhibiting shackles of super secrecy which impaired its efficiency in the field, and to put it directly under the army command".

At best, conditions were highly unfavourable. Far from finding the jungle neutral, most SOE agents experienced it as full of hostile or alien plants, insects, and animals. "Treat jungles with respect, even with fear," said an official SOE training manual. SOE gave its Force 136 agents special training to equip them for the jungle, both at Kharakvasla and at its Advanced Operations School on an island off Trincomalee in Ceylon, teaching them how to fend for themselves by eating plants, filtering marsh water, cutting pathways through the dense underbrush, and interpreting the smells and sights of the jungle so that they could "read it like a book". For the SOE agent in Asia, there were ten jungle commandments: *Thou Shalt Not*: Stay in Wet Clothes; Disregard Scratches; Sit on Bare Earth; Eat Fruit; Scratch Leech Bites; Sit up Late Talking. *Thou Shalt*: Look after Your Feet; Keep Your Boots Oiled; Carry Citronella Oil; Keep a Teaspoonful of Salt in Your Water Bottle. But the gap between training and experience was often large. Very little could actually minimize the dangers that agents faced operating in an adverse environment thousands of miles from safety.[22]

For Archambault, parachuted into Burma in April 1945, the dangers were to prove fatal.

By this time, General William Slim's Fourteenth Army had captured Mandalay and was poised for the advance south to Rangoon, driving the Japanese back between the Irrawaddy and Sittang rivers. To the east of the Sittang were the Karen Hills, inhabited by hill people who showed little fondness for the Japanese (or the Burmese) and who the British were convinced could be mobilized to help in the campaign. To the west of the Irrawaddy were the Arakan Mountains and then the ocean. Slim requested Force 136 to help his advance by providing tactical intelligence and by harassing any Japanese attempts to escape over the mountains towards Thailand to the east. Three SOE operations were mounted to help the Fourteenth Army: ELEPHANT, NATION, and CHARACTER. CHARACTER, the biggest and most successful, involved mobilizing the Karen hillsmen into guerrilla groups. Archambault was a member of this operation.

The Japanese had some 50,000 troops in the Karen Hills, and they were soon joined by the elements of the Japanese Fifteenth Army making for Thailand after the fall of Rangoon early in May. Working with the Karen, Archambault took part in guerrilla and sabotage attacks, carrying with him a supply of explosives. But the monsoon was approaching and the heavy moisture in the air damaged his supply. On May 17, less than two weeks after the end of the war in Europe, while attempting to dry out explosives in his tent, Archambault blew himself up. He survived for two days, propped against a tree in a jungle clearing while he wrote his final report. But with no medical help available, death was inevitable.

A Camp X survivor of Operation CHARACTER was another French Canadian recruited in the fall of 1943, Leonard Taschereau. Like Archambault, Taschereau spent his time in the Karen Hills of Burma harassing the retreating Japanese and using explosives to blow up mountain paths as convoys of stragglers attempted to reach Thailand. He, too, had served in France and, like Archambault, had volunteered for special operations in Asia when he got back to London.

Taschereau had been born in Saskatoon but had grown up in Montreal. For a while he worked as a mechanic in the Royal Canadian Air Force and then as a bush pilot in Quebec. But by the time the Canadian Army identified him in 1943 as potential material for secret operations, he was working in an aircraft plant in Montreal. A short and aggressive man in his mid-thirties, Taschereau was one of the few older French Canadian volunteers who did well at Camp X. On Boxing Day, 1943, he embarked from Halifax to take advanced training at SOE schools in England and Scotland.

The resistance circuit to which he was dropped just six days after D-Day was code-named DIPLOMAT. Its organizer was a Frenchwoman named Yvan Dupont, whom SOE had parachuted into the area around Troyes, in Champagne, several months beforehand to organize teams of railway saboteurs for operations against the important Paris-Belfort railway line. By the end of April 1944 Dupont had trained over a hundred men to isolate Troyes by road and rail when the D-Day signal came. When it did, Dupont's men were so successful that the Germans made a concentrated effort to wipe them out. It was almost into the middle of a pitched battle between the Germans and the resistance that Taschereau parachuted on the night of June 12.

Almost immediately Dupont gave him control of a hundred *Maquis*, and for the next few weeks, hiding out in local forests, Taschereau and his men launched a series of successful sabotage raids against the railway system and fought running battles with the Germans and the hated French *Milice*. Taschereau was particularly successful in using his radio to call up supply drops and ammunition for his men, and he was able to distribute equipment for over 1,000 members of the *Maquis*.

Eventually, in late August, advance units of the U.S. Third Army reached Troyes. But "his zest for adventure," noted Felix Walter, "seems not to have been quenched." Taschereau joined forces with the Americans. Organizing an army intelligence service using his local knowledge and many of the men he had fought with, he and his team of fifty agents bicycled ahead of the advancing Americans reporting on the movements of the retreating Germans. By the time SOE London finally ordered him to return to England, he was responsible for all agent intelligence in the three departments of Aube, Côte-d'Or, and Haute-Marne. Like Archambault, Taschereau was awarded the Military Cross for his work in France.

The third over-age Canadian recruited in Canada in the fall of 1943 and trained at Camp X, Joseph Benoit, also worked for SOE in both Europe and Asia. For much of the time his career paralleled that of Archambault, and the two men trained together at Camp X, at SOE schools in Britain, and then in the Eastern Warfare Schools in India and Ceylon. In peacetime an electrical engineer with the Montreal Tramway Company, Benoit parachuted into France just two weeks before D-Day to work as a wireless operator with a sabotage circuit code-named SILVERSMITH in the Champagne district close to Reims. A "dark decisive man with a poker face and remarkable skill at all card games",[23] Benoit specialized in blowing up ammunition and petrol dumps, and he twice cut the crucial Reims-Berlin telephone cable using sulphuric acid. But his most important victory was in establishing the location of V-1 rocket sites in the Champagne, where his reconnaissance was instrumental in helping to locate twelve kilometres of tunnel full of rockets and component parts. "I got a great satisfaction," Benoit told a newspaper reporter after he returned to Canada, "out of seeing the RAF come over soon and drop bombs on the spot." He also picked up information by pretending to be a collaborator and fraternizing with German officers. "I must have looked more French than a Frenchman," he recalled, "for German soldiers often stopped to talk to me on the street." Forced to leave the area when his driver, who had drunk and talked too much in a bar, was picked up and tortured by the Gestapo, Benoit then moved south and hid out in the forests close to Chaumont where he helped to organize a large force of *Maquis*. Finally, like Taschereau, he helped the liberating U.S. Third Army in mop-up operations before returning to SOE headquarters in London at the end of the year.

Along with Archambault and Taschereau, Benoit travelled out to India early in 1945, having volunteered for more SOE work in Asia. What he experienced provides a good example of how SOE's involvement with local guerrilla forces could lead to a political jungle.

Benoit operated in Burma for a month before being returned to Calcutta to prepare for a mission into Malaya as part of SOE's plan to help with Admiral Louis Mountbatten's planned attack on the Malay Peninsula, code-named ZIPPER. Mountbatten, the Allied commander in South-east Asia, originally timed ZIPPER for November 1945 but, after the German surrender, advanced it to August. Force 136 was given the role of arming and training guerrillas throughout the country ready to support ZIPPER when the moment arrived.

The main resistance force in Malaya was the anti-Japanese Union and Forces (AJUF), formed in 1943 by the Communist Party of Malaya, which was based almost exclusively on the large ethnic Chinese population of the Malay States. This presented the British with a problem similar to that in Yugoslavia: should they support this Communist resistance force in the common struggle against the enemy? The answer was as unavoidable as the one in Europe, and on New Year's Eve, 1943, SOE negotiated an agreement whereby the AJUF agreed to operate under the orders of the Allied commander-in-chief in return for supplies of arms, explosives, and money. The man with whom they negotiated, Chang-Hung, secretary-general of the Malayan Communist Party, later turned out to have been an informer of the Japanese. At the end of the war when this was discovered and he was denounced by the Party, Chang-Hung disappeared, taking with him a large amount of the Party's funds.

It was into this political as well as natural jungle that Benoit parachuted from a Liberator on August 5, 1945, his mission, code-named TIDEWAY GREEN, being to work with a group of Communist guerrillas in the northern region of Jahore State with a view both to collecting tactical intelligence and to blocking the Japanese retreat when Mountbatten's forces landed later that month. The atomic explosion at Hiroshima on Benoit's first day in Malaya rendered his mission redundant. Instead of finding himself working with the Communists, he now found himself working to prevent a Communist takeover, to preserve law and order in the interval between the Japanese surrender and the arrival of British troops, and to disarm the guerrillas. This was not just a question of preserving Malaya for the British. It was also necessary to prevent local massacres of the ethnic Chinese by the Malays and to keep peace between the two communities. To do this, Benoit's mission even resorted to using their former enemies, the Japanese, to patrol the area. Eventually, in November 1945, British forces were able to replace Force 136 and Benoit returned to Colombo for return to Canada.

But long before Hiroshima put an abrupt end to SOE activities in Asia, Camp X ceased to be a special agent-training school, assuming a new role that would be equally important in the rapidly cooling post-war climate.

CHAPTER 9

Final Secrets: Dossiers and a Defector

While many of the agents who passed through Camp X in 1943 were in Cairo, Bari, or London making the final preparations for their missions behind enemy lines, the general progress of the war and the prospect of impending victory, as well as the changing needs of SOE, introduced a significant shift in the Camp's life. From its principal role as an SOE training school for secret agents and partisan fighters, it was now transformed by decisions made in London in February 1944 into a communications centre.

Already the level of training activity had fallen drastically. Canada had been combed almost to the point of exhaustion for likely agents for use in Europe. OSS training schools were now fully functioning, OSS had finally got its own programme running smoothly, and American needs could no longer justify the Camp's existence. There remained for the most part only routine security courses for those working in Ottawa or at the BSC offices in New York and Washington. But here, too, things were beginning to wind down. South and Central America were no longer security threats, and with the tide of victory clearly moving in Allied favour, BSC's role was rapidly diminishing. The Americans had assumed many of BSC security functions in the Western Hemisphere, and much of the important liaison work on SOE and SIS affairs was taking place in London or North Africa. A number of top personnel left BSC, transferred to more important tasks in Europe or the Mediterranean. Of the remaining work, an increasing amount consisted of facilitating intelligence communications between Washington and London.

With the operational centre of gravity in the Anglo-American intelligence alliance shifting to Europe, the fate of SOE training courses at Camp X became deeply entangled in rivalries and disagreements between Gubbins and SOE headquarters in London on the one hand, and Stephenson and BSC in New York on the other. The widespread belief that Camp X was a Stephenson operation, as well as the equally powerful notion that he effectively pulled the intelligence strings in London, is amply disproved by material dealing with relations between SOE headquarters and BSC in New York that was made available to the author from the SOE archives in London.

The fate of Camp X had in fact been hanging in the balance since as early as the summer of 1942.

Gubbins had been a party to the original decision to set up Camp X. But he had become increasingly unhappy at arrangements that gave Stephenson in New York more authority over the school than himself. After all, it had been set up under the aegis of SOE, and he had let some of his most skilled instructors cross the Atlantic to get it going. Technically speaking, the school was only one among the many SOE training schools scattered around the world which he controlled from SOE headquarters and he kept a close eye on all of them through regular inspections by SOE officials from London. As early as March 1942, Camp X operations were scrutinized by John Keswick and Francis Glyn, the former a partner in the Far Eastern trading firm of Jardine Matheson and Company, the latter a merchant banker, and both leading SOE executives. Less than a month later, as we have seen, Lieutenant-Colonel "Jimmy" Munn, head of the Beaulieu schools, also went out to Camp X. Yet administratively it was BSC that ran the Camp, and in many ways London had little control over it. Skilbeck, for example, had no direct dealings with Gubbins once he became commandant, and the Camp ran virtually as an autonomous operation. This undoubtedly irked the irascible Gubbins. He also shared the general feeling in SOE that their organization in New York needed to be brought under tighter and more professional control than Stephenson could provide. In the summer of 1942, therefore, he decided that the Camp would be taken away from BSC and administered directly from London. At the same time, however, he was also considering more radical action to close it down altogether on the grounds that the new OSS schools had made it redundant, and that British security needs in Central and South America had diminished considerably. Viewed from London, Camp X was an expensive and unnecessary luxury.

Not surprisingly, Stephenson felt differently. Camp X was a splendid showroom with which to impress the Americans, and he saw no reason to give any of it up. Moreover, he argued, Camp X still had important tasks to perform. True, the Americans no longer needed it for training their own agents, but some of the originally secondary purposes of the school had now moved to the forefront. There was still a lot of work to be done in connection with South and Central America, and the Camp would provide a useful preliminary training for agents recruited in Canada or Latin America and then sent overseas for service in Europe. But the strongest card in Stephenson's hand was the situation in Latin America and the need to cultivate the Americans. Pointing out that Brazil and Argentina were "teeming with Axis agents, and other enemies of the Allies", a BSC report of June 2, 1942, entitled "S.O. in Latin America – its past history, present resources and future possibilities" emphasized the urgent need to mobilize American support.

> Above all, [it noted] there are powerful agencies among our friends in Washington who must be told, persuaded, and convinced, of what should be done. [In this connection, the report continued, SOE] should be particularly grateful to the training school [Camp X]; which by the hospitality accorded to numbers of C.O.I. F.B.I., P.W.D., etc. officials, has put all these U.S. Government agencies deeply in our debt. Of those Americans who have attended courses at the school, everyone without exception, has returned a friend of England and an admirer of S.O. It is the rule, rather than the exception for close and sincere friendships to be made between members of the S.O. New York office and their American 'schoolfellows'. Friendships, which in the possibilities they create for future co-operation can and should prove to be priceless.
>
> This, indeed, throws into relief the great task which lies ahead. It is the task of educating, guiding and co-operating with the Americans, in our common aim of preserving South America as an invaluable asset to the democratic cause, and in

preventing our enemies from gaining control of any part of its territory or economy.[1]

Stephenson argued this case personally with Gubbins and other SOE chiefs when he flew over to London in June 1942 in the company of Donovan. It was a critical time and a critical visit. OSS was formed in June, and the London Treaty with SOE followed immediately afterwards. BSC provided the hinge of much of their co-operation, and it would be foolish, Stephenson argued, to close down the Camp. In the end, London accepted Stephenson's case. Skilbeck, newly arrived in Oshawa that summer, heard vague rumours of these discussions through his main contact in New York, Herbert Sichel, but nothing happened to disturb the daily running of the Camp.

Still, the now-tenuous hold that Camp X had in London's mind can be clearly seen in terms of reference given to Colonel Louis Franck when he was appointed SOE chief in New York the following month. His official brief for Camp X read in part as follows: "You will examine the desirability of the continuation of STS 103...", and hardly had he arrived in New York than Gubbins sent him a letter dated July 17, 1942, repeating London's desire to have exclusive control over Camp X, "even if the school is only going to last another two or three months". Sir Charles Hambro, appointed the new head of SOE in April 1942, finally intervened personally to settle the Stephenson-Gubbins dispute. "The basic principle," he declared in an official directive of September 1942 preserved in the SOE archives, "will be that the Commandant of STS 103 will be directly responsible to Gubbins in regard to all technical aspects of the training establishment and its activities."[2] This was a decisive reaffirmation of London's primacy over BSC on the substance of Camp X's operations.

Camp X had been reprieved, but within four months its fate was again under discussion, this time prompted by major strategic decisions reached at the Casablanca Conference in January 1943. Roosevelt and Churchill met in Morocco to celebrate the successful Allied landings in North Africa and plot an agreed-upon course for the coming year. They and their chiefs of staff agreed to focus on the Mediterranean and the Italians as their next major target. Sicily would be invaded in July. In the Balkans, where Italian troops formed the main occupying garrisons, guerrilla activity would be stepped up.

These decisions profoundly affected SOE, which was already in contact with guerrilla movements in Greece and Yugoslavia. A greatly increased program of support involving large numbers of agents parachuted into the area placed a sudden huge burden on SOE training. Facilities in Britain had been stretched for some time, and indeed Brooker had been so aware of them that he had recently refrained from asking for more support from the Beaulieu or Arisaig centres. But in the light of new Balkan needs, the situation had gone far beyond anything he had envisaged. Gubbins, in London, decided that there would have to be a drastic re-allocation of resources.

Throughout the winter and into the spring of 1943 Gubbins and his staff at Baker Street in London discussed the fate of Camp X, with Gubbins arguing strongly that the Camp had more than fulfilled its original purpose, and what was the point of keeping an entire establishment going in Canada when the manpower was needed in Britain? Thus stated, the argument was irrefutable. Hambro agreed that it was desirable to close Camp X "for many reasons". In May, SOE London told Stephenson that the training school would close down on July 3. It would be rented to the Canadians, but SOE would retain the right to re-open it, in case needs changed, with six months' notice.[3]

In the summer of 1943, therefore, Camp X came within a hair's breadth of closing down. But just four days before BSC was to break the news to Skilbeck, its commanding officer, London gave it a dramatic last-minute reprieve. Ironically, events related to the Balkans had this time worked in its favour.

The decision coincided with de Chastelain's mission to Canada to find recruits to fight as agents behind enemy lines in the Balkans. On hearing of the proposed closure, de Chastelain immediately sent an urgent cable to London saying that he could not hold himself responsible for the selection of recruits if the Camp closed. It was simply impossible, he said, to evaluate recruits for guerrilla work with nothing more than an interview. Camp X had to be kept open as a holding school to give recruits some preliminary testing. This cable coincided with pressures also reaching London from Washington, where they had undoubtedly been stimulated by Stephenson and BSC headquarters. While the OSS had little further use for the school, U.S. military and naval intelligence felt that they could take advantage of its facilities, and they had succeeded in rounding up backing from the

British services for their request that the Camp be kept open. Once again, therefore, and most reluctantly, Gubbins yielded. He gave Camp X a three-month reprieve. But as he did so, he noted that this would probably turn out to be an underestimate, and it would very likely stay open until early 1944. He was right. On February 18, 1944, he cabled to Stephenson for the last time about the Camp. The manpower situation he was facing as head of SOE was extremely tense, he told Stephenson, and "SOE had given an undertaking to the War Office that they would at once close any establishment which was not vital to SOE work." SOE had gained as much benefit as it could from Camp X, and the time had come, he said, to close it once and for all. This time, Stephenson offered ño objection. Two months later, in April 1944, STS 103 closed down. It had functioned as an SOE training school for just a little over two years.

First among the regular instructional staff to go was the chief instructor, Paul Dehn, who by early March had already left for New York *en route* back to Europe. From Ottawa, Tommy Stone dropped him a note expressing genuine regret at his departure and unconsciously revealing how top officials in Ottawa had now come to think of Camp X as a primarily Canadian operation. "Thank you for all the assistance which you have given us at the school," he told Dehn; "it is my earnest hope that our paths may cross again in the near future. It has been a joy to know you."[4] The next to leave was Hamish Pelham-Burn, who had been told the previous fall that he was to be transferred elsewhere. In October 1943 SOE had selected as a replacement, Major Thomas Cook, whom they immediately sent for training at their specialist demolitions school at Brickondbury Manor in Hertfordshire, close to London. Officially known as Station XVII, it was run by George Rheam, an instructor of genius who has been described as the founder of modern industrial sabotage. "Anyone trained by him," writes M.R.D. Foot, "could look at a factory with quite new eyes, spot the few essential machines in it, and understand how to stop them with a few well-placed ounces of explosive." Unfortunately Cook had little time at Camp X to impart what he had learned from Rheam: barely two weeks after he arrived at Oshawa, Gubbins informed BSC of his final decision to close down the school. By May, Cook was on his way via San Francisco to help with SOE training in

Australia. Pelham-Burn, the man whom he replaced only too briefly at Camp X, stayed for three days to brief him, and then flew back to Britain from Montreal for a refresher course at Arisaig.[5]

Soon Skilbeck and Hannay were the only two British officers left to wind up the training school. They were helped by Art Bushell, who by this time had been promoted to the rank of acting major in the Canadian Army. When Skilbeck and Hannay finally left Camp X in early April, Bushell took over command of the remnant local staff and supplies. Two of the Canadian NCO instructors trained by Pelham-Burn were sent to an offshoot operation briefly established in the Okanagan Valley of British Columbia to train Chinese volunteers for special duties in East Asia. Some of the Camp's equipment was given to the OSS for use in its American training schools and the rest was returned to the Canadian Army, as were most of the Camp's administrative personnel. By the summer of 1944, when the Allied attack on Fortress Europe reached its crescendo with the D-Day landings, the huts of the training school stood empty and the sound of explosives and small-arms fire had ceased to trouble the residents of Oshawa and Whitby.

But if STS 103 was dead, Camp X lived on. It still had a role to play within the history of BSC, and events that later took place within its confines were to provide a dramatic interlude in the transition from World War to Cold War. Indeed, Camp X continued as a functioning military installation until the late 1960s, although for most of the post-war period its activities still remain shrouded in secrecy.

Camp X survived because, like the mythical monster after which it was named, the wireless operation HYDRA lived on even when its other head, STS 103, was severed. Not only did it survive; it flourished. At the same time, it took the first steps that eventually transformed it from a wartime British to a peacetime Canadian operation.

The secrecy that had surrounded Camp X from the beginning had obscured even from some of the Canadians most closely involved the full picture of what the British were up to. HYDRA's operation and its steady expansion in particular had caught some of them off balance. "I am really not very clear as to just what action is being taken at Whitby," complained Colonel L.M. Chesley, director of staff duties at the Canadian National Defence Headquarters and the man responsible for handling the top-secret 25-1-1 files, to Colonel W.W. Murray, the director of military intelligence, on July 12, 1944. "The whole set-up has become somewhat confusing," he went on, "and I request clarification."6 Murray had a much clearer picture based on Canadian intelligence co-operation with BSC, and he agreed that with the closure of STS 103 the arrangements for Camp X reached in the fall of 1941 should now be reassessed. He summoned a top-level meeting in Ottawa to discuss the future of Camp X and BSC activities in Canada.

On August 9, 1944, Tommy Drew-Brook, who was still BSC's representative in Canada, found himself attending that meeting. A dozen top Canadian defence officials were present, as well as Captain Herbert Rowland, a Canadian sent up by Stephenson from New York. Much of the time was taken up with discussion about the training school in British Columbia, now due to close down because its trainees were being transferred to East Asia. The remainder of the discussion concerned Camp X. Colonel Murray, who chaired the meeting, said that, although its training function had ended, Camp X was still needed as a communications unit. "Although its existence no longer needs to be kept such a closely guarded secret as that of the SOE training school," he said, "the work being done there is of a top-secret nature connected with intelligence service work and the operation will continue to need Canadian support in terms of administrative assistance and personnel."7

While this meeting did help to clarify the minds of Canadian officials in Ottawa about what was still going on at the Camp, they decided that new ministerial authorization was needed. As the chief of the general staff explained to Ralston, who was still the minister of national defence, on August 29, the Camp X radio station "is part of the extensive wireless network which, in conjunction with Intelligence Discrimination Units (Canadian, American, and British) are engaged in the securing of information from Japanese wireless messages. It need hardly be stressed that the information gained in this manner is of the utmost operational value in the prosecution of the war against Japan." He recommended that as an integral part of the Canadian war effort, the costs of running Camp X should be borne by the Canadians. Ralston approved the proposal, and from September 1944 the Canadian Army assumed the costs of all Canadian

Army personnel stationed at Camp X – a total of three officers and sixty other ranks – in the first step towards eventual Canadian take-over of the operation. At the same time the army changed the Camp's designation, for security reasons, to "No. 2 Military Research Centre."[8]

Simultaneously with his approval of the new arrangement on pay, Ralston agreed to a request submitted by BSC for a 50 per cent increase in the size of the staff that would bring the total number employed to approximately one hundred. As soon as approval was given, Stephenson sent Pat Bayly to Toronto to prepare the ground for the recruitment and employment of the extra personnel. "Lt-Col Bailey [sic] spent the last two days in the District," reported Major Frank Justin from Toronto to Colonel Chesley on August 21, 1944. "He has laid the grounds to enable the employment of approximately 25 to 30 more personnel."[9] As we have seen, HYDRA played an important part in the general SIGINT (Signals Intelligence) battle against enemy communications and then, after the Japanese surrendered, in the Cold War struggles with the Soviet Union.

HYDRA was not the only activity that continued at Camp X after the SOE training school had closed down. The Camp had been created in secrecy, and throughout its existence those who worked there had lived both literally and metaphorically a cloak-and-dagger existence. Therefore it was appropriate that the two final scenes played out on its diminishing stage should have been among the most secret and bizarre of all.

A casual visitor staying at the Genosha Hotel in Oshawa in the summer or fall of 1945 might have been intrigued by the daily and nocturnal routine of a small group of men and women who were obviously long-term residents. They kept to themselves, talked little, and were a cut above the average visitor to Oshawa's premier but nonetheless modest hostelry. More to the point, they kept peculiar hours. Just when most of the guests were relaxing for the evening after their dinner, the nine or ten civilian strangers would be picked up by an army truck outside the hotel and disappear into the night. The next morning they would reappear in time for breakfast, clearly having worked all night. They would then retreat to their rooms for the rest of the day until dinner time, when once again the routine would be repeated.

Oshawa was accustomed to mystery surrounding nearby Camp X. No doubt those who wondered about the guests at the Genosha concluded that they were connected with its curious affairs. Perhaps they were scientists working on the atom bomb, for ever since Hiroshima early in August rumour had swept the town that plutonium was being stored within the Camp's still-guarded perimeter. Or perhaps they were something to do with the CBC, for since the training school had closed there had been speculation that the remaining wireless station belonged to the national radio network. Neither guess could ever have been correct, for at no time was Camp X the site of nuclear experiments or of a CBC radio station. But that the mysterious visitors were connected with the Camp was true. In fact, they were intimately connected with William Stephenson and BSC itself, most of them having spent the war working at Rockefeller Center in New York. They were there to carry out a final mission personally commanded by Stephenson himself.

Their job was to write in absolute secrecy the history of BSC, a record of its activities that would be seen by only a handful of people who needed to know. Once completed, it would be the only record of what BSC had accomplished. Its participants, sworn to silence, would take their secrets to the grave. The dossiers would then be destroyed. Only between the carefully bound covers created in Oshawa that summer would secrets of BSC be preserved.

Stephenson's desire for a written record of BSC activities was motivated by more than concern for the curiosity of future generations. All British secret agencies produced histories of their wartime operations. They were intended for internal circulation only, and to this day *none* has been released to the populations in whose name they worked. Inevitably, they were designed to justify the agency's work and to put the activities of its leading personalities in the best possible light. Stephenson was no less moved by this concern than others. But from the beginning of the enterprise, there was also a hidden agenda. This was revealed only after the history was completed, when Stephenson's first representative in Canada, Charles Vining, returned briefly to centre stage for the final curtain call on the BSC drama.

Since his illness in 1943 Vining had played little active part in BSC affairs. But in January 1946 Stephenson again called on him to do a favour comparable to that of 1940, when he had persuaded Ralston to give BSC a free hand in Canada. Would Vining help him in a bid to set up and run a new Canadian intelligence agency? It seemed that Stephenson held a strong card for such a bid, and Vining agreed.

"[In] January 1946 I wrote a new foreword for [the history] in which WS [Stephenson] gave warning of the Communist-Russian menace (then realized by few)," Vining wrote later, "and stressed the need for intensified intelligence services as the first line of defence."10 Two weeks later Vining tried to sell the idea in Ottawa when he met Norman Robertson and Arnold Heeney, the clerk of the Privy Council, and went over the foreword, stressing that the BSC record made Stephenson the ideal man to head a new Canadian intelligence service. "But," recalled Vining, "we got nowhere with it." For the moment, therefore, the plan was dropped. But the BSC record has remained a weapon in the arsenal of subsequent campaigns to strengthen Western intelligence defences against what Stephenson and many supporters have always seen as the primary Communist threat.

The importance that Stephenson attached to the history is indicated by the people he selected and the way in which he arranged for it to be written. Even before the war in Europe was over, he had set the project in motion. The first person he chose was a member of his BSC staff, Gilbert Highet, a professor of classics at Columbia University and the husband of Helen McInnes, the well-known spy-fiction writer. Perhaps Stephenson felt that her writing skills would rub off on her husband. Highet certainly did a great deal of the essential spade work of sorting through the documents, and he even produced an outline for Stephenson to read. But it failed to provide Stephenson with what he wanted, which was a lively, dramatic, and readable account that highlighted in particular BSC achievements during the period of American neutrality. Thus he turned to two other members of BSC with proven writing skills.

The first was Tom Hill, the Canadian we have already met as one of the BSC staff sent up to Camp X for an introductory course who spent most of the war writing the *Western Hemisphere Weekly*

Intelligence Bulletin. After Highet's attempt had been rejected, Hill was a natural choice to be put in charge of the project.

The other writer that Stephenson chose was the famous British author Roald Dahl. Dahl, who had been wounded while flying with No. 80 Fighter Squadron on the Western Desert, was already making his name as a writer when he was posted to Washington as assistant British air attaché in 1943. Some of his early short stories had already appeared in the United States, and his children's book, *The Gremlins*, had just been published and was a favourite of Eleanor Roosevelt's grandchildren. So it was not surprising that Dahl quickly joined the Washington social circuit, where he was a frequent dinner guest of the Roosevelts, the Morgenthaus, and other members of the administration. Dahl's introduction to BSC happened by chance. One evening an American acquaintance who was a friend of the American vice-president, Henry Wallace, called to see Dahl. He happened to be carrying some papers for Wallace that had been prepared by Adolf Berle of the State Department, and he showed them to Dahl. They revealed American plans for the domination of the post-war commercial airline business. Dahl, immediately realizing their significance, was able to borrow the material, hand it over to a BSC man he knew for rapid copying, and return it to his acquaintance without the latter realizing what had happened. Eventually the document found its way to Stephenson, who forwarded it to London. Impressed by Dahl's quick wit, Stephenson asked him to work for BSC, and for the remainder of the war Dahl was officially assigned to the BSC Washington office as a liaison officer with the OSS.

But his selection as co-writer of the history was not a success. Oshawa was a far cry from Washington, and dinners at the Genosha Hotel no match for those at Hyde Park. And for a fiction writer with a brilliant career in the making, the lengthy and prosaic job of producing an official history under the supervision of someone else soon palled. Dahl grew restless and eventually, in his own words, he "copped out", leaving the bulk of the work to Hill.

Dahl's strongest recollection of this strange episode in his life is its opening scene. "The thing I always remember," he told the author forty years after the event, "was how Bill [Stephenson] had all these archives sent up from New York in some sort of wonderful security truck with an escort."[11] This indeed is how it was, for the operation was carried out with all the care, precision, and secrecy that surrounded the most sensitive SOE operation behind enemy lines.

It did not take Stephenson very long to decide that the operation was too sensitive to be carried out in New York. The plan called for the history to be printed, and in the United States this meant using a commercial printer. This was too risky. It was not just that official British secrets were involved; there was also a lot of sensitive material concerning the United States. This was mostly information about BSC's work during the period of American neutrality when intimate links had been made with elements of the Roosevelt administration and a great deal of subversive and undercover work had been carried out to counter the powerful isolationist forces in American life. Details of this activity, if published in the American press, could seriously hurt Anglo-American relations and have damaging repercussions inside the United States. Stephenson decided that the work would have to be done elsewhere and, as a further security measure, would be printed by BSC itself. It made sense to carry out both the writing and the printing in the same location. The only place suitable and under BSC control was Camp X.

This explains the convoy and its outriders that travelled from New York to Oshawa in the spring of 1945, just as the Germans were surrendering to the Allies in Europe. Inside the vans were the thousands of top-secret files needed to produce the history. There were also two small offset presses and several of the early IBM executive typewriters from which the final copy would be photographed. When the convoy arrived at Camp X, it was to find that a special concrete building had been constructed for the project, with a large vault to hold the files and special rooms for the writers, secretaries, and typists. It was another sign of the importance he attached to the project that Stephenson assigned his two private secretaries to the team: Grace Garner, a Canadian who had been his principal secretary since the beginning and was going to write up some of the early chapters, and Eleanor Fleming, another Canadian who had worked in his private office for most of the war. Merle Cameron, head of Stephenson's filing section, also accompanied them.

Camp X had changed considerably since Hill's visit in 1943 when the training school had been in full swing, and he found it rather depressing. But one thing had not changed. "People in the area were quite curious about Camp X," he remembers, "and, according to one story I heard, people got the impression that the Camp was involved in something to do with the atomic bomb. Once they brought in a load of asphalt to surface a tennis court. Somebody had heard that uranium came from an ore called pitchblende and jumped to the conclusion that the black stuff must be pitchblende, thus giving a little coherence to the cover story [that it was a research centre]."[12]

Hill worked hard on the history throughout the summer, and by September most of the writing was done. But Stephenson was still dissatisfied. He wanted yet more drama and colour, and the separate sections written by Dahl and Hill needed to be more closely woven together. So for a final editing he brought in still another British writer working for BSC. Giles Playfair, the son of actor-producer Sir Nigel Playfair, had narrowly escaped capture by the Japanese during the fall of Singapore, where he had been working for the Malaysian Broadcasting Company. His dramatic eyewitness account of these events, *Singapore Goes Off the Air*, had just been published in New York and London. For this reason, Stephenson thought him an excellent candidate for the job of producing a readable and exciting account of BSC. But Playfair also knew about BSC from the inside. On arriving in New York after his escape from Singapore, he had been recruited into BSC by Christopher Wren, the son of P.C. Wren, author of the incomparable story of Foreign Legion adventure, *Beau Geste*. For two years Playfair had worked on counter-espionage in the New York office. "So," he revealed to the author recently, "I had material of my own to add to the story." As each chapter of the history appeared, Playfair edited it and submitted his final version to Stephenson for approval.[13]

By this time the original plan of printing the book at the Camp had been abandoned as too time-consuming and complicated. Instead, the work was given to an Oshawa printing company. This required yet another layer of secrecy. As Tom Hill now recalls, "We had a monotype operator, a compositor and a pressman at our disposal, all of them interviewed by the RCMP and sworn to secrecy."

Everything was done under tight supervision. Each night a few pages of the typescript would be taken under guard to the printer's. At the end of the night the galleys of type and galley proofs made up by the operator would be escorted back to Camp X for proofreading. When this was completed, everything would be taken back to the printer's, again under guard, the compositor would make up pages of type, and the galleys were then destroyed. In Hill's words, "It became quite a little feat of logistics to keep all these things in balance, especially after we started printing and would be taking in the made-up pages of type for the pressman and bringing back the printed pages... together with more work for the monotype operator and more for the compositor. We also had to develop an index as we went along."

A complicating dimension was added when photographs, printed by photo-offset in yet another plant, were added, and more security screening had to be carried out. All this required considerable feats of logistics. "Our hotel," Hill remembers, "was only a couple of blocks from the print shop, but everything we worked with was stored out at the camp, about four miles away. So we were shuttled back and forth by army vehicles. There we would select what things we had to take in to the print shop that night, would load it into the car, and would be driven back to town. After the night in the print shop we would be picked up again and taken back to the camp, would put the night's work in the vault, then be driven back to town where we would have breakfast and go to bed for the day."

When all the printing was completed and everything but the final copies had been destroyed, Tommy Drew-Brook, still acting as Stephenson's man in Toronto, arranged for a bindery to open on a Sunday. This was no mean feat in the days when the city was still imbued with the Presbyterian ethic and street signs told children that play on Sunday was forbidden. To the Sabbath chill was added a January blizzard as Hill and his assistants – who included his wife – drove from Oshawa to deliver the boxes of typeset pages. At the bindery, twenty copies of the history were bound in leather. Each was then placed in a specially designed box with a lock, a precaution requested by Stephenson himself.

Finally, when the twenty copies had been delivered back to Oshawa and then forwarded to Stephenson, Hill's team took the final and irrevocable step in protecting the secrets of BSC, the destruction of the files. "We set up a furnace of sorts," Hill records, "a concrete block affair at the camp, with a grate in it and a screen over the top to keep any large pieces of charred paper from floating away in the draft.... Various trusted people watched the fire and fed it from time to time." Thus the secrets of BSC were consigned to the flames.

If the burning of the BSC files provides a historian's nightmare, the fate of the twenty leather-bound volumes presents us with a sleuth's delight. Stephenson had operated throughout his life on the principle that if you wanted something badly enough, you always went straight to the top. He took immediate possession of ten copies, kept at least one for himself, and then distributed the others to Churchill and the leaders of the services that BSC had represented, as well as to one or two carefully chosen confidants. Of these ten copies none has seen the public light of day in the forty years that have since passed. The copy sent to Norman Robertson has disappeared, and the one sent to Gubbins as head of SOE cannot be found in what remains of the SOE archives in London. The copy in the SIS archive, like all SIS documents, remains permanently unavailable and officially non-existent. No copy has surfaced in the United States. Sometimes referred to as "The Bible" by those who have seen it, the official BSC history continues to be for the most part a secret to all but a small and diminishing band of disciples. But this is how Stephenson wanted it. He made this clear by the fate he decreed for the remaining ten copies. Eventually he decided that he had no need of them. At first they were stored in a bank vault in Montreal. Then, some time in 1946, they were taken out to a farm in the Eastern Townships of Quebec and burned by Tom Hill and his wife. "In retrospect," he mused later, "I wonder why I didn't keep a copy for myself. I think I was so completely sold on the need for complete security that the thought never occurred to me."

Forty years later, we can understand the obsessively secret atmosphere surrounding the fate of the BSC history and its writing at Camp X better if we turn our gaze to the final scene being played out in the BSC drama. For even while Hill and his team of writers were travelling by moonlight between the guarded vaults of the Camp and the Genosha Hotel, the most bizarre of the many actors who passed through its gates had arrived to take up residence.

The Gouzenko case was the first important spy scandal of the postwar years and quickly gained status as a turning point in the emerging Cold War. As a result of Gouzenko's revelations several arrests were made in Canada. An atomic scientist, Alan Nunn May, was detained and then imprisoned in Britain, and in the United States investigations began that led ultimately to the executions of Julius and Ethel Rosenberg as Soviet spies in 1953.

In spite of the remarkable consequences of his act, Igor Gouzenko was a relatively insignificant figure. It was less what he knew than what he brought with him that was important, and even now, forty years later, reverberations of the Gouzenko affair are felt whenever allegations about the presence of Soviet moles in the West are raised. He was a twenty-six-year-old cipher clerk working for Soviet military intelligence (GRU) in the Soviet Embassy in Ottawa when, on the night of September 5, 1945 – less than a month after Hiroshima and Nagasaki – he left the embassy with documents revealing details of extensive espionage the USSR conducted against its wartime Allies. At first Gouzenko encountered great difficulty in interesting people in what he had to offer, and he was turned away from both newspaper and government offices. The events surrounding his defection, and the subsequent trials in Canada and elsewhere, are now well known, but at the time, when Canadian officials realized the significance of his material, the case was kept from public knowledge for a combination of operational and political reasons. From September on, Gouzenko and his family were kept under close wraps, under the protection of the RCMP. For cover purposes, those involved in the case were told that he had been taken "up north". In fact the exact opposite was true. For most of the time the Gouzenko family were well to the south, hidden away at Camp X. The reason lay in Stephenson's direct involvement in the whole affair.

By an accident of timing, which in retrospect must have appeared miraculous to those involved, Stephenson was on a routine visit to Ottawa the night Gouzenko spent wandering around looking in vain for asylum. From the exclusive Seigniory Club in Montebello, Stephenson phoned Norman Robertson, the under-secretary at External Affairs, to invite him for a drink. Instead, within hours he found himself closeted with Robertson and Tommy Stone while the "Man of Influence" poured out his troubles and sought his advice. The problem, as always, lay with the Canadian prime minister. Exhibiting his customary distaste for spying and undercover work, King had said that he did not want Canada to get involved with Gouzenko at all. So far as he was concerned, he had told Robertson, they should let Gouzenko wander around until he either went back to his embassy or committed suicide. "If suicide took place," King confided to his diary, "let the city police take charge and secure whatever there was in the way of documents, but on no account for us to take the initiative." [14] If Canada got involved officially, it could only mean a further deterioration of relations with the Russians.

Stephenson vigorously opposed King's view. Like SIS headquarters in London, BSC for most of the war had operated a counterespionage section to keep an eye on Communist subversion. While this had focused more on Communist political activities than on Soviet espionage, Stephenson harboured no benevolence towards the USSR. Moreover, he was convinced, even before the Gouzenko affair, that BSC could provide the nucleus of a post-war intelligence organization in the Western Hemisphere. The cipher clerk's defection provided him with a golden opportunity to keep BSC alive until its post-war existence could be guaranteed. For the next few months, therefore, he did his best to ensure that BSC played an active role in the Gouzenko affair.

His first step was to argue strongly against King's view that Gouzenko should be ignored. The Russian, he said, would certainly have information valuable not merely to Canada but also to Britain, the United States, and other Allies. Furthermore, Gouzenko's life was almost certainly in danger. They should act, and do so immediately by taking Gouzenko in from the cold and looking at his documents.

Stephenson's word carried weight in the Canadian capital. He had all the expertise represented by British Intelligence behind him, and had run a security operation in close co-operation with the RCMP for the previous five years. Robertson hardly needed convincing. Eventually, the two of them prevailed over King's initial hesitations and doubts. Robertson shortly afterwards telephoned RCMP headquarters and gave the Mounties permission to intervene in the case, and the next day they took Gouzenko into protective custody. Russian-language experts began to translate his documents. By that same afternoon an alarming picture had emerged, and Robertson was able to tell King that they were dealing with "an espionage system on a large scale". Not only were there Soviet sympathizers in high places in the Canadian government and civil service; they were also in the British

High Commission and among scientists working on atomic secrets.

This was too big for the Canadians to handle on their own. The RCMP was simply too ill equipped to deal with a major espionage case alone. Its headquarters Intelligence Branch consisted of only two men, neither of whom was well qualified for complex counter-espionage work. The man in charge was Inspector Charles Rivett-Carnac, the younger son of an English baronet who had made his way through the ranks and had thoroughly absorbed the Mountie ethos. His assistant, John Leopold, enjoyed a strong reputation within the Force as the man who had penetrated the Communist Party in the 1920s and been the Crown's star witness in the 1931 trial of its leading members on conspiracy charges. But the Czech-born Leopold knew little about Soviet intelligence, and his Russian was far from perfect. To help, Rivett-Carnac brought in two senior RCMP criminal investigators, one of whom, Cliff Harvison, had had some wartime experience dealing with a German double agent. But this had not been a success, and RCMP inexperience had led M.I.5 to intervene. The double agent, code-named "Watchdog", had first of all fooled the RCMP in the information he gave them about the *Abwehr*, and, without the RCMP noticing, had then succeeded in telling his German control in Hamburg that he was operating under duress. As a result, M.I.5 had him put in chains and shipped to Britain where he was kept in cold storage until the end of the war. From this and other experiences it was clear that the RCMP needed professional help.

BSC headquarters was still operating on its wartime schedule of a six-day week. So when two of its leading counter-espionage experts arrived for work on September 7, a sunny Saturday morning, they were undoubtedly looking forward to an early departure from the office and a pleasant weekend with family and friends. A phone call from Stephenson's private secretary quickly put an end to that. Did they have their passports ready? she asked. They should get to Ottawa as quickly as possible. The two men barely had time to pack overnight bags before they were flying north over Long Island Sound to Canada. As one of them looked down and saw the waters dotted with the white sails of countless yachts enjoying the last days of summer, it seemed the sort of afternoon when "God's in his Heaven – All's well with the world."[15]

They quickly learned that this was far from true for the world in Ottawa. They were met by George Glazebrook, who immediately took them to the Chateau Laurier Hotel. Safely ensconced in their room, they turned on the bathroom taps in true spy-novel fashion so that no one could overhear while Glazebrook explained what had happened over the last forty-eight hours. They then went on to RCMP headquarters for further briefing. To all intents and purposes, this became their home for the next few weeks.

The two men were Peter Dwyer and Jean-Paul Evans. Dwyer was the senior of the two and head of the counter-espionage division of BSC. His name is now remembered in Canada because he was the first co-ordinator of arts programmes of the Canada Council, the government-funded cultural organization established in 1957, and he eventually became its associate director. In the words of historian J.L. Granatstein, "it was really he who provided its heart and soul".[16] Shortly before Dwyer's premature death from a stroke in 1972, a citation read before the governor-general of Canada described him as "perhaps the best known figure in the Canadian arts community". But the man who impressed Ottawa with his love of the arts had also played an important part in the history of Anglo-Canadian secret intelligence.

Originally recruited into SIS in 1939, Dwyer had first worked in Paris; after the collapse of France in 1940 he was transferred to Panama as head of station. In late 1942 he moved to Washington and came under the aegis of BSC. His job was to run the SIS counter-espionage division (Section V) and to liaise with the FBI. As noted earlier, Stephenson and Hoover had not always seen eye to eye; Dwyer's skill and diplomacy helped considerably to improve the situation. In June 1945, when BSC was beginning to close down, Stephenson told Dwyer, "You laid the groundwork of a vastly improved general relationship." In the same letter Stephenson also told Dwyer that he might expect to be around in BSC for a little while yet. "There is still important work for you to do," he said.[17] He could have had little idea at the time of how true this was. In the event, Dwyer stayed in Washington working for SIS until 1949, where his main job was to liaise with the FBI, CIA, and RCMP.

His most distinguished contribution in Washington in that period was to analyse the evidence from intercepts of Soviet communications that pointed the finger at one of the most infamous of atomic spies, Klaus Fuchs. It was a skilled piece of analysis, and his successor as SIS liaison in Washington was deeply impressed by the man who so carefully briefed him on his new tasks. "I knew him for a brilliant wit, and was to learn that he had a great deal more to him than just wit," was how Kim Philby remembered Dwyer.

He was not alone in being impressed. Dwyer is still remembered by colleagues as a very good intelligence officer, and one M.I.6 source has recently described him as "one of the better people in BSC". After Philby took over in Washington, Dwyer resigned from the British service and settled in Ottawa, where he quickly found a job in the post-war Canadian security and intelligence community. He joined the Privy Council Office in 1952, and played a central role in bringing greater professionalism and coherence to the job as chairman of the Security Panel during the height of the Cold War era. His entry into the Ottawa scene was greatly facilitated by the impression he had made on Canadian officials during the Gouzenko affair.

Dwyer's colleague, Jean-Paul Evans, was another Englishman. He had joined what was then the Security Division of the British Purchasing Division in New York in 1940. When this eventually became part of BSC, Evans graduated into the counter-espionage division, where he specialized in Communist affairs. This brought him into close liaison with the FBI, and he made regular trips to Washington to discuss developments with Lish Whitson, the head of its Communist affairs division. He was to meet this man again in Ottawa, when the Americans sent their own experts to Canada to help assess the damage revealed by Gouzenko's documents.

Dwyer and Evans quickly became leading members of the investigating team. On the Sunday morning after their arrival in Ottawa, they were briefed in greater detail by Rivett-Carnac and Leopold, whom Evans later remembered as "short, inclined to stoutness, [and] at first...very removed from one's idea of a Canadian Mountie." The four men quickly worked out a routine to deal with the defector. Leopold would be the only direct contact with Gouzenko. "He would spend some time with him each day," Evans recalled, "going over the translations which he would have made to date and questioning him as required. He would bring the material to me each day and I would write it up and raise queries as they arose. Peter [Dwyer] would also study the results and generally deal with matters of liaison."[18]

After working out this routine, Dwyer and Evans met with Norman Robertson and then returned to the RCMP offices close to Parliament Hill for their first working session. Here they quickly learned that Gouzenko had worked for Colonel Zabotin, the Russian military attaché, who was also station chief for Red Army intelligence, and used the cover name "Grant". Zabotin, Gouzenko said, was running a spy network in Canada, and he could identify many of the agents. The most important of them, Dwyer and Evans learned, was an atomic scientist known as "Aleck". "This news chilled us," Evans said later. "The Atomic Age had scarcely begun and here we were involved in one of its most sensitive aspects."

The atomic scientist turned out to be Alan Nunn May, who had been working with the National Research Council in Montreal. He had just been posted to a new position in England at the time Gouzenko defected, and it was decided that he should be allowed to go in the hope that he would lead investigators to new contacts. But he was told that he should leave his possessions with the British High Commission, which would arrange for onward shipping. As soon as May had gone, an expert in surreptitious mail opening from the censorship department of BSC, sent to Ottawa specifically for the purpose, set to work. Over several days she meticulously opened and then carefully resealed every one of the packets and parcels that May had left behind. What Dwyer and Evans expected to find was less proof of any Soviet connection than evidence that May had made unauthorized notes of his atomic research. To help in the task, Professor John Cockcroft, director of the Atomic Research Division in Montreal and May's former boss, examined the notes and files as they emerged from the parcels. But nothing was found.

BSC also helped with communications, for several things had quickly become clear, as Jean-Paul Evans now remembers:

As translations of the cables from the Director commenced to cross my desk it became evident that we were indeed dealing with an extensive Russian spy network with links to the United

States, Britain and Switzerland. Among other things, this meant that the most important information had to be passed as quickly as possible to New York to be relayed to London and Washington. At first we did this by diplomatic bag, but Bill Stephenson quickly decided that a wire link was imperative. He arranged to send up a ciphering machine which I knew of as a telekrypton. Manned by one or two specially chosen Wrens, it solved at a stroke our main communication bottleneck....

The telekrypton machine encoded standard five-channel punched tape that could safely be put on the international cable network. Messages were sent from Ottawa to New York, where they were then decoded for Stephenson. He then passed the material on, again by a secure BSC channel, to SIS in London and the FBI in Washington.

For Evans, however, this new procedure almost ended in disaster, as he recently revealed to the author:

So far as I, the sender, was concerned, the tape was a sensitive part of the operation, because if anyone were able to get a copy of a message in clear and of the tape, cryptographic experts would be well on their way to breaking the cipher. (From what I now know, I'm not so sure this necessarily follows, but we were walking on quicksand and acutely security-conscious.) I determined to take no chances and, the first evening after the telekrypton was installed, went down religiously to collect my original message and the tape. So far, so good, but what to do with it? I thrust the loose tape into a metal waste-paper basket, added newspapers, took it to our private washroom, and set fire to the lot. What I hadn't counted on is the fact that punched tape is or was oil-impregnated to make it run more smoothly. Before I knew it, I was enveloped in thick acrid, black smoke, which billowed out of the small window. How it was not noticed and how I avoided setting fire to the headquarters of the Royal Canadian Mounted Police, I shall never know. It would have taxed my ingenuity to explain the circumstances to the fire brigade if they had been called out, and to find a story which would not have drawn the attention of the press.

But if communications security was one worry, the other major concern was the physical safety of Gouzenko himself. Right after he defected, the Russians broke into Gouzenko's apartment searching for the missing cipher clerk. Although their later explanation, in which they claimed to have used "a diplomatic passkey", was received in Ottawa with some hilarity as an ingenuous euphemism for a hefty Russian shoulder, no one regarded the threat to Gouzenko as a joke. At first he was hidden in various hotels or cottages in the countryside surrounding Ottawa. But it eventually became clear that, with winter approaching and the investigation dragging on, some better accommodation was needed. Ideally, it should be out of the Ottawa area.

George B. McClellan once again came to the rescue. He and Herb Spanton, another RCMP officer from the Toronto detachment, were summoned to Ottawa and fully briefed on the case. "We were asked to do a study to find a place to put him that was secure but not totally isolated – preferably in the Toronto area," Spanton recalled later in an interview. "We left Ottawa at around nine o'clock that night. George B. was driving and oddly enough we both thought of the same place at the same time. He said 'Camp X'. I said 'The old farmhouse'. He said 'Yes'. That's how we chose the farmhouse at Camp X as the place to lodge Gouzenko."[19] It was an obvious choice: HYDRA was still operational, the buildings of the vacated training school were in good condition, and the site was guarded.

By mid-October Gouzenko, his pregnant wife, and his young son were safely installed in the old farmhouse with their bodyguard of Mounties. "The location was perfect," said Spanton. "It was wide open so the security was good.... There were antennas and everybody looked upon it as a CBC broadcasting place. The odd time somebody would come down the road to the beach, but we had a very good view." Visitors had either to pass the remaining Camp X guardroom, still manned in order to protect HYDRA, or to approach through open fields and clamber over barbed wire fences. For those inside, the site offered the opportunity to go for walks and break the monotony of guarding the Gouzenkos day and night. Most of the Mounties

disliked the old farmhouse, and some of them found Gouzenko himself an unsympathetic character. But for the defector and his family
the farmhouse was pure luxury. There were plenty of rooms and
unlimited hot water and food. "It was a nice little farmhouse," said
Svetlana Gouzenko many years later; "the first thing I did was take a
bath. After three, four weeks, you can imagine that."[20]

But it was hardly a quiet retreat, and there was a lot of tension.
The RCMP officers slept with their revolvers, and investigators came
down constantly from Ottawa for long interrogations. Gouzenko
himself was profoundly suspicious; like everyone else, he feared
Soviet retribution. Even more than others, he saw Soviet spies everywhere and even became convinced that Inspector Leopold, the RCMP
Russian expert, was a Communist agent. Spanton recalled the day that
Leopold came down from Ottawa to see Gouzenko. "The next day we
left for Ottawa and Igor came with us, but he wouldn't ride in the
same car as Leopold. He said he was a spy. We stopped in Kingston
for lunch and Igor got up and left the table.... He had learned that
Leopold had been undercover for some time and I suppose he felt that
if he worked undercover there he would be working against me too."

George Mackay, another member of Gouzenko's RCMP bodyguard at Camp X, recalled that Gouzenko "was thoroughly frightened
as to what his fate might be. He and I would go on walks together, but
I was never that far away that he couldn't call me. He wanted
somebody with him all the time." In order to get him away from his
wife and child for quiet discussions, interrogators would often drive
him around in a car and talk in the back seat. On one occasion when
the RCMP was driving him to Ottawa, they stopped at a restaurant for
a chicken dinner, got salmonella poisoning, and were quite ill. "Of
course," remembered John Dean, one of the group, "he thought an
agent was involved. It was just lousy chicken in the restaurant."[21]

For all his fears, however, Gouzenko need not have worried.
Operating on a strict need-to-know principle, Stephenson kept the
defector's location from even his counter-espionage experts. Evans,
poring over Gouzenko's evidence in Ottawa, had no idea where he
was hidden. Nor did the team of BSC historians who travelled from
Oshawa to Camp X every night realize that Gouzenko was there. "I
didn't know anything about the Gouzenko case except what I read in
the papers," recalled Tom Hill later. Yet he had worked within a few

hundred yards of the defector and his family for some three months and was in regular touch with Stephenson.

Stephenson followed events closely. Shortly before Christmas – celebrated with a traditional turkey and a Christmas tree with lights (designed "to assimilate the Gouzenkos to the Canadian way of life", as George Mackay put it) – Mrs. Gouzenko gave birth to her second child. Stephenson's office provided a white layette bought at Saks Fifth Avenue in New York and taken to Camp X by Captain Herbert Rowland. But it was matters of high politics rather than personal welfare that soon began to bother Stephenson. His first intervention had turned Gouzenko's individual protest into a collective Allied investigation. His last transformed it into a highly publicized international spy scandal.

Early on, the three Allied governments had agreed that nothing should be made public while investigations were being pursued. This made good operational sense. But they also had a political calculation in mind. So long as there seemed hope of prolonging the wartime alliance with the Soviet Union into the peace, they were reluctant to give ammunition to any anti-Communist crusade or backlash. The three governments therefore deliberately kept Gouzenko out of the public eye.

Stephenson had little patience with this view and became increasingly restless as time passed with no apparent results. By the New Year no arrests had been made and Stephenson had begun to form some dark views of what might explain the inaction. He had little respect for Mackenzie King and was concerned that the prime minister's earnest desire for the whole Gouzenko affair to fade away masked some deeper machinations by sinister influences in Ottawa. Finally he took unilateral action, doing so in true BSC style by using what he called "the deterrent of publicity". "King refused to take the necessary action for fear of offending Stalin," Stephenson claimed later. "After consultation with Hoover and President Roosevelt's so-called brain-trust co-ordinator, Ernest Cuneo, we agreed that the story should be released by way of Drew Pearson."[22] BSC had used Pearson in a similar manner during the war in order to get pro-British material into the mainstream of American public opinion. On February 4, 1946, Pearson told his radio audience on *Nationwide* that Mackenzie King had told President Truman about a spy ring in Canada.

As Stephenson had hoped, this broadcast forced King's hand. The next day the prime minister for the first time told his Cabinet colleagues what had been happening in Ottawa since the previous September. He also announced that he was setting up a royal commission to investigate the evidence. A day later the Kellock-Taschereau Commission began its work in secret by reviewing the documentary evidence provided by Gouzenko. A few days after that, Gouzenko himself was driven to Ottawa from Camp X to give evidence. On St. Valentine's Day the commission recommended that several arrests be made. At seven o'clock the next morning a dozen suspects were picked up by the RCMP, and by that evening the affair had become public knowledge. The Cold War espionage battle had begun.

As for Gouzenko, he was soon moved from Camp X. Given a new identity and considerable financial help by the Canadian government, he and his family eventually settled in Mississauga, an anonymous suburban sprawl on the outskirts of Toronto. For years he was cultivated in certain circles as a guru on the Red Menace. He wrote several successful books, and occasionally he would appear on television, a paper bag or pillow case over his head, to talk about his experiences and regale his audiences with dire prophecies about the Soviet threat. He died in Mississauga in 1982.

The Drew Pearson leak was not quite the last chapter in Stephenson's involvement with the Gouzenko affair. He was determined to make what capital he could out of the whole business in order to prolong Anglo-American-Canadian intelligence co-operation into the post-war world. This was to be embodied in a peacetime organization resembling BSC. Donovan had attempted a similar thing in the United States, arguing strongly for the post-war continuation of OSS as a centralized intelligence agency. The effort had failed when President Truman signed the order dissolving the OSS on September 20, 1945 – just two weeks after Gouzenko's defection. But Donovan continued to lobby actively and persistently for a post-war OSS among his friends in Washington.

It is not surprising that Stephenson got in touch with Donovan. In October, at about the time Gouzenko was moved to Camp X, the two men made a private arrangement by which one of their joint secret networks in China would be kept going. But if Stephenson wished to win his argument, he had to convince Ottawa and London. The way to do this was to prove how indispensable BSC was in the Gouzenko case and then to articulate the lessons in the BSC history before it was distributed to top intelligence experts.

A "Gouzenko Appendix" was therefore inserted into the bound copies of the history. Based on the report made by the BSC officials involved in the affair, it received the same treatment as the rest of the history. Giles Playfair rewrote large portions and edited the story to Stephenson's satisfaction. Predictably, its conclusion was to the effect that the Gouzenko case demonstrated the need for co-ordinated American-British-Canadian intelligence to meet the Soviet challenge, and for a continuation of a BSC-type organization. As we have seen, when Charles Vining presented the argument on Stephenson's behalf to Norman Robertson and Arnold Heeney in Ottawa exactly a week after the Gouzenko case had been made public, it fell on deaf ears.

At around this time, too, Stephenson approached Churchill with a similar proposal. But the old lion was now out of power, and although the Labour government was strongly anti-Communist, it saw no need to re-invent BSC. There was certainly going to be post-war intelligence co-operation between the wartime allies. Only the next year the UKUSA agreement on cryptographic co-operation, which included Canada, was signed in great secrecy, and the United States established the CIA. But neither Stephenson nor his own organization was going to be involved. In 1946 BSC was finally wound up, and the Rockefeller Center headquarters, which had once housed hundreds of BSC personnel, was vacated.

Camp X, however, was not entirely abandoned even after it passed beyond the control of BSC. As Military Research Centre No. 2, the HYDRA complex was manned exclusively by Canadians even before the war had ended. Shortly after that, it formally became an operation of the Canadian armed forces. It formed part of the extensive network that worked with the Americans and the British to monitor Soviet communications in the post-war years. By 1947, $3 million a year was being spent on the operation, which had become a major part of the Cold War confrontation. Precisely what HYDRA contributed to the exercise remains a classified secret, and it continued in active operation until the 1960s. Rapidly developing technological advances in the communications field eventually made it redundant, and in 1969 the Department of National Defence sold the land to the townships of Whitby and Oshawa. For several years it remained derelict. The old buildings of Camp X deteriorated steadily under the onslaught of the weather and vandalism, and eventually they were pulled down. In 1977 the site was cleared by army bulldozers looking for live ammunition reputed to have been stored there during the war. At about the same time, fuelled by the sensational claims of *A Man Called Intrepid*, rumours about the Camp's significance began to filter into public consciousness. Beginning in 1978, a group of local citizens formed a Camp X Society and tried to raise more than $1 million to construct a memorial by reconstructing Camp X as it existed during wartime. The Society published a magazine devoted to the Camp under the title *25-1-1*, the number of the file that Ottawa kept on the Camp's activities. Oddly enough, its first issue was dedicated to a Canadian SOE agent who did not train at Camp X: Frank Pickersgill, executed by the Germans at Buchenwald in 1944. Stephenson's wife, Lady Mary Stephenson, who died in December 1978, received the dedication of its second issue, while the front cover of the fourth and final issue carried a portrait of Sir William Stephenson and the title "Intrepid". Articles included interviews with some of those who had worked at or passed through the Camp, news of the Camp X Society, and items of interest to *aficionados* of secret war. But it folded through lack of interest, and the museum idea died with it.

There is little now to remind the visitor to Oshawa and Whitby of the Camp's historic importance. At the local airport a small private aeronautical museum houses a few of the Camp's artifacts and some wartime photographs taken from inside the perimeter. On the lakeshore itself there is little evidence of the site's historic wartime role. Much of it has been covered with light industrial buildings, and the Ontario Liquor Control Board's warehouse roughly covers the site of the old officers' mess. While some of the old Camp X hands think in more frivolous moments that this is entirely appropriate, it is left to the small bronze plaque situated only a few feet away to record the Camp's more sober historic purpose.

CHAPTER 10

Camp X:
Myth and Reality

This time they trained James Bond thoroughly – first at a house in Hertfordshire at a course for saboteurs, then out in Canada. Bond was a prize trainee, winning high marks for fitness, unarmed combat, weaponry and personal initiative. In Hertfordshire he was given an A-plus mark and privately commended to the D.N.I.: in Canada he gave a judo instructor a mild concussion and took the range records at small arms and on the submachine guns.

The Canadian establishment was at a place called Oshawa, on Lake Ontario. It had been founded, late in 1940, by Sir William Stephenson as training ground for his American agents, and at the time it offered the most rigorous and thorough training of its sort anywhere outside the Soviet Union. Bond learnt a lot.

As an inventor in his own right – much of his fortune came from his prewar inventions in radio photography – Sir William was a technocrat of sabotage. It was from him that Bond became acquainted with the whole armoury of the modern agent – cyphers and electronics, explosives and radio and listening devices. The trainees used the lake for underwater exercises, and it was here that James Bond trained as a frogman, learning evasive tactics, underwater fighting, and techniques with limpet mines. Bond spent three months at Oshawa. When he returned to London D.N.I. had already received a confidential report, commending his success and ending with a single statement – "The agent is a lethal weapon of the highest calibre."

Thi3 passage, from John Pearson's *James Bond, The Authorised Biography of 007*, is a classic example of the public mythology now surrounding Camp X. The book, a fictional biography of the most famous secret agent of all time, was a sequel to Pearson's *Life of Ian Fleming*, in which he painted a vivid and dramatic picture of James Bond's creator himself undergoing secret agent training at the Camp. "One of the best pupils the school ever had," Sir William Stephenson is quoted as saying about Fleming. His training there, and the influence this had on his later creation of James Bond, is now widely accepted as historical fact.

Yet all the available documentary evidence suggests that this, like so many other stories surrounding Camp X, belongs to the realm of fantasy and fiction rather than historical fact.

Whatever the reality of Camp X, much of its significance lies in the realm of myth. People have "invented" Camp X to suit their own needs and purposes. They have interpreted its importance according to a view of the past that has little to do with reality as understood by the historian. This in itself leads us on an intriguing and mysterious path, which is worth following at least some of the way.

The "myth" of Camp X is inseparable from a greater myth, that of "Intrepid". Sir William Stephenson's important achievements in creating a liaison between the British and the American secret services, particularly in the early part of the war, have become clouded during the last decade by many extravagant claims that have assumed legendary proportions. In essence, the Intrepid myth asserts the centrality of BSC and William Stephenson in the Allied war effort, and in particular in the secret war of resistance and intelligence. It presents Stephenson as the master-mind and master-spy behind several major wartime operations, the key to the ULTRA breakthrough, the intimate confidant of Churchill and Roosevelt, and the living embodiment of the transatlantic alliance. It also presents him as the personal recipient from Churchill of the code-name "Intrepid", thus placing him in the great tradition of those warrior ships of British history such as *Dauntless*, *Indefatigable*, and *Redoutable*.

As the only site available to BSC for training, Camp X has inevitably become entangled in many of Intrepid's alleged exploits. It was, *A Man Called Intrepid* tells us, "the clenched fist preparing for the knockout." Yet if we examine only three of the major blows it is supposed to have swung at Nazi Germany, we find them to be completely phantom.

Myth One: The Heydrich Assassination

The most dramatic myth concerns Reinhard Heydrich, the Nazi "Protector" of Bohemia and Moravia and deputy head of Himmler's SS. On May 27, 1942, Heydrich was mortally wounded during a grenade attack on his car in the suburbs of Prague. The two men responsible were Czech agents who had been specially trained for the assassination. The death of this top Nazi leader at the hands of "a subservient people" provoked a terrible retribution. German forces destroyed the entire Czech village of Lidice, cold-bloodedly murdered its male population, and transported the women and children to concentration and extermination camps in Germany and Poland. They thus ensured that to this day Lidice remains a symbol of Fascist atrocities throughout Europe. Repression in the Protectorate severely weakened Czech resistance and it never fully recovered. But the Czechs could claim that alone of all the Nazi-occupied countries they had struck directly at the highest level of the Nazi leadership.

The Intrepid myth has placed Camp X at the centre of this drama by claiming that the assassins were flown from Britain to be trained there and that Stephenson took a leading part in planning the mission. Training exercises at Camp X, so the story goes, included such detailed work as constructing a scale model of the Prague area and reproducing the conditions in which Heydrich was said to live. Even more dramatically, *A Man Called Intrepid* claimed, "at Camp X a replica was made of the green Mercedes [Heydrich] used when not piloting himself to Berlin".

Logic alone should be enough to pour cold water on this version of events. Stephenson and BSC had no operational responsibility for Europe at all. Their job lay in North and South America, and Heydrich's fate and the strategy of the Czech resistance were far beyond the range of their concerns. Furthermore, why would Czech agents be flown all the way across the Atlantic from Britain, the site of SOE's most advanced training schools, to Camp X, which provided only preliminary training? When logic is then reinforced by documented historical facts, the story dissolves into pure fantasy. For what, after all, was the sequence of events?

President Eduard Benes of Czechoslovakia was determined to demonstrate to the world that his country possessed an active resistance. He had toyed with the idea of a dramatic assassination of a high Nazi official in his occupied homeland since 1939, but the plans finally crystallized only after Heydrich took up his position as Protector on October 1, 1941. By then, several Czech exiles in Britain were already being trained by SOE for a variety of missions. Benes discussed his plan with General Frantisek Moravec, the head of Czech intelligence, and with a very small number of top SOE and OSS officials. Moravec then chose two volunteers, Josef Gabcik and Karel Svoboda, for the mission – code-named ANTHROPOID – from among the Czechs already undergoing SOE training in England and Scotland. On October 3, 1941, he set the operation in motion at a careful briefing in London, telling the men that the target date was the Czech national holiday on October 28 – "the saddest national holiday our country has known".

Fate intervened to prevent this target date being met. Svoboda injured his ankle in training and was replaced by Jan Kubis. Two attempted drops in November had to be aborted due to bad weather. Finally, on December 28, 1941, the two men climbed aboard a Halifax bomber at Tangmere aerodrome in southern England and were dropped east of Prague in the early-morning hours of the next day. From there they made their way into the city and their eventual rendezvous with history.

This sequence of events reveals the full absurdity of the notion that the agents were trained at Camp X or that the mission was planned there – an account that has even passed into some academic history books. Nigel West argues in a recent essay on the Intrepid myth in his book *Unreliable Witness*, that the two Czech agents could not have visited Camp X in Canada because "the evidence of their attendance at various SOE training schools [in Britain] confirms that there could not have been time." This is true, but it misses the central point. *Camp X did not even exist at the time the mission was conceived or planned, or when the agents were being trained* . Nor did it exist when the first two unsuccessful attempts were made to infiltrate the ANTHROPOID mission in November. When they finally did land on Czech soil, Camp X, some 3,000 miles to the west across the Atlantic, had been operational as a preliminary training camp for only three weeks. Unusual things happen in war – but one of them is not that men are trained and operations planned *after* they have begun. It is not just that there is no evidence that these men were trained at Camp X: it was impossible, even if it had been plausible. But myth in its fantasies takes little account of possibility or plausibility.

Myth Two: Vemork

Another somewhat comparable story is that Camp X trained the Norwegian agents who destroyed the Norsk Hydro heavy-water plant at Vemork, near Rjukan, west of Oslo, thus destroying with one blow Nazi capacity to develop an atomic bomb. Four men were recruited, according to the Intrepid legend, "in a region of Toronto known as Little Norway and then trained at Camp X." Equipped with special ski equipment hand-crafted in Canada, they were then parachuted into Norway, where they changed the course of the Second World War. Again, however, historical facts get in the way.

SOE dropped four men into Norway in October 1942 as part of a combined operations plan to destroy the Vemork plant, their mission being to assist an attack spearheaded by glider-borne commando troops from Britain. But the glider expedition on November 19-20 was a disaster. Both gliders crashed and the surviving commandos were captured and executed. SOE then took charge, and in February 1943 dropped another SOE-trained team into Norway. This group linked up with the first four SOE men and then the combined party successfully attacked the plant on the night of February 27-28, 1943. Temporarily, at least, this model sabotage operation set back heavy-water production, although because Nazi research on the atomic bomb was considerably off-track this had little effect on the ultimate outcome. But at the time it was a considerable feather in SOE's cap because it had demonstrated what it could achieve when other means had failed.

But this *coup* owed absolutely nothing to Camp X. Again, one has to ask why agents in Britain would be flown across the Atlantic to Camp X to receive preliminary training. What sense did this make? Obviously, none. Furthermore, the leading witness on the Norwegian side denies any contact with Canada or Camp X. Knut Haukelid was the second-in-command of the second team that attacked Vemork and figured prominently in the account of the operation provided in *A Man Called Intrepid*. Yet after the war, when he wrote a dramatic account of the expedition in *Skis Against the Atom*, Camp X was conspicuous by its absence (as was any mention of BSC). In the early 1980s, when the Intrepid myth began to take public hold, Haukelid was still alive in Norway. Questioned closely about the Camp X claims, Haukelid was adamant that neither he nor any of the Norwegians involved was ever in Canada during the war.

Myth Three: Dieppe

Let us look briefly at one final example of the attempt to link Camp X with a major wartime operation: its alleged part in preparations for the ill-fated Dieppe raid in August 1942 (Operation JUBILEE). In this cross-Channel attack, where 60 per cent of the troops were Canadian, practically everything that could go wrong did. Fewer than half the Canadians who set out returned home. One purpose of the raid was to find out more about German radar. This is where Camp X comes into the story.

The myth claims that two British radar specialists were attached to the raid to accompany the troops ashore and then dismantle parts of the Freya radar station at Pourville, close to Dieppe, for further analysis in Britain. These two men were sent to Camp X for training. Here they met an FBI agent who would accompany them. His task, according to the story, was to shoot them if they appeared likely to fall into enemy hands. Once again, the account defies all common sense and logic. Why would two British scientists need to cross the Atlantic to Camp X to learn about radar? And if not to learn about radar, but about how to take part in a raid, why, once again, bother, when Camp X could teach them nothing that could not be done better in Britain? Why risk the lives of two scientists – and valuable transport resources – on such a crazy idea?

And once again historical evidence points to the story being a pure invention. There was, in fact, only one radar expert attached to the Dieppe raid. Although his mission to find out information about German radar failed, he did manage to cut the telephone wires linking the radar station with the outside world, thus forcing it to transmit messages over the air that were then intercepted in Britain. The man was Jack Nissenthall, a London-born RAF flight sergeant who had helped to set up the first top-secret radar school in Britain. After the war Nissenthall immigrated to South Africa and then, in 1978, settled in Canada. By that time the Intrepid myth had begun to take hold. Like Knut Haukelid, Nissenthall was bewildered by it all. He had never, he asserted, been trained at Camp X, nor was there any truth to other aspects of the story linking Camp X to the Dieppe tragedy. Once again, invention had replaced fact.[1]

Ian Fleming/James Bond

But the most compelling myth is the one we have already encountered about Fleming and James Bond. "[Camp X] not only provided him with a lot of tricks which he was to pass on to James Bond," wrote Pearson in his biography of Fleming, "but it helped him to decide, when the time came to decide, just what kind of an agent Bond must be." Supposedly, Fleming's visit to Camp X grew out of his friendship with Stephenson.

As noted earlier, Fleming's war was spent in British Naval Intelligence, where he was recruited by its director, Admiral John Godfrey, to be his personal assistant. It was a sensitive and difficult post in which Fleming did well, rising quickly to the rank of commander – the same rank he was later to give 007. The position also fed his craving to be at the centre of things among powerful people, and it stimulated his immature and essentially adolescent appetite for indulging in fantasies about secret agents and heroic action. As Godfrey's representative on a number of top-secret Whitehall committees, Fleming quickly came into contact with SOE, where he learned a great deal about its schemes to bring down the Nazis by sabotage and subversion. "For Fleming in the middle of it all," Pearson recognized, "it must have seemed like his youthful fantasies...all over again, with the machine-guns hidden in the exhaust pipes of fast sports cars and the prospect of long brave battles with enemy agents again in the mountain passes...." Fleming had a more personal link with SOE, too, because his elder brother, Peter, was actually recruited for special operations in the Middle East. These contacts fuelled all of

Fleming's Buchanesque romantic leanings. Before long he was proposing imaginative but impractical schemes for SOE activities that would have fitted ideally into the columns of the *Boys' Own Paper*. One of them, for example, would have had Fleming digging himself into one of the Frisian Islands off the northern coast of Germany watching for U-boats through a periscope. "What nonsense they were," Fleming admitted after the war was over, "those romantic, Red Indian daydreams so many of us indulged in at the beginning of the war." Nonsense or not, Fleming relished them, both at the time and later on in his life.

Further opportunities to satisfy his insatiable need for travel, adventure, and fantasy came in the summer of 1941 when he accompanied Admiral Godfrey on a high-level and top-secret visit to the still-neutral United States. Godfrey's ostensible mission was to establish closer relations with American naval intelligence to help in the intensifying North Atlantic struggle. He was also in the United States to encourage progress in the establishment of a more centralized and efficient intelligence service that would be prepared to work closely with the British.

One of the first visits Godfrey and Fleming made was to Stephenson, then busily working to help Donovan in his campaign to become intelligence *supremo* in Washington. Fleming's encounter with Stephenson left an indelible mark on his life. Fleming was always a hero-worshipper, and in the heightened emotions of war, presented with Britain's intelligence chief in North America, he quickly placed Stephenson in his private pantheon of heroes. "For Fleming," wrote Pearson, "Stephenson was almost everything a hero should be. He was very tough.... He was very rich.... He was single-minded and patriotic and a man of few words." "One of the great secret agents of the last war," is how Fleming described Stephenson in the foreword he wrote to the American edition of a biography of Stephenson that appeared some twenty years after their first meeting at Rockefeller Center.[2]

Through Stephenson, Fleming then met Donovan. This encounter provided Fleming with an unprecedented opportunity to indulge in a non-fictional imaginative exercise about secret service. Donovan was soliciting advice from various sources about what the intelligence agency he had in mind for the United States would need. Fleming did not hesitate. In two days he put down on paper everything he thought Donovan needed to know about the financing, organizing, controlling, and training of a secret service. Dated June 27, 1942, this memorandum has survived in the OSS records. Many of Fleming's recommendations were commonplace or unrealistic, as CIA historian Thomas Troy has revealed in *Donovan and the CIA*, and none of the people Fleming recommended to Donovan for service with COI were ever appointed. But there was a typical Fleming touch in his last piece of advice. "Make an example of someone at an early date for indiscretion," he told Donovan, "and continue to act ruthlessly where lack of security is concerned."[3] It was like a dry run for a James Bond series.

Later on, long after the war, Fleming claimed to Cornelius Ryan that he had helped Donovan write "the cornerstone of the future OSS". This was extravagant and typically Fleming, and various accounts of the episode are marked by odd inconsistencies of detail. Writing to Rex Applegate in 1957, Fleming said, "General Donovan was a close personal friend of mine [*sic*] and, as a matter of fact, I spent some time with him in his house in Washington writing the original charter of the OSS." Ivar Bryce, however, recorded a rather different account of his friend's exertions in *You Only Live Once*. "He had been whisked off to a room in the new annexe of the Embassy, locked in it with a pen and paper and the necessities of life, and had written, under armed guard around the clock, a document of some seventy pages covering every aspect of a giant secret intelligence and secret operational organisation." Richard Dunlop, whose biography of Donovan prefers the Rex Applegate version, nonetheless denies any suggestion that the paper Donovan presented to Roosevelt was authored by Fleming, as does Troy. Donovan's *Memorandum on the Establishment of a Service of Strategic Information* , the submission to Roosevelt that led the president to appoint him in June 1941 as Co-ordinator of Information (not head of OSS, which was established only a year later) was Donovan's own work. "Fleming was hardly Donovan's ghostwriter," Dunlop notes. Nonetheless, Donovan felt grateful enough to present Fleming with a .38 Colt revolver inscribed "For Special Services". Inevitably, Fleming would later take much pleasure in showing this to friends and hinting darkly that it was for services to OSS of a more practical and deadly kind.

At this point, enter Camp X. That Fleming was personally acquainted with the deadly skills of a secret agent was a story that grew in reputation and strength in the years following the first appearance of James Bond in *Casino Royale* in 1953. In Pearson's biography of Fleming, published two years after his death in 1964, he claimed that Fleming visited Camp X a year or two after he first met Stephenson and Donovan. This would have had to be the case, of course, because in the summer of 1941 Camp X was still only an idea in the minds of BSC and SOE planners. Therefore the visit must have been in 1942 or 1943 – 1944 is unlikely because the school closed down early that year. It took place, according to Pearson, at Fleming's specific request and as the result of Stephenson's personal intervention.

Again according to the story, Fleming flourished at Camp X. He enjoyed the self-defence and unarmed combat course as well as taking to the sub-machine-gun "with extraordinary relish". His top marks, however, were received for the underwater exercise. This involved Fleming in a long underwater swim by night from the beach of Camp X to an old tanker moored offshore, where he had to fix a limpet mine to the hull. It was remarkably like James Bond's later performance against Mr. Big in *Live and Let Die*, the second of Fleming's best sellers. Like his fictional hero, Fleming succeeded in putting the mine in place and then escaping undetected. Another of his outstanding achievements was in the "Agent's Initiative" test. Here, trainees had to place an imaginary bomb in the main Toronto power station. Their task was made more difficult because the station was heavily guarded and because the city police had been deliberately alerted. Those who tried by attempting to sneak past the guards in disguise were caught. Fleming alone succeeded. He did so by using the best disguise of all: himself. He telephoned the plant manager, explained in his best British accent and Old Etonian manner that he was a visiting expert from Britain, arranged for a formal tour, and was ushered through the gates by welcoming guards.

But in the final crucial test, Fleming failed. Would-be agents were told that a dangerous enemy spy had been located in a downtown hotel. Each was given a revolver, which he loaded himself with live ammunition, and was told to burst into the man's room and shoot him on sight. There was, of course, no such agent. Instead, the room was occupied by one of the Camp's instructors who was sufficiently skilled – so the story goes – to confuse his attackers and dodge the bullet. But Fleming fell for it. After arriving at the hotel he lingered for a long time outside the man's room and eventually went away without even having touched the door. "I couldn't kill a man that way," he later confessed. It meant that the man who invented James Bond would himself never have been licensed to kill. "He hadn't got the temperament to be an agent or a real man of action," said Stephenson later. But despite this, he described Fleming as "one of the best pupils the school ever had."[4]

All this makes a fascinating episode in the life of the man who gave the world James Bond. But did any of it really happen? There are enough oddities and inconsistencies about the story to suggest that it is no more real than the cover invented by the average SOE agent working behind enemy lines.

In the first place, neither Bill Brooker nor Cuthbert Skilbeck, the two living commandants of the Camp, has any recollection at all of Fleming having been there – and between them they were there for the entire lifetime of the Camp. Of course, Fleming at the time would have been just another short-term visitor from BSC sent down by Stephenson to air his lungs – his fame only came later when Bond arrived on the scene in the 1950s – and the name Fleming would have meant nothing at all. Or at least this would have been true had Fleming made no mark on the Camp. But the legend has him doing precisely the opposite. Stephenson said that he was one of the school's best pupils: outstanding at underwater swimming and the only one of his group to succeed in the Agent's Initiative exercise. Then, dramatically, he failed the final test by refusing to shoot a man in cold blood. Would such a high-profile student – particularly one who was there by special invitation – really have passed unnoticed by the Camp's regular staff? Especially when he had such an obviously British and Etonian manner? And even more especially when he was the personal assistant to Britain's director of naval intelligence? It seems highly unlikely. Official SOE documents support the point. "I have not been able to find any evidence in the SOE Archive," the official archivist has told the author, "to support the claim that Ian Fleming did a course at STS 103."[5]

Brooker and Skilbeck also challenge the very basis of the central episode in the story, the underwater exercise. It is intriguing to imagine that the underwater skills demonstrated by James Bond in *Live and Let Die* were based on training at Camp X. The problem is that the episode almost certainly never occurred. Brooker was chief instructor from the day Camp X opened until the summer of 1942, when he was succeeded by Skilbeck, who in turn succeeded Brooker as commandant, a position he retained until the training school closed. Each of them has categorically denied that any underwater exercises took place at the Camp, at any time. "Certainly not in my lifetime there," says Brooker. "Never," says Skilbeck. Unless we are to disbelieve these expert eyewitnesses to the Camp's activities, Fleming's underwater swimming feats were an invention.

There are other problems, too. As told in Pearson's biography, the training staff were "odd, but highly competent". Leaving aside the credibility of a story that has one of them dodging bullets, let us look at the two who are mentioned by name. Both were former members of the Shanghai police. One, "Murphy", was the firearms expert; the other, "Colonel Wallace", the unarmed combat expert. Again, however, there is a problem. Neither Brooker nor Skilbeck, nor anyone else who worked at the Camp, has any recollection of these people, and again, the SOE official records on the Camp's training staff have failed to turn up any evidence either. "I have not found records of any Murphy or Colonel Wallace having served as instructors at STS 103 or indeed at any other SOE training school," writes the SOE archivist. The only one from the Shanghai police to have been on the instructional staff was Fairbairn. He might have been there if Fleming visited the Camp in 1942 because he was not seconded to OSS until April of that year and then he sometimes returned to the Camp to give special courses. But Fairbairn is not mentioned in the story. And who was "Colonel Wallace"? Could Fairbairn have used a cover name? This was often the practice at Beaulieu. But other Camp X graduates had no problem recalling Fairbairn's name, and there is no evidence that he used one. Even if he had, his real name would have been known to the sources who told the post-war Fleming story. Fairbairn was something of a post-war legend. If he had been "Colonel Wallace", it is inconceivable his real name would not have been used.

Clearly, as we subject the Fleming-Camp X story to the sort of detailed interrogation that Fleming might have learned about, had he really taken a course there, the evidence increasingly points to the construction of a highly imaginative invention. Fleming was a notorious fantasist who loved to embellish stories about his own life to impress both himself and his friends. The need was so compulsive, indeed, that eventually he invented James Bond as his fictional *alter ego*. But as Bond grew in fame, so did the need for Fleming to hint that his character was based on realities in his own life.

It is not difficult to imagine the process. Fleming, an international celebrity by the late 1950s, entertains famous guests at "Goldeneye", his Jamaican hide-away, over endless rounds of cocktails. *Casino Royale* – that first "experiment in the autobiography of dreams" – has been followed by such best sellers as *From Russia With Love*, *Dr. No*, *Diamonds Are Forever*, *Moonraker*, and *Live and Let Die*. Guests and friends become curious about Fleming's knowledge of various arcane details of the secret agent's skills. Fleming at first demurs, appealing to the need for secrecy and discretion and hiding behind the mask of aloofness provided by his Anglo-Scottish upbringing. But eventually, as the internal and external pressures mount, he relents. In reality he knows all about agent training because of his wartime contacts with SOE and because he has talked to his brother about it. He also knows about Camp X because of his contacts with Stephenson and Donovan, and particularly because of his close friendship with Ivar Bryce. More to the point, perhaps, Stephenson is often present at these gatherings because the two men are neighbours on the north shore of Jamaica.

In such gatherings, Fleming's imagination could easily have transported him to Camp X and made him part of its history. The story then grew. Stephenson himself had been far too important and busy to know details of the Camp's life – he never even visited it while it was operational, according to Brooker and Skilbeck – and so inconsistencies and inaccuracies would have passed him by. In any case, it was a good story. Fleming was a celebrity, and celebrities were good for the story of BSC and its various activities. Time passed. The story was embellished. Eventually it reached the ears of his biographer and found its way into print. Significantly, however, it was after Fleming himself was dead, so it presented no real problem of authentication or denial.

What is interesting here is not that the Fleming-Camp X exploits never happened, although they provide a classic example of a story that quickly grows in the telling and then is unravelled equally quickly when confronted with historical evidence. The significance lies in the fact that it has become an essential part of the myth of Ian Fleming's life, used to explain the creation of James Bond himself, and also a central part of the Camp X story as it is constantly retailed by word of mouth and popular histories. These two myths have become deeply intertwined and mutually reinforcing. Camp X validates Fleming's claim to direct expertise in the creation of his secret-agent hero. Fleming's fame and fortune, along with James Bond's universal fame, validates some of the more extravagant claims made for the importance of Camp X. The combination makes a potent brew of mystery and speculation that has successfully helped to obscure what really happened. SOE instruction to its Camp X recruits on the importance of cover could hardly have found a better example than in the post-war myths that have surrounded its operations in Canada. Camp X has become a cipher for grandiose fantasies about spymasters and secret agents in the Second World War.

The reality is that Camp X played a modest but intriguing part in the story of American-British-Canadian co-operation during the Second World War. The great political and military victories of the alliance are part of history. But the close transatlantic alliance in intelligence affairs that was forged in that war is still a little-understood part of the present. Camp X provided an example of this alliance in action and a limited foretaste of what was to come. In conditions of great secrecy it gave substance to the rhetoric of transatlantic unity. Then as now, North America often appeared psychologically and politically isolated from momentous events in the wider world. "Action" was overseas. In its own way Camp X brought the war closer to home. There, for the first time, Americans and Canadians encountered the semblance of what secret war might be like – and, unintentionally, a foretaste of the shadow war that has since been fought between the superpowers.

Camp X also meant something to each of the powers separately.

To the British, it was a strand in the elaborate thread of co-operation in the secret war that they deliberately wove in the years of American neutrality in order to link the fate of the United States with their own in the struggle against Hitler; and, once American partic-ipation was guaranteed, it was also a means to ensure that American policy and practice in subversive war followed the British model de-veloped by SOE. "The British," wrote William Corson in *The Armies of Ignorance*, "provided the base from which the wartime OSS was able to apprentice its personnel; while there were frictions and con-tretemps between both parties, these were less important than the fact that 'Special Activities' were legitimized, if not institutionalized, in the minds of those who would come to dominate America's postwar intelligence community." Camp X was remarkably successful in help-ing to achieve this goal. The OSS depended heavily on the British expertise that lay close to hand across the Canadian border. "There is no doubt," acknowledged the post-war OSS training history, "that British aid helped to organise the training program in time to be effective during the important periods of American participation in the war." Almost all of the first generation of OSS instructors, and many of its executive staff, were first trained at Camp X or came under the influence of its British instructors. Bill Brooker played a dominant role in the shaping of the OSS training program during the second half of 1942. In the following year, during the crisis over OSS training, Skilbeck and Dehn partially filled the vacuum left by Brooker's posting back to Europe. Many of the Americans carried the lessons they had learned from these Camp X officers through the years of OSS and into the CIA. So Camp X belongs to the history of the CIA as well as to the history of SOE.

The British received something in return for this help. Apart from the general influence they were able to exert on Donovan, and the fact that for most of the war there was close OSS-SOE co-operation in such crucial strategic areas as Western Europe, SOE made practical gains in the way of supplies and hardware, which were easier to come by in the wartime United States than in Britain.

The Americans gained some very obvious advantages from Camp X. It was built largely to satisfy Donovan's desire for a training camp embodying British expertise close to American soil, and without both it and its SOE staff he would have had a much more difficult task than he did in creating a cadre of experienced personnel who could help to create the kind of operatives he wanted. Eventually, as the OSS acquired experience in the field, it was able to devise its own methods and principles of training that modified the inheritance from Camp X. One obvious drawback of the Camp was that as an SOE operation it was of limited use for learning about purely secret intelligence work. The stress on method rather than objective in the SOE training syllabus could be a hindrance, and it was only in 1943 and 1944 that OSS began to discard some of the "cloak-and-dagger" philosophy that Brooker in particular had emphasized. Despite this, Camp X played a critical part in fostering the OSS-SOE relationship embodied in the June 1942 agreement on co-operation. "The British taught us everything we knew about intelligence," Donovan once said, referring to his relationship with Stephenson. A major part of that story belongs to Camp X.

For the Canadians, Camp X provided an opportunity to demonstrate their commitment to the British war effort, their friendship for the United States, and their competence and independence in the face of both. Although the Camp was a British operation, it could never have worked without close Canadian co-operation. The administrative and support staff of the Camp were Canadian, supplies and equipment were provided by the local Canadian military authorities, the RCMP collaborated closely in many aspects of its work, and officials in the know in Ottawa opened all the necessary doors to ensure that it operated as smoothly and quietly as possible. Like BSC itself, Camp X was in some senses an Anglo-Canadian operation, and as such provided the Canadians with expertise and experience they were to develop after the war. If they failed to follow either in the steps of Britain in running an SIS, or in those of the United States in establishing a CIA, they nonetheless became deeply and intimately involved in the post-war transatlantic intelligence community and set up their own Signals Intelligence (SIGINT) operations. This was by no means only a result of their experience with HYDRA, but when the station was handed over to Canadian control at the end of the war it became part of Canada's history, too.

But in some ways Camp X was more symbol than substance. It had, after all, a relatively short life. Within a war that lasted over five years, the training school operated for barely two and for a good portion of that time was under notice to terminate. It was never a large-scale affair. Five hundred trainees spread over two years was a respectable but not a substantial figure. Of these, less than half were designated for action behind enemy lines, and none of this group actually completed their agent training there. All without exception went on to advanced OSS and SOE training schools in the United States, Britain, or operational theatres of war. Many failed this more rigorous experience. "It must always be recognized," Skilbeck insists, "that we were basically a preliminary school.... STS 103 provided, on the American continent, a place where two forms of active intelligence could be taught – operational sabotage (primary) or counter-intelligence (security). Also as a pool of experience to help the OSS schools get going...equally we were a showroom for Bill Stephenson and his great work at BSC." For those who visited the showroom, some were no more than weekend visitors sent to Canada for what might be called rest and relaxation, albeit of a fairly strenuous physical kind. For the BSC executive in New York, the Washington-based OSS staff officer, or the Ottawa bureaucrat, a few days' instruction in secret warfare at Camp X offered a welcome diversion from the more arduous paper campaigns of their bureaucratic wars. Measured against the SOE's world-wide network of training schools, or the OSS schools in the United States, the achievements of Camp X were inevitably modest.

The same might be said for HYDRA. It was an important facility and an essential component in BSC's communications network in North America. Its antennae received and transmitted signals between the Western Hemisphere and Great Britain, and were responsible for handling the bulk of BSC's transatlantic intelligence communications. But when all is said and done, HYDRA was little more than a technologically sophisticated postbox. It was not a centre of intelligence gathering, interception, or analysis, and practically all messages passed straight through on their way elsewhere. The important work was done in Ottawa, New York, Washington, and London. Like the SOE training school, HYDRA was used to train agents. But they were relatively few, their original mission was downgraded, and they were merely elements in a very much larger and more extensive Allied network.

Even as a symbol, Camp X is ambiguous. In many accounts it appears as the apogee of Allied, and especially Anglo-American, unity. Yet like the view in a kaleidoscope, the picture rapidly alters shape according to the twist given by the viewer. The Americans and the British, the OSS and SOE, certainly worked closely together at Camp X. But it was because the United States was neutral that in 1941 Stephenson, Donovan, and SOE concocted the idea of the Camp. Before Pearl Harbor, such an exercise in the United States was politically impossible. In this sense Camp X was as much a result of American delay in entering the war as it was an illustration of harmonious Allied unity. Ironically, once this unity had been forged, some who had created it decided Camp X was redundant. If from irony we create a paradox, it could be said that Camp X was as much a victim as it was a product of Anglo-American unity.

Why has the story of Camp X been so distorted by myth? Myths are not the same as untruths or falsehoods. What myths do is embellish the past either to justify the present or to simplify something that is otherwise incomprehensible. In both these senses the Intrepid and Camp X stories as they have taken hold in popular imagination are classic examples of the myth-making process.

SIS imposed a post-war silence on much of the secret story of the Second World War, or else selectively released episodes that reflected glory on its achievements. Stephenson, sensitive to his own reputation as well as that of BSC, came to resent this. By the late 1950s he was determined that BSC's highlights should become public knowledge, and he actively encouraged the writing of a popular history. Once again, he took care to place the project in the best hands. His first choice was his former wartime deputy, Dick Ellis, who still had a close relationship with SIS. But the history he produced disappointed Stephenson, who felt, as he had with the first version of the BSC history in 1945, that it lacked drama and readability. So he turned to another former BSC member, Harford Montgomery Hyde, who had worked for two years in the SIS section in New York and was now a professional writer. His book, *The Quiet Canadian* (in the United States it was entitled *Room 3603*), appeared in 1962. This semi-biographical history offered the first public account of BSC and remained, as Bradley Smith has put it, "within hailing distance of the documentary evidence".[6] For all that the book claimed that BSC was "the keystone of the successful Anglo-American partnership in the field of secret intelligence, counter-espionage and special operations", it retained some historical perspective by making no claims for Stephenson's sphere of influence beyond the boundaries of the Western Hemisphere.

By 1976, however, Stephenson had been transformed from "The Quiet Canadian" to "The Man Called Intrepid". This magical metamorphosis was accomplished by journalist William Stevenson, whose book on occasion had only a very tenuous connection to historical reality. If Hyde's was a moderate eulogy, Stevenson's was an immoderate hagiography. It was here that Stephenson became "Intrepid", Camp X became "the clenched fist", and BSC was elevated to the status of equality with, or even superiority to, the British War Cabinet and the brain behind a whole host of Allied victories in the secret war around the globe.

The intent of this exercise was doubtless to enshrine Stephenson in the pantheon of Western heroes. The result, at one level, was to do exactly the opposite. Historians in Britain and the United States were quick to point out countless errors of fact and interpretation, and participants in many of the events completely rejected Stevenson's account. When the film of the book appeared under the same title, only slightly embellishing many of the episodes reputed to have involved Camp X, Skilbeck wrote fiercely to *The Times* to denounce it as "a travesty of history". Privately, he referred to the book itself as "ghastly" and "pure fiction" – a sentiment that was echoed by Brooker. The very extravagance of the story rebounded against Stephenson. It is now difficult for the serious historian to give him credit for anything. "Little Bill's reputation," writes M.R.D. Foot with considerable understatement, "has not been well served by a host of sensationalist articles and a book that suggests he did a great deal more that lay quite outside his domain."[7]

On the other hand, the book was a popular success and the Intrepid myth seized the popular imagination. One result was the attempt to establish a permanent museum at the site of Camp X. Although this failed, the small park that now houses the Camp X

Memorial on the shores of Lake Ontario is called "Intrepid Park" –
graphic material testimony to the power of the myth.

But what about Camp X itself? As we have seen, the support staff
was Canadian, and it would never have existed but for the co-opera-
tion of the Canadian authorities. But myths have taken hold here, too.
Camp X, one popular view holds, "was a purely Canadian operation".
Truth has been embellished here in the service of nation building.
Canadians, anxious to decolonize their past, have thus rewritten their
history since the war to cleanse it of the imperial heritage. To see
Camp X as a Canadian enterprise helps to fulfil the mission. Yet such
a claim is fundamentally misguided. The Camp *was* essentially a
British training school based in Canada. It came under the control of
SOE, which chose its commanding and instructional staff appointed
from schools in Britain. This is not to say that the Camp was "British"
rather than "Canadian". To the generation of the Second World War,
the distinction was largely meaningless. The Canadians who worked
for BSC were proud to be Canadian and often resented the imperial
condescension of the British personnel they encountered; but they
were also conscious of being part of a wider imperial war effort, and
were often more patriotic about this than the British.

Another of the myths surrounding Camp X is that which grants it,
along with Intrepid and BSC, superstar ranking in the triumph of the
Western Allies over Hitler. The myth carries two major messages,
one having to do with the past, the other with the present.

So far as the past is concerned, it helps to simplify and make
comprehensible some complex and uncomfortable realities. To many
people the Second World War presents an almost miraculous victory
over evil. How is it, they ask, that the powerful Nazi and Japanese war
machines were destroyed by nations not only unready for war but
almost defeated at the very beginning? Dunkirk drove the British
from Europe and virtually destroyed its army, while Pearl Harbor
eliminated the American Pacific fleet and opened Asia to the
Japanese. How did the Allies recover and go on to defeat apparently
invincible forces within only four years?

The real answer, or at least something approximating it, was
given a decade ago by Leopold Trepper, former head of the Red
Orchestra, the Soviet intelligence ring that operated in underground
Europe. "Who was it," he asked in his memoirs, *The Great Game,*

"who defeated the Axis?" The master spymaster then answered his own question. "It was the Russian footsoldier with his feet frozen in the snows of Stalingrad; the American marine with his nose in the red sands of Omaha Beach; the Yugoslav or Greek partisan fighting in his mountains. No intelligence service determined the outcome of the conflict."

For many people this answer is either unappealing – who today in the United States wants to talk about the Russian contribution to victory over Nazism? and who in the Soviet Union, about the vast American effort? – or too brutally direct. For them, a more simple and appealing answer is that victory came through victories in the secret war, a war that, appealingly to those with a primitive faith in technology, was won by science and machines rather than by men and women numbering in the millions. Revelations about ULTRA and PURPLE, the great intelligence successes of the Second World War, have sponsored a veritable industry about their wartime triumphs. No wonder, therefore, that Camp X and BSC, whose official histories have so far remained shrouded in secrecy, should attract the attention of those drawn instinctively to the powerful explanatory devices of myth.

As for the present, the myth celebrates transatlantic unity against a totalitarian foe, presenting us with a picture of a Paradise Lost of Western unity. Only strong and decisive leadership can save us now, its message proclaims, because we are faced with the implacable foe of Soviet expansionism and international communism. Both implicitly and explicitly, Stephenson's association with Churchill, the foe of appeasement, places him in the front rank of conservative denunciations of *détente* with the Soviet Union. For those who see the world today in terms of the Europe of the 1930s, the Intrepid myth both embellishes and simplifies the historical past to justify the current mood of anti-liberalism and anti-internationalism that has swept the Western world since the late 1970s. In doing so, of course, it not only ignores the far stronger analogies between our contemporary situation and that of the catastrophe of 1914; it also overblows the role of BSC within the wider Anglo-American relationship, underrates the often-serious divergences of interest and perspective that characterized their competitive co-operation, and forgets that, while Churchill was a conservative, he was also a pragmatist whose knowledge of the past armed him with the powerful weapons of irony and historical understanding.

Celebration of the Intrepid myth along with uncritical glorification of Camp X and Allied agencies such as the OSS and SOE can also produce an over-glamorized view of both the power and the nature of subversive war. It is more than coincidence that recent biographies praising Donovan and the OSS have appeared, and the Intrepid myth has flourished, alongside attempts to rehabilitate the CIA in American opinion and to re-assert the legitimacy of covert operations as a major arm of American foreign policy. The implication is clear: if Donovan and Stephenson could accomplish so much forty years ago, secret operations can do as much as that, if not more, now. This is a dangerously simplistic view. All international morality aside, the SOE and OSS experience clearly shows that the power of subversive warfare is limited even in the context of a wider conventional war. The agents from Camp X who achieved the most were those who fought as auxiliaries in a broader military campaign. Covert operations provide no quick fix for the intractable problems of revolution and violence in an unstable world.

To glorify or romanticize secret operations is also to do a disservice to the veterans of Camp X. The veneration of violence is a popular spectator sport. But those who ran Camp X never deluded themselves about what they were doing. Training men in the skills of silent killing, sabotage, and theft was, Brooker admits, "a form of licensed crime. It was a dirty war, but evil had to be driven out with evil and the best you could do was to implant some kind of ethic of responsibility in the minds of those you trained." But neither Brooker nor Skilbeck pretended that it was anything other than a necessary evil, a duty imposed only by a greater imperative.

"We of STS 103," Skilbeck says now, "were motivated, in our various ways, by a strong feeling that we could contribute to a war that had to be fought on many 'fronts' and in many ways against the devil of Hitler." Only too aware of what they were doing, these men have made no attempt to glorify, romanticize, or exaggerate the achievements of Camp X. Far too much fiction has been woven around it. As we have revealed, truth is fully its equal.

NOTES

Abbreviations used in notes:

CCAC – Churchill College Archives Centre, Cambridge, England.

DND – Department of National Defence, Historical Division, Ottawa, Canada.

FCO – Foreign and Commonwealth Office, London, England.

NA – National Archives, Washington, D.C., United States.

PAC – Public Archives Canada.

PRO – Public Record Office, Kew, England.

See Bibliography for full details of sources quoted.

Chapter 1

1. M.R.D. Foot, *SOE in France*, p.221.

2. Anthony Cave Brown, *The Last Hero*, p.261.

3. Carleton S. Coon, *Adventures and Discoveries*, p.172.

4. Carleton S. Coon, *A North Africa Story*, p.3.

5. Cave Brown, *The Last Hero*, p.835.

6. Interview with Bill Brooker, Scotland, August 1985.

7. M.R.D. Foot, *SOE in France*, p.4.

8. Joan Bright Astley, *The Inner Circle*, p.34.

9. M.R.D. Foot, *SOE: The Special Operations Executive 1940-46*, p.63.

10. Ibid., p.64.

11. Interview with Brooker, August 1985.

12. J.A. Cross, *Lord Swinton*, p.225.

13. Diary of A.J. Taylor, 7 September 1941. In possession of Taylor family.

14. Ibid., 12 September 1940.

15. Tommy Davies, Report, 15 October 1941 (SOE Archives, FCO, London).

16. Archives of Ontario, Ontario County, Township of Whitby, GS 4893 (Microfilm), Abstract Index to Deeds, Vol. A, 1798-1958; also East Whitby Township, GS 4895 (Microfilm), Abstract Vol. A, 1798-1958.

Chapter 2

1. Richard Dunlop, *Donovan, America's Master Spy*, p.421.

2. Christopher Andrew, *Secret Service* (U.S. title: *Her Majesty's Secret Service*), p.467.

3. Directive, 15 February 1941, Hyde Papers (CCAC).

4. Thomas F. Troy, *Donovan and the CIA*, p.82.

5. Christopher M. Woods, SOE Adviser at the FCO, to author, 25 March 1985, 1 May 1985, 8 August 1985, 10 September 1985, 17 February 1986, 15 and 24 April 1986.

6. Tommy Davies, Report for SOE on his American visit, 15 October 1941 (SOE Archives, FCO), Woods to author, 10 September 1985.

7. Ibid.

8. J.W. Pickersgill and D.F. Forster, *The Mackenzie King Record*, 1:41.

9. Ibid., p.254.

10. J.L. Granatstein, *Canada's War: The Politics of the Mackenzie King Government 1939-1945*, p.14.

11. This and subsequent quotations of Vining are taken from a scrapbook he compiled after the war, now in the possession of his widow, Mrs. Charles Vining.

12. Peter St. John, "Canada's Accession to the Allied Intelligence Community 1940-45," *Conflict Quarterly* 4 (Fall 1984), pp.5-21; J.L. Granatstein, *A Man of Influence*, passim.

13. Lester Pearson, *Mike, the Memories of Lester B. Pearson*, 1:195.

14. "A History of the Examination Unit 1941-1945", ed. Gilbert de B. Robinson, p.76. Declassified by Department of National Defence, Ottawa, under Access to Information Request 1463-86/10047, March 1986.

15. Stone to Hume Wrong, 22 November 1941, ibid.

16. Interview with John Holmes, Toronto, April 1986.

17. Stone to Denniston, 2 October 1943. Stone Papers Private Source.

18. Diary of Gerald Wilkinson, 12 March 1944 (CCAC).

19. For much of this information, I am indebted to an interview with Mrs. Mabel Drew-Brook and her daughter Mrs. Barbara Harris, Toronto, April 1985, and to a tape-recorded memoir made by Tommy Drew-Brook, in the family's possession.

20. Interview with Brooker, August 1985.

21. Hyde Papers (CCAC).

22. Diary of A.J. Taylor, October-November 1941 entries.

23. DND 112.352009 (D41); 162.009 (D23); 112.352009 (D190); 325.009 (D251).

24. Diary of Gerald Wilkinson, 21 February 1944 (CCAC).

25. Colonel W.H.S. Macklin to Major-General C.F. Constantine, 31 October 1941, DND 112.352009 (D190).

26. Colonel W.H.S. Macklin to Major-General C.F. Constantine, 24 October 1941, ibid.

27. Ibid., 31 October 1941.

28. D.G. Whittle to F.J. Cameron, 25 November 1941, DND 112.352009 (D41).

29. Interview with Brooker, August 1985.

Chapter 3

1. *History of the Schools and Training Branch OSS* (rev. 20 August 1945), Pt. 1, A, SA/G – Special Activities, Goodfellow, p.2, NA Record Group 226, Entry 99, Box 78, Folder #60.

2. Interview with Brooker, August 1985; Major-General C.F. Constantine to Colonel W.H.S. Macklin, 7 December 1941, DND 325.009 (D251).

3. *History of the Schools and Training Branch OSS*, Pt. 1, B, SA/B – Special Activities, Bruce, p.2, NA, *loc. cit.*

4. Bradley F. Smith, *The Shadow Warriors*, p.112.

5. Nigel West, *M.I.6: British Secret Intelligence Operations 1909-1945*, p.208; William Corson, *The Armies of Ignorance*, p.179.

6. Winston S. Churchill, *The Second World War: The Grand Alliance*, p.573.

7. Interviews with Kenneth Downs, Washington, D.C., December 1985 and May 1986.

8. Report of W.J. Keswick and F.M.G. Glyn to SOE London, March 1942 (SOE Archives, FCO), C.M. Woods to author, 17 February 1986.

9. Richard Dunlop, *Behind Japanese Lines: With the OSS in Burma*, p.84.

10. Major-General C.F. Constantine to Colonel L.M. Chesley, 24 November 1942, DND 162.009 (D23).

11. Lieut.-Colonel T. Roper-Caldbeck to Major-General C.F. Constantine, 21 December 1941, DND 325.009 (D251).

12. Lieut.-Colonel T. Roper-Caldbeck to Major-General C.F. Constantine, 19 January 1942, DND 162.009 (D23).

13. Major-General C.F. Constantine to Lieut.-Colonel T. Roper-Caldbeck, 23 December 1941, DND 325.009 (D251); Roper-Caldbeck to Constantine, 24 August 1942, DND 162.009 (D23).

14. Interview by telephone with John Bross, Virginia, October 1985.

15. Hyde Papers (CCAC).

16. Kermit Roosevelt, *War Report of the OSS*, p.372.

17. Ibid., p.359.

18. Bickham Sweet-Escott, *Baker Street Irregular*, pp.142-43.

19. *History of the Schools and Training Branch OSS*, Pt. 1, A, SA/G, p.3, NA, *loc. cit.*

20. Anthony Cave Brown, *The Last Hero: Wild Bill Donovan*, p.751.

21. Kim Philby, *My Silent War*, p.19.

22. Baker to Brooker, n.d. (May) 1942, NA Record Group 226, Entry 136, Box 164.

23. "Schools and Training", memorandum, October 1943, NA Record Group 226, Entry 136, Box 158.

24. Ibid.

25. *History of the Schools and Training Branch OSS*, Pt. 2, C, "The British Constitution – Early Character of Training", p.4, NA, *loc. cit.*

26. Notes of Meeting with Geographic Desks, 3 September 1942, by John A. Bross, NA Record Group 226, Entry 136, Box 162.

27. Brooker to Baker, 14 December 1942, NA, *loc. cit.*

28. Letter in possession of Brooker.

Chapter 4

1. This and other quotations in this chapter are taken from the official STS 103 training manual, a copy of which is in the author's possession.

2. Interview with Brooker, August 1985.

3. W. Somerset Maugham, *Ashenden, or The British Secret Agent*, pp.53-54.

Chapter 5

1. Donovan to Joint Chiefs of Staff enclosing Monthly Report of OSS for period ending 31 October 1942, NA Record Group 226, Entry 99, Box 81, Folder 75.

2. R. Harris Smith, *OSS*, p.255.

3. H. Montgomery Hyde, *Secret Intelligence Agent*, p.182.

4. Interview with Brooker, August 1985.

5. Carleton S. Coon, *A North Africa Story*, pp.31-32.

6. Ibid., pp.125-26.

7. Ibid., p. 131.

8. Hambro's comments, and the texts of the agreements, NA Record Group 218, CCS 385.

Chapter 6

1. Interview with Norman Delahunty, Ottawa, April 1986; Marsh Jeanneret "One Spy Controlled", *The Canadian Amateur Radio Magazine*, March 1983, pp.29-33.

2. Eric Curwain, "Almost Top Secret" (unpublished manuscript), p.72. Toronto, Royal Canadian Military Institute.

3. Interviews with Eric Adams 1985-86; and Adams's taped reminiscences.

4. "Bill Hardcastle Interview, Part 2". *25-1-1* (Journal of the Camp X Museum Society) 1, no. 3 (August/September 1979):4; and personal discussion with the author, April 1985.

5. F.H. Hinsley et al., *British Intelligence in the Second World War*, 2:53.

6. Ronald Lewin, *The American Magic*, p.47.

7. Nigel West, *M.I.6*, p.207; Sir William Stephenson, "The Story of OSS", Appendix in H. Montgomery Hyde, *Secret Intelligence Agent*, pp.257-58.

8. Interview with Elizabeth Wood, Toronto, April 1985.

9. Gambier-Perry to Stephenson, 19 November 1941, Hyde Papers (CCAC).

10. "Bill Hardcastle Interview, Part 1", *25-1-1 1*, no. 2 (February 1979):9.

11. Interview with Cecily Gates (Cruess), Toronto, May 1986.

12. Interview with Bobbie Griffiths (O'Neill), Ottawa, June 1986.

13. Gordon Welchman, *The Hut Six Story*, p.172.

14. Interview with George Carruthers, Toronto, April 1985.

Chapter 7

1. F.W.D. Deakin, *The Embattled Mountain*, p.18.

2. Alexander Lebl, "From Canada to the Partisans", *Borba* (Belgrade) 1982; translation from the Serbo-Croat in DND 82/1037.

3. Interview with Cuthbert Skilbeck, May 1985.

4. Basil Davidson, *Special Operations Europe*, p.107.

5. Patrick Howarth, *Undercover*, p.90.

6. Davidson, *Special Operations Europe*, p.116.

7. Deakin, *The Embattled Mountain*, pp.211-12.

8. Jozo Tomasevich, *The Chetniks*, p.471.

9. "Cloak and Dagger", Report by Colonel Felix Walter, senior intelligence officer at Canadian headquarters in London, in 1946, p.19, DND 760.013 (D1).

10. This and other quotations from Cuthbert Skilbeck are either from the author's interviews with him in May 1985 or from subsequent correspondence in the author's possession.

11. JP(42)570, 3 June 1942, AIR 20/7964 (PRO). See also WO 193/634. I am grateful to Bradley F. Smith for drawing this material to my attention.

12. Sir William Deakin to author, 20 June 1985.

13. J.S.M. Washington to Chiefs of Staff, London, 21 September 1942, WO 193/634 (PRO).

14. Colonel Louis Franck (GM) to London, 21 November; London to Franck, 21 December 1942; SOE Report, 7 April 1943 (SOE Archives, FCO), C.M. Woods to author, 15 April 1986.

15. Bickham Sweet-Escott, *Baker Street Irregular*, p.142.

16. SOE Archives, (FCO), C.M. Woods to author, 15 April 1986.

17. Hyde Papers (CCAC).

18. Interview with Norman Delahunty, Ottawa, April 1986.

19. Tom Hill to author, 18 April 1985.

20. Tom Hill to author, 30 March 1985.

21. Cedric Belfrage to author, 10 February 1985.

22. Jean-Paul Evans to author, 14 April 1985.

23. Interview with Daniel Hadekel, Montreal, 17 March 1985.

24. Drew-Brook to National Defence Headquarters, Ottawa, 13 January 1943, DND 112.352009 (D41).

25. Keswick and Glyn to SOE London, March 1942 (SOE Archives, FCO), C.M. Woods to author, 17 February 1986; Hambro to Brooker, 31 December 1942, letter in possession of Bill Brooker.

26. Report by Major H.A. Benson (SOE Archives, FCO), quoted, C.M. Woods to author, 17 February 1986.

27. Hyde Papers (CCAC).

Chapter 8

1. Kim Philby, *My Silent War,* p.20.

2. C.M. Woods to author, May 1985.

3. *History of the Schools and Training Branch OSS,* Pt. 2, C, "The British Constitution", NA. *loc. cit.*

4. *New York Times,* 18 November 1958.

5. Paul Dehn, *The Fern on the Rock,* p.77.

6. Corey Ford, *Donovan of OSS,* p.125.

7. Report by S. Morell, 8 April 1943 (SOE Archives, FCO), C.M. Woods to author, 17 February 1986.

8. Cuthbert Skilbeck to author, 22 September 1985.

9. Letter in possession of Bill Brooker.

10. Major F.J. Justin to Colonel L.M. Chesley, 4 September 1943, DND 112.352009 (D41); Skilbeck to author, 22 September 1985.

11. Interview with Hamish Pelham-Burn, Scotland, August 1985.

12. Interview with Ramsay Rainsford Hannay, Scotland, August 1985.

13. Major F.J. Justin to Mr. R.J. McNeill, 2 July 1943, DND 162.009 (D23); Ivar Bryce, *You Only Live Once*, p.53.

14. M.R.D. Foot, *SOE: The Special Operations Executive 1940-46*, p.132; H.J. Giskes, *London Calling North Pole*, p.136.

15. This and other statements from SOE records about van Schelle in C.M. Woods letter to author, 15 April 1986.

16. Giskes, *London Calling North Pole*, p.128.

17. Durovecz (Daniels) interview in *25-1-1 1*, no. 4 (1980).

18. Bickham Sweet-Escott, *Baker Street Irregular*, pp.203-04; Basil Davidson, *Special Operations Europe*, p.175; Roy MacLaren, *Canadians Behind Enemy Lines*, pp.155-68.

19. Elisabeth Barker, *British Policy in South-East Europe in the Second World War*, p.140; David Stafford, *Britain and European Resistance*, pp.144-98.

20. MacLaren, *Canadians Behind Enemy Lines*, pp.86-104. See also memoranda to Ralston in DND 112.352009 (D190); and Foot, *SOE in France, passim*.

21. Colonel Felix Walker, "Cloak and Dagger", Report, p.14, DND 760.013 (D1).

22. Charles Cruikshank, *SOE in the Far East*, p.47.

23. MacLaren, *Canadians Behind Enemy Lines*, p.92.

Chapter 9

1. Report, 2 June 1942 (SOE Archives, FCO), C.M. Woods to
    author, 15 April 1986.

2. Terms of reference for Colonel Louis Franck, 8 July 1942, and
    Instructions on control of STS 103, issued by Hambro (SOE
    Archives, FCO), C.M. Woods to author, 17 February 1986.

3. SOE London to BSC New York, 11 May 1943 (SOE Archives,
    FCO), C.M. Woods to author, 10 September 1985.

4. Tommy Stone to Paul Dehn, 7 March 1944. Letter in possession
    of Mr. Eric Dehn.

5. M.R.D. Foot, *SOE*, p.70; C.M. Woods to author, 10 September
    1985.

6. Colonel L.M. Chesley to D.M.I., 12 July 1944, DND 112.352009
    (D190).

7. "Minutes of a meeting...to discuss the operation of 'Special 25-1-
    1'," 9 August 1944, DND 162.009 (D23).

8. C.G.S. to Colonel Ralston, 29 August 1944, DND 112.352009
    (D190).

9. Major F.J. Justin to Colonel L.M. Chesley, 21 August 1944, DND
    162.009 (D23).

10. Vining scrapbook in possession of Mrs. Charles Vining.

11. Roald Dahl to author in conversation, July 1985.

12. Tom Hill to author, 30 March 1985.

13. Interview with Giles Playfair, London, August 1985.

14. J.W. Pickersgill and D.F. Forster, *The Mackenzie King Record*, 3:9. See also Robert Bothwell and J.L. Granatstein, *The Gouzenko Transcripts*, p.9.

15. Jean-Paul Evans, "Corby", recollections in letter to author, 1 September 1985.

16. J.L. Granatstein, "Culture and Scholarship: The First Ten Years of the Canada Council," *Canadian Historical Review* LXV, no. 4 (1984):441-74.

17. W.S. Stephenson to P.M. Dwyer, 28 June 1945. Letter in possession of Chris Dwyer.

18. Evans, "Corby," pp.4-5.

19. John Sawatsky, *Gouzenko: The Untold Story*, p.58.

20. Ibid., p.59.

21. Ibid., pp.58-67 *passim*.

22. Ibid., p.75.

Chapter 10

1. For much of the above, I am grateful to Alois Vyhnak's unpublished manuscript, "Superagent", in Mr. Vyhnak's possession.

2. Ian Fleming, Foreword to H. Montgomery Hyde, *Room 3603*, p.x.

3. Thomas F. Troy, *Donovan and the CIA*, p.82.

4. John Pearson, *The Life of Ian Fleming*, pp.119-21.

5. C.M. Woods to author, 17 February 1986.

6. Bradley F. Smith, *The Shadow Warriors*, p.427.

7. M.R.D. Foot, *SOE*, p.42.

BIBLIOGRAPHY

A. Archival Sources

Cambridge, England
    Churchill College Archives Centre:
        H.M. Hyde Papers
        Gerald Wilkinson Papers

London, England
    Public Record Office:
        WO 193/631
        WO 193/634
        WO 20/7964

    Foreign and Commonwealth Office:
        SOE Records

Ottawa, Canada
    Department of National Defence, Directorate of History:
        82/1037; 112.352009 (D41); 162.009 (D23);
        112.352009 (D190); 162.009 (D27); 325.009 (D251);
        760.013 (D1).

    Public Archives Canada:
        Record Group 24, file HQS 8885-1 ("Project J")
        Mackenzie King Papers
        J.R. Ralston Papers
        War Cabinet Minutes

Stanford, California, U.S.A.
    Hoover Institution:
       Goodfellow Papers

Toronto, Canada
    Archives of Ontario:
       Land Records, Ontario County

Washington D.C., U.S.A.
    National Archives:
       Record Group 218 (Records of the Joint Chiefs of Staff)
       Record Group 226 (Records of the Office of Strategic Services)

B. Books and Periodicals

Alsop, Stewart, and Broden, Thomas. *Sub Rosa: The OSS and American Espionage*. New York: Harcourt Brace & World, 1946.

Ambrose, Stephen E. *Eisenhower*. Vol. 1. New York: Simon & Schuster, 1983.

——, with Immerman, Richard H. *Ike's Spies: Eisenhower and the Espionage Establishment*. New York: Doubleday & Co., 1981.

Andrew, Christopher. *Secret Service: The History of the British Intelligence Community*. London: Heinemann, 1985.

Astley, Joan. *The Inner Circle: A View of the War at the Top*. London: Hutchinson, 1971.

Auty, Phyllis, and Clogg, Richard. *British Policy towards Wartime Resistance in Yugoslavia and Greece*. London: Macmillan & Co., 1975.

Bamford, James. *The Puzzle Palace*. New York: Penguin Books, 1983.

Barclay, Glen. *Struggle for a Continent: A Diplomatic History of South America 1919-1945*. London: Sidgwick and Jackson, 1971.

Barker, Elisabeth. *British Policy in South-East Europe in the Second World War*. London: Macmillan & Co., 1976.

Bothwell, Robert, and Granatstein, J.L. *The Gouzenko Transcripts*. Ottawa: Deneau, 1982.

Bruce, Jean. *Back the Attack! Canadian Women during the Second World War – at Home and Abroad*. Toronto: Macmillan of Canada, 1985.

Bryce, Ivar. *You Only Live Once: Memories of Ian Fleming*. London: Weidenfeld & Nicholson, 1984.

Buck, Tim. *Yours in the Struggle: Reminiscences of Tim Buck*. Edited by William Beeching and Dr. Phyllis Clarke. Toronto: NC Press Ltd., 1977.

Calvocoressi, Peter, and Wint, Guy. *Total War*. Harmondsworth: Penguin Books, 1974.

Canada, Department of Veteran Affairs. *Uncommon Courage: Canadian Secret Agents in the Second World War* . Ottawa: Public Affairs Division, Veteran Affairs Canada, 1985.

Cassidy, William L. "Fairbairn in Shanghai: Profile of a SWAT Pioneer". *Soldier of Fortune*, September 1979, pp.65-71.

——. "Quick or Dead in Shanghai". *Soldier of Fortune*, March 1979, pp.30-37.

——. "The Art of Silent Killing". *Soldier of Fortune*, July 1979, pp.35-39.

——, ed. *History of the Schools and Training Branch, Office of Strategic Services*. San Francisco: Kingfisher Press, 1983.

Cave Brown, Anthony, ed. *The Secret War Report of the OSS*. New York: Berkley Medallion, 1976.

——. *The Last Hero: Wild Bill Donovan*. New York: Times Books, 1982.

Chapman, F. Spencer. *The Jungle Is Neutral*. London: The Reprint Society, 1950.

Churchill, Winston S. *The Second World War*. 6 vols. New York: Bantam Books, 1962.

Cline, Ray S. *The CIA under Reagan, Bush and Casey*. Washington, D.C.: Acropolis Books, 1976.

——. *Secrets, Spies and Scholars: Blueprint of the Essential CIA*. Washington, D.C.: Acropolis Books, 1976.

Cook, Fred J. *The FBI Nobody Knows*. New York: Macmillan & Co., 1964.

Cookridge, E.H. *Inside S.O.E.: The Story of Special Operations in Western Europe 1940-45*. London: Arthur Baker, 1966.

Coon, Carleton S. *Adventures and Discoveries: The Autobiography of Carleton S. Coon, Anthropologist and Explorer*. Englewood Cliffs, N.J.: Prentice-Hall, 1982.

——. *A North Africa Story*. Ipswich, Mass.: Gambit Publishers, 1980.

Corson, William R. *The Armies of Ignorance: The Rise of the American Intelligence Empire*. New York: The Dial Press, 1977.

Cross, J.A. *Lord Swinton*. Oxford: Clarendon, 1982.

Cruikshank, Charles. *SOE in the Far East*. New York: Oxford University Press, 1983.

Curwain, Eric. "Almost Top Secret" (unpublished manuscript). Toronto: Royal Military Institute, n.d.

Davidson, Basil. *Special Operations Europe: Scenes from the Anti-Nazi War*. London: Victor Gollancz, 1980.

Deakin, F.W.D. *The Embattled Mountain*. New York & London: Oxford University Press, 1971.

Dehn, Paul. *The Fern on the Rock. Collected Poems 1935-1965*. London: Hamish Hamilton, 1965.

de Toledano, Ralph. *J. Edgar Hoover: The Man in His Time*. New Rochelle, N.Y.: Arlington House, 1973.

Deschnet, Gunter. *Reinhardt Heydrich*. New York: Stein & Day, 1981.

Diubaldo, Richard J. *Stefansson and the Canadian North*. Montreal: McGill-Queen's University Press, 1978.

Dodds-Parker, Douglas. *Setting Europe Ablaze: Some Account of Ungentlemanly Warfare*. Windlesham, Surrey: Springwood Books, 1983.

Dunlop, Richard. *Donovan, America's Master Spy*. Chicago: Rand McNally, 1982.

——. *Behind Japanese Lines: With the OSS in Burma*. Chicago: Rand McNally, 1979.

Elliot, S.R. *Scarlet to Green; A History of Intelligence in the Canadian Army 1903-1963*. Toronto: Canadian Intelligence and Security Association, 1981.

Fairbairn, W.E., and Sykes, E.A. *Shooting to Live with the One Hand Gun.* Washington, D.C.: 1942.

Farago, Ladislas. *War of Wits: The Secrets of Espionage and Intelligence.* London: Hutchinson, 1954.

Fisher, David. *The War Magician.* New York: Coward McCann, 1983.

Flaherty, John J. *Inside the FBI.* Philadelphia: J.B. Lippincott Co., 1943.

Foot, M.R.D. *SOE in France: An Account of the Work of the British Special Operations Executive in France 1940-1944.* London: Her Majesty's Stationery Office, 1966.

——. *Resistance: An Analysis of European Resistance to Nazism 1940-45.* London: Eyre Methuen, 1978.

——. *Six Faces of Courage.* London: Eyre Methuen, 1978.

——. *SOE: The Special Operations Executive 1940-46.* London: British Broadcasting Corporation, 1984.

Ford, Corey. *Donovan of OSS.* Boston: Little Brown & Co., 1970.

—— and MacBain, Alastair. *Cloak and Dagger: The Secret Story of the Office of Strategic Services.* New York: Random House, 1945.

Giskes, H.J. *London Calling North Pole.* London: William Kimber, 1953.

Goldston, Robert. *Sinister Touches: The Secret War against Hitler.* New York: Dial Press, 1982.

Granatstein, J.L. *Canada's War: The Politics of the Mackenzie King Government 1939-1945.* Toronto: Oxford University Press, 1975.

——. *A Man of Influence: Norman Robertson and Canadian Statecraft 1929-68.* Toronto: Deneau, 1981.

——. *The Ottawa Men: The Civil Service Mandarins 1935-1957.* Toronto: Oxford University Press, 1982.

Haestrup, Jorgen. *European Resistance Movements 1939-1945.* Westport, Conn.: Meckler Publishing, 1981.

Harvison, C.W. *The Horsemen.* Toronto: McClelland & Stewart, 1967.

Haukelid, Knut. *Skis against the Atom.* London: William Kimber, 1954.

Hilton, Stanley. *Hitler's Secret War in South America 1939-1945.* New York: Ballantine, 1981.

Hinsley, F.H., et al. *British Intelligence in the Second World War: Its Influence on Strategy and Operations.* New York: Cambridge University Press. Vol. 1 (1979). Vol. 2 (1981). Vol. 3 (1984).

Hodges, Andrew. *Alan Turing: The Enigma of Intelligence.* London: Unwin, 1985.

Howarth, Patrick, ed. *Special Operations.* London: Routledge & Kegan Paul, 1955.

——. *Undercover: The Men and Women of the Special Operations Executive.* London: Routledge & Kegan Paul, 1980.

Hyde, H. Montgomery. *Room 3603: The Story of the British Intelligence Centre in New York during World War Two.* New

York: Farrar, Straus & Co., 1962. (Published in Great Britain as *The Quiet Canadian*.)

———. *The Atom Bomb Spies*. London: Hamish Hamilton, 1980.

———. *Secret Intelligence Agent*. London: Constable, 1982.

Ivanov, Miroslav. *The Assassination of Heydrich, 27 May 1942*. London: Hart-Davis, MacGibbon, 1973.

Jeanneret, Marsh. "One Spy Controlled". *Canadian Amateur Radio Magazine*, March 1983, pp.29-33.

Johns, Philip. *Within Two Cloaks*. London: William Kimber, 1979.

Kahn, David. *Kahn on Codes: Secrets of the New Cryptology*. New York: Macmillan & Co., 1983.

———. *Hitler's Spies: German Military Intelligence in World War Two*. New York: Macmillan & Co., 1978.

———. *The Codebreakers*. New York: Macmillan & Co., 1967.

Karalekas, Anne. *History of the Central Intelligence Agency*. Report prepared for the United States Senate (Church) Committee. Washington, D.C.: 1975.

Kluckner, Michael. *Vancouver – The Way It Was*. Vancouver: Whitecap Books, 1984.

Langelaan, George. *Knights of the Floating Silk*. London: Hutchinson, 1959.

Leary, William M., ed. *The Central Intelligence Agency: History and Documents*. University of Alabama Press, 1984.

Leasor, James. *Green Beach*. London: Heinemann, 1975.

Lewin, Ronald. *Ultra Goes to War: The Secret Story.* London: Arrow Books, 1980.

——. *The American Magic.* New York: Penguin Books, 1983.

Littleton, James. *Target Nation: Canada and the Western Intelligence Network.* Toronto: Lester & Orpen Dennys, 1986.

Lorain, Pierre. *Clandestine Operations: The Arms and Techniques of the Resistance 1941-1944.* New York: Macmillan & Co., 1983.

Lowenthal, Max. *The Federal Bureau of Investigation.* New York: William Sloane Associates, 1950.

McAleer, John. *Rex Stout: A Biography.* Boston: Little Brown & Co., 1977.

MacLaren, Roy. *Canadians Behind Enemy Lines 1939-1945.* Vancouver: University of British Columbia Press, 1981.

Maschwitz, Eric. *No Chip on My Shoulder.* London: Herbert Jenkins, 1957.

Maugham, W. Somerset. *Ashenden, or The British Secret Agent.* New York: Doubleday & Co., 1941.

Michel, Henri. *The Second World War.* New York: Praeger, 1975.

——. *The Shadow War.* London: Deutsch, 1972.

Moon, Thomas N., and Eifler, Carl F. *The Deadliest Colonel.* New York: Vantage Press, 1975.

Moravec, F. *Master of Spies.* London: The Bodley Head, 1975.

Murphy, Brendan. *The Butcher of Lyons.* New York: Empire Books, 1983.

Ogilvy, David. *Blood, Brains and Beer*. London: Hamish Hamilton, 1978.

Omtcanin, Ivo. *Enigma Tito*. Washington, D.C.: Samizdat Press, 1984.

Page, Don. "Tommy Stone and Psychological Warfare in World War Two". *Journal of Canadian Studies*, Fall/Winter 1981.

Pearson, John. *The Life of Ian Fleming*. London: Jonathan Cape, 1966.

——. *James Bond. The Authorized Biography of 007*. New York: Grove Press, 1986.

Pearson, Lester. *Mike: The Memoirs of the Rt. Hon. Lester B. Pearson* Vol. 1, 1897-1948. Toronto: University of Toronto Press, 1972.

Philby, Kim. *My Silent War*. London: MacGibbon & Kee, 1968.

Pickersgill, J.W., and Forster, D.F. *The Mackenzie King Record*. Toronto: University of Toronto Press, 1970.

Popov, Dusko. *Spy Counter-Spy: The Autobiography of Dusko Popov*. New York: Grosset & Dunlap, 1974.

Powers, Richard. *G-Men: Hoover's FBI in American Popular Culture*. Carbondale & Edwardville: Southern Illinois University Press, 1983.

Powers, Thomas. *The Man Who Kept the Secrets: Richard Helms and the CIA*. New York: Alfred Knopf, 1979.

Reynolds, David. *The Creation of the Anglo-American Alliance 1937-1941: A Study in Competitive Co-Operation*. London: Europa Publications, 1981.

Roberts, Walter R. *Tito, Mihailovic and the Allies 1941-1945*. New Brunswick, N.J.: Rutgers University Press, 1973.

Robertson, Terence. *The Shame and the Glory – Dieppe*. Toronto: McClelland & Stewart, 1962.

Roosevelt, Kermit. *War Report of the OSS*. New York: Walker & Co., 1976.

Sawatsky, John. *Gouzenko: The Untold Story*. Toronto: Macmillan of Canada, 1984.

——. *Men in the Shadows: The RCMP Security Service*. Toronto: Totem Books, 1983.

Sherwood, Robert E. *Roosevelt and Hopkins*. New York: Harper & Bros., 1948.

Smith, Bradley F. *The Shadow Warriors: OSS and the Origins of the CIA*. New York: Basic Books, 1983.

Smith, R. Harris. *OSS*. Berkeley: University of California Press, 1972

St. John, Peter. "Canada's Accession to the Allied Intelligence Community 1940-45". *Conflict Quarterly* 4, no. 4, Fall 1984, pp.5-21.

Stacey, C.P. *Arms, Men and Governments: The War Policies of Canada 1939-1945*. Ottawa: The Queen's Printer, 1970.

——. *Canada and the Age of Conflict*. Vol. 2, 1921-1948. Toronto: University of Toronto Press, 1981.

Stafford, David. *Britain and European Resistance 1940-1945: A Survey of the Special Operations Executive, with Documents*. London: Macmillan & Co., 1980; Toronto: University of Toronto Press, 1984.

Stefansson, V. *Discovery: The Autobiography of Vilhjalmar Stefansson*. New York: McGraw-Hill, 1964.

——. "Routes to Alaska". *Foreign Affairs* 19, July 1941, pp. 861-69.

Stevenson, W. *A Man Called Intrepid*. New York: Harcourt Brace Jovanovich, 1976.

——. *Intrepid's Last Case*. New York: Villard Books, 1984.

Sweet-Escott, Bickham. *Baker Street Irregular*. London: Methuen, 1965.

Tolstoi, Ilya. "Across Tibet from India to China". *National Geographic Magazine*, August 1946, pp.169-222.

Tomasevich, Jozo. *The Chetniks*. Stanford: Stanford University Press, 1975.

Tompkins, Peter. *The Murder of Admiral Darlan*. New York: Simon & Schuster, 1965.

Trepper, Leopold. *The Great Game*. London: Michael Joseph, 1977.

Troy, Thomas F. *Donovan and the CIA: A History of the Establishment of the Central Intelligence Agency*. Frederick, Md.: University Publications of America, Inc., 1981.

Tuchman, Barbara. *Stilwell and the American Experience in China 1911-45*. New York: Macmillan & Co., 1970.

Unger, Sanford. *FBI*. Boston: Little Brown & Co., 1975.

Vyhnak, A. "Superagent: Singular Travels, Campaigns and Adventures of a Man Called Intrepid" (unpublished manuscript in possession of A. Vyhnak, Toronto).

Welchman, Gordon. *The Hut Six Story: Breaking the Enigma Codes* . Harmondsworth: Penguin, 1984.

West, Nigel. *M.I.6: British Secret Intelligence Operations 1909-1945*. London: Weidenfeld & Nicholson, 1983.

——. *M.I.5: British Security Service Operations 1909-1945* . London: The Bodley Head, 1981.

——. *Unreliable Witness: Espionage Myths of the Second World War* . London: Weidenfeld & Nicholson, 1984.

Wheeler, Mark. *Britain and the War for Yugoslavia 1940-1943*. Boulder, Colo.: East European Monographs, 1980.

Whitehead, Don. *The FBI Story: A Report to the People* . New York: Random House, 1956.

INDEX

Abd-el-Krim, 130, 131
Access to Information Act, 39
Adams, Eric, 146-54
Adams, Lieutenant James ("Paddy"), 152, 160
Adventures and Discoveries (Coon), 4, 128, 133-34
Agate, James, 204
Agent Techniques in the Field (Dehn), 203
"Agent's Initiative" test, 280-81
American Black Chamber, The (Yardley), 40
Anderson, John, 21
Andreas (ship), 175
Andrew, Christopher, 27
ANTHROPOID (mission), 274-75
Anti-Japanese Union and Forces (AJUF), 241
"Apollo" (code-name). *See* van Schelle, Jan David Anton
Applegate, Rex, 71, 279
"Arcadia" discussions, 62
Archambault, Jean-Paul, 233, 236, 238
Area A (OSS school), 82
Area B (OSS school), 71, 81
Area E (OSS school), 81, 205
Arisaig, Scotland, Group A schools in, 8, 211, 213, 246, 248
Armies of Ignorance, The (Corson), 59, 136, 285
"Arnaud" (code-name), 220
"Arno" (code-name). *See* Christmann, Richard
Art of Guerrilla Warfare, The (Gubbins), 7

Ashenden (Maugham), 115-16
ASPIDISTRA (transmitter), 157-58
Astley, Joan Bright, 7
Athlone, Lord, 62
Audley End House (SOE school), 184
AUDREY,Operation, 134
AUTONOMOUS (mission), 230-31

BADMINTON RUGGER, Operation, 216
Badoglio, Marshal Pietro, 222
Bailey, Colonel S.W. ("Bill"), 171, 173, 176, 197, 198
Baker, Kenneth, 83-84, 85-86, 88-89, 199, 205
Baker Street Irregular (Sweet-Escott), 5-6, Balmaceda, Giliana, 217
Bamford, James, 166
Barbie, Klaus, 232-33
Barnes, Tracy, 75
Bavin, Ernest, 194
Bayly, Benjamin deForest, 158-60, 161, 163, 164-65
Bayly, Pat, 250
Beau Geste (Wren), 255
Beaulieu (SOE school), 8-10, 12, 72, 84, 92, 184, 185, 199, 203, 204, 209, 215, 243, 246
Beauregard, André 233
Belfrage, Cedric, 195
Benes, President Eduard, 274

oit, Joseph, 239-40, 241
son, Major H.A., 200
e, Adolf, 123-24, 253
lin Diary (Shirer), 115
nard, James, 206
sell, Richard, 75
tchley Park, 36, 42, 56, 156, 161, 163, 164: Hut Six, 163-64
od, Brains and Beer (Ogilvy), 196
lo, Gustav, 228-29
ssevain, Fred, 210-11
anier de la Chapelle, Fernand, 1-3, 131-32
aghey, Lieutenant-Colonel Peter, 229
yle, Air Commander Archie, 221
ANDON (mission), 132
ckondbury Manor (SOE demolitions school), 247
tish Commonwealth Air Training Plan (BCATP), 33
tish Pacific Properties, 19
tish Passport Control, 15
tish Security Co-ordination (BSC), 13,14,15-16, 18, 21, 28, 31, 36, 37, 38, 40, 43, 44, 46, 47, 72, 123, 137: and Gouzenko affair, 258-59; and South America, 139-43, 147-48, 187, 189-90, 244-45; and Yugoslav recruiting mission, 171, 173; relations with FBI, 122-26; role in SIGINT, 155-58, 250; secret history of, 251-57; SIS division, 157-58; specialized recruiting section, 184; winding down activities in 1944, 242
tish Supply Council, 19
tish War Cabinet, 135
ooker, Major Bill, 5, 10-12, 30, 45, 46, 53, 56, 57, 70, 72, 73, 74-76, 81, 83, 85, 87-89, 93, 122, 125, 137, 173-74, 183, 184, 186, 190, 198, 199-200, 202, 205, 209, 210, 211-12, 246, 281-82, 285, 292
oss, John, 75-76, 81, 90
owne, Gordon, 127, 128, 129-35
owne-Bartoli, Albert, 232
uce, David, 84
RUSA agreement, 164, 166
3rutus " (code-name), 216
yce, Ivar, 20, 21, 190, 214, 215, 279
uck, Tim, 174-75
uckmaster, Maurice, 235
ullitt, William C., 64
ULLSEYE (mission), 169
urgess, Captain Howard, 72-73
urma, OSS forces in, 78-80
ushell, Art, 72, 248
utt, Sonia, 235

Byng, Lord, 34
Byrnes, James, 71

"CD" (code-name). *See* Nelson, Sir Frank
Cameron, Merle, 254
Camp X: "Agent's Initiative" test at, 280-81; and Allied missions behind enemy lines, 202-41, 246-47; and BSC headquarters, 193-97; and destruction of Norsk Hydro plant at Vermork, 275-76; and expanded security effort in South America, 189-93; and Gouzenko case, 265-69; and Heydrich assassination, 273-75; and Ian Fleming/James Bond, 277-84; and National Defence Headquarters, 198; and Operation JUBILEE, 276-77; and OSS, 75-83; and secret history of BSC, 251-57; and SIS, 201; Anglo-American relations at, 76-78; BSC evaluation of achievement of, 200-01; Canadian takeover of, 249-50; cost of, 52; death of Fred Boissevain at, 210-11; designated as No. 2 Military Research Centre, 250; disciplinary problems at, 73; effect of London Agreement on, 137-38, 245; effect of U.S. entry into war on, 61-63; end of, 269-70; end of, as SOE training school, 247; establishment of, 20-24; FBI and, 125, 126; fieldcraft exercises at, 212-13; French Canadians at, 233-35; Gubbins-Stephenson conflict and, 243-47; Hungarian Canadians at, 224-29; HYDRA and, 123, 124, 161-66, 201, 213, 248, 250; idea for, 29-30; initial training staff of, 55-57; Italian Canadians at, 222-24; myths surrounding, 271-84, 288-92; operational propaganda at, 209-10; overall importance of, 284-92; recruiting, 183-86; Romanian Canadians at, 229-30; secrecy surrounding, 32-34, 46, 52-53; syllabus at, 90-116; training of Detachment 101 at, 78-81; transformation into communications centre in 1944, 242, 249; wireless personnel at, 143-54; Yugoslav Canadians at, 169, 170-75, 179, 182-83, 222
Camp X Society, 270
Canada Council, 261
Canadian-American Special Service Force, 234
Canadian Arctic Expedition, 17
Canadian Industries Ltd., 72
Canadian Intelligence Corps, 234
Canadian Tribune (Communist newspaper), 174
Canadians Behind Enemy Lines (MacLaren), 181
Canaris, Admiral Wilhelm, 214
Caravan (Coon), 3-4

Carruthers, George, 165
Casablanca Conference (1943), 245-46
Casino Royale (Fleming), 280, 283
Cassidy, William, 70, 93
Central Intelligence Agency (CIA), 75, 87-88
Chandler, Knox, 199
CHARACTER, Operation, 238
Chastelain, Alfred Gardyne de, 230-31, 246-47
Chesley, Colonel L.M., 248-49, 250
Chichely Hall, 56
Christmann, Richard, 218-21
Churchill, Randolph, 133
Churchill, Sir Winston, 5, 15, 16, 26, 32, 34,
    36, 61, 62, 78, 126, 127, 155-56, 167,
    169, 178-79, 187-88
Clark, General Mark, 133
Clark, Greg, 44
Clark, Joseph T., 44
Clark, Mabel, 44
Close combat, training in at Camp X, 94-97
Coates, John, 228-29
Cockcroft, John, 263
Codes and ciphers, training in at Camp X, 107-
    11
Coffey, Ed, 122, 125, 132
Cohen, Louis, 81
Coit, Richard, 20, 21
Collins, Michael, 91
Communications, training in at Camp X, 107
Communications Security Establishment, 162
Communist Party: Cambridge University, 176;
    Canadian, 172-73, 174; Central
    Committee, 172, 177; Malayan, 241;
    Yugoslav, 172
Confessions of an Advertising Man (Ogilvy),
    195
Constantine, Major-General, 50-51, 53, 57,
    72, 73, 221
Cook, Major Thomas, 247-48
Coon, Carleton S., 3-5, 126-27, 128-35
Co-ordinator of Information (COI), 27, 28-29,
    58-61, 64: activities in Northwest Africa,
    127; division for secret intelligence, 58,
    84; division for special operations, 58, 84;
    Foreign Information Service (FIS), 58,
    64, 135, 207, 208-09; Research and
    Analysis Branch, 58, 64, 83; Special
    Activities Division, 66; transformed into
    OSS, 135
Corps Franc d'Afrique, 3
Corson, William, 59, 61, 136, 285
Coughlin, John, 80
Counter-measures, training in at Camp X, 106-
    07
Court, Sergeant, 153
Cover creation, instruction in at Camp X, 105-
    06

Croatian Peasant Party, 180
Crowther, Bosley, 206
Cruikshank, Charles, 237
Cuneo, Ernest, 267
Cunliffe-Lister, Philip. See Swinton, Lord
Curwain, Eric, 144-46, 150-51, 153, 154,
    171, 174, 175, 224, 231

Dahl, Roald, 253-54
Daily Eagle (Brooklyn), 60
Dalai Lama, 117-18, 119-21
Dalton, Hugh, 5, 17, 26, 61
"Daniels" (cover name). See Durovecz, An
Dansey, Sir Claude, 15
Dark Invader (von Rintelen), 115
Darlan, Admiral François, 1-3, 131-32, 13
d'Artois, Lionel Guy, 233, 234-36
Davidson, Basil, 168, 173, 176, 177, 178,
    183, 228
Davies, Mostyn, 190
Davies, Tommy, 17, 18, 20, 21, 24, 30-32,
    49, 52, 136, 169
Deadliest Colonel, The (Moon and Eifler),
Deadly Affair, The (le Carré), 203
Deakin, Captain William, 172, 178, 180, 1
    82, 190,191
Dean, John, 266
DEERHURST (mission), 229
Defendu: Scientific Self-defence (Fairbairn)
Dehn, Paul, 203-07, 211, 214, 247, 285
Delahunty, Norman, 139-43, 144-46, 148-4
    192-93
Del Gaizo, August, 82-83
Denniston, Commander Alastair, 42
de Rewelyskow, Sergeant-Major George, 5
    I52
Detachment 101, 78-81
di Lucia, Giovanni, 223
Diamonds Are Forever (Fleming), 283
Diclich, George, 179, 183
Dieppe raid. See JUBILEE, Operation
DIPLOMAT (resistance circuit), 239
DITCHER (resistance circuit), 232-36
Doenitz, Admiral Karl, 188
Dolan, Lieutenant Brooke, 118-22
Donaldson, Dr. Blake, 17, 18
Donovan, General William ("Wild Bill"), 2,
    4, 18, 25-29, 30, 31, 52, 57-61, 63, 64,
    71, 76, 81, 82, 83, 86, 88, 89, 90, 117,
    118, 122, 125, 127, 129, 132, 135-36,
    137, 155, 156, 157-58, 169, 174, 189,
    199, 207-08, 245, 268, 278-79, 285-86
Donovan and the CIA (Troy), 279
Donovan of OSS (Ford), 82
Dorman-Smith, Sir Reginald, 78
Double Transpositon (cipher), 109-11
Dourlein, Pieter, 8

ns, Kenneth, 63-68, 74-75, 81, 90
Vo (Fleming), 283
-Brook, Tommy, 35, 43, 45, 46, 47-49,
  51, 52, 53, 57, 143-44, 150, 153, 154,
  162, 171, 197, 198, 203, 211, 222, 231,
  233, 249, 256
es, Allan, 29
top, Richard, 70, 279
ont, Yvan, 239
ovecz, Andre, 224-27
er, Peter, 261-64

ern Warfare Training School (SOE), 236
y, Colonel William, 128, 129
n, Anthony, 2
imann, Adolf, 226
er, Carl, 76-80, 114
nhower, General Dwight D., 1, 2
il (ship), 176
PHANT, Operation, 238
s, Colonel Charles H. ("Dick"), 15, 29, 60,
  83, 288
attled Mountain, The (Deakin), 179
gma (cipher), 156, 162
ljach, Petar, 180
ns, Jean-Paul, 196, 261, 262-65, 266
mination Unit (Ottawa), 39-43
ernal Affairs, Department of, 37, 38, 41,
  203

bairn, Captain William Ewart ("Fearless
  Dan"), 68-72, 83, 88, 93-96, 205, 206,
  282
East, SOE in, 236-39
e Farm" (OSS school). See RTU-11
eral Bureau of Investigation (FBI), 122-26:
  handling of Dusko Popov, 124-25; New
  York Bureau, 126; relations with BSC,
  122-26, 160; Special Intelligence Service
  for Latin America, 187,189
ld, Spike, 209-10
ld Security Police, 12
earms training, at Camp X, 97-100
ming, Elinor, 254
ming, Ian, 21, 22, 203, 277-84
ming, Peter, 277
ot, M.R.D., 7, 8, 214, 220, 247, 289
r Whom the Bell Tolls (Hemingway), 115
rce 136. See Special Operations Executive
rd, Corey, 82, 208
rd, John, 25
reign Information Service (FIS), 58, 64,
  135, 207, 208-09
rster, Major, 29-30
xworth, Percy J., 126
anck, Louis, 20, 137, 190, 191, 245
ench Section (SOE). See Special Operations

Executive
Friedmann, Colonel William, 156
From Russia With Love (Fleming), 283
Fuchs, Klaus, 262
FUNGUS (code-name), 180-81

Gabcik, Josef, 274
Gallup, Dr. George, 196
Gambier-Parry, Brigadier Richard, 156-58,
  159, 160
Garner, Grace, 254
Gates, Cecily, 162, 163
Gelleny, Joseph, 227, 229
Georgescu, George, 231
Gerson, Victor, 217-18, 220
Get Tough (Fairbairn), 115
Gingold, Hermione, 47
Giskes, H.J., 214, 218-21
Glazebrook, George, 38, 42-43, 203, 212,
  261
Glyn, Francis, 243
Go Spy the Land (Hill), 115
Godfrey, Admiral John, 277, 278
Goldfinger (film), 203
GOLF (code-name), 218-21
Goodfellow, Major Preston, 60, 63, 66, 78,
  84, 135, 136, 137
Gouzenko, Igor, 196, 257-69
Gouzenko, Svetlana, 266
Granatstein, J.L., 35-36, 261
Great Game, The (Trepper), 290-91
Gremlins, The (Dahl), 253
Griffiths, Bobbie, 162-63
Grindley, H.H., 139-43
Gubbins, Captain Michael, 131, 132
Gubbins, Colonel Colin McVeagh, 5-8, 10, 12-
  13, 30, 49, 50, 53-54, 55, 61, 90, 91,
  125, 133, 137, 199, 243-47
Guerrilla-warfare, training in at Camp X, 100-
  02

Hadekel, Daniel, 196-97
Hale, Captain Nathan, 58
Hall, Noel, 17, 18
Halliwell's Film Guide, 206
Hambro, Sir Charles, 136, 137, 192, 199,
  200, 245, 246
Hannay, Captain Ramsay Rainsford, 213, 214,
  248
Hardcastle, Bill, 151, 154, 160-61
Harvison, Cliff, 260
Haukelid, Knut, 276, 277
Hayden, Dr. Joseph, 83
Hearst International News Service, 63, 64
Heeney, Arnold, 36, 252, 269
Helms, Richard, 75, 205
Heydrich, Reinhard, 273-75

Highet, Gilbert, 252
Hill, Tom, 193-95, 252-53, 254-57, 266
HOATLEY (code-name), 179, 183
Home Defence (Security) Executive. *See*
      Security Executive (British)
Hoover, J. Edgar, 122-23, 126, 160, 187,
      189, 191
Hopkins, Harry, 209
Horthy, Admiral Miklos, 226, 227
Howarth, Patrick, 15, 177
Hudson, Captain D.T. ("Bill"), 169
Hungary, SOE in, 224, 226-29
Huot, Major Louis, 134
Hut Six, Bletchley Park, 163-64
Hut Six Story, The (Welchman), 164
Hyde, Harford Montgomery, 47, 124, 126,
      157, 288
HYDRA, 123, 124, 155-66, 186, 201, 213,
      248, 250, 269, 286, 287

"Installation J". *See* Camp X
Intelligence Staff College (Matlock), 12
Intelligence Training Centre (Matlock), 185
International Encyclopedia of Film, 205-06
International Labour Organization, 175
"Intrepid", myth of, 272-92
Italy, SOE involvement in, 226-27

"J Force". *See* Camp X
James Bond (Pearson), 271-72
Jennings, John, 21-22
Johns, Commander Philip, 16
Joint Intelligence Committee, 188
Joint Planning Staff of the British Chiefs,189
Jones, Major William, 180-81
JUBILEE, Operation, 276-77
Justin, Major Frank, 250

Kai-shek, Generalissimo Chiang, 78, 122
Kallay, Prime Minister Miklos, 226
Kasserine Pass, battle of (1943), 133-34
Keble, Colonel C.M. ("Bolo"), 177-78, 197
Kefauver Committee, 82
Kellock-Taschereau Commission, 268
Keswick, John, 243
KETTLEDRUM-ROLL, Operation. *See*
      PAUKENSCHLUG, Operation
Khan, Noor Inayat, 232
Kill or Get Killed (Applegate), 71
King, Admiral Ernest, 188
King, Mackenzie, 32-34, 35, 36, 169, 258-59,
      267
Klugmann, James, 176-77, 179
Knights of the Floating Silk (Langelaan), 68
Knox, Frank, 27
Kombol, Nikola, 182-83
Kovacevich, Nikola, 172-73, 175

Kubis, Jan, 274

Langelaan, George, 68-69
Langer, William L., 58
LATI airline, 47-49
Latin America: British intervention in, 1
      U.S. concern about German activity
      186-88, 189
Lauder, Harry, 213
le Carré, John, 168, 203
Leopold, John, 260, 262, 266
Lethbridge, Major R.F., 198, 224
Levin, George, 218, 220
Lewin, Ronald, 156
Lewis, John L., 82
"Lieutenant Vincent" (code-name). *See*
      Alexander
Life of Ian Fleming (Pearson), 272, 277,
      280
Lindsay, Major, 49-50, 53, 55
Live and Let Die (Fleming), 280, 283
London Advertiser, 34
London Agreement, 136-38
Lovell, Dr. Stanley, 82
Low, Frank, 120
Low, Robert, 67

"M" (code-name). *See* Gubbins, Colonel
      McVeagh
M.I.5, 14
M.I.6. *See* Secret Intelligence Service
M.I.6. (West), 61
MacArthur, Douglas, 26
McClellan, Inspector George B., 22-23, ⸱
      48, 171, 174, 265
McInnes, Helen, 252
Mackay, George, 266
Macklin, Colonel W.H.S., 50-51, 53
MacLaren, Roy, 181
McLaughlin, Samuel, 23
Maclean, Brigadier Fitzroy, 134
"Madeleine" (code-name). *See* Khan, Noo
      Inayat
MAGIC (code), 156
Malaya, SOE in, 241
Man Called Intrepid, A (Stevenson), 22, ⸱
      272-73, 276, 289-90
Man Who Kept the Secrets, The (Powers)
      71
Marshall, General George, 167, 188
"Martin" (cover name), 217-18
Maschwitz, Eric, 47-49
Massingham (mission), 3, 84
May, Alan Nunn, 258, 263
Memorandum on the Establishment of a S
      of Strategic Information (Donovan),
Men in the Shadows (Sawatsky), 45

...es, Sir Stewart, 14, 15, 26, 123, 155,
  59
...ovich, General, 169-70, 171, 176, 182,
  98
...ry District 2, 50, 51, 57, 173, 198, 224,
  34
...ry Intelligence, Research (MIR), 30
...r, Captain Fred, 56, 72, 195
...rand, Jacques, 218, 220
...ovan, Victor, 231
... *Is Down, The* (Steinbeck), 115
...*raker* (Fleming), 283
...le Operations (MO), 205
...vec, General Frantisek, 274
...ell, Sidney, 209
...atbatten, Admiral Louis, 240
...1, Lieutenant-Colonel "Jimmy", 84, 243
...*ler on the Orient Express* (film), 203
...hy, James, 135
...ay, Colonel W.W., 249
...ow, Ed, 57-58
...solini, Benito, 222
...*ilent War* (Philby), 10

...ction (SOE). *See* Special Operations
  Executive
...ION, Operation, 238
...onal Defence Headquarters, 50, 51, 198,
  248
...*onal Geographic*, 119, 121
...onal Institute for Economic and Social
  Research (London), 17
...on, Sir Frank, 5-6, 28, 31, 135
  York National Guard, Fighting 69th
  Regiment, 26
...*York Times*, 206
...enthall, Jack, 277
...*hip on My Shoulder* (Maschwitz), 47
...2 Military Research Centre. *See* Camp X
...RDPOL, Operation, 214-15, 218-21
...man, Herbert, 39-40
...sk Hydro plant (Vemork), 275-76
...h Africa, SOE activity in, 167-69
...*h Africa Story, A* (Coon), 132
...RTH POLE, Operation. *See* NORDPOL,
  Operation
...*osti* (Serbo-Croat newspaper), 171

...chner, Fred, 205
...ce of Policy Co-ordination (OPC), 75
...ce of Strategic Services (OSS), 3, 4, 10,
  25, 70-71, 74, 75, 83, 86-89, 117: and
  Latin America, 189; and London
  Agreement, 136-38; and missions behind
  enemy lines, 202; and pressure for co-
  operation with military, 198-200; Morale
  Operations, 205, 208; relations with SOE,

  135-38, 184; Special Operations Division,
  81, 135, 137; Training Directorate, 88, 92
Office of War Information (OWI), 135, 208-11
Office of War Mobilization, 71
Official Secrets Act, 48
Ogdensburg Agreement, 36
Ogilvy, David, 195-96
Oldfield, Maurice, 168
O'Neill, Kevin, 162
Orders to Kill (film), 203, 206
L'Organisateur (Belgium), 107
OVERLORD, Operation, 221

Paget, Captain Sir James, 126
Paine, Denis, 123-24
Palais d'Eté (Algiers), 1, 3, 132
Partisan Leader's Handbook (Gubbins), 7
PAUKENSCHLUG, Operation, 188
Pavlich, Paul, 180
Pearl Harbor, Japanese attack on, 61
Pearson, Drew, 267, 268
Pearson, John, 272
Pearson, Lester B., 20, 38-39, 40
Pelham-Burn, Captain Hamish, 210-13, 214,
  225, 247, 248
Pétain, Marshal Philippe, 2
Petrie, Sir David, 14
Philby, Kim, 10, 11, 84, 203, 204, 262
Pickersgill, Frank, 34, 270
Pickersgill, Jack, 34
"Pig Hill" (Djebel Hallouf), 132
Planet of the Apes (film series), 206
Playfair (cipher), 107-09
Playfair, Giles, 255, 269
Playfair, Sir John, 108
Plewman, Elaine, 232
Pleydell-Bouverie, Colonel "Barty", 83, 135,
  136
Police methods, training in at Camp X, 106-07
Popov, Dusko, 124-25
Power, Thomas, 70-71
Princess Patricia Canadian Light Infantry, 34
Project J. *See* Camp X
Propaganda, training in at Camp X, 111-14
PROSPER (resistance group), 218
Psychological Warfare Committee, 42
PURPLE (cipher machine), 156, 291
Puzzle Palace, The (Bamford), 166

Queen Elizabeth (ship) , 224
Quiet Canadian, The (Hyde), 47, 288-89

Radio College of Canada, 150
Radio Security Service (RSS), 157
Ralston, Colonel Layton, 35, 36, 50, 52-53,
  233, 249, 252
Red Star Over China (Snow), 115

Research and Analysis Branch (COI), 58, 64, 83
Revolution of Nihilism (Rauschning), 115
Rheam, George, 247
Rivett-Carnac, Inspector Charles, 260-62
Robertson, Norman, 36, 37-38, 40, 50, 252, 257, 258-59, 263, 269
Rockefeller, Nelson, 126, 187
Rockex (cipher machine), 161-63
Romania, SOE involvement in, 230-31
Roosevelt, Franklin Delano, 27, 32, 36, 63, 71, 126, 127, 167, 187, 189, 208
Roosevelt, James, 57
Roosevelt, Kermit, 79, 80
Roosevelt and Hopkins (Sherwood), 209
Roper-Caldbeck, Lieutenant-Colonel Terence, 55, 57, 65, 67, 72, 73, 118, 184
Ross-Smith, Bill, 196
Rowland, Captain Herbert, 249, 267
Royal Canadian Mounted Police (RCMP), 22, 37, 39-40, 43, 45, 46, 47, 50, 53,170-71, 174: and Gouzenko affair, 259-66; Security Service, 45; Special Branch, 45
Royal Canadian Institute, 158
Royal Signals Corps, 153, 160
RTU-11 (OSS school), 86-89, 193, 205
Rural Realty Company Ltd., 22
Rustem Buildings (Cairo), 168, 176, 180
Ryan, Cornelius, 279

Sawatsky, John, 45
Scott Polar Institute, 17
Scouting for Boys (Baden-Powell), 115
Secret inks, training in at Camp X, 111
Secret Intelligence Agent (Hyde), 123-24
Secret Intelligence Service (SIS), 6, 14, 15, 26: and Camp X, 201; interest in SIGINT, 155; Section D, 30, 47, 230; Section VIII, 156; Section V, 261
Section D, 30, 47
Section V (SIS), 261
Section VIII (SIS), 156
Security Executive (British), 13-14
Security Intelligence Service (Canada), 45
Selborne, Lord, 2, 192
Serdar, Stevan, 174, 176, 179, 183
Seton-Watson, Hugh, 168
Seven Days To Noon, (film), 203, 206-07
Shadow Warriors, The (Smith), 59, 135
Shanghai Defence Force, 56
Shanghai Riot Squad, 70
Shephardson,Whitney, 156, 157
Sherwood, Robert, 58, 207-11
Ships' Observers Scheme, 187, 189
Sichel, Herbert, 43, 245
Sikich, Karko. *See* Kovacevich, Nikola
SILVERSMITH (sabotage circuit), 240

Simich, Alexander, 180
Sinclair, Alexander, 23
Sinclair, Gordon, 18
Sinclair, Major, 127
Singapore Goes Off the Air (Playfair), 2
Six Faces of Courage (Foot), 217
Skilbeck, Major Cuthbert, 46, 160, 173, 86, 191-92, 200, 203, 204, 205, 20 210, 211, 214, 243, 245, 248, 281- 285, 287, 289, 292
Skis Against the Atom (Haukelid), 276
Skorzeny, Otto, 222
Slim, General William, 238
Smith, Bradley, 59, 135, 208, 289
S.O. in Latin America (BSC Report) 24
Special Operations Executive (SOE), 2, 14, 26, 28, 47, 52, 127:and LATI a 47-49;and London Agreement, 136 and missions behind enemy lines, 2 and pressure for co-operation with military, 198-200; Cairo base of, 1(176; effect of Casablanca Conferen 245-46; European escape lines of, 2 expansion of activities in North Am 28-30; French Section, 235; Gubbir Stephenson conflict and, 243-47; in East, 236-39; in Hungary, 226-29; i Italy, 222-23; in Malaya, 241; N Se 214-15; network in Latin America, 190; relations with OSS, 134-35, 18 resistance circuits, 231-36; training system, 8-10, 55-57, 85, 89, 90-92; Yugoslav Section, 168-70, 197-98
SOE in France (Foot), 216
SOE in the Far East (Cruikshank), 237
Solborg, Lieutenant Colonel Robert, 59- 127, 128
Spanton, Herb, 265-66
"Special Activities/Bruce" (SA/B), 84
Special Activities Division (COI), 66
"Special Activities/Goodfellow" (SA/G),
Special Communications Unit No. 3. *See* Security Service
Special Operations Division (OSS), 81, 137
Special Operations Europe (Davidson),
Special Operations Section (BSC), 20
"Special School J". *See* Camp X
Special Training School 41 (STS 41), 55-
Special Training School 46 (STS 46), 56
Special Training School 101 (STS 101),
Special Training School 102 (STS 102), 176
Special Training School 103 (STS 103). Camp X
Spy Who Came in From the Cold, The (le Carré), 203

...naster training, at Camp X, 102-04
of Alexandria, The (ship), 176
Weekly (Toronto), 34
...evich, Ivan, 182
...on XVII. *See* Brickondbury Manor
...on "M", 47-49
...ansson, Vilhjälmur, 17, 18
...henson, William, 15-17, 18, 19-20, 26-29,
    31, 35, 36, 37, 43, 44, 45, 49, 52, 53,
    57, 59, 72, 122-23, 125, 126, 135, 137,
    155, 156, 157-58, 159, 160, 169, 178,
    187, 190, 191, 193-94, 209, 243-47, 251-
    57, 258-59, 261, 266-69; *See also*
    "Intrepid", myth of
...henson, Lady Mary, 270
...enson, William, 289
...ell, "Vinegar Joe", 76, 78, 118
...e, Thomas Archibald ("Tommy"), 38, 41,
    247, 258
...ings" (code-name), 130
...ng, Philip, 81
...ng Medicine (Donaldson), 17
...art, Captain William, 171-72, 176, 181-
    82,197
...boda, Karel, 274
...eet-Escott, Bickham, 5-6, 10, 69, 74, 87,
    191, 227, 229
...nton, Lord, 13
...lassi, Ferenc, 227

...Li, General, 78
...ning of the Shrew, The (film), 203
...chereau, Leonard, 233, 238-39
...ssels" (code-name), 129-30
...lor, Alfred James Towle, 18-20, 21, 46,
    49, 53, 57, 59
...lor, E.G., 21
...ere Shall Be No Night (Sherwood), 207
...riert, Paul, 65-66
...'43 (radio circuit), 148-49
...irty Five" (Dehn), 207
...irty-Nine Steps, The (Buchan) , 115, 213
...DEWAY GREEN (mission), 241
...lstoy, Ilia, 117-22
...)RCH, Operation, 1
...ronto Daily Star, 34, 44, 154
...ronto Telegram, 37
...avis, Sir Edward, 161, 163, 164
...epper, Leopold, 290
...ibes of the Rif, The (Coon), 3
..."ricycle" (code-name). *See* Popov, Dusko
...iumph, H.M.S., 169
...oy, Thomas, 29, 279
...ue Glory (film), 47
...uman, Harry S., 75, 267
...JBE ALLOYS (code-name), 167
...rk, Michael, 229

25-1-1 (magazine), 270
TYPICAL (code-name), 182

UKUSA agreement, 166, 269
ULTRA (code), 155-56, 159, 163-65, 178,
    272, 291
Undercover (Howarth), 15
Unreliable Witness (West), 274

Van Deman, Major General Ralph, 58-59
van Schelle, Jan David Anton, 214-21
Vass, Alexander, 229
VIC line (France), 217-18, 219-20
Vickers, Colonel Geoffrey, 28, 29
Vingt-Deux Regiment, 234
Vining, Charles Arthur McLaren, 34-37, 43, 44-
    45, 48, 51-52, 269
von Arnim, General Jurgin, 133

Walter, Colonel Felix, 233, 234, 236, 239
Wallace, Henry, 253
War Report of the OSS (Roosevelt), 79
Wartime Information Board, 43
Wartime Prices and Trade Board, 43
Welchman, Gordon, 163, 164-65
West, Nigel, 61, 156, 274
*Western Hemisphere Weekly Intelligence
    Bulletin*, 194, 252-53
Weston, Garfield, 49
Wharton-Tigar, Edward, 129
White, George, 81-83
Wilkinson, Gerald, 44
Williams, Colonel Garland, 66-67, 78, 84, 135
Wiseman, Sir William, 213
Within Two Cloaks (Johns), 16
Wood, Elizabeth, 158
Wren, Christopher, 255

Yardley, Herbert, 40-41, 58-59
You Only Live Once (Bryce), 21, 279
Yours in the Struggle (Buck), 174
Yugoslavia, British involvement in, 169-83

"Z" network, 15
Zabotin, Colonel, 263
ZIPPER, Operation, 240-41